ON REVOLUTION

Edited by
• **William Lutz**
and
• **Harry Brent**

Winthrop Publishers, Inc.
Cambridge, Massachusetts

 Printed in the United States of America: 87626-644-2, 87626-628-6. Library of Congress Catalog Card Number: 70-145761. Current Printing (last number): 10 9 8 7 6 5 4 3 2 1.

Cover: Kay Larson

Photographs: LIBERATION NEWS SERVICE. 2, Howie Epstein; 65, Cinda Firestone; 67, Jeffrey Blankfort; 172, Howie Epstein; 174, Jeffrey Blankfort; 242, Barbara Rothkrug; 295, Howie Epstein; 323, Barbara Rothkrug.

Acknowledgements: "Imperialism", © 1939 by International Publishers Co., Inc., by permission; "The New Forms of Control", © 1964 by Herbert Marcuse, by permission of Beacon Press; "The Marxist Theory of Alienation," © 1970 by International Socialist Review, by permission; "The Political Economy of Women's Liberation", © 1969 by Monthly Review, Inc., by permission; "The Revolted", © 1967 by Carl Oglesby and Richard Shaull, by permission of The Macmillan Company; "Toward A Theory of Revolution", © by The American Sociological Review, by permission of the author; "The Limits of Revolution", © 1969 by Martin Oppenheimer, by permission of Quadrangle Books, Inc. and Penguin Books, Ltd.; "Marxism and Revolution", © 1969 by David Horowitz, by permission of Random House, Inc. and Deborah Rogers, Ltd.; "Can American Workers Make A Socialist Revolution?" © 1969 by International Socialist Review, by permission; "Socialism In One Country", by Oxford University Press under the auspices of the Royal Institute of International Affairs; "Selections – Trotsky", © 1957 by Pioneer Publishers, by permission of Pathfinder Press, Inc.; "The Permanent Revolution", © 1969 by Merit Publishers, by permission of Pathfinder Press, Inc.; "The Science of Revolutions and the Art of Making Them", © 1969 by International Socialist Review, by permission; "How to Commit Revolution In Corporate America", by permission of the author; "How To Make A Revolution In the United States", © 1969 by Merit Publishers, by permission of Pathfinder Press, Inc.; "Eldridge Cleaver", from the book *The Black Panthers Speak* edited by Philip S. Foner. Copyright © 1970 by Philip S. Foner. Reprinted by permission of J. B. Lippincott Company; "Guerrilla Warfare In Bolivia Is Not Dead", *The London Bulletin,* winter 1968, by permission The Bertrand Russell Peace Foundation; "What Is To Be Done?" © 1969 by International Publishers Co. Inc., by permission; "C'est Pour Toi Que Tu Fais La Revolution", © 1968 English translation by Andre Deutsch, Ltd. Used by permission of McGraw-Hill Book Company; "The Principal Lesson For the Present", © 1967 by Librarie Francois Maspero, by permission the Monthly Review Press, English translation © 1967 by Monthly Review Press; "The Function of a University", by permission of Counterpoint; "The New Radicals In the Multiversity", by permission of the author; "An End To History", by permission of Humanity; "We Want Revolution", © 1968 The Curtis Publishing Corp., by permission of The Saturday Evening Post; "Notes On Man And Socialism In Cuba", © 1967 by Merit Publishers, by permission of Pathfinder Press, Inc.; "A Day In the Life of A Socialist Citizen", © 1968, Dissent by permission.

To Bill, Beth Ann, Jimmy, and Miranda.
"O brave new world, That has such people in it!"

CONTENTS

REVOLUTIONARY PRACTICE

THE REVOLUTIONARY PARTY

THE REVOLUTION ON CAMPUS

AFTER THE REVOLUTION

INTRODUCTION

When we first started to work on this book our intention was to gather some current writings on a much used and abused word—*revolution*. But we quickly realized that the study of revolution cannot deal simply with current trends. Indeed, if one accepts the idea that revolution is a serious undertaking, then one will also accept the idea that revolution is proper matter for serious study. The obvious thing to do, then, was to put the subject of revolution into a proper framework for study, a framework that would include the historical as well as the current perspective. Our organization is admittedly arbitrary, but we feel that it brings together, in a coherent order, many disparate views on revolution. Certainly we have not provided a handbook for revolution or revolutionaries. What we hope we have provided is a serious, non-emotional approach to a valid subject of study.

This book brings history to the modern radical scene. It presents the ideas of Marx, Lenin, Trotsky, Stalin, Mao Tse-tung, and other Marxist and non-Marxist revolutionary theorists to the modern student. It replaces slogans with substance. It juxtaposes the heroes of the Old Left with those of the New and suggests what most New Leftists began to realize toward the end of the sixties—that no successful revolutionary movement can divorce itself from history; that rhetoric cannot substitute for analysis.

The organization of this collection of essays suggests an outline for that analysis. It proceeds from the basis of revolution to an analysis of the type of society that would exist after a successful revolution. Some of the questions it poses are: On what grounds is revolution necessary or desirable? Is there a theory of revolution that is tactically viable in the modern world? Who are the leaders of the revolution? Do contemporary upheavals on campus have anything to do with revolution? What are the fruits of a successful revolution? How will the new society differ from the old—what does *revolution* mean?

This reader incorporates widely varying answers by revolutionary theorists and activists to these questions. Marx and Lenin in their most classic works explain the economic and historically dialectic foundations of revolution. Herbert Marcuse and Ernest Mandel, developing a central theme of the *Communist Manifesto,* discuss in contemporary terms the psychological alienation which impels even the moderately affluent to rebel. In Section II, non-Marxist sociologists, James Davies and Martin Oppenheimer, bring their methodology to the study of revolution. David Horowitz then connects the major theses of Marx and Lenin to contemporary world politics and economics while George Novack presents his opinion of the possibility of revolution in the United States. The final four essays in Section II outline the debate between Leon Trotsky and Josef Stalin—world-wide revolution, or socialism in one country? Revolution directed from Moscow, or directed by the people who make it? Stalin's theoretical formulations as presented in the *Draft Program of the Sixth Congress of the Third International* are especially significant here. This document was not previously available to the general reader or student, and was not, within recent memory at least, published together with Trotsky's reply. Trotsky's reply, presented in two complementary selections from his major works, also takes issue with Mao Tse-tung on the question of alliances between Marxist revolutionaries and progressive capitalists.

While the selections from Trotsky, Stalin, and Mao form the nexus of modern debate about revolutionary theory, Sections III and IV contain essays which bring that debate, and recently evolved debates, to particular *ad hoc* situations. If revolutions are theoretically viable, what makes them succeed? What makes them fail? If revolution is theoretically practicable for America, which, if either, of the two practical models for revolution presented here—the straight Marxist analysis by Peter Camejo or the more empirical formulations in the paper by G. William Domhoff—seems to have the best chance for success? Are the predictions of Inti Peredo as accurate for guerrilla warfare in Latin America as some would argue Vo Nguyen Giap's have been for Southeast Asia? Does Lenin's model for the structure of a revolutionary party meet the conditions of the 1970's better than the anarchist formulations of Daniel Cohn-Bendit or the guerrilla *foco* theory of Régis Debray? Is Rosa Luxemburg in essential agreement with Lenin, or do her objections to the secretive, disciplined nature of Lenin's revolutionary party reinforce Martin Oppenheimer's earlier suggestion that the revolutionary personality is incapable of constructing a humanistic social order—questions debated in a larger context by Che Guevara, Michael Walzer, and Chinese Workers in the book's final section.

The authors realize that Section V—Revolution on the Campus—does not really fit the organic composition of the rest of the book. Like the essays on the position of women and Blacks in contemporary society—questions outlined more extensively in more specialized anthologies—it is included as a starting point for discussion and debate by the people who will most likely read the other essays here. We have included a special section on the campus because the American university, where this book is most likely to be read, is presently alive with radical and revolutionary ideas. To use a catch phrase, the universities are in "motion"; in motion with the increasingly massive drive against American military intervention throughout the world, with the struggles of Blacks, minorities, and women to determine their own destinies, and with the attempts of workers to organize in their own interests—all topics discussed in this section.

Most students who use this book will be familiar with radical and revolutionary slogans like "Power to the People." Most, especially students on the smaller campuses throughout America which have lately come into "motion," should be exposed to something more than revolutionary slogans. This book provides an opportunity to give serious analysis to the major arguments of and among revolutionaries; arguments which slogans often obscure. It also provides an opportunity to seriously and critically examine the whole idea of revolution itself.

We would like to thank all those who helped directly or indirectly in the preparation of this book. Special thanks are due to Paul O'Connell and Jim Murray who helped and encouraged us in the early stages of the book; to Professors Lewis Coser of the State University of New York, Stony Brook, Ted R. Gurr of Northwestern University, David Singer of the University of Michigan, and Michael Walzer of Harvard University who gave generously of their time to make helpful comments on the content and organization of the book; to Bradley University for funded leave used to gather materials for this book; to Professor Bernard Bray of Bradley University; to Rev. William Stickney, rector of St. Stephen's Episcopal Church of St. Louis, Missouri; to Patrick Quinn and to Robin Block; to Muriel Harman for her help in putting together the manuscript and the final appearance of the book; and finally to our wives, Maureen Brent and Kristen Lutz, for their consistently significant and constructive criticism.

THE GROUNDS FOR REVOLUTION

One - hundred twenty years and more after its initial publication, *The Communist Manifesto* by Marx and Engels remains *the* basic document for the study and practice of revolution. Though brief, it makes major theoretical formulations about those topics which concern most of the selections in this book. It is in this section because, whatever else the *Manifesto* says, it eloquently describes the physical and psychological bondage of workers in the nineteenth century, and, by extension and implication, the twentieth. It also posits a very accurate model of those class divisions within society which past revolutionaries have used to explain the cause of that bondage.

While Marx and Engels in the *Manifesto* addressed themselves principally to the plight of the European working class, Lenin, in his *Imperialism*, describes the methods by which the masters of European workers have become the overlords of the world. If future revolutions are to spring from the formerly colonial countries of Africa, Asia, and Latin America, as some respected revolutionary theorists predict, this essay will be the major guide to understanding the cause of that revolution.

Not all revolutionary thinkers would posit that revolution comes only to societies whose people are the most obviously oppressed. Herbert Marcuse and Ernest Mandel describe in their respective essays the feeling of boredom close to despair—the alienation—that characterizes even the lives of working people who live in moderate physical comfort. Both discuss the ways in which wealthy ruling classes in economically advanced countries drop a few crumbs of their affluence to working people to keep them from rebelling. They suggest that those who have tasted the crumbs may someday want to eat the entire meal. The essay by Carl Oglesby, a classic of the sixties, describes the outrage of the semi-affluent at their dehumanization.

2 We have included an essay on the liberation of women in this section—partially because women play a part in all the situations where there is ground for revolution; partially because historically revolutionary strategy, while at least aware of the oppression of individual minority groups, has been myopic with respect to the oppression of women. We might have included several other specialized essays dealing with the plight of Blacks, Chicanos, Indians, Palestinian refugees, French-speaking citizens of Quebec, poor Appalachian Whites, the Catholics of Northern Ireland, and other groups of oppressed peoples. However, there simply is not enough room here to adequately deal with all these problems in an *ad hoc* way. We hope that the entire book will help the reader to formulate abstract theoretical considerations applicable to these many particular situations.

THE COMMUNIST MANIFESTO

● *karl marx and frederick engels*

A spectre is haunting Europe—the spectre of Communism. All the Powers of old Europe have entered into a holy alliance to exorcise this spectre: Pope and Czar, Metternich and Guizot, French Radicals and German police-spies.

Where is the party in opposition that has not been decried as Communistic by its opponents in power? Where the Opposition that has not hurled back the branding reproach of Communism, against the more advanced opposition parties, as well as against its reactionary adversaries?

Two things result from this fact.

I. Communism is already acknowledged by all European Powers to be itself a Power.

II. It is high time that Communists should openly, in the face of the whole world, publish their views, their aims, their tendencies, and meet this nursery tale of the Spectre of Communism with a Manifesto of the party itself.

To this end, Communists of various nationalities have assembled in London, and sketched the following Manifesto, to be published in the English, French, German, Italian, Flemish and Danish languages.

bourgeois and proletarians

The history of all hitherto existing society is the history of class struggles.

Freeman and slave, patrician and plebeian, lord and serf, guild-master and journeyman, in a word, oppressor and oppressed, stood in constant opposition to one another, carried on an uninterrupted, now hidden, now open fight, a fight that each time ended, either in a revolutionary re-constitution of society at large, or in the common ruin of the contending classes.

In the earlier epochs of history, we find almost everywhere a complicated arrangement of society into various orders, a manifold gradation of social rank. In ancient Rome we have patricians, knights, plebeians, slaves; in the Middle Ages, feudal lords, vassals, guild-masters, journeymen, apprentices, serfs; in almost all of these classes, again, subordinate gradations.

The modern bourgeois society that has sprouted from the ruins of feudal society has not done away with class antagonisms. It has but established new classes, new conditions of oppression, new forms of struggle in place of the old ones.

Our epoch, the epoch of the bourgeoisie, possesses, however, this distinctive feature: it has simplified the class antagonisms. Society as a whole is more and more splitting up into two great hostile camps, into two great classes directly facing each other: Bourgeoisie and Proletariat.

From the serfs of the Middle Ages sprang the chartered burghers of the earliest towns. From these burgesses the first elements of the bourgeoisie were developed.

The discovery of America, the rounding of the Cape, opened up fresh ground for the rising bourgeoisie. The East-Indian and Chinese markets, the colonisation of America, trade with the colonies, the increase in the means of exchange and in commodities generally, gave to commerce, to navigation, to industry, an impulse never before known, and thereby, to the revolutionary element in the tottering feudal society, a rapid development.

The feudal system of industry, under which industrial production was monopolised by closed guilds, now no longer sufficed for the growing wants of the new markets. The manufacturing system took its place. The guild-masters were pushed on one side by the manufacturing middle class; division of labour between the different corporate guilds vanished in the face of division of labour in each single workshop.

Meantime the markets kept ever growing, the demand ever rising. Even manufacture no longer sufficed. Thereupon, steam and machinery revolutionized industrial production. The place of manufacture was taken by the giant, Modern Industry, the place of the industrial middle class, by industrial millionaires, the leaders of whole industrial armies, the modern bourgeois.

Modern industry has established the world market, for which the discovery of America paved the way. This market has given an immense development to commerce, to navigation, to communication by land. This development has, in its turn, reacted on the extension of industry; and in proportion as industry, commerce, navigation, railways extended, in the same proportion the bourgeoisie developed, increased its capital, and pushed into the background every class handed down from the Middle Ages.

We see, therefore, how the modern bourgeoisie is itself the product of a long course of development, of a series of revolutions in the modes of production and of exchange.

Each step in the development of the bourgeoisie was accompanied by a corresponding political advance of that class. An oppressed class under the sway of the feudal nobility, an armed and self-governing association in the mediaeval commune; here independent urban republic (as in Italy and Germany), there taxable "third estate" of the monarchy (as in France), afterwards, in the period of manufacture proper, serving either the semi-feudal or the absolute monarchy as a counterpoise against the nobility, and, in fact, corner stone of the great monarchies in general, the bourgeoisie has at last, since the establishment of Modern Industry and of the world market, conquered for itself, in the modern representative State, exclusive political sway. The executive of the modern State is but a committee for managing the common affairs of the whole bourgeoisie.

The bourgeoisie, historically, has played a most revolutionary part.

The bourgeoisie, wherever it has got the upper hand, has put an end to all feudal, patriarchal, idyllic relations. It has pitilessly torn asunder the motley feudal ties that bound man to his "natural superiors," and has left remaining no other nexus between man and man than naked self-interest, than callous "cash payment." It has drowned the most heavenly ecstasies of religious fervour, of chivalrous enthusiasm, of philistine sentimentalism, in the icy water of egotistical calculation. It has resolved personal worth into exchange value, and in place of the numberless indefeasible chartered freedoms, has set up that single, unconscionable freedom—Free Trade. In one word, for exploitation, veiled by religious and political illusions, it has substituted naked, shameless, direct, brutal exploitation.

The bourgeoisie has stripped of its halo every occupation hitherto honoured and looked up to with reverent awe. It has converted the physician, the lawyer, the priest, the poet, the man of science, into its paid wage-labourers.

The bourgeoisie has torn away from the family its sentimental veil, and has reduced the family relation to a mere money relation.

The bourgeoisie has disclosed how it came to pass that the brutal display of vigour in the Middle Ages, which Reactionists so much admire, found its fitting complement in the most slothful indolence. It has been the first to show what man's activity can bring about. It has accomplished wonders far surpassing Egyptian pyramids, Roman aqueducts, and Gothic cathedrals; it has conducted expeditions that put in the shade all former Exoduses of nations and crusades.

The bourgeoisie cannot exist without constantly revolutionising the instruments of production, and thereby the relations of production, and with them the whole relations of society. Conservation of the old modes of production in unaltered form, was, on the contrary, the first condition of existence for all earlier industrial classes. Constant revolutionising of production, uninterrupted disturbance of all social conditions, everlasting uncertainty and agitation distinguish the bourgeois epoch from all earlier ones. All fixed, fast-frozen relations, with their train of ancient and venerable prejudices and opinions, are swept away, all new-formed ones become antiquated before they can ossify. All that is solid melts into air, all that is holy is profaned, and man is at last compelled to face with sober senses, his real conditions of life, and his relations with his kind.

The need of a constantly expanding market for its products chases the bourgeoisie over the whole surface of the globe. It must nestle everywhere, settle everywhere, establish connexions everywhere.

The bourgeoisie has through its exploitation of the world market given a cosmopolitan character to production and consumption in every country. To the great chagrin of Reactionists, it has drawn from under the feet of industry the national ground on which it stood. All old-established national industries have been destroyed or are daily being destroyed. They are dislodged by new industries, whose introduction becomes a life and death question for all civilised nations, by industries that no longer work up indigenous raw material, but raw material drawn from the remotest zones; industries whose products are consumed, not only at home, but in every quarter of the globe. In place of the old wants, satisfied by the productions of the country, we find new wants, requiring for their satisfaction the products of distant lands and climes. In place of the old local and national seclusion and self-sufficiency, we have intercourse in every direction, universal interdependence of nations. And as in material, so also in intellectual production. The intellectual creations of individual nations become common property. National one-sidedness and narrow-mindedness become more and more impossible, and from the numerous national and local literatures there arises a world-literature.

The bourgeoisie, by the rapid improvement of all instruments of production, by the immensely facilitated means of communication, draws all, even the most barbarian, nations into civilisation. The cheap prices of its commodities are the heavy artillery with which it batters down all Chinese walls, with which it forces the barbarians' intensely obstinate hatred of foreigners to capitulate. It compels all nations, on pain of extinction, to adopt the bourgeois mode of production; it compels them to introduce what it calls civilisation into their midst, *i.e.*, to become bourgeois themselves. In one word, it creates a world after its own image.

The bourgeoisie has subjected the country to the rule of the towns. It has created enormous cities, has greatly increased the urban population as compared with the rural, and has thus rescued a considerable part of the population from the idiocy of rural life. Just as it has made the country dependent on the towns, so it has made barbarian and semi-barbarian countries dependent on the civilised ones, nations of peasants on nations of bourgeois, the East on the West.

The bourgeoisie keeps more and more doing away with the scattered state of the population, of the means of production, and of property. It has agglomerated population, centralised means of production, and has concentrated property in a few hands. The necessary consequence of this was political centralisation. Independent, or but loosely connected provinces, with separate interests, laws, governments and systems of taxation, became lumped together into one nation, with one government, one code of laws, one national class-interest, one frontier and one customs-tariff.

The bourgeoisie, during its rule of scarce one hundred years, has created more massive and more colossal productive forces than have all preceding generations together. Subjection of Nature's forces to man, machinery, application of chemistry to industry and agriculture, steam-navigation, railways, electric telegraphs, clearing of whole continents for cultivation, canalisation of rivers, whole populations conjured out of the ground—what earlier century had even a presentiment that such productive forces slumbered in the lap of social labour?

We see then: the means of production and of exchange, on whose foundation the bourgeoisie built itself up, were generated in feudal society. At a certain stage in the development of these means of production and of exchange, the conditions under which feudal society produced and exchanged, the feudal organisation of agriculture and manufacturing industry, in one word, the feudal relations of property became no longer compatible with the already developed productive forces; they became so many fetters. They had to be burst asunder; they were burst asunder.

Into their place stepped free competition, accompanied by a social and political constitution adapted to it, and by the economical and political sway of the bourgeois class.

A similar movement is going on before our own eyes. Modern bourgeois society with its relations of production, of exchange and of property, a society that has conjured up such gigantic means of production and of exchange, is like the sorcerer, who is no longer able to control the powers of the nether world whom he has called up by his spells. For many a decade past the history of industry and commerce is but the history of the revolt of modern productive forces against modern conditions of production, against the property relations that are the conditions for the existence of the bourgeoisie and of its rule. It is enough to mention the commercial crises that by their periodical return put on its trial, each time more threateningly, the existence of the entire bourgeois society. In these crises a great part not only of the existing products, but also of the previously created productive forces, are periodically destroyed. In these crises there breaks out an epidemic that, in all earlier epochs, would have seemed an absurdity—the epidemic of over-production. Society suddenly finds itself put back into a state of momentary barbarism; it appears as if a famine, a universal war of devastation had cut off the supply of every means of subsistence; industry and commerce seem to be destroyed; and why? Because there is too much civilisation, too much means of subsistence, too much industry, too much commerce. The productive forces at the disposal of society no longer tend to further the development of the conditions of bourgeois property; on the contrary, they have become too powerful for these conditions, by which they are fettered, and so soon as they overcome these fetters, they bring disorder into the whole of bourgeois society, endanger the existence of bourgeois property. The conditions of bourgeois society are too narrow to comprise the wealth created by them. And how does the bourgeoisie get over these crises? On the one hand by enforced destruction of a mass of productive forces; on the other, by the conquest of new markets, and by the more thorough exploitation of the old ones. That is to say, by paving the way for more extensive and more destructive crises, and by diminishing the means whereby crises are prevented.

The weapons with which the bourgeoisie felled feudalism to the ground are now turned against the bourgeoisie itself.

But not only has the bourgeoisie forged the weapons that bring death to itself; it has also called into existence the men who are to wield those weapons—the modern working class—the proletarians.

In proportion as the bourgeoisie, *i.e.*, capital, is developed, in the same proportion is the proletariat, the modern working class, developed—a class of labourers, who live only so long as they find work, and who find work only so long as their labour increases capital. These labourers, who must sell themselves piecemeal, are a commodity, like every other article of commerce, and are consequently exposed to all the vicissitudes of competition, to all the fluctuations of the market.

Owing to the extensive use of machinery and to division of labour, the work of the proletarians has lost all individual character, and, consequently, all charm for the workman. He becomes an appendage of the machine, and it is only the most simple, most monotonous, and most easily acquired knack, that is required of him. Hence, the cost of production of a workman is restricted, almost entirely, to the means of subsistence that he requires for his maintenance, and for the propagation of his race. But the price of a commodity, and therefore also of labour, is equal to its cost of production. In proportion, therefore, as the repulsiveness of the work increases, the wage decreases. Nay more, in proportion as the use of machinery and division of labour increases, in the same proportion the burden of toil also increases, whether by prolongation of the working hours, by increase of the work exacted in a given time or by increased speed of the machinery, etc.

Modern industry has converted the little workshop of the patriarchal master into the great factory of the industrial capitalist. Masses of labourers, crowded into the factory, are organised like soldiers. As privates of the industrial army they are placed under the command of a perfect hierarchy of officers and sergeants. Not only are they slaves of the bourgeois class, and of the bourgeois State; they are daily and hourly enslaved by the machine, by the overlooker, and, above all, by the individual bourgeois manufacturer himself. The more openly this despotism proclaims gain to be its end and aim, the more petty, the more hateful and the more embittering it is.

The less the skill and exertion of strength implied in manual labour, in other words, the more modern industry becomes developed, the more is the labour of men superseded by that of women. Differences of age and sex have no longer any distinctive social validity for the working class. All are instruments of labour, more or less expensive to use, according to their age and sex.

No sooner is the exploitation of the labourer by the manufacturer, so far, at an end, that he receives his wages in cash, than he is set upon by the other portions of the bourgeoisie, the landlord, the shopkeeper, the pawnbroker, etc.

The lower strata of the middle class—the small tradespeople, shopkeepers, and retired tradesmen generally, the handicraftsmen and peasants—all these sink gradually into the proletariat, partly because their diminutive capital does not suffice for the scale on which Modern Industry is carried on, and is swamped in the competition with the large capitalists, partly because their specialised skill is rendered worthless by new methods of production. Thus the proletariat is recruited from all classes of the population.

The proletariat goes through various stages of development. With its birth begins its struggle with the bourgeoisie. At first the contest is carried on by individual labourers, then by the workpeople of a factory, then by the operatives of one trade, in one locality, against the individual bourgeois who directly exploits them. They direct their attacks not against the bourgeois conditions of production, but against the instruments of production themselves; they destroy imported wares that compete with their labour, they smash to pieces machinery, they set factories ablaze, they seek to restore by force the vanished status of the workman of the Middle Ages.

At this stage the labourers still form an incoherent mass scattered over the whole country, and broken up by their mutual competition. If anywhere they unite to form more compact bodies, this is not yet the consequence of their own active union, but of the union of the bourgeoisie, which class, in order to attain its own political ends, is compelled to set the whole proletariat in motion, and is moreover yet, for a time, able to do so. At this stage, therefore, the proletarians do not fight their enemies, but the enemies of their enemies, the remnants of absolute monarchy, the landowners, the non-industrial bourgeois, the petty bourgeoisie. Thus the whole historical movement is concentrated in the hands of the bourgeoisie; every victory so obtained is a victory for the bourgeoisie.

But with the development of industry the proletariat not only increases in number; it becomes concentrated in greater masses, its strength grows, and it feels that strength more. The various interests and conditions of life within the ranks of the proletariat are more and more equalised, in proportion as machinery obliterates all distinctions of labour, and nearly everywhere reduces wages to the same low level. The growing competition among the bourgeois, and the resulting commercial crises, make the wages of the workers ever more fluctuating. The unceasing improvement of machinery, ever more rapidly developing, makes their livelihood more and more precarious; the collisions between individual workmen and individual bourgeois take more and more the character of collisions between two classes. Thereupon the workers begin to form combinations (Trades' Unions) against the bourgeois; they club together in order to keep up the rate of wages; they found permanent associations in order to make provision beforehand for these occasional revolts. Here and there the contest breaks out into riots.

Now and then the workers are victorious, but only for a time. The real fruit of their battles lies, not in the immediate result, but in the ever-expanding union of the workers. This union is helped on by the improved means of communication that are created by modern industry, and that place the workers of different localities in contact with one another. It was just this contact that was needed to centralise the numerous local struggles, all of the same character, into one national struggle between classes. But every class struggle is a political struggle. And that union, to attain which the burghers of the Middle Ages, with their miserable highways, required centuries, the modern proletarians, thanks to railways, achieve in a few years.

This organisation of the proletarians into a class, and consequently into a political party, is continually being upset again by the competition between the workers themselves. But it ever rises up again, stronger, firmer, mightier. It compels legislative recognition of particular interests of the workers, by taking advantage of the divisions among the bourgeoisie itself. Thus the ten-hours' bill in England was carried.

Altogether collisions between the classes of the old society further, in many ways, the course of development of the proletariat. The bourgeoisie finds itself involved in a constant battle. At first with the aristocracy; later on, with those portions of the bourgeoisie itself, whose interests have become antagonistic to the progress of industry; at all times, with the bourgeoisie of foreign countries. In all these battles it sees itself compelled to appeal to the proletariat, to ask for its help, and thus, to drag it into the political arena. The bourgeoisie itself, therefore, supplies the proletariat with its own elements of political and general education, in other words, it furnishes the proletariat with weapons for fighting the bourgeoisie.

Further, as we have already seen, entire sections of the ruling classes are, by the advance of industry, precipitated into the proletariat, or are at least threatened in their conditions of existence. These also supply the proletariat with fresh elements of enlightenment and progress.

Finally, in times when the class struggle nears the decisive hour, the process of dissolution going on within the ruling class, in fact within the whole range of old society, assumes such a violent, glaring character, that a small section of the ruling class cuts itself adrift, and joins the revolutionary class, the class that holds the future in its hands. Just as, therefore, at an earlier period, a section of the nobility went over to the bourgeoisie, so now a portion of the bourgeoisie goes over to the proletariat, and in particular, a portion of the bourgeois ideologists, who have raised themselves to the level of comprehending theoretically the historical movement as a whole.

Of all the classes that stand face to face with the bourgeoisie to-day, the proletariat alone is a really revolutionary class. The other classes decay and finally disappear in the face of modern industry; the proletariat is its special and essential product.

The lower middle class, the small manufacturer, the shopkeeper, the artisan, the peasant, all these fight against the bourgeoisie, to save from extinction their existence as fractions of the middle class. They are therefore not revolutionary, but conservative. Nay more, they are reactionary, for they try to roll back the wheel of history. If by chance they are revolutionary, they are so only in view of their impending transfer into the proletariat, they thus defend not their present, but their future interests, they desert their own standpoint to place themselves at that of the proletariat.

The "dangerous class," the social scum, that passively rotting mass thrown off by the lowest layers of old society, may, here and there, be swept into the movement by a proletarian revolution; its conditions of life, however, prepare it far more for the part of a bribed tool of reactionary intrigue.

In the conditions of the proletariat, those of old society at large are already virtually swamped. The proletarian is without property; his relation to his wife and children has no longer anything in common with the bourgeois family-relations; modern industrial labour, modern subjection to capital, the same in England as in France, in America as in Germany, has stripped him of every trace of national character. Law, morality, religion, are to him so many bourgeois prejudices, behind which lurk in ambush just as many bourgeois interests.

All the preceding classes that got the upper hand, sought to fortify their already acquired status by subjecting society at large to their conditions of appropriation. The proletarians cannot become masters of the productive forces of society, except by abolishing their own previous mode of appropriation, and thereby also every other previous mode of appropriation. They have nothing of their own to secure and to fortify; their mission is to destroy all previous securities for, and insurances of, individual property.

All previous historical movements were movements of minorities, or in the interest of minorities. The proletarian movement is the self-conscious, independent movement of the immense majority, in the interest of the immense majority. The proletariat, the lowest stratum of our present society, cannot stir, cannot raise itself up, without the whole superincumbent strata of official society being sprung into the air.

Though not in substance, yet in form, the struggle of the proletariat with the bourgeoisie is at first a national struggle. The proletariat of each country must, of course, first of all settle matters with its own bourgeoisie.

In depicting the most general phases of the development of the proletariat, we traced the more or less veiled civil war, raging within existing society, up to the point where that war breaks out into open revolution, and where the violent overthrow of the bourgeoisie lays the foundation for the sway of the proletariat.

Hitherto, every form of society has been based, as we have already seen, on the antagonism of oppressing and oppressed classes. But in order to oppress a class, certain conditions must be assured to it under which it can, at least, continue its slavish existence. The serf, in the period of serfdom, raised himself to membership in the commune, just as the petty bourgeois, under the yoke of feudal absolutism, managed to develop into a bourgeois. The modern labourer, on the contrary, instead of rising with the progress of industry, sinks deeper and deeper below the conditions of existence of his own class. He becomes a pauper, and pauperism develops more rapidly than population and wealth. And here it becomes evident, that the bourgeoisie is unfit any longer to be the ruling class in society, and to impose its conditions of existence upon society as an over-riding law. It is unfit to rule because it is incompetent to assure an existence to its slave within his slavery, because it cannot help letting him sink into such a state, that it has to feed him, instead of being fed by him. Society can no longer live under this bourgeoisie, in other words, its existence is no longer compatible with society.

The essential condition for the existence, and for the sway of the bourgeois class, is the formation and augmentation of capital; the condition for capital is wage-labour. Wage-labour rests exclusively on competition between the labourers. The advance of industry, whose involuntary promoter is the bourgeoisie, replaces the isolation of the labourers, due to competition, by their revolutionary combination, due to association. The development of Modern Industry, therefore, cuts from under its feet the very foundation on which the bourgeoisie produces and appropriates products. What the bourgeoisie, therefore, produces, above all, are its own grave-diggers. Its fall and the victory of the proletariat are equally inevitable.

proletarians and communists

In what relation do the Communists stand to the proletarians as a whole?

The Communists do not form a separate party opposed to other working-class parties.

They have no interests separate and apart from those of the proletariat as a whole.

They do not set up any sectarian principles of their own, by which to shape and mould the proletarian movement.

The Communists are distinguished from the other working-class parties by this only: 1. In the national struggles of the proletarians of the different countries, they point out and bring to the front the common interests of the entire proletariat, independently of all nationality. 2. In the various stages of development which the struggle of the working class against the bourgeoisie has to pass through, they always and everywhere represent the interests of the movement as a whole.

The Communists, therefore, are on the one hand, practically, the most advanced and resolute section of the working-class parties of every country, that section which pushes forward all others; on the other hand, theoretically, they have over the great mass of the proletariat the advantage of clearly understanding the line of march, the conditions, and the ultimate general results of the proletarian movement.

The immediate aim of the Communists is the same as that of all the other proletarian parties: formation of the proletariat into a class, overthrow of the bourgeois supremacy, conquest of political power by the proletariat.

The theoretical conclusions of the Communists are in no way based on ideas or principles that have been invented, or discovered, by this or that would-be universal reformer.

They merely express, in general terms, actual relations springing from an existing class struggle, from a historical movement going on under our very eyes. The abolition of existing property relations is not at all a distinctive feature of Communism.

All property relations in the past have continually been subject to historical change consequent upon the change in historical conditions.

The French Revolution, for example, abolished feudal property in favour of bourgeois property.

The distinguishing feature of Communism is not the abolition of property generally, but the abolition of bourgeois property. But modern bougeois private property is the final and most complete expression of the system of producing and appropriating products, that is based on class antagonisms, on the exploitation of the many by the few.

In this sense, the theory of the Communists may be summed up in the single sentence: Abolition of private property.

We Communists have been reproached with the desire of abolishing the right of personally acquiring property as the fruit of a man's own labour, which property is alleged to be the ground work of all personal freedom, activity and independence.

Hard-won, self-acquired, self-earned property! Do you mean the property of the petty artisan and of the small peasant, a form of property that preceded the bourgeois form? There is no need to abolish that; the development of industry has to a great extent already destroyed it, and is still destroying it daily.

Or do you mean modern bourgeois private property?

But does wage-labour create any property for the labourer? Not a bit. It creates capital, *i.e.*, that kind of property which exploits wage-labour, and which cannot increase except upon condition of begetting a new supply of wage-labour for fresh exploitation. Property, in its present form, is based on the antagonism of capital and wage-labour. Let us examine both sides of this antagonism.

To be a capitalist, is to have not only a purely personal, but a social *status* in production. Capital is a collective product, and only by the united action of many members, nay, in the last resort, only by the united action of all members of society, can it be set in motion.

Capital is, therefore, not a personal, it is a social power.

When, therefore, capital is converted into common property, into the property of all members of society, personal property is not thereby transformed into social property. It is only the social character of the property that is changed. It loses its class character.

Let us now take wage-labour.

The average price of wage-labour is the minimum wage, *i.e.*, that quantum of the means of subsistence, which is absolutely requisite to keep the labourer in bare existence as a labourer. What, therefore, the wage-labourer appropriates by means of his labour, merely suffices to prolong and reproduce a bare existence. We by no means intend to abolish this personal appropriation of the products of labour, an appropriation that is made for the maintenance and reproduction of human life, and that leaves no surplus wherewith to command the labour of others. All that we want to do away with is the miserable character of this appropriation, under which the labourer lives merely to increase capital, and is allowed to live only in so far as the interest of the ruling class requires it.

In bourgeois society, therefore, the past dominates the present; in Comlabour. In Communist society, accumulated labour is but a means to widen, to enrich, to promote the existence of the labourer.

In bourgeois society, therefore, the past dominates the present; in Communist society, the present dominates the past. In bourgeois society capital is independent and has individuality, while the living person is dependent and has no individuality.

And the abolition of this state of things is called by the bourgeois, abolition of individuality and freedom! And rightly so. The abolition of bourgeois individuality, bourgeois independence, and bourgeois freedom is undoubtedly aimed at.

By freedom is meant, under the present bourgeois conditions of production, free trade, free selling and buying.

But if selling and buying disappears, free selling and buying disappears also. This talk about free selling and buying, and all the other "brave words" of our bourgeoisie about freedom in general, have a meaning, if any, only in contrast with restricted selling and buying, with the fettered traders of the Middle Ages, but have no meaning when opposed to the Communistic abolition of buying and selling, of the bourgeois conditions of production, and of the bourgeoisie itself.

You are horrified at our intending to do away with private property. But in your existing society, private property is already done away with for nine-tenths of the population; its existence for the few is solely due to its non-existence in the hands of those nine-tenths. You reproach us, therefore, with intending to do away with a form of property, the necessary condition for whose existence is, the non-existence of any property for the immense majority of society.

In one word, you reproach us with intending to do away with your property. Precisely so; that is just what we intend.

From the moment when labour can no longer be converted into capital, money, or rent, into a social power capable of being monopolised, *i.e.*, from the moment when individual property can no longer be transformed into bourgeois property, into capital, from that moment, you say, individuality vanishes.

You must, therefore, confess that by "individual" you mean no other person than the bourgeois, than the middle-class owner of property. This person must, indeed, be swept out of the way, and made impossible.

Communism deprives no man of the power to appropriate the products of society; all that it does is to deprive him of the power to subjugate the labour of others by means of such appropriation.

It has been objected that upon the abolition of private property all work will cease, and universal laziness will overtake us.

According to this, bourgeois society ought long ago to have gone to the dogs through sheer idleness; for those of its members who work, acquire nothing, and those who acquire anything, do not work. The whole of this objection is but another expression of the tautology: that there can no longer be any wage-labour when there is no longer any capital.

All objections urged against the Communistic mode of producing and appropriating material products, have, in the same way, been urged against the Communistic modes of producing and appropriating intellectual products. Just as, to the bourgeois, the disappearance of class property is the disappearance of production itself, so the disappearance of class culture is to him identical with the disappearance of all culture.

That culture, the loss of which he laments, is, for the enormous majority, a mere training to act as a machine.

But don't wrangle with us so long as you apply, to our intended abolition of bourgeois property, the standard of your bourgeois notions of freedom, culture, law, etc. Your very ideas are but the outgrowth of the conditions of your bourgeois production and bourgeois property, just as your jurisprudence is but the will of your class made into a law for all, a will, whose essential character and direction are determined by the economical conditions of existence of your class.

The selfish misconception that induces you to transform into eternal laws of nature and of reason, the social forms springing from your present mode of production and form of property—historical relations that rise and disappear in the progress of production—this misconception you share with every ruling class that has preceded you. What you see clearly in the case of ancient property, what you admit in the case of feudal property, you are of course forbidden to admit in the case of your own bourgeois form of property.

Abolition of the family! Even the most radical flare up at this infamous proposal of the Communists.

On what foundation is the present family, the bourgeois family, based? On capital, on private gain. In its completely developed form this family exists only among the bourgeoisie. But this state of things finds its complement in the practical absence of the family among the proletarians, and in public prostitution.

The bourgeois family will vanish as a matter of course when its complement vanishes, and both will vanish with the vanishing of capital.

Do you charge us with wanting to stop the exploitation of children by their parents? To this crime we plead guilty.

But, you will say, we destroy the most hallowed of relations, when we replace home education by social.

And your education! Is not that also social, and determined by the social conditions under which you educate, by the intervention, direct or indirect, of society, by means of schools, etc.? The Communists have not invented the intervention of society in education; they do but seek to alter the character of that intervention, and to rescue education from the influence of the ruling class.

The bourgeois clap-trap about the family and education, about the hallowed co-relation of parent and child, becomes all the more disgusting, the more, by the action of Modern Industry, all family ties among the proletarians are torn asunder, and their children transformed into simple articles of commerce and instruments of labour.

But you Communists would introduce community of women, screams the whole bourgeoisie in chorus.

The bourgeois sees in his wife a mere instrument of production. He hears that the instruments of production are to be exploited in common, and, naturally, can come to no other conclusion than that the lot of being common to all will likewise fall to the women.

He has not even a suspicion that the real point aimed at is to do away with the status of women as mere instruments of production.

For the rest, nothing is more ridiculous than the virtuous indignation of our bourgeois at the community of women which, they pretend, is to be openly and officially established by the Communists. The Communists have no need to introduce community of women; it has existed almost from time immemorial.

Our bourgeois, not content with having the wives and daughters of their proletarians at their disposal, not to speak of common prostitutes, take the greatest pleasure in seducing each others' wives.

Bourgeois marriage is in reality a system of wives in common and thus, at the most, what the Communists might possibly be reproached with, is that they desire to introduce, in substitution for a hypocritically concealed, an openly legalised community of women. For the rest, it is self-evident that the abolition of the present system of production must bring with it the abolition of the community of women springing from that system, *i.e.*, of prostitution both public and private.

The Communists are further reproached with desiring to abolish countries and nationality.

The working men have no country. We cannot take from them what they have not got. Since the proletariat must first of all acquire political supremacy, must rise to be the leading class of the nation, must constitute itself *the* nation, it is, so far, itself national, though not in the bourgeois sense of the word.

National differences and antagonisms between peoples are daily more and more vanishing, owing to the development of the bourgeoisie, to freedom of commerce, to the world market, to uniformity in the mode of production and in the conditions of life corresponding thereto.

The supremacy of the proletariat will cause them to vanish still faster. United action, of the leading civilised countries at least, is one of the first conditions for the emancipation of the proletariat.

In proportion as the exploitation of one individual by another is put an end to, the exploitation of one nation by another will also be put an end to. In proportion as the antagonism between classes within the nation vanishes, the hostility of one nation to another will come to an end.

The charges against Communism made from a religious, a philosophical, and, generally, from an ideological standpoint, are not deserving of serious examination.

Does it require deep intuition to comprehend that man's ideas, views and conceptions, in one word, man's consciousness, changes with every change in the conditions of his material existence, in his social relations and in his social life?

What else does the history of ideas prove, than that intellectual production changes its character in proportion as material production is changed? The ruling ideas of each age have ever been the ideas of its ruling class.

When people speak of ideas that revolutionise society, they do but express the fact, that within the old society, the elements of a new one have been created, and that the dissolution of the old ideas keeps even pace with the dissolution of the old conditions of existence.

When the ancient world was in its last throes, the ancient religions were overcome by Christianity. When Christian ideas succumbed in the 18th century to rationalist ideas, feudal society fought its death-battle with the then revolutionary bourgeoisie. The ideas of religious liberty and freedom of conscience, merely gave expression to the sway of free competition within the domain of knowledge.

"Undoubtedly," it will be said, "religious, moral, philosophical and juridical ideas have been modified in the course of historical development. But religion, morality, philosophy, political science, and law, constantly survived this change."

"There are, besides, eternal truths, such as Freedom, Justice, etc., that are common to all states of society. But Communism abolishes eternal truths, it abolishes all religion, and all morality, instead of constituting them on a new basis; it therefore acts in contradiction to all past historical experience."

What does this accusation reduce itself to? The history of all past society has consisted in the development of class antagonisms, antagonisms that assumed different forms at different epochs.

But whatever form they may have taken, one fact is common to all past ages, *viz.,* the exploitation of one part of society by the other. No wonder, then, that the social consciousness of past ages, despite all the multiplicity and variety it displays, moves within certain common forms, or general ideas, which cannot completely vanish except with the total disappearance of class antagonisms.

The Communist revolution is the most radical rupture with traditional property relations; no wonder that its development involves the most radical rupture with traditional ideas.

But let us have done with the bourgeois objections to Communism.

We have seen above, that the first step in the revolution by the working class, is to raise the proletariat to the position of ruling class, to win the battle of democracy.

The proletariat will use its political supremacy to wrest, by degrees, all capital from the bourgeoisie, to centralise all instruments of production in the hands of the State, *i.e.,* of the proletariat organised as the ruling class; and to increase the total of productive forces as rapidly as possible.

Of course, in the beginning, this cannot be effected except by means of despotic inroads on the rights of property, and on the conditions of bourgeois production; by means of measures, therefore, which appear economically insufficient and untenable, but which, in the course of the movement, outstrip themselves, necessitate further inroads upon the old social order, and are unavoidable as a means of entirely revolutionising the mode of production.

These measures will of course be different in different countries.

Nevertheless in the most advanced countries, the following will be pretty generally applicable.

1. Abolition of property in land and application of all rents of land to public purposes.
2. A heavy progressive or graduated income tax.
3. Abolition of all right of inheritance.
4. Confiscation of the property of all emigrants and rebels.
5. Centralisation of credit in the hands of the State, by means of a national bank with State capital and an exclusive monopoly.
6. Centralisation of the means of communication and transport in the hands of the State.
7. Extension of factories and instruments of production owned by the State; the bringing into cultivation of waste lands, and the improvement of the soil generally in accordance with a common plan.
8. Equal liability of all to labour. Establishment of industrial armies, especially for agriculture.
9. Combination of agriculture with manufacturing industries; gradual abolition of the distinction between town and country, by a more equable distribution of the population over the country.
10. Free education for all children in public schools. Abolition of children's factory labour in its present form. Combination of education with industrial production, etc., etc.

When, in the course of development, class distinctions have disappeared, and all production has been concentrated in the hands of a vast association of the whole nation, the public power will lose its political character. Political power, properly so called, is merely the organised power of one class for oppressing another. If the proletariat during its contest with the bourgeoisie is compelled, by the force of circumstances, to organise itself as a class, if, by means of a revolution, it makes itself the ruling class, and, as such, sweeps away by force the old conditions of production, then it will, along with these conditions, have swept away the conditions for the existence of class antagonisms and of classes generally, and will thereby have abolished its own supremacy as a class.

In place of the old bourgeois society, with its classes and class antagonisms, we shall have an association, in which the free development of each is the condition for the free development of all.

socialist and communist literature

reactionary socialism

feudal socialism

Owing to their historical position, it became the vocation of the aristocracies of France and England to write pamphlets against modern bourgeois society. In the French revolution of July, 1830, and in the English reform agitation, these aristocracies again succumbed to the hateful upstart. Thenceforth, a serious political contest was altogether out of the question. A literary battle alone remained possible. But even in the domain of literature the old cries of the restoration period had become impossible.

In order to arouse sympathy, the aristocracy were obliged to lose sight, apparently, of their own interests, and to formulate their indictment against the bourgeoisie in the interest of the exploited working class alone. Thus the aristocracy took their revenge by singing lampoons on their new master, and whispering in his ears sinister prophecies of coming catastrophe.

In this way arose feudal Socialism: half lamentation, half lampoon; half echo of the past, half menace of the future; at times, by its bitter, witty and incisive criticism, striking the bourgeoisie to the very heart's core; but always ludicrous in its effect, through total incapacity to comprehend the march of modern history.

The aristocracy, in order to rally the people to them, waved the proletarian alms-bag in front for a banner. But the people, so often as it joined them, saw on their hindquarters the old feudal coats of arms, and deserted with loud and irreverent laughter.

One section of the French Legitimists and "Young England" exhibited this spectacle.

In pointing out that their mode of exploitation was different to that of the bourgeoisie, the feudalists forget that they exploited under circumstances and conditions that were quite different, and that are now antiquated. In showing that, under their rule, the modern proletariat never existed, they forget that the modern bourgeoisie is the necessary offspring of their own form of society.

For the rest, so little do they conceal the reactionary character of their criticism that their chief accusation against the bourgeoisie amounts to this, that under the bourgeois *régime* a class is being developed, which is destined to cut up root and branch the old order of society.

What they upbraid the bourgeoisie with is not so much that it creates a proletariat, as that it creates a *revolutionary* proletariat.

In political practice, therefore, they join in all coercive measures against the working class; and in ordinary life, despite their high-falutin phrases, they stoop to pick up the golden apples dropped from the tree of industry, and to barter truth, love, and honour for traffic in wool, beetroot-sugar, and potato spirits.

As the parson has ever gone hand in hand with the landlord, so has Clerical Socialism with Feudal Socialism.

Nothing is easier than to give Christian asceticism a Socialist tinge. Has not Christianity declaimed against private property, against marriage, against the State? Has it not preached in the place of these, charity and poverty, celibacy and mortification of the flesh, monastic life and Mother Church? Christian Socialism is but the holy water with which the priest consecrates the heart-burnings of the aristocrat.

petty-bourgeois socialism

The feudal aristocracy was not the only class that was ruined by the bourgeoisie, not the only class whose conditions of existence pined and perished in the atmosphere of modern bourgeois society. The mediaeval burgesses and the small peasant proprietors were the precursors of the modern bourgeoisie. In those countries which are but little developed, industrially and commercially, these two classes still vegetate side by side with the rising bourgeoisie.

In countries where modern civilisation has become fully developed, a new class of petty bourgeois has been formed, fluctuating between proletariat and bourgeoisie, and ever renewing itself as a supplementary part of bourgeois society. The individual members of this class, however, are being constantly hurled down into the proletariat by the action of competition, and, as modern industry develops, they even see the moment approaching when they will completely disappear as an independent section of modern society, to be replaced, in manufactures, agriculture and commerce, by over-lookers, bailiffs and shopmen.

In countries like France, where the peasants constitute far more than half of the population, it was natural that writers who sided with the proletariat against the bourgeoisie, should use, in their criticism of the bourgeois *regime,* the standard of the peasant and petty bourgeois, and from the standpoint of these intermediate classes should take up the cudgels for the working class. Thus arose petty-bourgeois Socialism. Sismondi was the head of this school, not only in France but also in England.

This school of Socialism dissected with great acuteness the contradictions in the conditions of modern production. It laid bare the hypocritical apologies of economists. It proved, incontrovertibly, the disastrous effects of machinery and division of labour; the concentration of capital and land in a few hands; overproduction and crises; it pointed out the inevitable ruin of the petty bourgeois and peasant, the misery of the proletariat, the anarchy in production, the crying inequalities in the distribution of wealth, the industrial war of extermination between nations, the dissolution of old moral bonds, of the old family relations, of the old nationalities.

In its positive aims, however, this form of Socialism aspires either to restoring the old means of production and of exchange, and with them the old property relations, and the old society, or to cramping the modern means of production and of exchange, within the framework of the old property relations that have been, and were bound to be, exploded by those means. In either case, it is both reactionary and Utopian.

Its last words are: corporate guilds for manufacture; patriarchal relations in agriculture.

Ultimately, when stubborn historical facts had dispersed all intoxicating effects of self-deception, this form of Socialism ended in a miserable fit of the blues.

german, or "true," socialism

The Socialist and Communist literature of France, a literature that originated under the pressure of a bourgeoisie in power, and that was the expression of the struggle against this power, was introduced into Germany at a time when the bourgeoisie, in that country, had just begun its contest with feudal absolutism.

German philosophers, would-be philosophers, and *beaux esprits,* eagerly seized on this literature, only forgetting, that when these writings immigrated from France into Germany, French social conditions had not immigrated along with them. In contact with German social conditions, this French literature lost all its immediate practical significance, and assumed a purely literary aspect. Thus, to the German philosophers of the Eighteenth Century, the demands of the first French Revolution were nothing more than the demands of "Practical Reason" in general, and the utterance of the will of the revolutionary French bourgeoisie signified in their eyes the laws of pure Will, of Will as it was bound to be, of true human Will generally.

The work of the German *literati* consisted solely in bringing the new French ideas into harmony with their ancient philosophical conscience, or rather, in annexing the French ideas without deserting their own philosophic point of view.

This annexation took place in the same way in which a foreign language is appropriated, namely, by translation.

It is well known how the monks wrote silly lives of Catholic Saints *over* the manuscripts on which the classical works of ancient heathendom had been written. The German *literati* reversed this process with the profane French literature. They wrote their philosophical nonsense beneath the French original. For instance, beneath the French criticism of the economic functions of money, they wrote "Alienation of Humanity," and beneath the French criticism of the bourgeois State they wrote, "Dethronement of the Category of the General," and so forth.

The introduction of these philosophical phrases at the back of the French historical criticisms they dubbed "Philosophy of Action," "True Socialism," "German Science of Socialism," "Philosophical Foundation of Socialism," and so on.

The French Socialist and Communist literature was thus completely emasculated. And, since it ceased in the hands of the German to express the struggle of one class with the other, he felt conscious of having overcome "French one-sidedness" and of representing, not true requirements, but the requirements of Truth; not the interests of the proletariat, but the interests of Human Nature, of Man in general, who belongs to no class, has no reality, who exists only in the misty realm of philosophical fantasy.

This German Socialism, which took its school-boy task so seriously and solemnly, and extolled its poor stock-in-trade in such mountebank fashion, meanwhile gradually lost its pedantic innocence.

The fight of the German, and, especially, of the Prussian bourgeoisie, against feudal aristocracy and absolute monarchy, in other words, the liberal movement, became more earnest.

By this, the long-wished-for opportunity was offered to "True" Socialism of confronting the political movement with the Socialist demands, of hurling the traditional anathemas against liberalism, against representative government, against bourgeois competition, bourgeois freedom of the press, bourgeois legislation, bourgeois liberty and equality, and of preaching to the masses that they had nothing to gain, and everything to lose, by this bourgeois movement. German Socialism forgot, in the nick of time, that the French criticism, whose silly echo it was, presupposed the existence of modern bourgeois society, with its corresponding economic conditions of existence, and the political constitution adapted thereto, the very things whose attainment was the object of the pending struggle in Germany.

To the absolute governments, with their following of parsons, professors, country squires and officials, it served as a welcome scarecrow against the threatening bourgeoisie.

It was a sweet finish after the bitter pills of floggings and bullets with which these same governments, just at that time, dosed the German working-class risings.

While this "True" Socialism thus served the governments as a weapon for fighting the German bourgeoisie, it, at the same time, directly represented a reactionary interest, the interest of the German Philistines. In Germany the *petty-bourgeois* class, a relic of the 16th century, and since then constantly cropping up again under various forms, is the real social basis of the existing state of things.

To preserve this class is to preserve the existing state of things in Germany. The industrial and political supremacy of the bourgeoisie threatens it with certain destruction; on the one hand, from the concentration of capital; on the other, from the rise of a revolutionary proletariat. "True" Socialism appeared to kill these two birds with one stone. It spread like an epidemic.

The robe of speculative cobwebs, embroidered with flowers of rhetoric, steeped in the dew of sickly sentiment, this transcendental robe in which the German Socialists wrapped their sorry "eternal truths," all skin and bone, served to wonderfully increase the sale of their goods amongst such a public.

And on its part, German Socialism recognised, more and more, its own calling as the bombastic representative of the petty-bourgeois Philistine.

It proclaimed the German nation to be the model nation, and the German petty Philistine to be the typical man. To every villainous meanness of this model man it gave a hidden, higher, Socialistic interpretation, the exact contrary of its real character. It went to the extreme length of directly opposing the "brutally destructive" tendency of Communism, and of proclaiming its supreme and impartial contempt of all class struggles. With very few exceptions, all the so-called Socialist and Communist publications that now (1847) circulate in Germany belong to the domain of this foul and enervating literature.

conservative, or bourgeois, socialism

A part of the bourgeoisie is desirous of redressing social grievances, in order to secure the continued existence of bourgeois society.

To this section belong economists, philanthropists, humanitarians, improvers of the condition of the working class, organisers of charity, members of societies for the prevention of cruelty to animals, temperance fanatics, hole-and-corner reformers of every imaginable kind. This form of Socialism has, moreover, been worked out into complete systems.

We may cite Proudhon's *Philosophie de la Misere* as an example of this form.

The Socialistic bourgeois want all the advantages of modern social conditions without the struggles and dangers necessarily resulting therefrom. They desire the existing state of society minus its revolutionary and disintegrating elements. They wish for a bourgeoisie without a proletariat. The bourgeoisie naturally conceives the world in which it is supreme to be the best; and bourgeois Socialism develops this comfortable conception into various more or less complete systems. In requiring the proletariat to carry out such a system, and thereby to march straightway into the social New Jerusalem, it but requires in reality, that the proletariat should remain within the bounds of existing society, but should cast away all its hateful ideas concerning the bourgeoisie.

A second and more practical, but less systematic, form of this Socialism sought to depreciate every revolutionary movement in the eyes of the working class, by showing that no mere political reform, but only a change in the material conditions of existence, in economical relations, could be of any advantage to them. By changes in the material conditions of existence, this form of Socialism, however, by no means understands abolition of the bourgeois relations of production, an abolition that can be effected only by a revolution, but administrative reforms, based on the continued existence of these relations; reforms, therefore, that in no respect affect the relations between capital and labour, but, at the best, lessen the cost, and simplify the administrative work, of bourgeois government.

Bourgeois Socialism attains adequate expression, when, and only when, it becomes a mere figure of speech.

Free trade: for the benefit of the working class. Protective duties: for the benefit of the working class. Prison Reform: for the benefit of the working class. This is the last word and the only seriously meant word of bourgeois Socialism.

It is summed up in the phrase: the bourgeois is a bourgeois—for the benefit of the working class.

critical-utopian socialism and communism

We do not here refer to that literature which, in every great modern revolution, has always given voice to the demands of the proletariat, such as the writings of Babeuf and others.

The first direct attempts of the proletariat to attain its own ends, made in times of universal excitement, when feudal society was being overthrown, these attempts necessarily failed, owing to the then undeveloped state of the proletariat, as well as to the absence of the economic conditions for its emancipation, conditions that had yet to be produced, and could be produced by the impending bourgeois epoch alone. The revolutionary literature that accompanied these first movements of the proletariat had necessarily a reactionary character. It inculcated universal asceticism and social levelling in its crudest form.

The Socialist and Communist systems properly so called, those of St. Simon, Fourier, Owen and others, spring into existence in the early undeveloped period, described above, of the struggle between proletariat and bourgeoisie (see Section I. Bourgeois and Proletarians).

The founders of these systems see, indeed, the class antagonisms, as well as the action of the decomposing elements in the prevailing form of society. But the proletariat, as yet in its infancy, offers to them the spectacle of a class without any historical initiative or any independent political movement.

Since the development of class antagonism keeps even pace with the development of industry, the economic situation, as they find it, does not as yet offer to them the material conditions for the emancipation of the proletariat. They therefore search after a new social science, after new social laws, that are to create these conditions.

Historical action is to yield to their personal inventive action, historically created conditions of emancipation to fantastic ones, and the gradual, spontaneous class-organisation of the proletariat to an organisation of society specially contrived by these inventors. Future history resolves itself, in their eyes, into the propaganda and the practical carrying out of their social plans.

In the formation of their plans they are conscious of caring chiefly for the interests of the working class, as being the most suffering class. Only from the point of view of being the most suffering class does the proletariat exist for them.

The undeveloped state of the class struggle, as well as their own surroundings, causes Socialists of this kind to consider themselves far superior to all class antagonisms. They want to improve the condition of every member of society, even that of the most favoured. Hence, they habitually appeal to society at large, without distinction of class; nay, by preference, to the ruling class. For how can people, when once they understand their system, fail to see in it the best possible plan of the best possible state of society?

Hence, they reject all political, and especially all revolutionary, action; they wish to attain their ends by peaceful means, and endeavour, by small experiments, necessarily doomed to failure, and by the force of example, to pave the way for the new social Gospel.

Such fantastic pictures of future society, painted at a time when the proletariat is still in a very undeveloped state and has but a fantastic conception of its own position, correspond with the first instinctive yearnings of that class for a general reconstruction of society.

But these Socialist and Communist publications contain also a critical element. They attack every principle of existing society. Hence they are full of the most valuable materials for the enlightenment of the working class. The practical measures proposed in them—such as the abolition of the distinction between town and country, of the family, of the carrying on of industries for the account of private individuals, and of the wage system, the proclamation of social harmony, the conversion of the functions of the State into a mere superintendence of production, all these proposals point solely to the disappearance of class antagonisms which were, at that time, only just cropping up, and which, in these publications, are recognised in their earliest, indistinct and undefined forms only. These proposals, therefore, are of a purely Utopian character.

The significance of Critical-Utopian Socialism and Communism bears an inverse relation to historical development. In proportion as the modern class struggle develops and takes definite shape, this fantastic standing apart from the contest, these fantastic attacks on it, lose all practical value and all theoretical justification. Therefore, although the originators of these systems were, in many respects, revolutionary, their disciples have, in every case, formed mere reactionary sects. They hold fast by the original views of their masters, in opposition to the progressive historical development of the proletariat. They, therefore, endeavour, and that consistently, to deaden the class struggle and to reconcile the class antagonisms. They still dream of experimental realisation of their social Utopias, of founding isolated "*phalansteres,*" of establishing "Home Colonies," of setting up a "Little Icaria"—duodecimo editions of the New Jerusalem—and to realise all these castles in the air, they are compelled to appeal to the feelings and purses of the bourgeois. By degrees they sink into the category of the reactionary conservative Socialists depicted above, differing from these only by more systematic pedantry, and by their fanatical and superstitious belief in the miraculous effects of their social science.

They, therefore, violently oppose all political action on the part of the working class; such action, according to them, can only result from blind unbelief in the new Gospel.

The Owenites in England, and the Fourierists in France, respectively oppose the Chartists and the *Reformistes*.

position of the communists in relation to the various existing opposition parties

Section II has made clear the relations of the Communists to the existing working-class parties, such as the Chartists in England and the Agrarian Reformers in America.

The Communists fight for the attainment of the immediate aims, for the enforcement of the momentary interests of the working class; but in the movement of the present, they also represent and take care of the future of that movement. In France the Communists ally themselves with the Social-Democrats, against the conservative and radical bourgeoisie, reserving, however, the right to take up a critical position in regard to phrases and illusions traditionally handed down from the great Revolution.

In Switzerland they support the Radicals, without losing sight of the fact that this party consists of antagonistic elements, partly of Democratic Socialists, in the French sense, partly of radical bourgeois.

In Poland they support the party that insists on an agrarian revolution as the prime condition for national emancipation, that party which fomented the insurrection of Cracow in 1846.

In Germany they fight with the bourgeoisie whenever it acts in a revolutionary way, against the absolute monarchy, the feudal squirearchy, and the petty bourgeoisie.

But they never cease, for a single instant, to instil into the working class the clearest possible recognition of the hostile antagonism between bourgeoisie and proletariat, in order that the German workers may straightway use, as so many weapons against the bourgeoisie, the social and political conditions that the bourgeoisie must necessarily introduce along with its supremacy, and in order that, after the fall of the reactionary classes in Germany, the fight against the bourgeoisie itself may immediately begin.

The Communists turn their attention chiefly to Germany, because that country is on the eve of a bourgeois revolution that is bound to be carried out under more advanced conditions of European civilisation, and with a much more developed proletariat, than that of England was in the seventeenth, and of France in the eighteenth century, and because the bourgeois revolution in Germany will be but the prelude to an immediately following proletarian revolution.

In short, the Communists everywhere support every revolutionary movement against the existing social and political order of things.

In all these movements they bring to the front, as the leading question in each, the property question, no matter what its degree of development at the time.

Finally, they labour everywhere for the union and agreement of the democratic parties of all countries.

The Communists disdain to conceal their views and aims. They openly declare that their ends can be attained only by the forcible overthrow of all existing social conditions. Let the ruling classes tremble at a Communistic revolution. The proletarians have nothing to lose but their chains. They have a world to win.

WORKING MEN OF ALL COUNTRIES, UNITE!

IMPERIALISM: THE LAST STAGE OF CAPITALISM—SELECTIONS

● *v. i. lenin*

imperialism as a special stage of capitalism

We must now try to sum up and put together what has been said above on the subject of imperialism. Imperialism emerged as the development and direct continuation of the fundamental attributes of capitalism in general. But capitalism only became capitalist imperialism at a definite and very high stage of its development, when certain of its fundamental attributes began to be transformed into their opposites, when the features of a period of transition from capitalism to a higher social and economic system began to take shape and reveal themselves all along the line. Economically, the main thing in this process is the substitution of capitalist monopolies for capitalist free competition. Free competition is the fundamental attribute of capitalism, and of commodity production generally. Monopoly is exactly the opposite of free competition; but we have seen the latter being transformed into monopoly before our very eyes, creating large-scale industry and eliminating small industry, replacing large-scale industry by still larger-scale industry, finally leading to such a concentration of production and capital that monopoly has been and is the result: cartels, syndicates and trusts, and merging with them, the capital of a dozen or so banks manipulating thousands of millions. At the same time monopoly, which has grown out of free competition, does not abolish the latter, but exists over it and alongside of it, and thereby gives rise to a number of very acute, intense antagonisms, friction and conflicts. Monopoly is the transition from capitalism to a higher system.

If it were necessary to give the briefest possible definition of imperialism we should have to say that imperialism is the monopoly stage of capitalism. Such a definition would include what is most important, for, on the one hand, finance capital is the bank capital of a few big monopolist banks, merged with the capital of the monopolist combines of manufacturers; and, on the other hand, the division of the world is the transition from a colonial policy which has extended without hindrance to territories unoccupied by any capitalist power, to a colonial policy of monopolistic possession of the territory of the world which has been completely divided up.

But very brief definitions, although convenient, for they sum up the main points, are nevertheless inadequate, because very important features of the phenomenon that has to be defined have to be especially deduced. And so, without forgetting the conditional and relative value of all definitions, which can never include all the concatenations of a phenomenon in its complete development, we must give a definition of imperialism that will embrace the following five essential features:

1) The concentration of production and capital developed to such a high stage that it created monopolies which play a decisive role in economic life.

2) The merging of bank capital with industrial capital, and the creation, on the basis of this "finance capital," of a "financial oligarchy."

3) The export of capital, which has become extremely important, as distinguished from the export of commodities.

4) The formation of international capitalist monopolies which share the world among themselves.

5) The territorial division of the whole world among the greatest capitalist powers is completed.

Imperialism is capitalism in that stage of development in which the dominance of monopolies and finance capital has established itself; in which the export of capital has acquired pronounced importance; in which the division of the world among the international trusts has begun; in which the division of all territories of the globe among the great capitalist powers has been completed. . . .

the place of imperialism in history

We have seen that the economic quintessence of imperialism is monopoly capitalism. This very fact determines its place in history, for monopoly that grew up on the basis of free competition, and precisely out of free competition, is the transition from the capitalist system to a higher social-economic order. We must take special note of the four principal forms of monopoly, or the four principal manifestations of monopoly capitalism, which are characteristic of the epoch under review.

Firstly, monopoly arose out of the concentration of production at a very advanced stage of development. This refers to the monopolist capitalist combines, cartels, syndicates and trusts. We have seen the important part that these play in modern economic life. At the beginning of the twentieth century, monopolies acquired complete supremacy in the advanced countries. And although the first steps towards the formation of the cartels were first taken by countries enjoying the protection of high tariffs (Germany, America), Great Britain, with her system of free trade, was not far behind in revealing the same basic phenomenon, namely, the birth of monopoly out of the concentration of production.

Secondly, monopolies have accelerated the capture of the most important sources of raw materials, especially for the coal and iron industries, which are the basic and most highly cartelised industries in capitalist society. The monopoly of the most important sources of raw materials has enormously increased the power of big capital, and has sharpened the antagonism between cartelised and non-cartelised industry.

Thirdly, monopoly has sprung from the banks. The banks have developed from modest intermediary enterprises into the monopolists of finance capital. Some three or five of the biggest banks in each of the foremost capitalist countries have achieved the "personal union" of industrial and bank capital, and have concentrated in their hands the disposal of thousands upon thousands of millions which form the greater part of the capital and income of entire countries. A financial oligarchy, which throws a close net of relations of dependence over all the economic and political institutions of contemporary bourgeois society without exception—such is the most striking manifestation of this monopoly.

Fourthly, monopoly has grown out of colonial policy. To the numerous "old" motives of colonial policy, finance capital has added the struggle for the sources of raw materials, for the export of capital, for "spheres of influence," *i.e.*, for spheres for profitable deals, concessions, monopolist profits and so on; in fine, for economic territory in general. When the colonies of the European powers in Africa, for instance, comprised only one-tenth of that territory (as was the case in 1876), colonial policy was able to develop by methods other than those of monopoly—by the "free grabbing" of territories, so to speak.

 But when nine-tenths of Africa had been seized (approximately by 1900), when the whole world had been divided up, there was inevitably ushered in a period of colonial monopoly and, consequently, a period of particularly intense struggle for the division and the redivision of the world.

The extent to which monopolist capital has intensified all the contradictions of capitalism is generally known. It is sufficient to mention the high cost of living and the oppression of the cartels. This intensification of contradictions constitutes the most powerful driving force of the transitional period of history, which began from the time of the definite victory of world finance capital.

Monopolies, oligarchy, the striving for domination instead of the striving for liberty, the exploitation of an increasing number of small or weak nations by an extremely small group of the richest or most powerful nations—all these have given birth to those distinctive characteristics of imperialism which compel us to define it as parasitic or decaying capitalism. More and more prominently there emerges, as one of the tendencies of imperialism, the creation of the "bondholding" (rentier) state, the usurer state, in which the bourgeoisie lives on the proceeds of capital exports and by "clipping coupons." It would be a mistake to believe that this tendency to decay precludes the possibility of the rapid growth of capitalism. It does not. In the epoch of imperialism, certain branches of industry, certain strata of the bourgeoisie and certain countries betray, to a more or less degree, one or other of these tendencies. On the whole, capitalism is growing far more rapidly than before. But this growth is not only becoming more and more uneven in general; its unevenness also manifests itself, in particular, in the decay of the countries which are richest in capital (such as England). . . .

In its turn, this finance capital which has grown so rapidly is not unwilling (precisely because it has grown so quickly) to pass on to a more "tranquil" possession of colonies which have to be seized—and not only by peaceful methods—from richer nations. In the United States, economic development in the last decades has been even more rapid than in Germany, and *for this very reason* the parasitic character of modern American capitalism has stood out with particular prominence. On the other hand, a comparison of, say, the republican American bourgeoisie with the monarchist Japanese or German bourgeoisie shows that the most pronounced political distinctions diminish to an extreme degree in the epoch of imperialism—not because they are unimportant in general, but because in all these cases we are discussing a bourgeoisie which has definite features of parasitism. . . .

THE NEW FORMS OF CONTROL

● *herbert marcuse*

A comfortable, smooth, reasonable, democratic unfreedom prevails in advanced industrial civilization, a token of technical progress. Indeed, what could be more rational than the suppression of individuality in the mechanization of socially necessary but painful performances; the concentration of individual enterprises in more effective, more productive corporations; the regulation of free competition among unequally equipped economic subjects; the curtailment of prerogatives and national sovereignties which impede the international organization of resources. That this technological order also involves a political and intellectual coordination may be a regrettable and yet promising development.

The rights and liberties which were such vital factors in the origins and earlier stages of industrial society yield to a higher stage of this society: they are losing their traditional rationale and content. Freedom of thought, speech, and conscience were—just as free enterprise, which they served to promote and protect—essentially *critical* ideas, designed to replace an obsolescent material and intellectual culture by a more productive and rational one. Once institutionalized, these rights and liberties shared the fate of the society of which they had become an integral part. The achievement cancels the premises.

To the degree to which freedom from want, the concrete substance of all freedom, is becoming a real possibility, the liberties which pertain to a state of lower productivity are losing their former content. Independence of thought, autonomy, and the right to political opposition are being deprived of their basic critical function in a society which seems increasingly capable of satisfying the needs of the individuals through the way in which it is organized. Such a society may justly demand acceptance of its principles and institutions, and reduce the opposition to the discussion and promotion of alternative policies *within* the status quo. In this respect, it seems to make little difference whether the increasing satisfaction of needs is accomplished by an authoritarian or a non-authoritarian system. Under the conditions of a rising standard of living, non-conformity with the system itself appears to be socially useless, and the more so when it entails tangible economic and political disadvantages and threatens the smooth operation of the whole. Indeed, at least in so far as the necessities of life are involved, there seems to be no reason why the production and distribution of goods and services should proceed through the competitive concurrence of individual liberties.

Freedom of enterprise was from the beginning not altogether a blessing. As the liberty to work or to starve, it spelled toil, insecurity, and fear for the vast majority of the population. If the individual were no longer compelled to prove himself on the market, as a free economic subject, the disappearance of this kind of freedom would be one of the greatest achievements of civilization. The technological processes of mechanization and standardization might release individual energy into a yet uncharted realm of freedom beyond necessity. The very structure of human existence would be altered; the individual would be liberated from the work world's imposing upon him alien needs and alien possibilities. The individual would be free to exert autonomy over a life that would be his own. If the productive apparatus could be organized and directed toward the satisfaction of the vital needs, its control might well be centralized; such control would not prevent individual autonomy, but render it possible.

This is a goal within the capabilities of advanced industrial civilization, the "end" of technological rationality. In actual fact, however, the contrary trend operates: the apparatus imposes its economic and political requirements for defense and expansion on labor time and free time, on the material and intellectual culture. By virtue of the way it has organized its technological base, contemporary industrial society tends to be totalitarian. For "totalitarian" is not only a terroristic political coordination of society, but also a non-terroristic economic-technical coordination which operates through the manipulation of needs by vested interests. It thus precludes the emergence of an effective opposition against the whole. Not only a specific form of government or party rule makes for totalitarianism, but also a specific system of production and distribution which may well be compatible with a "pluralism" of parties, newspapers, "countervailing powers," etc.

Today political power asserts itself through its power over the machine process and over the technical organization of the apparatus. The government of advanced and advancing industrial societies can maintain and secure itself only when it succeeds in mobilizing, organizing, and exploiting the technical, scientific, and mechanical productivity available to industrial civilization. And this productivity mobilizes society as a whole, above and beyond any particular individual or group interests. The brute fact that the machine's physical (only physical?) power surpasses that of the individual, and of any particular group of individuals, makes the machine the most effective political instrument in any society whose basic organization is that of the machine process. But the political trend may be reversed; essentially the power of the machine is only the stored-up and projected power of man. To the extent to which the work world is conceived of as a machine and mechanized accordingly, it becomes the *potential* basis of a new freedom for man.

Contemporary industrial civilization demonstrates that it has reached the stage at which "the free society" can no longer be adequately defined in the traditional terms of economic, political, and intellectual liberties, not because these liberties have become insignificant, but because they are too significant to be confined within the traditional forms. New modes of realization are needed, corresponding to the new capabilities of society.

Such new modes can be indicated only in negative terms because they would amount to the negation of the prevailing modes. Thus economic freedom would mean freedom *from* the economy—from being controlled by economic forces and relationships; freedom from the daily struggle for existence, from earning a living. Political freedom would mean liberation of the individuals *from* politics over which they have no effective control. Similarly, intellectual freedom would mean the restoration of individual thought now absorbed by mass communication and indoctrination, abolition of "public opinion" together with its makers. The unrealistic sound of these propositions is indicative, not of their utopian character, but of the strength of the forces which prevent their realization. The most effective and enduring form of warfare against liberation is the implanting of material and intellectual needs that perpetuate obsolete forms of the struggle for existence.

The intensity, the satisfaction and even the character of human needs, beyond the biological level, have always been preconditioned. Whether or not the possibility of doing or leaving, enjoying or destroying, possessing or rejecting something is seized as a *need* depends on whether or not it can be seen as desirable and necessary for the prevailing societal institutions and interests. In this sense, human needs are historical needs and, to the extent to which the society demands the repressive development of the individual, his needs themselves and their claim for satisfaction are subject to overriding critical standards.

We may distinguish both true and false needs. "False" are those which are superimposed upon the individual by particular social interests in his repression: the needs which perpetuate toil, aggressiveness, misery, and injustice. Their satisfaction might be most gratifying to the individual, but this happiness is not a condition which has to be maintained and protected if it serves to arrest the development of the ability (his own and others) to recognize the disease of the whole and grasp the chances of curing the disease. The result then is euphoria in unhappiness. Most of the prevailing needs to relax, to have fun, to behave and consume in accordance with the advertisements, to love and hate what others love and hate, belong to this category of false needs.

Such needs have a societal content and function which are determined by external powers over which the individual has no control; the development and satisfaction of these needs is heteronomous. No matter how much such needs may have become the individual's own, reproduced and fortified by the conditions of his existence; no matter how much he identifies himself with them and finds himself in their satisfaction, they continue to be what they were from the beginning—products of a society whose dominant interest demands repression.

The prevalence of repressive needs is an accomplished fact, accepted in ignorance and defeat, but a fact that must be undone in the interest of the happy individual as well as all those whose misery is the price of his satisfaction. The only needs that have an unqualified claim for satisfaction are the vital ones—nourishment, clothing, lodging at the attainable level of culture. The satisfaction of these needs is the prerequisite for the realization of *all* needs, of the unsublimated as well as the sublimated ones.

For any consciousness and conscience, for any experience which does not accept the prevailing societal interest as the supreme law of thought and behavior, the established universe of needs and satisfactions is a fact to be questioned—questioned in terms of truth and falsehood. These terms are historical throughout, and their objectivity is historical. The judgment of needs and their satisfaction, under the given conditions, involves standards of *priority*—standards which refer to the optimal development of the individual, of all individuals, under the optimal utilization of the material and intellectual resources available to man. The resources are calculable. "Truth" and "falsehood" of needs designate objective conditions to the extent to which the universal satisfaction of vital needs and, beyond it, the progressive alleviation of toil and poverty, are universally valid standards. But as historical standards, they do not only vary according to area and stage of development, they also can be defined only in (greater or lesser) *contradiction* to the prevailing ones. What tribunal can possibly claim the authority of decision?

In the last analysis, the question of what are true and false needs must be answered by the individuals themselves, but only in the last analysis; that is, if and when they are free to give their own answer. As long as they are kept incapable of being autonomous, as long as they are indoctrinated and manipulated (down to their very instincts), their answer to this question cannot be taken as their own. By the same token, however, no tribunal can justly arrogate to itself the right to decide which needs should be developed and satisfied. Any such tribunal is reprehensible, although our revulsion does not do away with the question: how can the people who have been the object of effective and productive domination by themselves create the conditions of freedom?

The more rational, productive, technical, and total the repressive administration of society becomes, the more unimaginable the means and ways by which the administered individuals might break their servitude and seize their own liberation. To be sure, to impose Reason upon an entire society is a paradoxical and scandalous idea—although one might dispute the righteousness of a society which ridicules this idea while making its own population into objects of total administration. All liberation depends on the consciousness of servitude, and the emergence of this consciousness is always hampered by the predominance of needs and satisfactions which, to a great extent, have become the individual's own. The process always replaces one system of preconditioning by another; the optimal goal is the replacement of false needs by true ones, the abandonment of repressive satisfaction.

The distinguishing feature of advanced industrial society is its effective suffocation of those needs which demand liberation—liberation also from that which is tolerable and rewarding and comfortable—while it sustains and absolves the destructive power and repressive function of the affluent society. Here, the social controls exact the overwhelming need for the production and consumption of waste; the need for stupefying work where it is no longer a real necessity; the need for modes of relaxation which soothe and prolong this stupefication; the need for maintaining such deceptive liberties as free competition at administered prices, a free press which censors itself, free choice between brands and gadgets.

Under the rule of a repressive whole, liberty can be made into a powerful instrument of domination. The range of choice open to the individual is not the decisive factor in determining the degree of human freedom, but *what* can be chosen and what *is* chosen by the individual. The criterion for free choice can never be an absolute one, but neither is it entirely relative. Free election of masters does not abolish the masters or the slaves. Free choice among a wide variety of goods and services does not signify freedom if these goods and services sustain social controls over a life of toil and fear—that is, if they sustain alienation. And the spontaneous reproduction of superimposed needs by the individual does not establish autonomy; it only testifies to the efficacy of the controls.

Our insistence on the depth and efficacy of these controls is open to the objection that we overrate greatly the indoctrinating power of the "media," and that by themselves the people would feel and satisfy the needs which are now imposed upon them. The objection misses the point. The preconditioning does not start with the mass production of radio and television and with the centralization of their control. The people enter this stage as preconditioned receptacles of long standing; the decisive difference is in the flattening out of the contrast (or conflict) between the given and the possible, between the satisfied and the unsatisfied needs. Here, the so-called equalization of class distinctions reveals its ideological function. If the worker and his boss enjoy the same television program and visit the same resort places, if the typist is as attractively made up as the daughter of her employer, if the Negro owns a Cadillac, if they all read the same newspaper, then this assimilation indicates not the disappearance of classes, but the extent to which the needs and satisfactions that serve the preservation of the Establishment are shared by the underlying population.

Indeed, in the most highly developed areas of contemporary society, the transplantation of social into individual needs is so effective that the difference between them seems to be purely theoretical. Can one really distinguish between the mass media as instruments of information and entertainment, and as agents of manipulation and indoctrination? Between the automobile as nuisance and as convenience? Between the horrors and the comforts of functional architecture? Between the work for national defense, and the work for corporate gain? Between the private pleasure and the commercial and political utility involved in increasing the birth rate?

We are again confronted with one of the most vexing aspects of advanced industrial civilization: the rational character of its irrationality. Its productivity and efficiency, its capacity to increase and spread comforts, to turn waste into need, and destruction into construction, the extent to which this civilization transforms the object world into an extension of man's mind and body makes the very notion of alienation questionable. The people recognize themselves in their commodities; they find their soul in their automobile, hi-fi set, split-level home, kitchen equipment. The very mechanism which ties the individual to his society has changed, and social control is anchored in the new needs which it has produced.

The prevailing forms of social control are technological in a new sense. To be sure, the technical structure and efficacy of the productive and destructive apparatus has been a major instrumentality for subjecting the population to the established social division of labor throughout the modern period. Moreover, such integration has always been accompanied by more obvious forms of compulsion: loss of livelihood, the administration of justice, the police, the armed forces. It still is. But in the contemporary period, the technological controls appear to be the very embodiment of Reason for the benefit of all social groups and interests—to such an extent that all contradiction seems irrational and all counteraction impossible.

No wonder then that, in the most advanced areas of this civilization, the social controls have been introjected to the point where even individual protest is affected at its roots. The intellectual and emotional refusal "to go along" appears neurotic and impotent. This is the socio-psychological aspect of the political event that marks the contemporary period: the passing of the historical forces which, at the preceding stage of industrial society, seemed to represent the possibility of new forms of existence.

But the term "introjection" perhaps no longer describes the way in which the individual by himself reproduces and perpetuates the external controls exercised by his society. Introjection suggests a variety of relatively spontaneous processes by which a Self (Ego) transposes the "outer" into the "inner." Thus introjection implies the existence of an inner dimension distinguished from and even antagonistic to the external exigencies—an individual consciousness and an individual unconscious *apart from* public opinion and behavior.[1] The idea of "inner freedom" here has its reality: it designates the private space in which man may become and remain "himself."

Today this private space has been invaded and whittled down by technological reality. Mass production and mass distribution claim the *entire* individual, and industrial psychology has long since ceased to be confined to the factory. The manifold processes of introjection seem to be ossified in almost mechanical reactions. The result is, not adjustment but *mimesis:* an immediate identification of the individual with *his* society and, through it, with the society as a whole.

This immediate, automatic identification (which may have been characteristic of primitive forms of association) reappears in high industrial civilization;

[1] The change in the function of the family here plays a decisive role: its "socializing" functions are increasingly taken over by outside groups and media. See my *Eros and Civilization* (Boston: Beacon Press, 1955), p. 96 ff.

 its new "immediacy," however, is the product of a sophisticated, scientific management and organization. In this process, the "inner" dimension of the mind in which opposition to the status quo can take root is whittled down. The loss of this dimension, in which the power of negative thinking—the critical power of Reason—is at home, is the ideological counterpart to the very material process in which advanced industrial society silences and reconciles the opposition. The impact of progress turns Reason into submission to the facts of life, and to the dynamic capability of producing more and bigger facts of the same sort of life. The efficiency of the system blunts the individuals' recognition that it contains no facts which do not communicate the repressive power of the whole. If the individuals find themselves in the things which shape their life, they do so, not by giving, but by accepting the law of things—not the law of physics but the law of their society.

I have just suggested that the concept of alienation seems to become questionable when the individuals identify themselves with the existence which is imposed upon them and have in it their own development and satisfaction. This identification is not illusion but reality. However, the reality constitutes a more progressive stage of alienation. The latter has become entirely objective; the subject which is alienated is swallowed up by its alienated existence. There is only one dimension, and it is everywhere and in all forms. The achievements of progress defy ideological indictment as well as justification; before their tribunal, the "false consciousness" of their rationality becomes the true consciousness.

This absorption of ideology into reality does not, however, signify the "end of ideology." On the contrary, in a specific sense advanced industrial culture is *more* ideological than its predecessor, inasmuch as today the ideology is in the process of production itself.[2] In a provocative form, this proposition reveals the political aspects of the prevailing technological rationality. The productive apparatus and the goods and services which it produces "sell" or impose the social system as a whole. The means of mass transportation and communication, the commodities of lodging, food, and clothing, the irresistible output of the entertainment and information industry carry with them prescribed attitudes and habits, certain intellectual and emotional reactions which bind the consumers more or less pleasantly to the producers and, through the latter, to the whole. The products indoctrinate and manipulate; they promote a false consciousness which is immune against its falsehood. And as these beneficial products become available to more individuals in more social classes, the indoctrination they carry ceases to be publicity; it becomes a way of life. It is a good way of life—much better than before—and as a good way of life, it militates against qualitative change. Thus emerges a pattern of *one-dimensional thought and behavior* in which ideas, aspirations, and objectives that, by their content, transcend the established universe of discourse and action are either repelled or reduced to terms of this universe. They are redefined by the rationality of the given system and of its quantitative extension.

The trend may be related to a development in scientific method: operationalism in the physical, behaviorism in the social sciences. The common feature is a total empiricism in the treatment of concepts; their meaning is

[2] Theodor W. Adorno, *Prismen. Kulturkritik und Gesellschaft.* (Frankfurt: Suhrkamp, 1955), p. 24 f.

restricted to the representation of particular operations and behavior. The operational point of view is well illustrated by P. W. Bridgman's analysis of the concept of length:[3]

> *We evidently know what we mean by length if we can tell what the length of any and every object is, and for the physicist nothing more is required. To find the length of an object, we have to perform certain physical operations. The concept of length is therefore fixed when the operations by which length is measured are fixed: that is, the concept of length involves as much and nothing more than the set of operations by which length is determined. In general, we mean by any concept nothing more than a set of operations;* the concept is synonymous with the corresponding set of operations.

Bridgman has seen the wide implications of this mode of thought for the society at large:[4]

> *To adopt the operational point of view involves much more than a mere restriction of the sense in which we understand 'concept,' but means a far-reaching change in all our habits of thought, in that we shall no longer permit ourselves to use as tools in our thinking concepts of which we cannot give an adequate account in terms of operations.*

Bridgman's prediction has come true. The new mode of thought is today the predominant tendency in philosophy, psychology, sociology, and other fields. Many of the most seriously troublesome concepts are being "eliminated" by showing that no adequate account of them in terms of operations or behavior can be given. The radical empiricist onslaught . . . thus provides the methodological justification for the debunking of the mind by the intellectuals—a positivism which, in its denial of the transcending elements of Reason, forms the academic counterpart of the socially required behavior.

Outside the academic establishment, the "far-reaching change in all our habits of thought" is more serious. It serves to coordinate ideas and goals with those exacted by the prevailing system, to enclose them in the system, and to repel those which are irreconcilable with the system. The reign of such a one-dimensional reality does not mean that materialism rules, and that the spiritual, metaphysical, and bohemian occupations are petering out. On the contrary, there is a great deal of "Worship together this week," "Why not try God;" Zen, existentialism, and beat ways of life, etc. But such modes of protest and transcendence are no longer contradictory to the status quo and no longer negative. They are rather the ceremonial part of practical behaviorism, its harmless negation, and are quickly digested by the status quo as part of its healthy diet.

One-dimensional thought is systematically promoted by the makers of politics and their purveyors of mass information. Their universe of discourse is populated by self-validating hypotheses which, incessantly and monopo-

[3] P. W. Bridgman, *The Logic of Modern Physics* (New York: Macmillan, 1928), p. 5. The operational doctrine has since been refined and qualified. Bridgman himself has extended the concept of "operation" to include the "paper-and-pencil" operations of the theorist (in Philipp J. Frank, *The Validation of Scientific Theories* [Boston: Beacon Press, 1954], Chap. II). The main impetus remains the same: it is "desirable" that the paper-and-pencil operations "be capable of eventual contact, although perhaps indirectly, with instrumental operations."

[4] P. W. Bridgman, *The Logic of Modern Physics,* loc. cit., p. 31.

 listically repeated, become hypnotic definitions or dictations. For example, "free" are the institutions which operate (and are operated on) in the countries of the Free World; other transcending modes of freedom are by definition either anarchism, communism, or propaganda. "Socialistic" are all encroachments on private enterprises not undertaken by private enterprise itself (or by government contracts), such as universal and comprehensive health insurance, or the protection of nature from all too sweeping commercialization, or the establishment of public services which may hurt private profit. This totalitarian logic of accomplished facts has its Eastern counterpart. There, freedom is the way of life instituted by a communist regime, and all other transcending modes of freedom are either capitalistic, or revisionist, or leftist sectarianism. In both camps, non-operational ideas are non-behavioral and subversive. The movement of thought is stopped at barriers which appear as the limits of Reason itself.

Such limitation of thought is certainly not new. Ascending modern rationalism, in its speculative as well as empirical form, shows a striking contrast between extreme critical radicalism in scientific and philosophic method on the one hand, and an uncritical quietism in the attitude toward established and functioning social institutions. Thus Descartes' *ego cogitans* was to leave the "great public bodies" untouched, and Hobbes held that "the present ought always to be preferred, maintained, and accounted best." Kant agreed with Locke in justifying revolution *if and when* it has succeeded in organizing the whole and in preventing subversion.

However, these accommodating concepts of Reason were always contradicted by the evident misery and injustice of the "great public bodies" and the effective, more or less conscious rebellion against them. Societal conditions existed which provoked and permitted real dissociation from the established state of affairs; a private as well as political dimension was present in which dissociation could develop into effective opposition, testing its strength and the validity of its objectives.

With the gradual closing of this dimension by the society, the self-limitation of thought assumes a larger significance. The interrelation between scientific-philosophical and societal processes, between theoretical and practical Reason, asserts itself "behind the back" of the scientists and philosophers. The society bars a whole type of oppositional operations and behavior; consequently, the concepts pertaining to them are rendered illusory or meaningless. Historical transcendence appears as metaphysical transcendence, not acceptable to science and scientific thought. The operational and behavioral point of view, practiced as a "habit of thought" at large, becomes the view of the established universe of discourse and action, needs and aspirations. The "cunning of Reason" works, as it often did, in the interest of the powers that be. The insistence on operational and behavioral concepts turns against the efforts to free thought and behavior *from* the given reality and *for* the suppressed alternatives. Theoretical and practical Reason, academic and social behaviorism meet on common ground: that of an advanced society which makes scientific and technical progress into an instrument of domination.

"Progress" is not a neutral term; it moves toward specific ends, and these ends are defined by the possibilities of ameliorating the human condition. Advanced industrial society is approaching the stage where continued progress would demand the radical subversion of the prevailing direction and organization of progress. This stage would be reached when material production (including the necessary services) becomes automated to the extent that all vital needs can be satisfied while necessary labor time is reduced to marginal time. From this point on, technical progress would transcend the realm of necessity, where it served as the instrument of domination and exploitation which thereby limited its rationality; technology would become subject to the free play of faculties in the struggle for the pacification of nature and of society.

Such a state is envisioned in Marx's notion of the "abolition of labor." The term "pacification of existence" seems better suited to designate the historical alternative of a world which—through an international conflict which transforms and suspends the contradictions within the established societies—advances on the brink of a global war. "Pacification of existence" means the development of man's struggle with man and with nature, under conditions where the competing needs, desires, and aspirations are no longer organized by vested interests in domination and scarcity—an organization which perpetuates the destructive forms of this struggle.

Today's fight against this historical alternative finds a firm mass basis in the underlying population, and finds its ideology in the rigid orientation of thought and behavior to the given universe of facts. Validated by the accomplishments of science and technology, justified by its growing productivity, the status quo defies all transcendence. Faced with the possibility of pacification on the grounds of its technical and intellectual achievements, the mature industrial society closes itself against this alternative. Operationalism, in theory and practice, becomes the theory and practice of *containment.* Underneath its obvious dynamics, this society is a thoroughly static system of life: self-propelling in its oppressive productivity and in its beneficial coordination. Containment of technical progress goes hand in hand with its growth in the established direction. In spite of the political fetters imposed by the status quo, the more technology appears capable of creating the conditions for pacification, the more are the minds and bodies of man organized against this alternative.

The most advanced areas of industrial society exhibit throughout these two features: a trend toward consummation of technological rationality, and intensive efforts to contain this trend within the established institutions. Here is the internal contradiction of this civilization: the irrational element in its rationality. It is the token of its achievements. The industrial society which makes technology and science its own is organized for the ever-more-effective domination of man and nature, for the ever-more-effective utilization of its resources. It becomes irrational when the success of these efforts opens new dimensions of human realization. Organization for peace is different from organization for war; the institutions which served the struggle for existence cannot serve the pacification of existence. Life as an end is qualitatively different from life as a means.

Such a qualitatively new mode of existence can never be envisaged as the mere by-product of economic and political changes, as the more or less spontaneous effect of the new institutions which constitute the necessary prerequisite. Qualitative change also involves a change in the *technical* basis on which this society rests—one which sustains the economic and political institutions through which the "second nature" of man as an aggressive object of administration is stabilized. The techniques of industrialization are political techniques; as such, they prejudge the possibilities of Reason and Freedom.

To be sure, labor must precede the reduction of labor, and industrialization must precede the development of human needs and satisfactions. But as all freedom depends on the conquest of alien necessity, the realization of freedom depends on the *techniques* of this conquest. The highest productivity of labor can be used for the perpetuation of labor, and the most efficient industrialization can serve the restriction and manipulation of needs.

When this point is reached, domination—in the guise of affluence and liberty—extends to all spheres of private and public existence, integrates all authentic opposition, absorbs all alternatives. Technological rationality reveals its political character as it becomes the great vehicle of better domination, creating a truly totalitarian universe in which society and nature, mind and body are kept in a state of permanent mobilization for the defense of this universe.

THE MARXIST THEORY OF ALIENATION

● *ernest mandel*

It was by studying Hegel that Marx first came across the concept of alienation. But, oddly enough, it was not the theory of alienated labor that he originally picked up from Hegel's works. It was the alienation of man as a citizen in his relationship with the state that became the starting point of Marx's philosophical, political and social thought.

The social contract theory maintained that in organized society the individual must forfeit a certain number of individual rights to the state as the representative of the collective interest of the community. Hegel especially had developed this idea which was so strongly enunciated by the theoreticians of the natural rights philosophy. That also served as the starting point of Marx's critique of Hegel and his beginning as a critical social thinker in general.

Some small incidents which happened in the Rhine province of western Germany around 1842-43 (the increase in the number of people who stole wood and the intervention of the government against these people) led Marx to conclude that the state, which purports to represent the collective interest, instead represented the interests of only one part of the society, that is to say, those who own private property. Therefore the forfeiture of individual rights to that state represented a phenomenon of alienation: the loss of rights by people to institutions which were in reality hostile to them.

Starting from that political-philosophical platform, Marx, who in the meantime had been expelled from Germany and gone into exile in France, got in contact with the first socialist and workers organizations there and began to study economics, especially the classical writers of British political economy, the Adam Smith-Ricardo school. This was the background for Marx's first attempt in 1844 at a synthesis of philosophical and economic ideas in the so-called *Economic and Philosophic Manuscripts of 1844,* also called the *Parisian Manuscripts.* This was an attempt to integrate his ideas about labor in bourgeois society with ideas about the fate of man, man's position in history, and his existence on earth.

This initial youthful attempt at synthesis was carried out with very inadequate means. At that period Marx did not yet have a thorough knowledge of political economy; he had only started to acquaint himself with some of the basic notions of the classical school in political economy; and he had little direct or indirect experience with the modern industrial system. He would obtain all that only during the next ten years.

This unfinished early work was unknown for a very long time. It was first published in 1932, nearly one hundred years after it was written. Accordingly, much of the discussion which had been going on in economic as well as philosophic circles, about what he thought in his youth and how he arrived at a certain number of his basic concepts, was very much distorted by an ignorance of this specific landmark in his intellectual development.

Immature as parts of it might seem and are, especially the economic part, it nevertheless represents both a major turning point in Marx's intellectual development and in the intellectual history of mankind. Its importance, which I will try to explain, is linked with the concept of alienation.

Alienation is a very old idea which has religious origins and is almost as old as organized religion itself. It was taken over by nearly all the classical philosophical trends in the West as in the East. This concept turns around what one could call the tragic fate of man. Hegel, who was one of the greatest German philosophers, took over the idea from his predecessors but gave it a new slant and a new basis which denoted momentous progress. He did this by changing the foundation of that concept of the tragic fate of man from a vague anthropological and philosophical concept into a concept rooted in labor.

Hegel, before Marx, said that man is alienated because human labor is alienated. He gave two explanations for this general alienation of human labor. One is what he called the dialetics of need and labor. Human needs, he said, are always one step ahead of the available economic resources; men will therefore always be condemned to work very hard to fulfill unsatisfied needs. However, the attempt to equalize the organization of material resources with the necessity of satisfying all human needs is an impossible task, a goal which can never be attained. That was one aspect of what Hegel called alienated labor.

The other side of his philosophical analysis was a bit more complicated. It is summarized in a difficult word, the word "externalization" (*Entäusserung*). Though the term is complicated and sounds foreign, its content is easier to understand. Hegel meant by the philosophical concept of externalization the fact that every man who works, who produces something, really reproduces in his work an idea which he initially had in his head. Some of you might be astonished if I immediately add that Marx shared that opinion. You will find this same idea, that any work which man performs lives in his head before being realized in material reality, in the first chapter of *Capital.* Hegel, as well as Marx, thereby drew a basic distinction between men, and, let us say, ants or other creatures which seem to be busily at work but do things purely on instinct. Man, on the other hand, first develops an idea about what he aims to do and then tries to realize that idea.

Hegel goes a step farther when he asks, what do we do in reality when we try to express, in material, what first lives in us as an idea? We inevitably separate ourselves from the product of our labor. Anything which we project out of ourselves, anything which we fabricate, anything which we produce, we project out of our own body and it becomes separated from us. It cannot remain as much part and parcel of our being as an idea which continues to live in our head. That was for Hegel the main, let us say, anthropological, definition of alienated labor. He therefore arrived at the conclusion that every and any kind of labor is alienated labor because in any society and under any conditions men will always be condemned to become separated from the products of their labor.

When Marx takes up these two definitions of alienated labor given by Hegel, he contradicts both of them. He says that the discrepancy between needs and material resources, the tension between needs and labor, is a limited one, conditioned by history. It is not true that man's needs can develop in an unlimited way or that the output of his collective labor will always remain inferior to these needs. He denies this most emphatically on the basis of a historical analysis. He especially rejects Hegel's idealistic identification of externalization with alienation. Marx says that when we separate ourselves from the product of our labor it does not necessarily follow that the product of our labor then oppresses us or that any material forces whatsoever turn against men. Such alienation is not the result of the projection of things out of our body as such, which first live in us as ideas and then take on a material existence as objects, as products of our labor.

Alienation results from a certain form of organization of society. More concretely, only in a society which is based on commodity production and only under the specific economic and social circumstances of a market economy, can the objects which we project out of us when we produce acquire a socially oppressive existence of their own and be integrated in an economic and social mechanism which becomes oppressive and exploitative of human beings.

The tremendous advance in human thought which I referred to in this critique of Hegel consists in the fact that Marx rejects the idea of the alienation of labor as being an anthropological characteristic, that is, an inherent and ineradicable curse of mankind. He says that the alienation of labor is not bound to human existence in all places and for all future time. It is a specific result of specific forms of social and economic organization. In other words, Marx transforms Hegel's notion of alienated labor from an eternal anthropological into a transitory historical notion.

This reinterpretation carries a message of hope for mankind. Marx says that mankind is not condemned to live "by the sweat of his brow" under alienated conditions throughout his whole term on earth. He can become free, his labor can become free, he is capable of self-emancipation, though only under specific historical conditions. Later I will define what specific social and economic conditions are required for the disappearance of alienated labor.

Let us now pass from the first systematic exposition of his theory of alienation in the *Economic and Philosophic Manuscripts of 1844* to his main work, *Capital,* which was published over twenty years later. It is true that the word alienation hardly appears there.

A new profession has sprung up in the last thirty years which is called "Marxology." Its practitioners read through the works of Marx and put on small index cards all the words he uses in his books and then try to draw some conclusions about his thought from their philological statistics. Some people have even used computers in this type of formal analysis. These "Marx-philologists" have so far discovered six places in *Capital* where the word "alienation" is used either as a noun or as a verb. I certainly will not dispute that colossal discovery though somebody may find a seventh spot or there could be some dispute about the sixth one.

On the basis of such an analysis of *Capital*, done in a purely verbal and superficial way, it could be concluded that the mature Marx did not have a real theory of alienation. Marx would then have discarded it after his youth, after his immature development, especially when, around 1856-57, he became thoroughly convinced of the correctness of the labor theory of value and perfected that labor theory of value himself.

When the *Economic and Philosophic Manuscripts of 1844* were published for the first time in 1932, a big controversy arose around these issues. At least three trends can be distinguished in the debate. I will not cite the names of all the authors who have participated in it since more than a hundred people have written on the subject and the controversy is far from having ended. Some said there is a contradiction between the youthful and the mature works and Marx abandoned his original theories when his own views were fully developed.

Others said the opposite. The real Marx is to be found in the youthful works and he later degenerated by restricting the scope of his understanding to purely economic problems. He thus fell victim to the deviation of economism.

Still other people tried to deny that Marx's ideas underwent any significant or substantial evolution whatsoever. Among these are the American Erich Fromm, the French Marxist scholar Maximilien Rubel, and two French Catholic priests, Fathers Bigo and Colvez. They maintain that the same ideas are contained in his early as in his later works.

I think all three of these opinions are wrong. There was an important evolution, not an identical repetition, in Marx's thought from decade to decade. Any person who thinks, and continues to think and live, will not say exactly the same thing when he is sixty as when he was twenty-five. Even if it is conceded that the basic concepts remain the same, there is obviously some progress, some change. In this concrete case the evolution is all the more striking, as I said before, because the Marx of 1844 had not yet accepted the labor theory of value which is a cornerstone of the economic theory he developed ten or fifteen years later.

One of the pivotal questions in this continuing debate is whether the mature Marx held a theory of alienation or whether he altogether abandoned his original theory of alienation. This dispute, which can be resolved on a documentary basis, would not have gone on so long and inconclusively if it had not been for another unfortunate accident.

It happened that another major work of Marx, *Grundrisse der Kritik der Politischen Ökonomie* (Fundamental Outlines of a Critique of Political Economy), a thirteen-hundred-page work written in 1857-58, which is a kind of laboratory where all the major ideas of *Capital* were first elaborated and tested, was also not published until a century after it was written. Its first publication occurred at the beginning of the second world war in Russia, but most of the copies were destroyed as a result of the war. I believe only two copies arrived in the United States and none were available in Western Europe. The Russians under Stalin were not eager to reproduce it a second time. Thus it was not until the nineteen-fifties, almost a century after it had been originally written, that the book was reprinted and became known to a certain number of experts in a few countries.

Sad to say, this major work of Marx has still to be translated into English, although one has been announced. It appeared in French only a short time ago. So some of the participants in this dispute did have the excuse that they did not know that key work. For anybody who reads it can at once see that a Marxist theory of alienation exists because in the *Grŭndrisse* the word, the concept, and the analysis appear dozens and dozens of times.

What then is this theory of alienation as it was developed by the mature Marx, not by the young Marx? And how can we relate it to what is set down in *Capital?* There is first a purely formal difficulty here because Marx uses three different terms in this connection and he uses them in an interchangeable manner. One is the concept of alienation; another is the concept of reification, a complicated word; and a third is the concept of commodity fetishism, which is still more complicated. However, these three concepts are not so difficult to explain, and I will try to clarify their meaning for you.

Let us start this analysis with a definition of economic alienation. I must immediately state that in the comprehensive Marxist theory of alienation, economic alienation is only one part of a much more general phenomenon which covers practically all fields of human activity in class society. But it is the most decisive element. So let's start from economic alienation. We will approach it in successive stages. The first and most striking feature of economic alienation is the separation of men from free access to the means of production and means of subsistence.This is a rather recent development in human history. As late as the nineteenth century free access to the means of production in agriculture survived in some countries of the world, among others, in the United States and Canada. Until after the American Civil War it was not impossible for masses of people to find some unpreempted spot of land and to establish themselves on that acreage as free farmers, as homesteaders. In Europe that possibility had ceased to exist for two hundred years, and in some countries there even three or four hundred years earlier.

That historical factor is the starting point for any theory of alienation because the institution of wage labor in which men are forced to sell their labor power to another person, to their employer, can come into existence on a large scale only when and where free access to the means of production and subsistence is denied to an important part of society. Thus the first precondition for the alienation of labor occurs when labor becomes separated from the basic means of production and subsistence.

I said this is a relatively new phenomenon. A second example may illuminate this more sharply. The classical historical criticism made by liberal thought in the nineteenth century about the society of the middle ages, feudal society, was the lack of freedom of the cultivators of the soil. I won't take exception to that criticism which I think was correct. The direct producers in that society, the peasants and serfs, were not free people. They could not move about freely; they were tied to the land.

But what the bourgeois liberal critics of feudal society forgot was that tying men to the land was a two-sided phenomenon. If man was tied to the land, the land was also tied to man. And because the land was tied to man, there wasn't any important part of the people living within feudal relations who could be forced to become wage laborers and sell their labor power to owners of capital. They had access to the land, they could produce their own means of subsistence and keep part of it for themselves. Only people outside organized feudal society, in reality outlaws, because that is what they were originally, could become the starting point for new social classes—wage laborers on the one hand, merchants on the other.

The second stage in the alienation of labor came about when part of society was driven off the land, no longer had access to the means of production and means of subsistence, and, in order to survive, was forced to sell its labor power on the market. That is the main characteristic of alienated labor. In the economic field it is the institution of wage labor, the economic obligation of people who cannot otherwise survive to sell the only commodity they possess, their labor power, on the labor market.

What does it mean to sell your labor power to a boss? In Marx's analysis, both in his youthful and his mature work, behind this purely formal and legal contractual relation—you sell your labor power, part of your time, to another for money to live on—is in reality something of deepgoing consequence for all human existence and particularly for the life of the wage laborer. It first of all implies that you lose control over a large part of your waking hours. All the time which you have sold to the employer belongs to him, not to you. You are not free to do what you want at work. It is the employer who dictates what you will and will not do during this whole time. He will dictate what you produce, how you produce it, where you produce it. He will be master over your activity.

And the more the productivity of labor increases and the shorter the work-week becomes, the stricter will be the control of the employer over every hour of your time as a wage laborer. In time and motion studies—the ultimate and most perfected form of this control—the boss even tries to control every second, *literally* every second, of the time which you spend in his employ.

Alienation thereupon acquires a third form. When a wage earner has sold his labor power for a certain part of his life to his employer, the products of his labor are not his own. The products of his labor become the property of the employer.

The fact that the modern wage earner owns none of the products of his own labor, obvious as it may appear to people who are accustomed to bourgeois society, is not at all so self-evident from the viewpoint of human history as a whole. It was not like that for thousands upon thousands of years of human existence. Both the medieval handicraftsman and the handicraftsman of antiquity were the proprietors of their own products. The peasant, and even the serf of the middle ages, remained in possession of at least 50 per cent, sometimes 60 and 70 per cent, of the output of their own labor.

Under capitalism not only does the wage earner lose possession of the product of his labor, but these products can function in a hostile and injurious manner against him. This happened with the machine. This remarkable product of human ingenuity becomes a source of tyranny against the worker when the worker serves as an appendage of the machine and is forced to adapt the cadence of his life and work to the operation of the machine. This can become a serious source of alienation in shift work when part of the working class has to work during the night or at odd hours in conflict with the normal rhythm of human life between day and night. Such an abnormal schedule causes all sorts of psychological and nervous disorders.

Another aspect of the oppressive nature which the products of labor can acquire once society is divided into hostile classes of capitalists and wage workers are the crises of overproduction, depressions or, as it is nowadays more prudently put, recessions. Then people consume less because they produce too much. And they consume less, not because their labor is inadequately productive, but because their labor is too productive.

We come now to a final form of alienated labor in the economic field which derives from the conclusions of the points I have noted. The alienation of the worker and his labor means that something basic has changed in the life of the worker. What is it? Normally everybody has some creative capacity, certain talents lodged in him, untapped potentialities for human development which should be expressed in his labor activity.

However, once the institution of wage labor is prevalent, these possibilities become nullified. Work is no longer a means of self-expression for anybody who sells his labor time. Work is just a means to attain a goal. And that goal is to get money, some income to be able to buy the consumer goods necessary to satisfy your needs.

In this way a basic aspect of man's nature, his capacity to perform creative work, becomes thwarted and distorted. Work becomes something which is not creative and productive for human beings but something which is harmful and destructive. Catholic priests and Protestant pastors who have worked in factories in Western Europe, the so-called "worker-priests," who have written books about their experiences, have arrived at conclusions on this point that are absolutely identical with those of Marxism. They declare that a wage earner considers the hours passed in factories or in offices as time lost from his life. He must spend time there in order to get freedom and capacity for human development outside the sphere of production and of work.

Ironically, this hope for fulfillment during leisure time turns out to be an illusion. Many humanitarian and philanthropic reformers of liberal or social-democratic persuasion in the nineteenth and the beginning of the twentieth centuries thought that men could become liberated when their leisure time would increase. They did not understand that the nature of leisure was likewise determined by the nature of wage labor and by the conditions of a society based on commodity production and wage labor.

Once socially necessary labor time became shorter and leisure time greater, a commercialization of leisure took place. The capitalist society of commodity production, the so-called "consumer society" did its utmost to integrate leisure time into the totality of economic phenomena at the basis of commodity production, exploitation and accumulation.

At this point the notion of alienation is extended from a purely economic to a broader social phenomenon. The first bridge to this wider application is the concept of alienation of the consumer. Thus far we have spoken only about the consequences of alienated labor. But one of the cardinal characteristics of capitalist society, as Marx understood as early as 1844, is its built-in contradiction regarding human needs. On the one hand, each capitalist entrepreneur tries to limit the human needs of his own wage earners as much as possible by paying as little wages as possible. Otherwise he would not make enough profit to accumulate.

On the other hand, each capitalist sees in the work force of all the other capitalists not wage earners but potential consumers. He would therefore like to expand the capacity of consumption of these other wage earners to the limit or otherwise he cannot increase production and sell what his own workers produce. Thus capitalism has a tendency to constantly extend the needs of people.

Up to a certain point this expansion can cover genuine human needs, such as the elementary requirements of feeding, housing and clothing everybody in more or less decent circumstances. Very quickly, however, capitalism in its efforts to commercialize everything and sell as many gadgets as possible, goes beyond any rational human needs and starts to spur and stimulate artificial needs in a systematic, large-scale manner. Some of these are absurd and grotesque. Let me give one example. An American author, Jessica Mitford, has written an amusing book, called the *American Way of Death*. It describes the practices of morticians who seek to induce people to buy more expensive coffins so that the beloved dead can rest not only peacefully, but lightly, on foam mattresses. The sales pitchmen say this satisfies, not the corpse, but the feelings of the consumer.

Is it necessary to observe that no real need is involved in this grotesque attempt of the burial business to make money? It is scandalous to feed in this mercenary manner upon the feelings of grief of people who have lost members of their family.

Such alienation is no longer purely economic but has become social and psychological in nature. For what is the motivation of a system for constantly extending needs beyond the limits of what is rational? It is to create, purposely and deliberately, permanent and meretricious dissatisfactions in human beings. Capitalism would cease to exist if people were fully and healthily satisfied. The system must provoke continued artificial dissatisfaction in human beings because without that dissatisfaction the sale of new gadgets which are more and more divorced from genuine human needs cannot be increased.

A society which is turned toward creating systematic frustration of this kind generates the bad results recorded in the crime pages of the daily newspapers. A society which breeds worthless dissatisfaction will also breed all kinds of antisocial attempts to overcome this dissatisfaction.

Beyond this alienation of human beings as consumers, there are two very important aspects of alienation. One is the alienation of human activity in general. The other is the alienation of human beings in one of their most fundamental features, the capacity to communicate.

What is meant by the extension of the concept of alienation to human activity in general? We live in a society based on commodity production and a social division of labor pushed to the limits of over-specialization. As a result, people in a particular job or doing a certain type of activity for a living will incline to have an extremely narrow horizon. They will be prisoners of their trade, seeing only the problems and preoccupations of their specialty. They will also tend to have a restricted social and political awareness because of this limitation.

Along with this shut-in horizon will go something which is much worse, the tendency to transform relations between human beings into relations between things. This is that famous tendency toward "reification," the transformation of social relations into things, into objects, of which Marx speaks in *Capital*.

This way of looking at phenomena is an extension of this theory of alienation. Here is an example of this transformation which I witnessed the other day in this country. The waiters and waitresses in restaurants are poor working people who are the victims and not the authors of this process of reification. They are even unaware of the nature of their involvement in this phenomenon.

 While they are under heavy pressure to serve the maximum number of customers on the job imposed upon them by the system and its owners, they look upon the customers solely under the form of the orders they put in. I heard one waitress address herself to a person and say, "Ah, you are the corned-beef and cabbage." You are not Mr. or Mrs. Brown, not a person of a certain age and with a certain address. You are "corned-beef and cabbage" because the waitress has on her mind the orders taken under stress from so many people.

This habit of reification is not the fault of the inhumanity or insensitivity of the workers. It results from a certain type of human relation rooted in commodity production and its extreme division of labor where people engaged in one trade tend to see their fellows only as customers or through the lenses of whatever economic relations they have with them.

This outlook finds expression in everyday language. I have been told that in the city of Osaka, the main commercial and industrial capital of Japan, the common mode of addressing people when you meet is not "how do you do?" but "how is business?" or "are you making money?" This signifies that bourgeois economic relations have so completely pervaded ordinary human relations as to dehumanize them to an appreciable extent.

I come now to the ultimate and most tragic form of alienation, which is alienation of the capacity to communicate. The capacity to communicate has become the most fundamental attribute of man, of his quality as a human being. Without communication, there can be no organized society because without communication, there is no language, and without language, there is no intelligence. Capitalist society, class society, commodity-producing society tends to thwart, divert and partially destroy this basic human capacity.

Let me give three examples of this process at three different levels, starting with a most commonplace case. How do men learn to communicate? While they are infants they go through what psychologists call a process of socialization and learn to speak. For a long time one of the main methods of socializing young children has been through playing with dolls. When a child plays with dolls, he duplicates himself, projects himself outside his own individuality, and carries on a dialogue with that other self. He speaks two languages, his own language and the language of the doll, thereby bringing into play an artificial process of communication which, through its spontaneous nature, facilitates the development of language and intelligence.

Recently, industry started to produce dolls which speak. This is supposed to be a mark of progress. But once the doll speaks, the dialogue is limited. The child no longer speaks in two languages, or with the same spontaneity. Part of its speech is induced, and induced by some capitalist corporation.

That corporation may have hired the biggest educators and psychologists who make the doll speak more perfectly than any of the babble which could come out of the child's mind itself—although I have some doubts on that subject. Nevertheless, the spontaneous nature of the dialogue is partially thwarted, suppressed or detoured. There is less development of dialogue, of capacity for communication, and therefore a lesser formation of intelligence than in more backward times when dolls did not speak and children had to give them a language of their own.

A second example is taken from a more sophisticated level. Any class society which is divided by social-material interests and in which class struggle goes on suppresses to a certain extent the capacity for communication between people standing on different sides of the barricades. This is not a matter of lack of intelligence, of understanding or honesty, from any individual point of view. This is simply the effect of the inhibitive pressures that substantial divisive material interests exercise on any group of individuals.

Anybody who has ever been present at wage bargaining where there is severe tension between workers' and employers' representatives—I'm talking about real wage bargaining, not sham wage bargaining—will understand what I am referring to. The employers' side simply cannot sympathize with or understand what the workers are talking about even if they have the utmost good will and liberal opinions, because their material-social interests prevent them from understanding what the other side is most concerned with.

There was a very striking example of this inhibition on another level (because workers and not employers were involved) in the tragic strike of the United Federation of Teachers in New York in 1968 against the decentralization of control over the school system. People of bad will, fools or stupid people were not so much involved. Indeed, most of them would have been called liberal or even left some time ago. But through very strong pressures of social interest and social milieu, they were simply incapable of understanding what the other side, the Black and Puerto Rican masses who wanted community control over the education of their children, was talking about.

Thus the Marxist notion of alienation extends far beyond the oppressed classes of society, properly speaking. The oppressors are also alienated from part of their human capacity through their inability to communicate on a human basis with the majority of society. And this divorcement is inevitable as long as class society and its deep differentiations exist.

Another terrible expression of this alienation on the individual scale is the tremendous loneliness which a society based on commodity production and division of labor inevitably induces in many human beings. Ours is a society based on the principle, every man for himself. Individualism pushed to the extreme also means loneliness pushed to the extreme.

It is simply not true, as certain existentialist philosophers contend, that man has always been an essentially lonely human being. There have been forms of integrated collective life in primitive society where the very notion of loneliness could not arise. It arises out of commodity production and division of labor only at a certain stage of human development in bourgeois society. And then unfortunately it acquires a tremendous extension which can go beyond the limits of mental health.

Psychologists have gone around with tape recorders and listened to certain types of dialogues between people in shops or on the street. When they play these dialogues afterwards they discover that there has been no exchange whatsoever. The two people have talked along parallel lines without once meeting with each other. Each talks because he welcomes the occasion to unburden himself, to get out of his loneliness, but he is incapable of listening to what the other person is saying.

The only meeting place is at the end of the dialogue when they say goodbye. Even that farewell is saddening because they want to save the possibility of unburdening themselves of their loneliness the next time they meet. They carry on what the French call *dialogue de sourds,* dialogues between deaf people, that is, dialogues between people who are incapable of understanding or listening to other people.

This is of course an extreme and marginal illustration. Happily, the majority of members of our society are not yet in that situation or otherwise we would be on the brink of a complete breakdown of social relations. Nonetheless, capitalism tends to extend the zone of this extreme loneliness with all its terrible implications.

This looks like a very dim picture, and the dim picture undoubtedly corresponds to the dim reality of our times. If the curve of mental sickness has climbed parallel with the curve of material wealth and income in most of the advanced countries of the West, this dismal picture has not been invented by Marxist critics but corresponds to very deep-rooted aspects of the social and economic reality in which we live.

But, as I said before, this grim situation is not at all without hope. Our optimism comes from the fact that, after all this analysis of the roots of the alienation of labor and the specific expressions of the alienation of man in bourgeois society is completed, there emerges the inescapable conclusion that a society can be envisaged in which there will be no more alienation of labor and alienation of human beings. This is a historically produced and man-made evil, not an evil rooted in nature or human nature. Like everything else which has been made by man, it can also be unmade by man. This condition is a product of history and it can be destroyed by history or at least gradually overcome by further progress.

Thus the Marxist theory of alienation implies and contains a theory of disalienation through the creation of conditions for the gradual disappearance and eventual abolition of alienation. I stress "gradual disappearance" because such a process or institution can no more be abolished by fiat or a stroke of the pen than commodity production, the state, or the division of society into classes can be eliminated by a government decree or proclamation.

Marxists understand that the social and economic preconditions for a gradual disappearance of alienation can be brought about only in a classless society ushered in by a world socialist revolution. And when I say a classless socialist society, I obviously do not mean the societies which exist in the Soviet Union, Eastern Europe or China. In the best cases these are transitional societies somewhere halfway between capitalism and socialism. Though private property has been abolished, they have not yet abolished the division of society into classes, they still have different social classes and different social layers, division of labor and commodity production. As a consequence of these conditions, they still have alienated labor and alienated men.

The prerequisites for the disappearance of human alienation, of alienated labor and the alienated activities of human beings, can only be created precisely through the continuation of those processes I have just named: the withering away of commodity production, the disappearance of economic scarcity, the withering away of social division of labor through the disappearance of private ownership of the means of production and the elimination of the difference between manual and intellectual labor, between producers and administrators. All of this would bring about the slow transformation of the very nature of labor from a coercive necessity in order to get money, income and means of consumption into a voluntary occupation that people want to do because it covers their own internal needs and expresses their talents. This transformation of labor into all-sided creative human activity is the ultimate goal of socialism. Only when that goal is attained will alienated labor and all its pernicious consequences cease to exist.

THE POLITICAL ECONOMY OF WOMEN'S LIBERATION

● *margaret benston*

The position of women rests, as everything in our complex society, on an economic base.

—*Eleanor Marx and Edward Aveling*

The "woman question" is generally ignored in analyses of the class structure of society. This is so because, on the one hand, classes are generally defined by their relation to the means of production and, on the other hand, women are not supposed to have any unique relation to the means of production. The category seems instead to cut across all classes; one speaks of working-class women, middle-class women, etc. The status of women is clearly inferior to that of men,[1] but analysis of this condition usually falls into discussing socialization, psychology, interpersonal relations, or the role of marriage as a social institution.[2] Are these, however, the primary factors? In arguing that the roots of the secondary status of women are in fact economic, it can be shown that women as a group do indeed have a definite relation to the means of production and that this is different from that of men. The personal and psychological factors then follow from this special relation to production, and a change in the latter will be a necessary (but not sufficient) condition for changing the former.[3] If this special relation of women to production is accepted, the analysis of the situation of women fits naturally into a class analysis of society.

The starting point for discussion of classes in a capitalist society is the distinction between those who own the means of production and those who sell their labor power for a wage. As Ernest Mandel says:

> *The proletarian condition is, in a nutshell, the lack of access to the means of production or means of subsistence which, in a society of generalized commodity production, forces the proletarian to sell his labor power. In exchange for this labor power he receives a wage which then enables him to acquire the means of consumption necessary for satisfying his own needs and those of his family.*
>
> *This is the structural definition of wage earner, the proletarian. From it necessarily flows a certain relationship to his work, to the products of his work, and to his overall situation in society, which can be summarized by the catchword alienation. But there does not follow from this structural definition any necessary conclusions as to the level of his consumption . . . the extent of his needs, or the degree to which he can satisfy them.*[4]

[1] Marlene Dixon, "Secondary Social Status of Women." (Available from U.S. Voice of Women's Liberation Movement, 1940 Bissell, Chicago, Illinois 60614.)

[2] The biological argument is, of course, the first one used, but it is not usually taken seriously by socialist writers. Margaret Mead's *Sex and Temperament* is an early statement of the importance of culture instead of biology.

[3] This applies to the group or category as a whole. Women as individuals can and do free themselves from their socialization to a great degree (and they can even come to terms with the economic situation in favorable cases), but the majority of women have no chance to do so.

[4] Ernest Mandel, "Workers Under Neocapitalism," paper delivered at Simon Fraser University. (Available through the Department of Political Science, Sociology and Anthropology, Simon Fraser University, Burnaby, B.C., Canada.)

 We lack a corresponding structural definition of women. What is needed first is not a complete examination of the symptoms of the secondary status of women, but instead a statement of the material conditions in capitalist (and other) societies which define the group "women." Upon these conditions are built the specific superstructures which we know. An interesting passage from Mandel points the way to such a definition:

> *The commodity . . . is a product created to be exchanged on the market, as opposed to one which has been made for direct consumption.* Every commodity must have both a use-value and an exchange-value.
>
> *It must have a use-value or else nobody would buy it. . . . A commodity without a use-value to anyone would consequently be unsalable, would constitute useless production, would have no exchange-value precisely because it had no use-value.*
>
> *On the other hand, every product which has use-value does not necessarily have exchange-value. It has an exchange-value only to the extent that the society itself, in which the commodity is produced, is founded on exchange, is a society where exchange is a common practice. . . .*
>
> *In capitalist society, commodity production, the production of exchange-values, has reached its greatest development. It is the first society in human history where the major part of production consists of commodities. It is not true, however, that all production under capitalism is commodity production. Two classes of products still remain simple use-value.*
>
> *The first group consists of all things produced by the peasantry for its own consumption, everything directly consumed on the farms where it is produced. . . .*
>
> *The second group of products in capitalist society which are not commodities but remain simple use-value consists of all things produced in the home. Despite the fact that considerable human labor goes into this type of household production, it still remains a production of use-values and not of commodities. Every time a soup is made or a button sewn on a garment, it constitutes production, but it is not production for the market.*
>
> *The appearance of commodity production and its subsequent regularization and generalization have radically transformed the way men labor and how they organize society.*[5]

What Mandel may not have noticed is that his last paragraph is precisely correct. The appearance of commodity production has indeed transformed the way that *men* labor. As he points out, most household labor in capitalist society (and in the existing socialist societies, for that matter) remains in the pre-market stage. This is the work which is reserved for women and it is in this fact that we can find the basis for a definition of women.

In sheer quantity, household labor, including child care, constitutes a huge amount of socially necessary production. Nevertheless, in a society based on commodity production, it is not usually considered "real work" since it is outside of trade and the market place. It is pre-capitalist in a very real sense. This assignment of household work as the function of a special category "women" means that this group *does* stand in a different relation to production than the group "men." We will tentatively define women, then, as that group of people who are responsible for the production of simple use-values in those activities associated with the home and family.

[5] Ernest Mandel, *An Introduction to Marxist Economic Theory* (New York: Merit Publishers, 1967), pp. 10-11.

Since men carry no responsibility for such production, the difference between the two groups lies here. Notice that women are not excluded from commodity production. Their participation in wage labor occurs but, as a group, they have no structural responsibility in this area and such participation is ordinarily regarded as transient. Men, on the other hand, are responsible for commodity production; they are not, in principle, given any role in household labor. For example, when they do participate in household production, it is regarded as more than simply exceptional; it is demoralizing, emasculating, even harmful to health. (A story on the front page of the *Vancouver Sun* in January 1969 reported that men in Britain were having their health endangered because they had to do too much housework!)

The material basis for the inferior status of women is to be found in just this definition of women. In a society in which money determines value, women are a group who work outside the money economy. Their work is not worth money, is therefore valueless, is therefore not even real work. And women themselves, who do this valueless work, can hardly be expected to be worth as much as men, who work for money. In structural terms, the closest thing to the condition of women is the condition of others who are or were also outside of commodity production, i.e., serfs and peasants.

In her recent paper on women, Juliet Mitchell introduces the subject as follows: "In advanced industrial society, women's work is only marginal to the total economy. Yet it is through work that man changes natural conditions and thereby produces society. Until there is a revolution in production, the labor situation will prescribe women's situation within the world of men."[6] The statement of the marginality of women's work is an unanalyzed recognition that the work women do is *different* from the work that men do. Such work is not marginal, however; it is just not wage labor and so is not counted. She even says later in the same article, "Domestic labor, even today, is enormous if quantified in terms of productive labor." She gives some figures to illustrate: In Sweden, 2,340 million hours a year are spent by women in housework compared with 1,290 million hours spent by women in industry. And the Chase Manhattan Bank estimates a woman's overall work week at 99.6 hours.

However, Mitchell gives little emphasis to the basic economic factors (in fact she condemns most Marxists for being "overly economist") and moves on hastily to superstructural factors, because she notices that "the advent of industrialization has not so far freed women." What she fails to see is that no society has thus far industrialized housework. Engels points out that the "first premise for the emancipation of women is the reintroduction of the entire female sex into public industry. . . . And this has become possible not only as a result of modern large-scale industry, which not only permits the participation of women in production in large numbers, but actually calls for it and, moreover, strives to convert private domestic work also into a public industry."[7] And later in the same passage: "Here we see already that the emancipation of women and their equality with men are

[6] Juliet Mitchell, "Women: The Longest Revolution," *New Left Review*, December 1966.

[7] Frederick Engels, *Origin of the Family, Private Property and the State* (Moscow: Progress Publishers, 1968), Chapter IX, p. 158. The anthropological evidence known to Engels indicated primitive woman's dominance over man. Modern anthropology disputes this dominance but provides evidence for a more nearly equal position of women in the matrilineal societies used by Engels as examples. The arguments in this work of Engels do not require the former dominance of women but merely their former equality, and so the conclusions remain unchanged.

 impossible and must remain so as long as women are excluded from socially productive work and restricted to housework, which is private." What Mitchell has not taken into account is that the problem is not simply one of getting women into *existing* industrial production but the more complex one of converting private production of household work into public production.

For most North Americans, domestic work as "public production" brings immediate images of Brave New World or of a vast institution—a cross between a home for orphans and an army barracks—where we would all be forced to live. For this reason, it is probably just as well to outline here, schematically and simplistically, the nature of industrialization.

A pre-industrial production unit is one in which production is small-scale and reduplicative; i.e., there are a great number of little units, each complete and just like all the others. Ordinarily such production units are in some way kin-based and they are multi-purpose, fulfilling religious, recreational, educational, and sexual functions along with the economic function. In such a situation, desirable attributes of an individual, those which give prestige, are judged by more than purely economic criteria: for example, among approved character traits are proper behavior to kin or readiness to fulfill obligations.

Such production is originally not for exchange. But if exchange of commodities becomes important enough, then increased efficiency of production becomes necessary. Such efficiency is provided by the transition to industrialized production which involves the elimination of the kin-based production unit. A large-scale, non-reduplicative production unit is substituted which has only one function, the economic one, and where prestige or status is attained by economic skills. Production is rationalized, made vastly more efficient, and becomes more and more public—part of an integrated social network. An enormous expansion of man's productive potential takes place. Under capitalism such social productive forces are utilized almost exclusively for private profit. These can be thought of as *capitalized* forms of production.

If we apply the above to housework and child rearing, it is evident that each family, each household, constitutes an individual production unit, a pre-industrial entity, in the same way that peasant farmers or cottage weavers constitute pre-industrial production units. The main features are clear, with the reduplicative, kin-based, private nature of the work being the most important. (It is interesting to notice the other features: the multi-purpose functions of the family, the fact that desirable attributes for women do not center on economic prowess, etc.) The rationalization of production effected by a transition to large-scale production has not taken place in this area.

Industrialization is, in itself, a great force for human good: exploitation and dehumanization go with capitalism and not necessarily with industrialization. To advocate the conversion of private domestic labor into a public industry under capitalism is quite a different thing from advocating such conversion in a socialist society. In the latter case the forces of production would operate for human welfare, not private profit, and the result should be liberation, not dehumanization. In this case we can speak of *socialized* forms of production.

These definitions are not meant to be technical but rather to differentiate between two important aspects of industrialization. Thus the fear of the barracks-like result of introducing housekeeping into the public economy is most realistic under capitalism. With socialized production and the removal of the profit motive and its attendant alienated labor, there is no reason why, *in an industrialized society,* industrialization of housework should not result in better production, i.e., better food, more comfortable surroundings, more intelligent and loving child-care, etc., than in the present nuclear family.

The argument is often advanced that, under neocapitalism, the work in the home has been much reduced. Even if this is true, it is not structurally relevant. Except for the very rich, who can hire someone to do it, there is for most women, an irreducible minimum of necessary labor involved in caring for home, husband, and children. For a married woman without children this irreducible minimum of work probably takes fifteen to twenty hours a week; for a woman with small children the minimum is probably seventy or eighty hours a week.[8] (There is some resistance to regarding child-rearing as a job. That labor is involved, i.e., the production of use-value, can be clearly seen when exchange-value is also involved—when the work is done by baby sitters, nurses, child-care centers, or teachers. An economist has already pointed out the paradox that if a man marries his housekeeper, he reduces the national income, since the money he gives her is no longer counted as wages.) The reduction of housework to the minimums given is also expensive; for low-income families more labor is required. In any case, household work remains structurally the same—a matter of private production.

One function of the family, the one taught to us in school and the one which is popularly accepted, is the satisfaction of emotional needs: the needs for closeness, community, and warm secure relationships. This society provides few other ways of satisfying such needs; for example, work relationships or friendships are not expected to be nearly as important as a man-woman-with-children relationship. Even other ties of kinship are increasingly secondary. This function of the family is important in stabilizing it so that it can fulfill the second, purely economic, function discussed above. The wage-earner, the husband-father, whose earnings support himself, also "pays for" the labor done by the mother-wife and supports the children. The wages of a man buy the labor of two people. The crucial importance of this second function of the family can be seen when the family unit breaks down in divorce. The continuation of the economic function is the major concern where children are involved; the man must continue to pay for the labor of the woman. His wage is very often insufficient to enable him to support a second family. In this case his emotional needs are sacrificed to the necessity to support his ex-wife and children. That is, when there is a conflict the economic function of the family very often takes precedence over the emotional one. And this in a society which teaches that the major function of the family is the satisfaction of emotional needs.[9]

As an economic unit, the nuclear family is a valuable stabilizing force

[8] Such figures can easily be estimated. For example, a married woman without children is expected each week to cook and wash up (10 hours), clean house (4 hours), do laundry (1 hour), and shop for food (1 hour). The figures are *minimum* times required each week for such work. The total, 16 hours, is probably unrealistically low; even so, it is close to half of a regular work week. A mother with young children must spend at least six or seven days a week working close to 12 hours.

[9] For evidence of such teaching, see any high school text on the family.

 in capitalist society. Since the production which is done in the home is paid for by the husband-father's earnings, his ability to withhold his labor from the market is much reduced. Even his flexibility in changing jobs is limited. The woman, denied an active place in the market, has little control over the conditions that govern her life. Her economic dependence is reflected in emotional dependence, passivity, and other "typical" female personality traits. She is conservative, fearful, supportive of the status quo.

Furthermore, the structure of this family is such that it is an ideal consumption unit. But this fact, which is widely noted in Women's Liberation literature, should not be taken to mean that this is its primary function. If the above analysis is correct, the family should be seen primarily as a production unit for housework and child-rearing. *Everyone* in capitalist society is a consumer; the structure of the family simply means that it is particularly well suited to encourage consumption. Women in particular *are* good consumers; this follows naturally from their responsibility for matters in the home. Also, the inferior status of women, their general lack of a strong sense of worth and identity, make them more exploitable than men and hence better consumers.

The history of women in the industrialized sector of the economy has depended simply on the labor needs of that sector. Women function as a massive reserve army of labor. When labor is scarce (early industrialization, the two world wars, etc.) then women form an important part of the labor force. When there is less demand for labor (as now under neocapitalism) women become a surplus labor force—but one for which their husbands and not society are economically responsible. The "cult of the home" makes its reappearance during times of labor surplus and is used to channel women out of the market economy. This is relatively easy since the pervading ideology ensures that no one, man or woman, takes women's participation in the labor force very seriously. Women's real work, we are taught, is in the home; this holds whether or not they are married, single, or the heads of households.

At all times household work is the responsibility of women. When they are working outside the home they must somehow manage to get both outside job and housework done (or they supervise a substitute for the housework). Women, particularly married women with children, who work outside the home simply to do two jobs; their participation in the labor force is only allowed if they continue to fulfill their first responsibility in the home. This is particularly evident in countries like Russia and those in Eastern Europe where expanded opportunities for women in the labor force have not brought about a corresponding expansion in their liberty. Equal access to jobs outside the home, while one of the preconditions for women's liberation, will not in itself be sufficient to give equality for women; as long as work in the home remains a matter of private production and is the responsibility of women, they will simply carry a double work-load.

A second prerequisite for women's liberation which follows from the above analysis is the conversion of the work now done in the home as private production into work to be done in the public economy.[10] To be more specific, this means that child-rearing should no longer be the responsibility solely of the parents. Society must begin to take responsibility for children;

[10] This is stated clearly by early Marxist writers besides Engels. Relevant quotes from Engels have been given in the text. . . .

the economic dependence of women and children on the husband-father must be ended. The other work that goes on in the home must also be changed—communal eating places and laundries for example. When such work is moved into the public sector, then the material basis for discrimination against women will be gone.

These are only preconditions. The idea of the inferior status of women is deeply rooted in the society and will take a great deal of effort to eradicate. But once the structures which produce and support that idea are changed then, and only then, can we hope to make progress. It is possible, for example, that a change to communal eating places would simply mean that women are moved from a home kitchen to a communal one. This *would* be an advance, to be sure, particularly in a socialist society where work would not have the inherently exploitative nature it does now. Once women are freed from private production in the home, it will probably be very difficult to maintain for any long period of time a rigid definition of jobs by sex. This illustrates the interrelation between the two preconditions given above: true equality in job opportunity is probably impossible without freedom from housework, and the industrialization of housework is unlikely unless women are leaving the home for jobs.

The changes in production necessary to get women out of the home might seem to be, in theory, possible under capitalism. One of the sources of women's liberation movements may be the fact that alternative capitalized forms of home production now exist. Day care is available, even if inadequate and perhaps expensive; convenience foods, home delivery of meals, and take-out meals are widespread; laundries and cleaners offer bulk rates. However, cost usually prohibits a complete dependence on such facilities, and they are not available everywhere, even in North America. These should probably then be regarded as embryonic forms rather than completed structures. However, they clearly stand as alternatives to the present system of getting such work done. Particularly in North America, where the growth of "service industries" is important in maintaining the growth of the economy, the contradictions between these alternatives and the need to keep women in the home will grow.

The need to keep women in the home arises from two major aspects of the present system. First, the amount of unpaid labor performed by women is very large and very profitable to those who own the means of production. To pay women for their work, even at minimum wage scales, would imply a massive redistribution of wealth. At present, the support of a family is a hidden tax on the wage earner—his wage buys the labor power of two people. And second, there is the problem of whether the economy can expand enough to put all women to work as a part of the normally employed labor force. The war economy has been adequate to draw women partially into the economy but not adequate to establish a need for all or most of them. If it is argued that the jobs created by the industrialization of housework will create this need, then one can counter by pointing to (1) the strong economic forces operating for the status quo and against capitalization discussed above, and (2) the fact that the present service industries, which somewhat counter these forces, have not been able to keep up with the growth of the labor force as presently constituted. The present trends in the service industries simply create "underemployment" in the home; they do not create new jobs for women. So long as this situation exists, women remain a very convenient and elastic part of the industrial reserve army. Their incorporation into the labor force on terms of equality—which would create pressure for capitalization of housework—is possible only with an economic expansion so far achieved by neocapitalism only under conditions of full-scale war mobilization.

In addition, such structural changes imply the complete breakdown of the present nuclear family. The stabilizing consuming functions of the family, plus the ability of the cult of the home to keep women out of the labor market, serve neocapitalism too well to be easily dispensed with. And, on a less fundamental level, even if these necessary changes in the nature of household production were achieved under capitalism it would have the unpleasant consequence of including *all* human relations in the cash nexus. The atomization and isolation of people in Western society is already sufficiently advanced to make it doubtful if such complete psychic isolation could be tolerated. It is likely in fact that one of the major negative emotional responses to women's liberation movements may be exactly such a fear. If this is the case, then possible alternatives—cooperatives, the kibbutz, etc.—can be cited to show that psychic needs for community and warmth can in fact be better satisfied if other structures are substituted for the nuclear family.

At best the change to capitalization of housework would only give women the same limited freedom given most men in capitalist society. This does not mean, however, that women should wait to demand freedom from discrimination. There *is* a material basis for women's status; we are not merely discriminated against, we are exploited. At present, our unpaid labor in the home is necessary if the entire system is to function. Pressure created by women who challenge their role will reduce the effectiveness of this exploitation. In addition, such challenges will impede the functioning of the family and may make the channeling of women out of the labor force less effective. All of these will hopefully make quicker the transition to a society in which the necessary structural changes in production can actually be made. That such a transition will require a revolution I have no doubt; our task is to make sure that revolutionary changes in the society do in fact end women's oppression.

THE REVOLTED

● *carl oglesby*

Killing is evil. . . . All countries are different and progress should be achieved by peaceful means whenever possible.

—Che Guevara

The young men joining them [the NLF] have been attracted by the excitement of the guerrilla life.

—Robert S. McNamara

Everyone in the rich world has heard that there is another world out there, almost out of sight, where two thirds of all of us are living, where misery and violence are routine, where Mozart has not been widely heard nor Plato and Shakespeare much studied.

There is a world, that is, which, according to the mainstream intuitions of mainstream middle-class America, must be somebody's exaggeration, a world which is fundamentally implausible. For the most part, we really believe in it, this poor world, only to the extent that we have it to blame for certain of our troubles. It is the "breeding ground," we say (a favorite term, packed with connotations of the plague), of those discontents which harass us. Most ordinary rich-world people would much prefer never even to have heard of Vietnam or Mozambique, not to mention the nearly thirty other states of the world where long-term insurgencies are under way.

The main fact about the revolutionary is that he demands total change. The corresponding fact about most Americans is that they are insulted by that demand. But what of that demand's moral force? When the statistics of world poverty reach us, as they now and then do, we can respond in several characteristic ways. Sometimes we cluck our tongues, shake our heads, and send a check off to CARE. Sometimes we tell tales about brave missionaries of either the Baptist or the AID persuasion. Someone might name the Alliance for Progress. And someone else might cough. When the statistics are voiced by the poor man's machine-gun fire, we are more decisive. While waiting for our bombers to warm up, we develop our poor-devils theory, according to which the wretched have been duped by Communist con men. It is a bad thing to be hungry; we can see that. But it is better to be hungry and patient than hungry and Red, for to be Red proves to us that all this hunger was really just a trick. It is probably the case that a Communist *has* no hunger.

In the land of remote-controlled adventure, the office-dwelling frontiersman, the automated pioneer—how can matters be seen otherwise?

Middle-class America is the nation to which the forthcoming obsolescence of the moral choice has been revealed.

Middle-class America is the condition of mind which supposes that a new, plastic Eden has been descried upon a calm sea, off our bow. A point here and there, a firm rudder, a smart following breeze, a bit of pluck, and we shall make port any time now in this "American Century."

Middle-class America regards itself as the Final Solution. Its most intense desire is not to be bothered by fools who disagree about that.

What must be difficult for any nation seems out of the question for us: To imagine that we may from time to time be the enemies of men who are just, smart, honest, courageous, and *correct*—Who could think such a thing? Since we love rose arbors and pretty girls, our enemies must be unjust, stupid, dishonest, craven, and *wrong*.

Such conceptions are sometimes shaken. After the 1965 battle of Plei Me, Special Forces Major Charles Beckwith described NLF guerrilla fighters as "the finest soldiers I have ever seen in the world except Americans. I wish we could recruit them." After the same battle, another American said of a captured Viet Cong, "We ought to put this guy on the north wall and throw out these Government troops. He could probably hold it alone. If we could get two more, we would have all the walls [of the triangular camp] taken care of." Major Beckwith was intrigued with the "high motivation" and "high dedication" of this enemy force and suggested an explanation: "I wish I knew what they were drugging them with to make them fight like that."

That curiosity, at least, is good. Why do men rebel? Let us try to find out what could possibly be so wrong with so many of the world's men and women that they should fight so hard to stay outside the Eden we think we are offering them.

I make three assumptions. First, everyone who is now a rebel *became* a rebel; he was once upon a time a child who spoke no politics. The rebel is someone who has changed.

Second, men do not imperil their own and others' lives for unimpressive reasons. They are sharp accountants on the subject of staying alive. When they do something dangerous, they have been convinced that not to do it was more dangerous. There are always a few who can evidently be persuaded by some combination of statistics and principles to put their lives on the line. Lenin, for example, did not materially *need* the Russian Revolution. His commitment was principled and it originated from a basic detachment. But I am not trying to describe the Lenins. I am after those nameless ones but for whom the Lenins would have remained only philosophers, those who (as Brecht put it) grasp revolution first in the hand and only later in the mind.

Third, I assume that the rebel is much like myself, someone whom I can understand. He is politically extraordinary. That does not mean that he is psychologically so. My assumption is that what would not move me to the act of rebellion would not move another man.

It is safe to say first that revolutionary potential exists only in societies where material human misery is the denominating term in most social relationships. No one thinks that bankers are going to make disturbances in the streets. Less obviously, this also implies that privation can be political only if it is not universal. The peasant who compares his poverty to someone else's richness is able to conceive that his poverty is special, a social identity. To say that hunger does not become a rebellious sensation until it coexists with food is to say that rebellion has less to do with scarcity than with maldistribution. This states a central theme: revolutionary anger is not produced by privation, but by understood injustice.

But the self-recognized victim is not at once his own avenger. He is first of all a man who simply wants to reject his humiliation. He will therefore recreate his world via social pantomimes which transfigure or otherwise discharge that humiliation. "They whipped Him up the hill," sang the black slave, "and He never said a mumbling word." That divine reticence is clearly supposed to set an example. But it also does much more. In such a song, the slave plays the role of himself and thus avoids himself, puts his realities at the distance of a pretense which differs from the realities only to the extent that it *is* a pretense. The slave creates for the master's inspection an exact replica of himself, of that slave which he is; and even as the master looks, the slave escapes behind the image. It is not that he pretends to be other than a slave. Such an act would be quickly punished. He instead pretends to be what he knows himself to be, acts out the role of the suffering and humiliated, in order to place a psychic foil between himself and the eyes of others. The American Negro's older Steppinfetchit disguise, or the acutely ritualized violence of ghetto gangs: these are intentional lies which intentionally tell the truth. The victim-liar's inner reality, his demand for freedom, precludes telling the truth. His outer reality, his victimhood, precludes telling a lie. Therefore he *pretends* the truth, pretends to hold the truth in his hand and to pass judgment on it. And by choosing to enact what he *is* he disguises from himself the fact that he had no choice.

A crucial moment comes when something ruptures this thin membrane of pretense. What can do that? A glimpse of weakness in his master sometimes; sometimes the accidental discovery of some unsuspected strength in himself. More often it will be the master's heightened violence that confronts the slave with the incorrigible authenticity of his slave act. A black man sings blues about his powerlessness, his loneliness; he has taken refuge behind that perfect image of himself. The white master, for no reason, in mid-song, takes the guitar away, breaks it, awaits the slave's reaction. The slave is at that moment forced into his self-image space, is psychologically fused with this truth-telling pretense of his: He *is* powerless; he *is* lonely. He cannot now enact himself; he must *be* that man of whom he had tried to sing. This encounter strips life of its formality and returns it to pure, primitive substance. For the victim, there is no longer even the fragile, rare escape of the simultaneous re-enactment of reality. He lives wholly now in his victim space, without manners, not even allowed to mimic the horror of victimhood in the same gesture that expresses it. He is nothing now but the locus of injustice.

Grown less random, injustice becomes more coherent. Confronted at every instant by that coherence, the victim may find that it is no longer so easy to avoid the truth that his suffering is *caused*, that it is not just an accident that there are so many differences between his life and the life of the round, white-suited man in the big hillside house. He begins to feel singled out. He rediscovers the idea of the system of power.

And at that same moment he discovers that he also may accuse. When the victim sees that what had seemed universal is local, that what had seemed God-given is man-made, that what had seemed quality is mere condition—his permanent immobility permanently disappears. Being for the first time in possession of the stark idea that his life could be different were it not for others, he is for the first time someone who might move. His vision of change will at this point be narrow and mundane, his politics naive: Maybe he only wants a different landlord, a different mayor, a different sheriff. The important element is not the scope or complexity of his vision but the sheer existence of the idea that change can happen.

Then who is to be the agent of this change? Surely not the victim himself. He has already seen enough proof of his impotence, and knows better than anyone else that he is an unimportant person. What compels him to hope nevertheless is the vague notion that his tormentor is answerable to a higher and fairer authority. This sheriff's outrageous conduct, that is, belongs strictly to this particular sheriff, not to sheriffness. Further, this sheriff represents only a local derangement within a system which the victim barely perceives and certainly does not yet accuse, a hardship which High Authority did not intend to inflict, does not need, and will not allow. (Once Robin Hood meets King Richard, the Sheriff of Nottingham is done for.)

We meet in this the politics of the appeal to higher power, which has led to some poignant moments in history. It is the same thing as prayer. Its prayerfulness remains basic even as it is elaborated into the seemingly more politically aggressive mass petition to the king, a main assumption of which is that the king is not bad, only uninformed. This way of thinking brought the peasants and priests to their massacre at Kremlin Square in 1905. It prompted the so-called Manifesto of the Eighteen which leading Vietnamese intellectuals published in 1960. It rationalized the 1963 March on Washington for Jobs and Freedom. The Freedom Rides, the nonviolent sit-ins, and the various Deep South marches were rooted in the same belief: that there was indeed a higher power which was responsive and decent.

Sometimes mass-based secular prayer has resulted in change. But more often it has only shown the victim-petitioners that the problem is graver and change harder to get than they had imagined. The bad sheriffs turn out to be everywhere; indeed, there seems to be no other kind. It turns out that the king is on their side, that the state's administrative and coercive-punitive machinery exists precisely to serve the landlords. It turns out that the powerful know perfectly well who their victims are and why there should be victims, and that they have no intention of changing anything. This recognition is momentous, no doubt the spiritual low point of the emergent revolutionary's education. He finds that the enemy is not a few men but a whole system whose agents saturate the society, occupying and fiercely protecting its control centers. He is diverted by a most realistic despair.

But this despair contains within itself the omen of that final shattering reconstitution of the spirit which will prepare the malcontent, the fighter, the wino, the criminal for the shift to insurgency, rebellion, revolution. He had entertained certain hopes about the powerful: They can tell justice from injustice, they support the first, they are open to change. He is now instructed that these hopes are whimsical. At the heart of his despair lies the new certainty that there will be no change which he does not produce by himself.

The man who believes that change can only come from his own initiative will be disinclined to believe that change can be less than total. Before he could see matters otherwise, he would have to accept on some terms, however revised, the power which he now opposes. The compromises which will actually be made will be arranged by his quietly "realistic" leaders and will be presented to him as a total victory. He himself is immoderate and unconciliatory. But the more important, more elusive feature of this immoderation is that he may be powerless to change it. He could only compromise with rebelled-against authority if he were in possession of specific "solutions" to those "problems" that finally drove him to revolt. Otherwise there is nothing to discuss. But the leap into revolution has left these "solutions" behind because it has collapsed and wholly redefined the "problems" to which they referred. The rebel is an incorrigible absolutist who has replaced all "problems" with the one grand claim that the entire system is

[1] What was new was the way these forms enlarged the concept of petition. Instead of merely writing down the tale of grievance, they reproduced the grievance itself in settings that forced everyone to behold it, tzar included, and to respond. The Vietnam war protest demonstrations are no different. The speeches they occasion may sometimes seem especially pugnacious. But inasmuch as the antiwar movement has never been able to dream up a threat which it might really make good, this fiercer face-making has remained basically a kind of entertainment. The main idea has always been to persuade higher authority—Congress, the UN, Bobby Kennedy—to do something. Far from calling higher authority into question, these wildly militant demonstrations actually dramatize and even exaggerate its power.

an error, all "solutions" with the single irreducible demand that change shall be total, all diagnoses of disease with one final certificate of death. To him, total change means only that those who now have all power shall no longer have any, and that those who now have none—the people, the victimized—shall have all. Then what can it mean to speak of compromise? Compromise is whatever absolves and reprieves an enemy who has already been sentenced. It explicitly restores the legitimacy of the very authority which the rebel defines himself by repudiating. This repudiation being total, it leaves exactly no motive—again, not even the *motive*—for creating that fund of specific proposals, that *conversation,* without which a compromise is not even *technically* possible.

"What do you want?" asks the worried, perhaps intimidated master. "What can I give you?" he inquires, hoping to have found in this rebel a responsible, realistic person, a man of the world like himself. But the rebel does not fail to see the real meaning of this word *give*. Therefore he answers, "I cannot be purchased." The answer is meant mainly to break off the conference. But at one level, it is a completely substantive comment, not at all just a bolt of pride. It informs the master that he no longer exists, not even in part.

At another level, however, this answer is nothing but an evasion. The master seems to have solicited the rebel's views on the revolutionized, good society. The rebel would be embarrassed to confess the truth: that he has no such views. Industry? Agriculture? Foreign trade? It is not such matters that drive and preoccupy him. The victorious future is at the moment any society in which certain individuals no longer have power, no longer exist. The rebel fights for something that will not be like *this*. He cannot answer the question about the future because that is not his question. It is not the future that is victimizing him. It is the present. It is not an anticipated Utopia which moves him to risk his life. It is pain. "Turn it over!" he cries, because he can no longer bear it as it is. The revolutionary is not *by type* a Lenin, a Mao, a Castro, least of all a Brezhnev. He is neither an economist nor a politician nor a social philosopher. He may become these; ultimately he must. But his motivating vision of change is at root a vision of something absent—not of something that *will* be there, but of something that will be there *no longer*. His good future world is elementally described by its empty spaces: a missing landlord, a missing mine owner, a missing sheriff. Who or what will replace landlord, owner, sheriff? Never mind, says the revolutionary, glancing over his shoulder. Something better. If he is thereupon warned that this undefined "something" may turn out to make things worse than ever, his response is a plain one: "Then we should have to continue the revolution."

The fundamental revolutionary motive is not to construct a Paradise but to destroy an Inferno. In time, Utopian ideas will appear. Because the world now has a revolutionary past, it may seem that they appear at the same moment as destructive anger, or even that they precede and activate or even cause it. This is always an illusion produced by the predictive social analytic which revolutionist intellectuals claim to have borrowed from history. We may be sure that the people have not said: Here is a plan for a better life—socialism, Montes called it. He has proved to us that it is good. In its behalf, we shall throw everything to the wind and risk our necks. Rather, they have said: What we have here in the way of life cannot be put up with anymore. Therefore, we must defend ourselves.

It happens that at least the spirit of socialism will be implied by the inner dynamics of mass revolt: What was collectively won should be collectively owned. But it cannot be too much emphasized that the interest in developing other social forms, however acute it will become, follows, *does not precede,* the soul-basic explosion against injustice which is the one redemption of the damned. When Turcios takes his rebel band to a Guatemalan village for "armed propaganda," there is no need to talk of classless societies. Someone kneels in the center of the circle and begins to speak of his life, the few cents pay for a hard day's labor, the high prices, the arrogance of the *patrón,* the coffins of the children. It is this talk—very old talk, unfortunately always new—which finally sets the circle ringing with the defiant cry, *"Si, es cierto!"* Yes, it is true. Something will have to be done.

Revolutionary consciousness exists for the first time when the victim elaborates his experience of injustice into an inclusive definition of the society in which he lives. *The rebel is someone for whom injustice and society are only different words for the same thing.* Nothing in the social world of the master is spared the contempt of this definition, which, as soon as it exists, absorbs everything in sight. No public door is marked overnight with a device that permits its survival. The loanshark's corner office and the Chase Manhattan Bank, Coney Island and Lincoln Center, look very much the same from 137th Street. They are all owned by someone else.

Everywhere he looks, the man-who-is-being-revolted sees something which is not his. The good land which the *campesino* works belongs to the *hacienda.* That belongs to the *patrón.* As often as not, the *patrón* belongs to the United Fruit Company. And that prime mover unmoved belongs to nothing. It can only be for a brief moment that the *campesino* gazes with unashamed wonder at these skyscrapers. For all the justice they promise him, they might as well be so many rocks. He is soon unimpressed and grows apathetic toward Western grandeur. *The rebel is someone who has no stakes.* He is an unnecessary number, a drifter into a life that will be memorable chiefly for its humiliations. No use talking to him about the need to sustain traditions and preserve institutions or to help society evolve in an orderly way toward something better bit by bit. He very well knows that it is not in his name that the virtue of this orderliness is being proved. *The rebel is an irresponsible man whose irresponsibility has been decreed by others.* It is no doing of his own that his fantasy is now filled with explosions and burning Spanish lace.

But this new consciousness, this radical alienation from past and present authority, does not lead straightway to political action. A commitment to violence has only just become possible at this point. We have a man who certainly will not intervene in a streetcorner incident in behalf of the "law and order" of which he considers himself the main victim. He will even betray a government troop movement or shelter an "outlaw." But he may also find a tactical rationale for joining a "moderate" march or applauding a "reasonable" speech or doing nothing at all. At odd moments, he will abide talk of reform. Maybe things left to themselves will get better. He will keep the conversation open and the switchblade closed.

What is wrong with this man who thinks things can change without being changed? Who knows everything and does nothing?

Nothing is wrong with him but the fact that he is a human being. All these excuses, these cautions and carefully rationalized delays, add up to one thing: *He wants to be free.* He therefore temporizes with freedom. His desire for an independent private life has been intensified everywhere by the conditions that prohibit it. He has understood his situation and the demands it makes. He knows he is being asked to become a historical object. But he seems to recognize in this demand an old familiar presence. He has been drafted before by this history, has he not? Is the new allurement of rebellion really so different at bottom from the old coercion of slavery? Are his privacy and freedom not pre-empted equally by both? Is the rebel anything more than the same unfree object in a different costume, playing a new role? When the slave kills the master, argues Sartre, two men die. He meant that the slave dies too and the free man materializes in his place. Very well, the image is nearly overwhelming. But where is the freedom of this ex-slave who, instead of cutting cane, is now sharpening knives? That he has removed himself from one discipline to another does not hide the fact that he remains under discipline. It will be said that he at least chose the new one. But that does not diminish the servitude. When the slave conceives rebellion and remains a slave, one may say that he has chosen his slavery. That makes him no less a slave, no more a free man. In fact, the free man was glimpsed only in the moment at which he said: *I can! I may!* At that moment, the whole world shook with his exhilaration. Everywhere, he saw commotion and uncertainty where there had been only stillness and routine before. He stops at the window of a firearms dealer. He does not go in. He proceeds to the window of an agency of escape. This is not irresolution; it is freedom, the liquidity of choice. When he changes *I may* into *I will,* when he has taken the rifle and changed *I will* into *I am,* this man who was for one moment a profuse blur of possibilities, a fleeting freedom, has disappeared into another pose, has transformed himself into another image: that of the rebel.

Of all people, Sartre should have been distant enough from his partisanship to see that in this case freedom was only the possibility of transition from one binding contract to another—*and therefore not freedom.* As the slave found himself isolated from freedom by the master's power, so the rebel finds himself isolated from it by the decision which his life has forced upon him not merely to be a slave no longer, but *to be this rebel.* Once again, he is not his own man. Once again his future, which was for one moment molten, has hardened into a specific object.

Do not be deceived by the high-mindedness of these concepts. Freedom is not an ecstasy reserved for enlightened Europeans. It is not as if its subtleties confine their influence to the bourgeois radicals who anatomize and name them. The psychiatric appendices to Fanon's *The Wretched of the Earth* often read like case-study illustrations for Sartre's *Being and Nothingness.* Drop-outs on Lexington Avenue are jangling and illumined with this torment. Freedom is not something which only certain men will discover only under certain conditions, and its goodness is not limited by the well-known fact that there are better and worse, nobler and baser ways in which it can be lost. We must not get it into our heads that the rebel *wants* to be a rebel. We must not think that he hurls his Molotov cocktails with a howl of glee, much less with a smirk on his face. We have to catch the wince, the flinch, those moments when he unaccountably turns aside. For the slave, there is simply no way to put an end to his current servitude except to exchange it for another. He is not at liberty to be just a nonslave. He is only free to choose between two hard masters. He will struggle to escape this fork, to liberate himself from these titles, to balance on the peak between them. But always he is about to be blown off on one side or the other. For him, it is a clear case of either/or.

I think Camus misses this. I cannot otherwise understand how he could believe himself to be making a useful, relevant moral point when he affirms that men should be "neither victims nor executioners." This is excellent advice for the executioner. It is less illuminating for the victim, perhaps even beyond his depth. The victim does not belong to that category of men for whom action can be regulated by such advice. This does *not* mean that he will recognize himself as the object of Camus's brilliant epithet, "privileged executioner," much less that he somehow prefers to be such a thing. What is so poignant about the victim, in fact, is the desperation with which he seeks to *enter* that category, to become *available* to Camus, for that is the category of free men. It is ruthless to assume that not ourselves but others are so appallingly strange as to choose shattered lives—as if pursuit, revenge, estrangement made up a career.

On the contrary. The rebel will have resisted his rebellion fiercely. The same inner agility that guarded his spirit from his body's subjugation, the same good guile that kept him from becoming for himself that slave which he could not help being for others—this talent for inner survival now stands up to ward off the new version of the old threat. At the moment at which he is most accelerated by his revulsion, he may also be most alarmed to see that he is about to be *reduced* to that revulsion, that he is in danger of becoming it—of becoming a revolted one, a revolutionary. He will for a long time affect a kind of reserve; he will not permit the loss of what Harlem has named his "cool," a word which could only be translated into the languages of oppressed people—"native tongues." To be cool is to float upon one's decisions, to remain positioned just barely beyond the reach of one's commitments. To be cool is to act freedom out without quite denying that there is a hoax involved. It is to tantalize oneself with the possibility that one may do *nothing,* at the same time never letting anyone forget the *fatefulness* of one's situation. Since he wants to be free, the slave cannot renounce rebellion. Since he cannot renounce rebellion, he craves freedom all the more hungrily. That tension can only be controlled by irony: The slave-rebel evades both captivities by refusing to destroy either.

But the evasion is only a more precarious form of the older ritualized self-enacting, and it dooms itself. As soon as the slave defines himself as *other* than the slave, he has already defined himself as the rebel, since the slave is precisely that person who cannot otherwise define himself without committing the act of rebellion.

How can he be said to make a choice when to choose anything at all is already to stand in rebellion?

This man's predicament can almost be touched with the hands. He wants nothing but freedom. That simple demand pits him against the injustice of being defined by the master. It also pits him against the internal and external forces that pressure him to define himself. The choice seems to lie between submitting to murder and committing suicide. Freedom is always escaping him in the direction of his anger or his fatigue. Desiring only that his objective life can have some of the variousness and elasticity of his subjective life, he is always rediscovering that this will be possible only if he forgoes variousness for concentration, elasticity for discipline. *The revolutionary is someone who is nothing else in order to be everything else.*

"We have come to the point," writes someone from the Brazilian underground, "of making a rigorous distinction between being leftist—even radically leftist—and being revolutionary. In the critical situation through which we are now living, there is all the difference in the world between the two. We are in dead earnest. At stake is the humanity of man."

Anyone who wants to know where revolution's strange capacity for terror and innocence comes from will find the answer vibrating between these last two sentences. How can ordinary men be at once warm enough to want what revolutionaries say they want (humanity), cold enough to do without remorse what they are capable of doing (cutting throats), and poised enough in the turbulence of their lives to keep the aspiration and the act both integrated and distinct? How is it that one of these passions does not invade and devour the other? How is it that the knife that is still wet from a second person's blood and a third person's tears can be raised in an intimate salute to "humanity"?

Thus the rebel's picture of himself: a dead-earnest soldier for the humanity of man. If we join him in accepting that picture, if we take the rebel's *machismo* as offered, then we shall probably convince ourselves that he is trapped in a deadly moral contradiction which can be resolved in only one of two ways. Most sympathetically, stressing his aspirations, we should then decide that he is *tragic,* someone driven to disfigure what he most highly prizes. Least sympathetically, stressing his actions, we should find in him the hypocrite *criminal* who cynically pretends that death is only relatively evil.

Both views are wrong. When the "criminal" affirms that he is "in dead earnest," his tone of voice attributes to himself a decision that has originated elsewhere. "In dead earnest" is a euphemism for "desperate." When the "tragic" figure affirms that his cause is "the humanity of man," he has either forgotten the way he came or he has failed to see that negating one thing is not the same as affirming its opposite. "The humanity of man" is a euphemism for "survival."

This abstract man has come through a good many changes. From one whose reaction to his own victimhood was resignation and ritual flight, he has become a self-conscious victim who understands that no one will change things for him, that he may himself take action, and that there is such a thing as revolution. Wretched man has come to the edge of violence. But he is not yet revolutionary man. He may very well piece together an entire habit of life out of hesitation, ambiguity, reserve. He is oblique, ironic, elegant, and cool, someone whose detachment tries not to become treachery, whose sympathy tries not to become irreversible involvement.

What drives him over the divide? What is the difference between the Guatemalan, Mozambiquan, Brazilian farmers who have joined Turcios, Mondlane, Alepio in the mountains, and those likeminded ones who have remained onlookers in the villages? What is the difference between the "revolutionary" and the "radical leftist" which the Brazilian informs us is so critical?

If I am correct in assuming that men resist danger and want freedom from *all* servitudes, then it follows that rebellion does not take place until it has become compulsory. The rebel is someone who is no longer free to choose even his own docile servitude. He has been driven to the wall. Somebody is even trying to pound him through it. He has been reduced from the slave to the prisoner, from the prisoner to the condemned. It is no longer a matter of standing before two objects and choosing which he shall be. Totally possessed by his predicament, and therefore in its command, he is no longer able to make even a subjective distinction between that predicament and himself. His anger, like his previous humiliation, was for awhile still something which he could set beside himself and contemplate or enact: his *situation,* not his *person.* But this changes. In spite of himself, he is pushed into the same space which he formerly quarantined off for his anger. He is fused with it—with the poverty, estrangement, futurelessness which gave it its murderous content. He is turned into the venom from which he has tried to stand apart. Except for rebellion, there is nothing. The strange apparent freedom of the rebel, and hence that pride of his which is so enormous when it arrives as to dwarf everything else, a psychic flood which sweeps everything before it, lie in his having finally affirmed the only life that is available to him: *The rebel is someone who has accepted death.*

It is this deprivation of choice that makes the difference between the "revolutionary," who may not be at all "radical," and the "radical," who may never become "revolutionary."

Who determined that this most severe and absolute of reductions should have taken place? We contented Westerners prefer to think that it was the rebel himself. This gives us the right to treat him as though he were a criminal. This is what allows us to single out for pity those "innocent women and children" whom our bombs also destroy, as if there is nothing wrong in killing adult male rebels. But this distinction, because it presupposes that the rebel has had a choice, obliges us to concoct a whole new second definition of man, a definition to place beside the one which we reserve for ourselves. The rebel will in that case be for us the very astounding slave who found it in his power to walk away from his slavery.

There is a more mundane explanation.

Here is someone who was lucky. He was *educated.* It was systematically driven into his head that justice is such and such, truth this, honor that. One day he surfaced from his education. Powerless not to do so, he observed his world. Having no measures other than those that had been nailed into his brain, and unable to detach them, he found himself possessed by certain conclusions: There is no justice here. Innocently, meaning no harm, he spoke the names of the guilty. No doubt he vaguely expected to be thanked for this, congratulated for having entered the camp of Socrates and Bruno. Matters were otherwise and now he is in prison making plans. This happened.

Here is another, a humbler person. Belly rumbling but hat in hand, he goes before the mighty; does not accuse them of being mighty, far from it; points out politely that there is unused grain in the silos, and untilled land; makes a modest suggestion. His son is dragged from bed the following dawn to see someone whipped for having dangerous ideas. This happened.

A third spoke of a union. He survived the bomb that destroyed his family, but it appears that no one will accept his apologies.

Another who joined a freedom march believing that men were good; he saw an old black man fall in the heat, where he was at once surrounded by white men who said, "Watch him wiggle. Let him die." This is memorable.

A quiet one who spoke for peace between the city and the countryside. It is whispered to him that he must hide; the police have his name; he has committed the crime of neutralism. Where shall this quiet one go now that he is a criminal?

A scholar speculates in a public article that aspects of his nation's foreign-trade system are disadvantageous to development. A week later he hears that his name has been linked with the names of certain enemies of society. Another week, and he finds that he may no longer teach.

One day someone's telephone develops a peculiar click.

Two bombs go off in San Francisco. No clues are found. Two pacifists are shot in Richmond. The police are baffled. Gang beatings of a political nature occur in New York. There are no arrests. The murder toll in Dixie mounts year by year. There are no convictions. One group proposes to rethink the idea of nonviolence. Its supporters are alarmed. Another group arms itself. Its supporters disaffiliate.

Stability, after all, must be ensured. The *peace* must be kept.

But the master seems to grow less and less confident with each of his victories. Now he requires the slave to affirm his happiness. Suspicion of unhappiness in the slave becomes ground for his detention; proved unhappiness constitutes a criminal assault upon the peace. The master is unsure of something. He wants to see the slave embracing his chains.

Trying only to reduce his pain for a moment, the slave forces his body to fade away. The backward faction acquires hard proof from this that its assessment of the situation has been correct. "See this docility? After all, the whip is the best pacifier."

Exasperated, the slave spits out a curse. Shocked to discover that a slave can have learned to curse, the advanced faction hastens forward with a principled rebuke: "Bad tactics! No way to change the hearts of men!"

It is almost comic. As though he were really trying to produce the angry backlash, the master grinds the slave's face deeper and deeper into the realities of his situation. Yet the master must be blameless, for he is only trying to satisfy his now insatiable appetite for security, an appetite which has actually become an addiction. He only wants to know that he is still respected, if not loved, that matters stand as matters should, and that no threat to the peace is being incubated here. "I love you, master," whispers the slave, squinting up between the two huge boots, thinking to steal a moment's relief. To no one's real surprise, he is promptly shot. The master's explanation rings true: "He was a liar. He *must* have been. Liars are untrustworthy and dangerous."

The rebel is the man for whom it has been decreed that there is only one way out.

The rebel is also the man whom America has called "the Communist" and taken as her enemy. The man whom America now claims the right to kill.

REVOLUTIONARY THEORY

Revolutionary Theory as a chapter heading implies two major considerations. The first is the possibility of constructing any viable theory of revolution. The second is, given the discovery of more than one apparently workable theory, the choice of the correct one. James Davies seriously challenges the possibility of imminent revolution in advanced capitalist countries. Martin Oppenheimer, on the other hand, agrees that such revolutions are possible, but suggests that the new revolutionary order is likely to be marred by scars left from the violence and anti-humanistic modes of organization necessary to achieve basic revolutionary change. The remaining selections all argue or presuppose the possibility of progressive social transformation through revolution. George Novack makes a case for a successful working-class led revolution in the United States.

The considerations which are raised in the selections on Mao, Stalin, and Trotsky are at the heart of the twentieth century's major theoretical discussions about revolution. Can socialism be successfully built in a single country without the socialist transformation of the entire world? Can revolution be made through the alliance of communist parties with the bourgeoisie? Trotsky answers *no* to both questions, and we are left to speculate on what the political face of the world would look like now if his *no* had won out in the twenties. To bring the debate to our decade, we may ask whether revolutionaries should follow the line of supporting socialism by implementing the foreign policy of the Soviet Union or China, or whether they should seek to adapt revolutionary theory to their particular nation's or continent's specific situations, perhaps then expanding their revolution beyond its original borders. Success for contemporary revolutionary movements may also depend on whether, given necessary objective conditions, revolutionaries attempt to move the working class to the forefront of the revolutionary struggle or allow the more liberal members of the capitalist class to share that leadership role. As a reading of the selections in section III, which follows, should indicate revolutionary theory must precede revolutionary practice.

TOWARD A THEORY OF REVOLUTION

● *james c. davies*

Revolutions are most likely to occur when a prolonged period of objective economic and social development is followed by a short period of sharp reversal. People then subjectively fear that ground gained with great effort will be quite lost; their mood becomes revolutionary. The evidence from Dorr's Rebellion, the Russian Revolution, and the Egyptian Revolution supports this notion; tentatively, so do data on other civil disturbances. Various statistics—as on rural uprisings, industrial strikes, unemployment, and cost of living—may serve as crude indexes of popular mood. More useful, though less easy to obtain, are direct questions in cross-sectional interviews. The goal of predicting revolution is conceived but not yet born or matured.

In exhorting proletarians of all nations to unite in revolution, because they had nothing to lose but their chains, Marx and Engels most succinctly presented that theory of revolution which is recognized as their brain child. But this most famed thesis, that progressive degradation of the industrial working class would finally reach the point of despair and inevitable revolt, is not the only one that Marx fathered. In at least one essay he gave life to a quite antithetical idea. He described, as a precondition of widespread unrest, not progressive degradation of the proletariat but rather an improvement in workers' economic condition which did not keep pace with the growing welfare of capitalists and therefore produced social tension.

> *A noticeable increase in wages presupposes a rapid growth of productive capital. The rapid growth of productive capital brings about an equally rapid growth of wealth, luxury, social wants, social enjoyments. Thus, although the enjoyments of the workers have risen, the social satisfaction that they give has fallen in comparison with the increased enjoyments of the capitalist, which are inaccessible to the worker, in comparison with the state of development of society in general. Our desires and pleasures spring from society; we measure them, therefore, by society and not by the objects which serve for their satisfaction. Because they are of a social nature, they are of a relative nature.*[1]

Marx's qualification here of his more frequent belief that degradation produces revolution is expressed as the main thesis by de Tocqueville in his study of the French Revolution. After a long review of economic and social decline in the seventeenth century and dynamic growth in the eighteenth, de Tocqueville concludes:

> *So it would appear that the French found their condition the more unsupportable in proportion to its improvement. . . . Revolutions are not always brought about by a gradual decline from bad to worse. Nations that*

[1] The *Communist Manifesto* of 1848 evidently antedates the opposing idea by about a year. See Edmund Wilson, *To the Finland Station* (Anchor Books edition), New York: Doubleday & Co. (n.d.), p. 157; Lewis S. Feuer, *Karl Marx and Friedrich Engels: Basic Writings on Politics and Philosophy*, N. Y.: Doubleday & Co., Inc., 1959, p. 1. The above quotation is from Karl Marx and Frederick Engels, "Wage Labour and Capital," *Selected Works in Two Volumes*, Moscow: Foreign Languages Publishing House, 1955, vol. 1, p. 94.

have endured patiently and almost unconsciously the most overwhelming oppression often burst into rebellion against the yoke the moment it begins to grow lighter. The regime which is destroyed by a revolution is almost always an improvement on its immediate predecessor. . . . Evils which are patiently endured when they seem inevitable become intolerable when once the idea of escape from them is suggested.[2]

On the basis of de Tocqueville and Marx, we can choose one of these ideas or the other, which makes it hard to decide just when revolutions are more likely to occur—when there has been social and economic progress or when there has been regress. It appears that both ideas have explanatory and possibly predictive value, if they are juxtaposed and put in the proper time sequence.

Revolutions are most likely to occur when a prolonged period of objective economic and social development is followed by a short period of sharp reversal.[3] The all-important effect on the minds of people in a particular society is to produce, during the former period, an expectation of continued ability to satisfy needs—which continue to rise—and, during the latter, a mental state of anxiety and frustration when manifest reality breaks away from anticipated reality. The actual state of socio-economic development is less significant than the expectation that past progress, now blocked, can and must continue in the future.

Political stability and instability are ultimately dependent on a state of mind, a mood, in a society. Satisfied or apathetic people who are poor in goods, status, and power can remain politically quiet and their opposites can revolt, just as, correlatively and more probably, dissatisfied poor can revolt and satisfied rich oppose revolution. It is the dissatisfied state of mind rather than the tangible provision of "adequate" or "inadequate" supplies of food, equality, or liberty which produces the revolution. In actuality, there must be a joining of forces between dissatisfied, frustrated people who differ in their degree of objective, tangible welfare and status. Well-fed, well-educated, high-status individuals who rebel in the face of apathy among the objectively deprived can accomplish at most a coup d'état. The objectively deprived, when faced with solid opposition of people of wealth, status, and power, will be smashed in their rebellion as were peasants and Anabaptists by German noblemen in 1525 and East Germans by the Communist élite in 1953.

Before appraising this general notion in light of a series of revolutions, a word is in order as to why revolutions ordinarily do not occur when a society is generally impoverished—when, as de Tocqueville put it, evils that seem inevitable are patiently endured. They are endured in the extreme case because the physical and mental energies of people are totally employed in the process of merely staying alive. The Minnesota starvation studies conducted during World War II[4] indicate clearly the constant pre-occupation of very hungry

[2] A. de Tocqueville, *The Old Regime and the French Revolution* (trans. by John Bonner), N. Y.: Harper & Bros., 1856, p. 214. The Stuart Gilbert translation, Garden City: Doubleday & Co., Inc., 1955, pp. 176-177, gives a somewhat less pungent version of the same comment. *L'Ancien régime* was first published in 1856.

[3] Revolutions are here defined as violent civil disturbances that cause the displacement of one ruling group by another that has a broader popular basis for support.

[4] The full report is Ancel Keys *et al.*, *The Biology of Human Starvation,* Minneapolis: University of Minnesota Press, 1950. See J. Brozek, "Semi-starvation and Nutritional Rehabilitation," *Journal of Clinical Nutrition,* 1, (January, 1953), pp. 107-118 for a brief analysis.

 individuals with fantasies and thoughts of food. In extremis, as the Minnesota research poignantly demonstrates, the individual withdraws into a life of his own, withdraws from society, withdraws from any significant kind of activity unrelated to staying alive. Reports of behavior in Nazi concentration camps indicate the same preoccupation.[5] In less extreme and barbarous circumstances, where minimal survival is possible but little more, the preoccupation of individuals with staying alive is only mitigated. Social action takes place for the most part on a local, face-to-face basis. In such circumstances the family is a —perhaps the major—solidarity unit[6] and even the local community exists primarily to the extent families need to act together to secure their separate survival. Such was life on the American frontier in the sixteenth through nineteenth centuries. In very much attenuated form, but with a substantial degree of social isolation persisting, such evidently is rural life even today. This is clearly related to a relatively low level of political participation in elections.[7] As Zawadzki and Lazarsfeld have indicated,[8] preoccupation with physical survival, even in industrial areas, is a force strongly militating against the establishment of the community-sense and consensus on joint political action which are necessary to induce a revolutionary state of mind. Far from making people into revolutionaries, enduring poverty makes for concern with one's solitary self or solitary family at best and resignation or mute despair at worst. When it is a choice between losing their chains or their lives, people will mostly choose to keep their chains, a fact which Marx seems to have overlooked.[9]

It is when the chains have been loosened somewhat, so that they can be cast off without a high probability of losing life, that people are put in a condition of proto-rebelliousness. I use the term proto-rebelliousness because the mood of discontent may be dissipated before a violent outbreak occurs. The causes for such dissipation may be natural or social (including economic and political). A bad crop year that threatens a return to chronic hunger may be succeeded by a year of natural abundance. Recovery from sharp economic dislocation may take the steam from the boiler of rebellion.[10] The slow, grudging grant of reforms, which has been the political history of England since at least the Industrial Revolution, may effectively and continuously prevent the degree of frustration that produces revolt.

A revolutionary state of mind requires the continued, even habitual but dynamic expectation of greater opportunity to satisfy basic needs, which may

[5] E. A. Cohen, *Human Behavior in the Concentration Camp,* New York: W. W. Norton & Co., 1953, pp. 123-125, 131-140.

[6] For community life in such poverty, in Mezzogiorno Italy, see E. C. Banfield, *The Moral Basis of a Backward Society,* Glencoe, Ill.: The Free Press, 1958. The author emphasizes that the nuclear family is a solidary, consensual, moral unit (see p. 85) but even within it, consensus appears to break down, in outbreaks of pure, individual amorality—notably between parents and children (see p. 117).

[7] See Angus Campbell *et al., The American Voter,* New York: John Wiley & Sons, 1960, Chap. 15, "Agrarian Political Behavior."

[8] B. Zawadzki and P. F. Lazarsfeld, "The Psychological Consequences of Unemployment," *Journal of Social Psychology,* 6 (May, 1935), pp. 224-251.

[9] A remarkable and awesome exception to this phenomenon occurred occasionally in some Nazi concentration camps, e.g., in a Buchenwald revolt against capricious rule by criminal prisoners. During this revolt, one hundred criminal prisoners were killed by political prisoners. See Cohen, *op. cit.,* p. 200.

[10] See W. W. Rostow, "Business Cycles, Harvests, and Politics: 1790-1850," *Journal of Economic History,* 1 (November, 1941), pp. 206-221 for the relation between economic fluctuation and the activities of the Chartists in the 1830s and 1840s.

range from merely physical (food, clothing, shelter, health, and safety from bodily harm) to social (the affectional ties of family and friends) to the need for equal dignity and justice. But the necessary additional ingredient is a persistent, unrelenting threat to the satisfaction of these needs: not a threat which actually returns people to a state of sheer survival but which puts them in the mental state where they believe they will not be able to satisfy one or more basic needs. Although physical deprivation in some degree may be threatened on the eve of all revolutions, it need not be the prime factor, as it surely was not in the American Revolution of 1775. The crucial factor is the vague or specific fear that ground gained over a long period of time will be quickly lost. This fear does not generate if there is continued opportunity to satisfy continually emerging needs; it generates when the existing government suppresses or is blamed for suppressing such opportunity.

Three rebellions or revolutions are given considerable attention in the sections that follow: Dorr's Rebellion of 1842, the Russian Revolution of 1917, and the Egyptian Revolution of 1952. Brief mention is then made of several other major civil disturbances, all of which appear to fit the J-curve pattern.[11] After considering these specific disturbances, some general theoretical and research problems are discussed.

No claim is made that all rebellions follow the pattern, but just that the ones here presented do. All of these are "progressive" revolutions in behalf of greater equality and liberty. The question is open whether the pattern occurs in such markedly retrogressive revolutions as Nazism in Germany or the 1861 Southern rebellion in the United States. It will surely be necessary to examine other progressive revolutions before one can judge how universal the J-curve is. And it will be necessary, in the interests of scientific validation, to examine cases of serious civil disturbance that fell short of producing profound revolution—such as the Sepoy Rebellion of 1857 in India, the Pullman Strike of 1894 in America, the Boxer Rebellion of 1900 in China, and the Great Depression of the 1920s and 1930s as it was experienced in Austria, France, Great Britain, and the United States. The explanation for such still-born rebellions—for revolutions that might have occurred—is inevitably more complicated than for those that come to term in the "normal" course of political gestation.

dorr's rebellion of 1842

Dorr's Rebellion[12] in nineteenth-century America was perhaps the first of many civil disturbances to occur in America as a consequence, in part, of the Industrial Revolution. It followed by three years an outbreak in England that had similar roots and a similar program—the Chartist agitation. A machine-operated textile industry was first established in Rhode Island in 1790 and grew rapidly as a consequence of domestic and international demand, notably during the Napoleonic Wars. Jefferson's Embargo Act of 1807, the War of 1812, and a high tariff in 1816 further stimulated American industry.

[11] This curve is of course not to be confused with its prior and altogether different use by Floyd Allport in his study of social conformity. See F. H. Allport, "The J-Curve Hypothesis of Conforming Behavior," *Journal of Social Psychology,* 5 (May, 1934), pp. 141-183, reprinted in T. H. Newcomb & E. L. Hartley, *Readings in Social Psychology,* N. Y.: Henry Holt & Co., 1947, pp. 55-67.

[12] I am indebted to Beryl L. Crowe for his extensive research on Dorr's Rebellion while he was a participant in my political behavior seminar at the University of California, Berkeley, Spring 1960.

Rapid industrial growth meant the movement of people from farms to cities. In Massachusetts the practice developed of hiring mainly the wives and daughters of farmers, whose income was thereby supplemented but not displaced by wages. In Rhode Island whole families moved to the cities and became committed to the factory system. When times were good, industrialized families earned two or three times what they got from the soil; when the mills were idle, there was not enough money for bread.[13] From 1807 to 1815 textiles enjoyed great prosperity; from 1834 to 1842 they suffered depression, most severely from 1835 to 1840. Prosperity raised expectations and depression frustrated them, particularly when accompanied by stubborn resistance to suffrage demands that first stirred in 1790 and recurred in a wave-like pattern in 1811 and then in 1818 and 1820 following suffrage extension in Connecticut and Massachusetts. The final crest was reached in 1841, when suffrage associations met and called for a constitutional convention.[14]

Against the will of the government, the suffragists held an election in which all adult males were eligible to vote, held a constitutional convention composed of delegates so elected and in December 1841 submitted the People's Constitution to the same electorate, which approved it and the call for an election of state officers the following April, to form a new government under this unconstitutional constitution.[15]

These actions joined the conflict with the established government. When asked—by the dissidents—the state supreme court rendered its private judgment in March 1842 that the new constitution was "of no binding force whatever" and any act "to carry it into effect by force will be treason against the state." The legislature passed what became known as the Algerian law, making it an offense punishable by a year in jail to vote in the April election, and by life imprisonment to hold office under the People's Constitution.

The rebels went stoutly ahead with the election, and on May 3, 1842 inaugurated the new government. The next day the People's legislature met and respectfully requested the sheriff to take possession of state buildings, which he failed to do. Violence broke out on the 17th of May in an attempt to take over a state arsenal with two British cannon left over from the Revolutionary War. When the cannon misfired, the People's government resigned. Sporadic violence continued for another month, resulting in the arrest of over 500 men, mostly textile workers, mechanics, and laborers. The official legislature called for a new constitutional convention, chosen by universal manhood suffrage, and a new constitution went into effect in January, 1843. Altogether only one person was killed in this little revolution, which experienced violence, failure, and then success within the space of nine months.

[13] Joseph Brennan, *Social Conditions in Industrial Rhode Island: 1820-1860,* Washington, D. C.: Catholic University of America, 1940, p. 33.

[14] The persistent demand for suffrage may be understood in light of election data for 1828 and 1840. In the former year, only 3600 votes were cast in Rhode Island, whose total population was about 94,000. (Of these votes, 23 per cent were cast for Jackson and 77 per cent for Adams, in contrast to a total national division of 56 per cent for Jackson and 44 per cent for Adams.) All votes cast in the 1828 election amount to 4 per cent of the total Rhode Island population and 11 per cent of the total U. S. population excluding slaves. In 1840, with a total population of 109,000 only 8300 votes—8 per cent—were cast in Rhode Island, in contrast to 17 per cent of the national population excluding slaves.

[15] A. M. Mowry, *The Dorr War,* Providence, R. I.: Preston & Rounds Co., 1901, p. 114.

It is impossible altogether to separate the experience of rising expectations among people in Rhode Island from that among Americans generally. They all shared historically the struggle against a stubborn but ultimately rewarding frontier where their self-confidence gained strength not only in the daily process of tilling the soil and harvesting the crops but also by improving their skill at self-government. Winning their war of independence, Americans continued to press for more goods and more democracy. The pursuit of economic expectations was greatly facilitated by the growth of domestic and foreign trade and the gradual establishment of industry. Equalitarian expectations in politics were satisfied and without severe struggle—in most Northern states—by suffrage reforms.

In Rhode Island, these rising expectations—more goods, more equality, more self-rule—were countered by a series of containing forces which built up such a head of steam that the boiler cracked a little in 1842. The textile depression hit hard in 1835 and its consequences were aggravated by the Panic of 1837. In addition to the frustration of seeing their peers get the right to vote in other states, poor people in Rhode Island were now beset by industrial dislocation in which the machines that brought them prosperity they had never before enjoyed now were bringing economic disaster. The machines could not be converted to produce food and in Rhode Island the machine tenders could not go back to the farm.

When they had recovered from the preoccupation with staying alive, they turned in earnest to their demands for constitutional reform. But these were met first with indifference and then by a growing intransigence on the part of the government representing the propertied class. Hostile action by the state supreme court and then the legislature with its Algerian law proved just enough to break briefly the constitutional structure which in stable societies has the measure of power and resilience necessary to absorb social tension.

the russian revolution of 1917

In Russia's tangled history it is hard to decide when began the final upsurge of expectations that, when frustrated, produced the cataclysmic events of 1917. One can truly say that the real beginning was the slow modernization process begun by Peter the Great over two hundred years before the revolution. And surely the rationalist currents from France that slowly penetrated Russian intellectual life during the reign of Catherine the Great a hundred years before the revolution were necessary, lineal antecedents of the 1917 revolution.

Without denying that there was an accumulation of forces over at least a 200-year period,[16] we may nonetheless date the final upsurge as beginning with the 1861 emancipation of serfs and reaching a crest in the 1905 revolution.

The chronic and growing unrest of serfs before their emancipation in 1861 is an ironic commentary on the Marxian notion that human beings are what social institutions make them. Although serfdom had been shaping their personality since 1647, peasants became increasingly restive in the second

[16] There is an excellent summary in B. Brutzkus, "The Historical Peculiarities of the Social and Economic Development of Russia," in R. Bendix and S. M. Lipset, *Class, Status, and Power*, Glencoe, Ill.: The Free Press, 1953, pp. 517-540.

 quarter of the nineteenth century.[17] The continued discontent of peasants after emancipation is an equally ironic commentary on the belief that relieving one profound frustration produces enduring contentment. Peasants rather quickly got over their joy at being untied from the soil after two hundred years. Instead of declining, rural violence increased.[18] Having gained freedom but not much free land, peasants now had to rent or buy land to survive: virtual personal slavery was exchanged for financial servitude. Land pressure grew, reflected in a doubling of land prices between 1868 and 1897.

It is hard thus to tell whether the economic plight of peasants was much lessened after emancipation. A 1903 government study indicated that even with a normal harvest, average food intake per peasant was 30 per cent below the minimum for health. The only sure contrary item of evidence is that the peasant population grew, indicating at least increased ability of the land to support life, as the following table shows.

TABLE 1. POPULATION OF EUROPEAN RUSSIA
(1480-1895)

	Population in Millions	Increase in Millions	Average Annual Rate of Increase*
1480	2.1	—	—
1580	4.3	2.2	1.05%
1680	12.6	8.3	1.93%
1780	26.8	14.2	1.13%
1880	84.5	57.7	2.15%
1895	110.0	25.5	2.02%

* Computed as follows: dividing the increase by the number of years and then dividing this hypothetical annual increase by the population at the end of the preceding 100-year period.

Source for gross population data: *Entsiklopedicheskii Slovar,* St. Petersburg, 1897, vol. 40, p. 631. Russia's population was about 97% rural in 1784, 91% in 1878, and 87% in 1897. See Masaryk, *op. cit.,* p. 162n.

The land-population pressure pushed people into towns and cities, where the rapid growth of industry truly afforded the chance for economic betterment. One estimate of net annual income for a peasant family of five in the rich blackearth area in the late nineteenth century was 82 rubles. In contrast, a "good" wage for a male factory worker was about 168 rubles per year. It was this difference in the degree of poverty that produced almost a doubling of the urban population between 1878 and 1897. The number of industrial workers increased almost as rapidly. The city and the factory gave new hope. Strikes in the 1880s were met with brutal suppression but also with the beginning of factory legislation, including the requirement that wages be paid regularly and the abolition of child labor. The burgeoning

[17] Jacqueries rose from an average of 8 per year in 1826-30 to 34 per year in 1845-49. T. G. Masaryk, *The Spirit of Russia,* London: Allen and Unwin, Ltd., 1919, Vol. 1, p. 130. This long, careful, and rather neglected analysis was first published in German in 1913 under the title *Zur Russischen Geschichts- und Religionsphilosophie.*

[18] Jacqueries averaged 350 per year for the first three years after emancipation. *Ibid.,* pp. 140-141.

proletariat remained comparatively contented until the eve of the 1905 revolution.[19]

There is additional, non-economic evidence to support the view that 1861 to 1905 was the period of rising expectations that preceded the 1917 revolution. The administration of justice before the emancipation had largely been carried out by noblemen and landowners who embodied the law for their peasants. In 1864 justice was in principle no longer delegated to such private individuals. Trials became public, the jury system was introduced, and judges got tenure. Corporal punishment was alleviated by the elimination of running the gauntlet, lashing, and branding; caning persisted until 1904. Public joy at these reforms was widespread. For the intelligentsia, there was increased opportunity to think and write and to criticize established institutions, even sacrosanct absolutism itself.

But Tsarist autocracy had not quite abandoned the scene. Having inclined but not bowed, in granting the inevitable emancipation as an act not of justice but grace, it sought to maintain its absolutist principle by conceding reform without accepting anything like democratic authority. Radical political and economic criticism surged higher. Some strong efforts to raise the somewhat lowered floodgates began as early as 1866, after an unsuccessful attempt was made on the life of Alexander II, in whose name serfs had just gained emancipation. When the attempt succeeded fifteen years later, there was increasing state action under Alexander III to limit constantly rising expectations. By suppression and concession, the last Alexander succeeded in dying naturally in 1894.

When it became apparent that Nicholas II shared his father's ideas but not his forcefulness, opposition of the intelligentsia to absolutism joined with the demands of peasants and workers, who remained loyal to the Tsar but demanded economic reforms. Starting in 1904, there developed a "League of Deliverance" that coordinated efforts of at least seventeen other revolutionary, proletarian, or nationalist groups within the empire. Consensus on the need for drastic reform, both political and economic, established a many-ringed circus of groups sharing the same tent. These groups were geographically distributed from Finland to Armenia and ideologically from liberal constitutionalists to revolutionaries made prudent by the contrast between their own small forces and the power of Tsardom.

Events of 1904–5 mark the general downward turning point of expectations, which people increasingly saw as frustrated by the continuation of Tsardom. Two major and related occurrences made 1905 the point of no return. The first took place on the Bloody Sunday of January 22, 1905, when peaceful proletarian petitioners marched on the St. Petersburg palace and were killed by the hundreds. The myth that the Tsar was the gracious protector of his subjects, however surrounded he might be by malicious advisers, was quite shattered. The reaction was immediate, bitter, and prolonged and was not at all confined to the working class. Employers, merchants, and white-collar officials joined in the burgeoning of strikes which brought the economy

[19] The proportion of workers who struck from 1895 through 1902 varied between 1.7 per cent and 4.0 per cent per year. In 1903 the proportion rose to 5.1 per cent but dropped a year later to 1.5 per cent. In 1905 the proportion rose to 163.8 per cent, indicating that the total working force struck, on the average, closer to twice than to once during that portentous year. In 1906 the proportion dropped to 65.8 per cent; in 1907 to 41.9 per cent; and by 1909 was down to a "normal" 3.5 per cent. *Ibid.*, p. 175n.

 to a virtual standstill in October. Some employers even continued to pay wages to strikers. University students and faculties joined the revolution. After the great October strike, the peasants ominously sided with the workers and engaged in riots and assaults on landowners. Until peasants became involved, even some landowners had sided with the revolution.

The other major occurrence was the disastrous defeat of the Russian army and navy in the 1904–5 war with Japan. Fundamentally an imperialist venture aspiring to hegemony over the people of Asia, the war was not regarded as a people's but as a Tsar's war, to save and spread absolutism. The military defeat itself probably had less portent than the return of shattered soldiers from a fight that was not for them. Hundreds of thousands, wounded or not, returned from the war as a visible, vocal, and ugly reminder to the entire populace of the weakness and selfishness of Tsarist absolutism.

The years from 1905 to 1917 formed an almost relentless procession of increasing misery and despair. Promising at last a constitutional government, the Tsar, in October, 1905, issued from on high a proclamation renouncing absolutism, granting law-making power to a duma, and guaranteeing freedom of speech, assembly, and association. The first two dumas, of 1906 and 1907, were dissolved for recalcitrance. The third was made pliant by reduced representation of workers and peasants and by the prosecution and conviction of protestants in the first two. The brief period of a free press was succeeded in 1907 by a reinstatement of censorship and confiscation of prohibited publications. Trial of offenders against the Tsar was now conducted by courts martial. Whereas there had been only 26 executions of the death sentence, in the 13 years of Alexander II's firm rule (1881–94), there were 4,449 in the years 1905-10, in six years of Nicholas II's soft regimen.[20]

But this "white terror," which caused despair among the workers and intelligentsia in the cities, was not the only face of misery. For the peasants, there was a bad harvest in 1906 followed by continued crop failures in several areas in 1907. To forestall action by the dumas, Stolypin decreed a series of agrarian reforms designed to break up the power of the rural communes by individualizing land ownership. Between these acts of God and government, peasants were so preoccupied with hunger or self-aggrandizement as to be dulled in their sensitivity to the revolutionary appeals of radical organizers.

After more than five years of degrading terror and misery, in 1910 the country appeared to have reached a condition of exhaustion. Political strikes had fallen off to a new low. As the economy recovered, the insouciance of hopelessness set in. Amongst the intelligentsia the mood was hedonism, or despair that often ended in suicide. Industrialists aligned themselves with the government. Workers worked. But an upturn of expectations, inadequately quashed by the police, was evidenced by a recrudescence of political strikes which, in the first half of 1914—on the eve of war—approached the peak of 1905. They sharply diminished during 1915 but grew again in 1916 and became a general strike in February 1917.[21]

. . . [T]he lesser waves in the tidal wave [are those whose] first trough is at the

[20] *Ibid.*, p. 189n.

[21] In his *History of the Russian Revolution,* Leon Trotsky presents data on political strikes from 1903 to 1917. In his *Spirit of Russia,* Masaryk presents comparable data from 1905 through 1912. The figures are not identical but the reported yearly trends are consistent. Masaryk's figures are somewhat lower, except for 1912. Cf. Trotsky, *op. cit.*, Doubleday Anchor Books ed., 1959, p. 32 and Masaryk, *op. cit. supra,* p. 197n.

end of serfdom in 1861 and whose second is at the end of Tsardom in 1917. This fifty-six year period appears to constitute a single long phase in which popular gratification at the termination of one institution (serfdom) rather quickly was replaced with rising expectations which resulted from intensified industrialization and which were incompatible with the continuation of the inequitable and capricious power structure of Tsarist society. The small trough of frustration during the repression that followed the assassination of Alexander II seems to have only briefly interrupted the rise in popular demand for more goods and more power. The trough in 1904 indicates the consequences of war with Japan. The 1905–6 trough reflects the repression of January 22, and after, and is followed by economic recovery. The final downturn, after the first year of war, was a consequence of the dislocations of the German attack on all kinds of concerted activities other than production for the prosecution of the war. Patriotism and governmental repression for a time smothered discontent. The inflation that developed in 1916 when goods, including food, became severely scarce began to make workers self-consciously discontented. The conduct of the war, including the growing brutality against reluctant, ill-provisioned troops, and the enormous loss of life, produced the same bitter frustration in the army.[22] When civilian discontent reached the breaking point in February, 1917, it did not take long for it to spread rapidly into the armed forces. Thus began the second phase of the revolution that really started in 1905 and ended in death to the Tsar and Tsardom—but not to absolutism—when the Bolsheviks gained ascendancy over the moderates in October. A centuries-long history of absolutism appears to have made this post-Tsarist phase of it tragically inevitable.

the egyptian revolution of 1952

The final slow upsurge of expectations in Egypt that culminated in the revolution began when that society became a nation in 1922, with the British grant of limited independence. British troops remained in Egypt to protect not only the Suez Canal but also, ostensibly, to prevent foreign aggression. The presence of foreign troops served only to heighten nationalist expectations, which were excited by the Wafd, the political organization that formed public opinion on national rather than religious grounds and helped establish a fairly unified community—in striking contrast to late-nineteenth century Russia.

But nationalist aspirations were not the only rising expectations in Egypt of the 1920s and 1930s. World War I had spurred industrialization, which opened opportunities for peasants to improve, somewhat, their way of life by working for wages in the cities and also opened great opportunities for entrepreneurs to get rich. The moderately wealthy got immoderately so in commodity market speculation, finance, and manufacture, and the uprooted peasants who were now employed, or at any rate living, in cities were relieved of at least the notion that poverty and boredom must be the will of Allah. But the incongruity of a money-based modern semi-feudality that was like a chariot with a gasoline engine evidently escaped the attention of ordinary people. The generation of the 1930s could see more rapid

[22] See Trotsky, *op cit.*, pp. 18-21 for a vivid picture of rising discontent in the army.

 progress, even for themselves, than their parents had even envisioned. If conditions remained poor, they could always be blamed on the British, whose economic and military power remained visible and strong.

Economic progress continued, though unevenly, during World War II. Conventional exports, mostly cotton, actually declined, not even reaching depression levels until 1945, but direct employment by Allied military forces reached a peak of over 200,000 during the most intense part of the African war. Exports after the war rose steadily until 1948, dipped, and then rose sharply to a peak in 1951 as a consequence of the Korean war. But in 1945 over 250,000 wage earners [23]—probably over a third of the working force—became jobless. The cost of living by 1945 had risen to three times the index of 1937.[24] Manual laborers were hit by unemployment; white collar workers and professionals probably more by inflation than unemployment. Meanwhile the number of millionaires in pounds sterling had increased eight times during the war.[25]

Frustrations, exacerbated during the war by German and thereafter by Soviet propaganda, were at first deflected against the British [26] but gradually shifted closer to home. Egyptian agitators began quoting the Koran in favor of a just, equalitarian society and against great differences in individual wealth. There was an ominous series of strikes, mostly in the textile mills, from 1946-8.

At least two factors stand out in the postponement of revolution. The first was the insatiable postwar world demand for cotton and textiles and the second was the surge of solidarity with king and country that followed the 1948 invasion of the new state of Israel. Israel now supplemented England as an object of deflected frustration. The disastrous defeat a year later, by a new nation with but a fifteenth of Egypt's population, was the beginning of the end. This little war had struck the peasant at his hearth, when a shortage of wheat and of oil for stoves provided a daily reminder of a weak and corrupt government. The defeat frustrated popular hopes for national glory and—with even more portent—humiliated the army and solidified it against the bureaucracy and the palace which had profiteered at the expense of national honor. In 1950 began for the first time a direct and open propaganda attack against the king himself. A series of peasant uprisings, even on the lands of the king, took place in 1951 along with some 49 strikes in the cities. The skyrocketing demand for cotton after the start of the Korean War in June, 1950 was followed by a collapse in March, 1952. The uncontrollable or uncontrolled riots in Cairo, on January 26, 1952, marked the fiery start of the revolution. The officers' coup in the early morning of July 23 only made it official.

[23] C. Issawi, *Egypt at Mid-Century: An Economic Survey*, London: Oxford University Press, 1954, p. 262. J. & S. Lacouture in their *Egypt in Transition*, New York: Criterion Books, 1958, p. 100, give a figure of over 300,000. Sir R. Bullard, editor, *The Middle East: A Political and Economic Survey*, London: Oxford University Press, 1958, p. 221 estimates total employment in industry, transport, and commerce in 1957 to have been about 750,000.

[24] International Monetary Fund, *International Financial Statistics*, Washington, D. C. See monthly issues of this report, 1950-53.

[25] J. and S. Lacouture, *op. cit.*, p. 99.

[26] England threatened to depose Farouk in February 1942, by force if necessary, if Egypt did not support the Allies. Capitulation by the government and the Wafd caused widespread popular disaffection. When Egypt finally declared war on the Axis in 1945, the prime minister was assassinated. See J. & S. Lacouture, *op. cit.*, pp. 97-98 and Issawi, *op. cit.*, p. 268.

The J-curve of rising expectations followed by their effective frustration is applicable to other revolutions and rebellions than just the three already considered. Leisler's Rebellion in the royal colony of New York in 1689 was a brief dress-rehearsal for the American Revolution eighty-six years later. In an effort to make the colony serve the crown better, duties had been raised and were being vigorously collected. The tanning of hides in the colony was forbidden, as was the distillation of liquor. An embargo was placed on unmilled grain, which hurt the farmers. After a long period of economic growth and substantial political autonomy, these new and burdensome regulations produced a popular rebellion that for a year displaced British sovereignty.[27]

The American Revolution itself fits the J-curve and deserves more than the brief mention here given. Again prolonged economic growth and political autonomy produced continually rising expectations. They became acutely frustrated when, following the French and Indian War (which had cost England so much and the colonies so little), England began a series of largely economic regulations having the same purpose as those directed against New York in the preceding century. From the 1763 Proclamation (closing to settlement land west of the Appalachians) to the Coercive Acts of April, 1774 (which among other things, in response to the December, 1773 Boston Tea Party, closed tight the port of Boston), Americans were beset with unaccustomed manifestations of British power and began to resist forcibly in 1775, on the Lexington-Concord road. A significant decline in trade with England in 1772 [28] may have hastened the maturation of colonial rebelliousness.

The curve also fits the French Revolution, which again merits more mention than space here permits. Growing rural prosperity, marked by steadily rising land values in the eighteenth century, had progressed to the point where a third of French land was owned by peasant-proprietors. There were the beginnings of large-scale manufacture in the factory system. Constant pressure by the bourgeoisie against the state for reforms was met with considerable hospitality by a government already shifting from its old landed-aristocratic and clerical base to the growing middle class. Counter to these trends, which would *per se* avoid revolution, was the feudal reaction of the mid-eighteenth century, in which the dying nobility sought in numerous nagging ways to retain and reactivate its prerequisites against a resentful peasantry and importunate bourgeoisie.

But expectations apparently continued rising until the growing opportunities and prosperity rather abruptly halted, about 1787. The fiscal crisis of the government is well known, much of it a consequence of a 1.5 billion livre deficit following intervention against Britain in the American war of independence. The threat to tax the nobility severely—after its virtual tax immunity—and the bourgeoisie more severely may indeed be said to have precipitated the revolution. But less well-known is the fact that 1787 was a bad harvest year and 1788 even worse; that by July, 1789 bread prices were higher than they had been in over 70 years; that an ill-timed trade treaty with England depressed the prices of French textiles; that a concurrent

[27] See J. R. Reich, *Leisler's Rebellion,* Chicago: University of Chicago Press, 1953.

[28] See U. S. Bureau of the Census, *Historical Statistics of the United States, Colonial Times to 1957,* Washington, D. C., 1960, p. 757.

 bumper grape crop depressed wine prices—all with the result of making desperate the plight of the large segment of the population now dependent on other producers for food. They had little money to buy even less bread. Nobles and bourgeoisie were alienated from the government by the threat of taxation; workers and some peasants by the threat of starvation. A long period of halting but real progress for virtually all segments of the population was now abruptly ended in consequence of the government's efforts to meet its deficit and of economic crisis resulting from poor crops and poor tariff policy.[29]

The draft riots that turned the city of New York upside down for five days in July, 1863 also follow the J-curve. This severe local disturbance began when conscription threatened the lives and fortunes of workingmen whose enjoyment of wartime prosperity was now frustrated not only by military service (which could be avoided by paying $300 or furnishing a substitute—neither means being available to poor people) but also by inflation.[30]

Even the riots in Nyasaland, in February and March, 1959, appear to follow the pattern of a period of frustration after expectations and satisfactions have risen. Nyasaland workers who had enjoyed the high wages they were paid during the construction of the Kariba dam in Rhodesia returned to their homes and to unemployment, or to jobs paying $5 per month at a time when $15 was considered a bare minimum wage.[31]

One negative case—of a revolution that did not occur—is the depression of the 1930s in the United States. It was severe enough, at least on economic grounds, to have produced a revolution. Total national private production income in 1932 reverted to what it had been in 1916. Farm income in the same year was as low as in 1900; manufacturing as low as in 1913. Construction had not been as low since 1908. Mining and quarrying was back at the 1909 level.[32] For much of the population, two decades of economic progress had been wiped out. There were more than sporadic demonstrations of unemployed, hunger marchers, and veterans. In New York City, at least 29 people died of starvation. Poor people could vividly contrast their own past condition with the present—and their own present condition with that of those who were not seriously suffering. There were clearly audible rumbles of revolt. Why, then, no revolution?

Several forces worked strongly against it. Among the most depressed, the mood was one of apathy and despair, like that observed in Austria by Zawadzki and Lazarsfeld. It was not until the 1936 election that there was an increased turnout in the national election. The great majority of the public shared a set of values which since 1776 had been official dogma—not the dissident program of an alienated intelligentsia. People by and large were in agreement, whether or not they had succeeded economically, in a belief in individual hard work, self-reliance, and the promise of success. (Among

[29] See G. Lefebvre, *The Coming of the French Revolution*, Princeton: Princeton University Press, 1947, pp. 101-109, 145-148, 196. G. Le Bon, *The Psychology of Revolution*, New York: G. Putnam's Sons, 1913, p. 143.

[30] The account by Irving Werstein, *July 1863*, New York: Julian Messner, Inc., 1957, is journalistic but to my knowledge the fullest yet available.

[31] E. S. Munger, "The Tragedy of Nyasaland," American Universities Field Staff Reports Service, vol. 7, no. 4 (August 1, 1959), p. 9.

[32] See U. S. Bureau of the Census, *Historical Statistics of the United States: 1789-1945*, Washington, D. C.: 1949, p. 14.

workers, this non-class orientation had greatly impeded the establishment of trade unions, for example.) Those least hit by the depression—the upper-middle class businessmen, clergymen, lawyers, and intellectuals—remained rather solidly committed not only to equalitarian values and to the established economic system but also to constitutional processes. There was no such widespread or profound alienation as that which had cracked the loyalty of the nobility, clergy, bourgeoisie, armed forces, and intelligentsia in Russia. And the national political leadership that emerged had constitutionalism almost bred in its bones. The major threat to constitutionalism came in Louisiana; this leadership was unable to capture a national party organization, in part because Huey Long's arbitrariness and demagogy were mistrusted.

The major reason that revolution did not nonetheless develop probably remains the vigor with which the national government attacked the depression in 1933, when it became no longer possible to blame the government. The ambivalent popular hostility to the business community was contained by both the action of government against the depression and the government's practice of publicly and successfully eliciting the cooperation of businessmen during the crucial months of 1933. A failure then of cooperation could have intensified rather than lessened popular hostility to business. There was no longer an economic or a political class that could be the object of widespread intense hatred because of its indifference or hostility to the downtrodden. Had Roosevelt adopted a demagogic stance in the 1932 campaign and gained the loyalty to himself personally of the Army and the F.B.I., there might have been a Nazi-type "revolution," with a potpourri of equalitarian reform, nationalism, imperialism, and domestic scapegoats. Because of a conservatism in America stemming from strong and long attachment to a value system shared by all classes, an anti-capitalist, leftist revolution in the 1930s is very difficult to imagine.

some conclusions

The notion that revolutions need both a period of rising expectations and a succeeding period in which they are frustrated qualifies substantially the main Marxian notion that revolutions occur after progressive degradation and the de Tocqueville notion that they occur when conditions are improving. By putting de Tocqueville before Marx but without abandoning either theory, we are better able to plot the antecedents of at least the disturbances here described.

Half of the general, if not common, sense of this revised notion lies in the utter improbability of a revolution occurring in a society where there is the continued, unimpeded opportunity to satisfy new needs, new hopes, new expectations. Would Dorr's rebellion have become such if the established electorate and government had readily acceded to the suffrage demands of the unpropertied? Would the Russian Revolution have taken place if the Tsarist autocracy had, quite out of character, truly granted the popular demands for constitutional democracy in 1905? Would the Cairo riots of January, 1952 and the subsequent coup actually have occurred if Britain had departed from Egypt and if the Egyptian monarchy had established an equitable tax system and in other ways alleviated the poverty of urban masses and the shame of the military?

 The other half of the sense of the notion has to do with the improbability of revolution taking place where there has been no hope, no period in which expectations have risen. Such a stability of expectations presupposes a static state of human aspirations that sometimes exists but is rare. Stability of expectations is not a stable social condition. Such was the case of American Indians (at least from our perspective) and perhaps Africans before white men with Bibles, guns, and other goods interrupted the stability of African society. Egypt was in such a condition, vis-à-vis modern aspirations, before Europe became interested in building a canal. Such stasis was the case in Nazi concentration camps, where conformism reached the point of inmates cooperating with guards even when the inmates were told to lie down so that they could be shot.[33] But in the latter case there was a society with externally induced complete despair, and even in these camps there were occasional rebellions of sheer desperation. It is of course true that in a society less regimented than concentration camps, the rise of expectations can be frustrated successfully, thereby defeating rebellion just as the satisfaction of expectations does. This, however, requires the uninhibited exercise of brute force as it was used in suppressing the Hungarian rebellion of 1956. Failing the continued ability and persistent will of a ruling power to use such force, there appears to be no sure way to avoid revolution short of an effective, affirmative, and continuous response on the part of established governments to the almost continuously emerging needs of the governed.

To be predictive, my notion requires the assessment of the state of mind—or more precisely, the mood—of a people. This is always difficult, even by techniques of systematic public opinion analysis. Respondents interviewed in a country with a repressive government are not likely to be responsive. But there has been considerable progress in gathering first-hand data about the state of mind of peoples in politically unstable circumstances. One instance of this involved interviewing in West Berlin, during and after the 1948 blockade, as reported by Buchanan and Cantril. They were able to ascertain, however crudely, the sense of security that people in Berlin felt. There was a significant increase in security after the blockade.[34]

Another instance comes out of the Middle Eastern study conducted by the Columbia University Bureau of Applied Social Research and reported by Lerner.[35] By directly asking respondents whether they were happy or unhappy with the way things had turned out in their life, the interviewers turned up data indicating marked differences in the frequency of a sense of unhappiness between countries and between "traditional," "transitional," and "modern" individuals in these countries.[36] There is no technical reason why such comparisons could not be made chronologically as well as they have been geographically.

Other than interview data are available with which we can, from past experience, make reasonable inferences about the mood of a people. It was

[33] Eugen Kogon, *The Theory and Practice of Hell,* New York: Farrar, Straus & Co., 1950, pp. 284-286.

[34] W. Buchanan, "Mass Communication in Reverse," *International Social Science Bulletin,* 5 (1953), pp. 577-583, at 578. The full study is W. Buchanan and H. Cantril, *How Nations See Each Other,* Urbana: University of Illinois Press, 1953, esp. pp. 85-90.

[35] Daniel Lerner, *The Passing of Traditional Society,* Glencoe, Ill.: Free Press, 1958.

[36] *Ibid.,* pp. 101-103. See also F. P. Kilpatrick & H. Cantril, "Self-Anchoring Scaling, A Measure of Individuals' Unique Reality Words," *Journal of Individual Psychology,* 16 (November, 1960), pp. 158-173.

surely the sense for the relevance of such data that led Thomas Masaryk before the first World War to gather facts about peasant uprisings and industrial strikes and about the writings and actions of the intelligentsia in nineteenth-century Russia. In the present report, I have used not only such data—in the collection of which other social scientists have been less assiduous than Masaryk—but also such indexes as comparative size of vote as between Rhode Island and the United States, employment, exports, and cost of living. Some such indexes, like strikes and cost of living, may be rather closely related to the mood of a people; others, like value of exports, are much cruder indications. Lest we shy away from the gathering of crude data, we should bear in mind that Durkheim developed his remarkable insights into modern society in large part by his analysis of suicide rates. He was unable to rely on the interviewing technique. We need not always ask people whether they are grievously frustrated by their government; their actions can tell us as well and sometimes better.

In his *Anatomy of Revolution,* Crane Brinton describes "some tentative uniformities" that he discovered in the Puritan, American, French, and Russian revolutions.[37] The uniformities were: an economically advancing society, class antagonism, desertion of intellectuals, inefficient government, a ruling class that has lost self-confidence, financial failure of government, and the inept use of force against rebels. All but the last two of these are long-range phenomena that lend themselves to studies over extended time periods. The first two lend themselves to statistical analysis. If they serve the purpose, techniques of content analysis could be used to ascertain trends in alienation of intellectuals. Less rigorous methods would perhaps serve better to ascertain the effectiveness of government and the self-confidence of rulers. Because tensions and frustrations are present at all times in every society, what is most seriously needed are data that cover an extended time period in a particular society, so that one can say there is evidence that tension is greater or less than it was N years or months previously.

We need also to know how long is a long cycle of rising expectations and how long is a brief cycle of frustration. We noted a brief period of frustration in Russia after the 1881 assassination of Alexander II and a longer period after the 1904 beginning of the Russo-Japanese War. Why did not the revolution occur at either of these times rather than in 1917? Had expectations before these two times not risen high enough? Had the subsequent decline not been sufficiently sharp and deep? Measuring techniques have not yet been devised to answer these questions. But their unavailability now does not forecast their eternal inaccessibility. Physicists devised useful temperature scales long before they came as close to absolute zero as they have recently in laboratory conditions. The far more complex problems of scaling in social science inescapably are harder to solve.

We therefore are still not at the point of being able to predict revolution, but the closer we can get to data indicating by inference the prevailing mood in a society, the closer we will be to understanding the change from gratification to frustration in people's minds. That is the part of the anatomy, we are forever being told with truth and futility, in which wars and revolutions always start. We should eventually be able to escape the embarrassment

[37] See the revised edition of 1952 as reprinted by Vintage Books, Inc., 1957, pp. 264-275.

 that may have come to Lenin six weeks after he made the statement in Switzerland, in January, 1917, that he doubted whether "we, the old [will] live to see the decisive battles of the coming revolution." [38]

[38] Quoted in E. H. Carr, *A History of Soviet Russia*, vol. 1, *The Bolshevik Revolution: 1917-23*, London: Macmillan, 1950, p. 69.

THE LIMITS OF REVOLUTION

● *martin oppenheimer*

Several factors inhibit the democratic development of even an urban revolution: (1) problems of ideology inherent in all revolutionary *thought;* (2) problems of the revolutionary *personality;* and (3) problems of revolutionary *organization.* First, the tendency on the one hand to dominate action with ideology is subversive of democracy; on the other hand, the reverse is equally dangerous. Second, the kind of people who become active in insurrections and survive it *tend* not to be the kind of people who will create a positive, humanistic order; and third, the kind of organization seemingly required to conduct a violent effort is inherently subversive of such an order. To put it into a sort of folk saying (if Barrington Moore will forgive me): ". . . it is a good working rule to be suspicious about political and intellectual leaders who talk mainly about moral values; many poor devils are liable to be badly hurt." [1]

Norman Mailer is not the first to note a profound distinction between the Old American Left and the New Left: the Old Left, whether communist, Trotskyist, or socialist, proceeded, and proceeds, in a deductive fashion, always detailing "the sound-as-brickwork logic in the next step in some new . . . program." The New Left induces from its experience "that you created the revolution first and learned from it, learned of what your revolution might consist and where it might go out of the intimate truth of the way it presented itself to your experience." For the traditional, Marxist left, understanding and analysis, plan and program precede action and revolution; for the new, Freudian-Marxist revolutionists, the idea is "of a revolution which preceded ideology," so that day-to-day practice creates the ideology, inductively.[2]

For the radical, the relationship between action and ideology is always the most difficult of all problems; especially so, then, when it comes to trying to plan the form of the culmination, the terminal point of radical action, the revolution itself. There is no easy solution. For a real radical, this is a dialectical struggle in which program and practice constantly affect one another, leading to the development and, hopefully, progress of the movement. In one way, it is a struggle to be welcomed because of its very difficulty, because it insures

[1] Moore, *Social Origins of Dictatorship and Democracy,* p. 492.
[2] Norman Mailer, "The Steps of the Pentagon," *Harper's,* March 1968.

that the program will be real and at the same time that practice will not simply
be based on momentary whim or opportunity. It is a struggle to be welcomed, as well, because it insures the *democratic* development of the movement as the program is hammered out in day-to-day confrontation with the practical needs of the masses who are, in theory, to be involved in their own emancipation.

One aspect of the history of radicalism is the history of this struggle as it takes place in the context of specific social and economic conditions. Too much emphasis on the immediate, on practice, and the goals are lost sight of; the movement, because it has no program, often becomes social-democratic, liberal, a tool of the status quo, led by "betrayers." Too much emphasis on program and the movement becomes isolated, sectarian, populated by adventurers, and profoundly elitist as it substitutes fancy blueprints for programs that are developed in the course of interaction with the system, the problems it creates, and the people it disaffects.

It is in particularly difficult and frustrating times, when the masses with whom radicals interact are not on the move, as in the United States, or are frightened into apathy, as sometimes in Latin America, that the utopian or left-wing adventuristic tendencies so neatly described in Lenin's *Left-Wing Communism, An Infantile Disorder,* appear strongest. Lacking faith in the masses' moving on their own behalf, such radicals often take into their own hands the decisions as to what is best for others, and so make plans, create utopias, and even seek violent short-cuts to change in the face of apathy.

But for a real radical such short-cuts are not a solution because they create more problems than they solve, divert energies from the development of the movement, and, most important of all, turn the movement into elitist, anti-democratic directions. Why is the utopian tendency elitist? Because, as Marx said in the *Communist Manifesto,* "Historical action is to yield to their [the utopians'] personal inventive action, historically created conditions of emancipation to fantastic ones, and the gradual, spontaneous class-organization of the proletariat to an organization of society specially contrived by these inventors. Future history resolves itself, in their eyes, into the propaganda and the practical carrying out of their social plans."

Just as it is true for radicalism in general that the revolutionary program should develop from struggle but also be informed by history and theory, so it is true for the insurrectionary movement. Neither an insurrection initiated with preconceived ideas nor one which negates the role of ideas can have a democratic outcome—apart from obstacles to democracy inherent in para-military organizational structure. The trouble is that in violent times the apparent "payoffs" for short-cuts are the highest; violence and elitism fit together very nicely.

the mystique of action

It is not necessary to have a plan in order to be an elitist. The movement that has no program tends, as I have said, to opportunism, and that too is elitist. But opportunists rarely make insurrections, so we are not really concerned with that facet of the left. Debray is an elitist not because he is an opportunist, nor because he has a plan. He is an elitist because he proposes to exclude the masses from decision-making over the revolutionary movement until, by some mystical process,the guerrilla band decides the masses are ready. At this point, somehow, the program will develop out of action.

This view is related to Debray's basic attitude toward the importance of ideas and rationality as against feeling and action—another way of saying the urban tradition against the rural, or, in one sense, Marx versus Marcuse. The party-less, program-less movement of action (labeled by some "confrontation politics") is related, therefore, to the *Gemeinschaft* concept common to those pro-peasant views . . . Moore, for example, describes the "Catonic" view of peasant life, the denigration of rational analysis characteristic of the peasant mystique.[3] Bertrand Russell attacks D. H. Lawrence's approach, which is closely related, terming it "thinking with the blood," and arguing that this denial of the intellect "led straight to Auschwitz."

This issue has become one of the divisive generational factors in the American left. There are some, particularly those "over thirty," who are bound by the traditions of linear, rational thinking which involves a concern for the consequences of action, no matter how moral actions may seem in themselves. There are others for whom action, love, feeling, expression are important in themselves, a kind of existential reaction to an overly rationalized and technological society. For these, Debray's mystique of action holds a certain attraction; they share his mistrust of conventional political ideologies. On the American scene, the incessant betrayals and seeming betrayals by so-called liberals and socialists of their announced aspirations seems more than adequate evidence of the futility of theories and ideologies for many alienated students and desperate ghetto blacks. For them, one action is worth a thousand words, and the Marcusian admonition to drop out so you can't cop out falls on eager ears.

It is not surprising, therefore, that Herbert Marcuse suggests that the only really revolutionary class consists of "the outcasts and outsiders, the exploited and persecuted of other races and other colors, the unemployed and the unemployable . . . [who] exist outside the democratic process . . ."[4] This is precisely that under class . . . "pseudo-*Gemeinschaft*," that element most susceptible to total revolution, to "thinking with the blood." We have, then, a strange alliance between humanistic politics and the worship of those less rational bases of politics which have traditionally been the source of support for . . . fascism.

Denigration of rational thought and worship of action has led, historically, to worship of violence and the concept of violence as a therapeutic force. For the traditional Marxist, violence was always a dependent variable, a tool, a tactic to be used under certain limited historical circumstances, usually in defense against violence mounted against a workers' movement by counter-revolutionary elements. At best it was tragic. But with the rise of revolutionary independence movements in the Third World, and with the failure of non-violent movements in American race relations, violence has once again become respectable, even a mark of prestige in left-wing circles. Guevara, Fanon, and Debray have become New Left heroes, and Sartre and D. H. Lawrence have replaced Rosa Luxemburg and Lenin as patron saints of revolution. Violence has become, in short, an independent variable, and the same circumstances that create an alliance between humanism and the denigration of thought also lead to frightening convergences between motorcycle gangs and Stormtroopers, and between Fanon's mystique of violence

[3] Moore, *Social Origins of Dictatorship and Democracy,* Epilogue.
[4] Herbert Marcuse, *One-Dimensional Man,* Boston, Beacon Press, 1964, p. 256.

and the attack on Western Enlightenment by Hitlerism and its philosophical antecedents. The worship of action for the sake of action, the support of feeling over rational thought, the generalized attack on the Western tradition (as opposed to the Marxian attack on specific aspects of Western thought), often encountered in the ranks of hippiedom and some black nationalism and New Leftism, cannot help but remind those over thirty of some of these sentiments:

> *Fascism is, above all, action and sentiment and that it must continue to be . . . Only because it is feeling and sentiment, only because it is the unconscious reawakening of our profound racial instinct, has it the force to stir the soul of a people . . .*[5]

> *National socialism is action pure and simple, dynamics* in vacuo *. . . one thing it is not—doctrine or philosophy.*[6] *Fascism has not been wholly successful with the intellectual classes (because of the fixity of their acquired rational culture) . . . it has been very successful with young people, with women, in rural districts, and among men of action unencumbered by a fixed and set social and political education.*[7]

These are precisely the alienated, marginal elements of society which have been shown to form the backbone of the "radical right," and in some respects also of the non-traditional left, particularly that element which seems to be gravitating to the guerrilla mystique.

The quest for community in the form of the fighting group, which is seen as being the ultimate in comradeship and romance, is related to the worship of violence. So is the Latin American concept of *machismo,* or manliness. As Irving Louis Horowitz recently pointed out, the guerrilla mystique is the incarnation of "virility in speech, action, and dress, virility expressed by bravado, courage, and ruthlessness," precisely those qualities denied, for example, the black male by American society.[8] For the young ghetto black, paramilitary posturing may soon replace the juvenile fighting gang as his way of finding the masculinity denied him by white society. The same thing would be true of young men in the oppressed sectors of the world—it is an idea closely related to Fanon's concept of violence as a psychologically liberating force, so that it is no wonder that Fanon has been so avidly read by opponents of non-violence in the civil rights movement. Violence, according to Fanon, is potent, virile—non-violence is castrating. Of course, we should remember that there is no clinical evidence one way or the other except Fanon's own cases, which are somewhat contradictory. And sociological evidence would seem to point strongly to the conclusion that even if violence occasionally is cathartic for the individual, at the same time it undermines the creation of anything approaching a "therapeutic community," if by that we mean a humanistically oriented community of brotherhood.

Violence, for one thing, is a symptom of bitterness and frustration when it takes political form. For certain alienated groups in this and other societies, violence is seen as the only remaining device, the only device that is not

[5] Alfredo Rocco, *The Political Doctrine of Fascism,* New York, Carnegie Endowment for International Peace, 1926, p. 10.

[6] Hermann Rauschning, *The Revolution of Nihilism,* New York, Alliance Book Corp., 1939, p. 92.

[7] Rocco, *Political Doctrine of Fascism,* p. 25.

[8] Irving L. Horowitz, "Cuban Communism," *Trans-action,* vol. 4 (October 1967), 9.

 co-optable, in a situation where all other measures have failed. It is for this reason that Fanon sees violence as cleansing and that Debray distrusts even radical political parties—all else results in betrayal. Only violence can lead to what is, in a way, a "final solution." The same situation applies to many younger urban blacks—"better to die on your feet than live on your knees." But this is a solution which by definition precludes a plan for the future, much less a democratic one. Once one has accepted a solution by suicide, one has already stopped discussing the "means-ends" problem.

The problem of ideology is that overplanning leads to separation from the masses, hence to elitism; underplanning leads either to opportunism or to thinking-by-feeling, hence to the kind of movement that denies the valid contributions of the Western Enlightenment. Even worse, an ideology of action for-the-sake-of-action tends to glorify violence for its own sake: both in terms of personality and organization, violence, far from being therapeutic, endangers when it does not utterly destroy the humanistic component of a social movement.

the revolutionary personality

Fanon was not the first to point out that oppressed people, frustrated and unable to focus their discontent in a political fashion, frequently aggress against each other (in-group hostility) or engage in various kinds of cathartic motor behavior in which their violent feelings in some way find means of harmless expression (dancing, religious possession, and so forth). That is, if aggression against the true source of oppression is excluded because it would mean instant retaliation and death, aggression must take place in some other way. Rioting, even though the oppressed group ends up as chief victim, serves a similar function although it is politically one step more advanced: "American Negro rioters . . . seem to share one basic psychological dynamic with striking French farmers, Guatemalan guerrillas, and rioting Indonesian students: most of them feel frustrated in the pursuit of their goals, they are angered as a consequence, and because of their immediate social circumstances they feel free enough, or desperate enough, to act on that anger."[9]

Once the historical stage of in-group aggression (high murder rates, for example both in the American ghetto and in Algeria), religious ecstasy, and rioting has passed, violence takes the form of various kinds of paramilitary activity, including terrorism. It may involve a mass revolutionary movement, in which case, according to Fanon, violence serves the function of unifying the people, of nation-building.[10] For the individual, it "is a cleansing force. It frees the native from his inferiority complex and from his despair and inaction; it makes him fearless and *restores his self-respect*" (my emphasis).

The story is confirmed by various observers. Recounts a member of the Nazi party, ". . . I recovered the exhilarating sense of comradery I had known in the army"; said another, "We were united by the terrorism raging around us;" a third, ". . . I always felt happy to see the little groups of

[9] Ted Gurr, "Urban Disorder: Perspectives from the Comparative Study of Civil Strife," *American Behavioral Scientist,* vol. 77 (March-April 1968), 50.

[10] Fanon, *The Wretched of the Earth,* p. 73.

brown-clad soldiers march through the city with rhythmic strides and straightforward mien."[11] Says Eldridge Cleaver, upon first seeing members of the Black Panther Party for Self-Defense, "I . . . saw the most beautiful sight I had ever seen: four black men wearing black berets, powder-blue shirts, black leather jackets, black trousers . . . and each with a gun!"[12] Similar sentiments have come from others, for example immigrants or Jewish visitors to Israel upon first seeing Israeli soldiers.

The question should, however, be raised as to whether this therapeutic effect stems from violence or from the effect of struggling against oppression, regardless of violent or non-violent content. The argument has been made by a number of authors, among others Reverend Martin Luther King, Jr. (in various writings and speeches), that the fact of fighting for one's rights non-violently is therapeutic also—it is, then, standing up that counts, not standing up with gun in hand. Compare, for example, this statement from Nehru, describing a non-violent campaign, with those just quoted: " . . . we had a sense of freedom and a pride in that freedom. The old feeling of oppression and frustration was completely gone . . . We had . . . an agreeable sense of moral superiority over our opponents, in regard to both our goals and our methods . . ."[13]

The negative consequences of violence for the health of the personality also must be mentioned, even though in many ways they should by now be obvious. Fanon's cases, cited in the closing section of *The Wretched of the Earth,* in fact refute his arguments as to the therapy of violence in many instances. The internal conflict over orders to kill, resulting in psychiatric disturbances, has been noted in populations ranging from concentration camp guards to American GI's. And structural consequences must be noted with those to the individual: the losses to society of the skills of those killed or exiled, the setbacks in economic growth, the acute losses of population (perhaps 150,000 in the Algerian War), the undermining of social structures such as family, village, and community, and, of course, the dangers to the society of the future, originating in the violent strategies of the past. B. H. Liddell Hart observes how even effective guerrilla campaigns such as those in Spain against Napoleon were "followed by an epidemic of armed revolutions that continued in quick succession for half a century . . ."[14]

Violence, therefore, is of questionable value in creating a liberating personality. Furthermore, because it is illegal and dangerous, it attracts a different kind of person than is attracted to a conventional reform movement. The underground figure is dedicated and self-sacrificing; prison is an honor, a proof of trust, of great political value after the revolution. But the high level of motivation required in such endeavors implies an unusual personality, a deviant (because tiny minority) type. Nechayev describes him: "The revolutionist is a doomed man. He has no personal interests, no affairs, sentiments, attachments, property, not even a name of his own. Everything in him is absorbed by one exclusive interest, one thought, one passion—the

[11] Abel, *Why Hitler Came into Power,* pp. 176, 179, 180.

[12] Eldridge Cleaver "A Letter from Jail," *Ramparts,* June 1968, p. 19.

[13] Jawaharlal Nehru, *Toward Freedom,* Boston, Beacon Press, 1958, p. 69.

[14] B. H. Liddell Hart, "Lessons from Resistance Movements—Guerrilla and Non-violent," in Adam Roberts, ed., *Civilian Resistance as a National Defense,* Harrisburg, Pa., Stackpole, 1968, p. 204.

 revolution." [15] Not all revolutionists go to Gandhi's extreme, that of taking the vow of celibacy, but one cannot help but shudder at least slightly at the thought of the humorless type described by Nechayev ruling post-revolutionary society. "On the New Left, too, among all these young Dantons, Desmoulins, Marats of fantasy and possibility, one can already pick out here and there the tight-lipped manner, the careful dress, and the touch of pedantry of the potential Robespierre. The play-actors have returned to the stage, but the Puritans are waiting their turn." [16]

One can go further. As one military observer has noted, "the heaviest handicap of all, and the most lasting one, was of a moral kind. The armed resistance movement [of the European undergrounds] attracted many 'bad-hats.' It gave them license to indulge their vices and work off their grudges under the cloak of patriotism . . . This left a disrespect for 'law and order' that inevitably continued after the invaders had gone." [17] The release of aggression sanctioned by revolution, that release deemed therapeutic by Fanon, is not therapeutic in the society after a revolution. This feeling that violence is sanctioned simply does not disappear when the revolution is over; as J. K. Zawodny puts it, "No political leadership can satisfy all aspirations of guerrillas . . . consequently, each movement relying on violence contains a potential seed of future counter-revolution in those of its own rank and file who emerge from the struggle dissatisfied and who are *conditioned to use violence as a means for solving their problems*" (my emphasis). [18]

This particular aspect of revolutionary struggle is sometimes termed "the principle of the transfer of total opposition." It works this way: Before the revolution any opposition to a totalitarian or authoritarian regime (for example, a colonial power) is considered by the regime to be subversive by definition; hence any opposition must be total opposition, prepared for prison, exile, and, hopefully, ultimately revolution. The politics of absolute opposition imposed by a police state leads to the disappearance of all middle-of-the-roaders. "The symbol 'compromise' enjoys a bad reputation, almost on a par with 'opportunism.' " [19] Compromisers are therefore perceived as betrayers. When independence or liberation is achieved, the moderates are dealt with; objectively, they had sided with the enemy. The new rulers, cloaked with the mantle of revolutionary legitimacy, are the only possible rulers—by definition those who did not participate, those who are not with the rulers, are excluded. But the rulers often end up disagreeing, especially where there are latent conflicts among various strata in the population as to how the power is to be divided. Those who go into opposition thereby separate themselves from revolutionary legitimacy and are treated as if they were counter-revolutionaries, in league with those who have just been replaced. If opposition is to be maintained, it must be outside of legitimate channels, which are monopolized by the new government; so that any new opposition becomes revolutionary in turn. All other avenues being closed to

[15] Nechayev, quoted in Gross, *Seizure of Political Power,* p. 342.

[16] Conor Cruse O'Brien, "Confessions of the Last American" (a review of Norman Mailer's *The Armies of the Night*), *New York Review of Books,* June 20, 1968.

[17] Hart, in Roberts, *Civilian Resistance,* p. 203.

[18] J. K. Zawodny, "Guerrilla and Sabotage: Organization, Operations, Motivations, Escalation," in *Annals of the American Academy of Political and Social Science,* vol. 341 (May 1962), special issue on "Unconventional Warfare," ed. by J. K. Zawodny, 15.

[19] Gross, *Seizure of Political Power,* p. 343.

it, the new opposition is left with no alternative than to make another revolution, to take up arms against the state it had helped to create.

the revolutionary organization

This principle of the transfer of total opposition is related to the form of organization used by a movement in the pre-revolutionary period, including its organization of violence. Sociological studies of complex organizations have often made the point that the most idealistic goals tend to be undermined by the organizations set up to achieve those goals, or simply, that the ends are implied in the means, or that the ends do not justify the means because the means change the ends. This is even more true of revolutionary movements which, whether they will it or not, must protect themselves against repression in a police state society. Doing so, they emulate the police state, building structures that maximize security precautions.

A revolution is a war; a revolutionary organization must therefore be military in nature. It is endangered constantly by spies and provocateurs. It must be able to make decisions quickly and have them carried out without question; it cannot, therefore, permit lengthy discussions and debates, or loose organization without a clear-cut chain of command. It must prevent the enemy from uncovering the whole operation if one part of it is uncovered; therefore, only small teams are safe, and the less people know, the better. Such an organization is the very antithesis of democracy. People trained in it, and comfortable within its confines, cannot, no matter how ardently they try, create a humanistic society. It was for this reason that Moses was only permitted to see, but not enter, the Promised Land.

What is particularly odious about the revolutionary organization is the constant fear that many of the participants justifiably must have of infiltrators and informers. Secret societies are made to order for the police in an interesting way: they enable the police to justify their own existence. The line is by now familiar, especially when it comes to asking for increased budgets: "The threat from subversive elements is great and we are doing a lot to solve the problem." (Hence, a few arrests and trials.) "But the problem is still very large." (Unprovable, since measures taken are secret.) "Therefore we need still more funds and facilities."

For the revolutionary organization as for democratic society, suspicion of informers, whether based on reality or not, poisons the atmosphere. It undermines such discussion as may exist and therefore promotes the further subversion of the organization's democratic procedures, however limited they may be. The danger from provocation is always present, so every person's credentials are constantly under scrutiny. "Does he advocate this or that because this would be exactly what the police would like, or not?"

A revolutionary organization operating clandestinely is also open to a counter-measure called the "pseudo-gang."[20] This is an operation in which the government recruits a group to *pose* as an independent revolutionary organization. This group then carries out several illegal acts and is contacted by the regular underground which seeks an alliance or some degree of control

[20] Andrew R. Molnar, William A. Lybrand, Lorna Hahn, James L. Kirkman, and Peter B. Riddleberger, *Undergrounds in Insurgent, Revolutionary, and Resistance Warfare*, Washington, American University, Special Operations Research Office, 1963, p. 184.

 or coordination with it. Thus the government obtains, through the pseudo-gang, valuable information about the real illicit organization. Sometimes the pseudo-gang is absorbed into the regular organization, thus saturating it with informers. Rumors concerning possible pseudo-gangs of ultra-militant black nationalists have, in fact, already begun to circulate in the United States.

The secret organization's vulnerability to police agents, provocation, and entrapment, is easy to see. In the spring of 1968 a New York City detective testified how he had infiltrated the Revolutionary Action Movement, a black nationalist group, and become a member of a three-man terrorist cell that was to murder several prominent moderate civil rights leaders. He had himself played a part in the alleged conspiracy, so that the police department had, in effect, assisted the plot. It was his word against the defendants'. They were convicted. Secret societies are made to order for that kind of "set-up," and really have no way of protecting themselves against it.

The only form of revolutionary organization not susceptible to this basic disease is the non-violent one, in which the revolution need not have a military organization because, first of all, it does not need to organize violence, and, second, because it has no secrets (thereby openly accepting repression). By its very nature ". . . non-violence is inherently a democratizing influence. For learning the techniques and philosophy of non-violence means that (the participant) must become intimately involved with his subject, hence must become deeply aware of himself, of the people who work with him and against him, and of his environment. Such an awareness on the part of large numbers . . . precludes or at least sharply limits the development of narrow elites." [21] Non-violence works best when large numbers participate. In order to motivate them, given the high risks involved, serious education must take place. In a sense, a *Gemeinschaft* or community must be created in which the non-violent practitioner is far more involved as a person than would be the case for a violent practitioner. The latter's role is often far more limited in the total picture (for example, he may only store ammunition in his cellar), so his motivation can also be more limited. Violence, in short, does not require either large numbers or as deep a commitment: it depends on the task. Non-violence requires commitment regardless of task, for all tasks are risky, thus education is essential.

In summary, the types of personalities, as well as the forms of organization, that usually emerge in a violent revolutionary struggle, regardless of its level (coup, terrorism, guerrilla warfare, or urban revolution), are those which undercut the humanistic hopes of such endeavors. Violent transitions of power, unhappily, make for conditions in which the "transfer of total opposition principle" works out so that the violent conditions of struggle before the revolution carry over and hamper the task of reconstruction. This seems to be true not only for movements which in any case are elitist-oriented —although it will be worse in conditions where there is no consciousness of this problem, or where, indeed the very raising of the issue is considered subversive (as in many Communist parties); [22] it is true, alas, for even the most benign, consciously motivated, humanistically inclined movements. The problem can be partially offset, perhaps balanced, by trying to build in democratic mechanisms, but so far in history no movement has managed

[21] Oppenheimer and Lakey, *Manual for Direct Action*, p. viii.
[22] Philip Selznick, *The Organizational Weapon*, New York, McGraw-Hill, 1952.

successfully to solve it. Some kind of Thermidorean reaction[23] has always set in, and somehow, following a violent revolution or uprising, some of the survivors always end up standing in the rubble asking, "Is this what we did it for?" and "Was it worth it?" History cannot unmake revolutions, and such questions can never be answered.

[23] Brinton, *Anatomy of Revolution*, chap. 8.

MARXISM AND REVOLUTION: THE MODERN REVOLUTIONARY FRAMEWORK

● *david horowitz*

i.

Without revolutionary theory, there can be no revolutionary movement.
—Lenin, 1902

To understand Bolshevism as a revolutionary perspective, it must be distinguished, first, from the image of Marxism that has been established during half a century by the orthodoxies of the Second and Third Internationals, and their anti-Marxist critics. Thus, in the orthodox image, Marxism appears as a straightforward economic determinism for which revolutionary changes in the structure of society occur as the simple reflex of revolutionary changes in the economic "base." If this view of Marx's theoretical perspective were as balanced and accurate as it is familiar, however, one would be compelled to conclude that the Bolsheviks were not "Marxists" at all. For the Bolshevik stress on the need to *create* a revolutionary consciousness, and to forge a vanguard party (shaped specifically for the revolutionary struggle), and above all the Bolsheviks' actual decision to seize power by a planned revolutionary insurrection can hardly be made to fit the framework of a theory of historical inevitability.

There are, in fact, two distinct strains of determinism which can be discerned in Marx's writings: one, the familiar *causal* determinism; the other, a *conditional* determinism, a theory of social action in terms of the possible.

The essence of this "conditional" perspective, as absorbed by the Bolsheviks, was most lucidly expressed by Marx in his historical essay on the coup d'état of Louis Napoleon: "Men make their own history," he wrote, "but they do not make it just as they please; they do not make it under circumstances chosen by themselves, but under circumstances directly encountered, given

[1] Several Communist writers have begun in recent years, however, to modify their own previous orthodoxy.

 and transmitted from the past."[2] In Lenin's writings, the same "conditional" perspective is evident, and if anything even more pronounced: "The idea of historical necessity," he observed in an early essay, "does not in the least undermine the role of the individual in history," for "all history is made up of the actions of individuals, who are undoubtedly active figures." But the "real question [that arises] in appraising the social activity of an individual is: *what conditions ensure the success of his actions, what guarantee is there that these actions will not remain an isolated act lost in a welter of contrary acts?*"[3]

Lenin's attitude toward the question of determinism was perhaps even more emphatically expressed in an interview which he gave in London in the year 1902: "The Mensheviks ['orthodox' Russian Marxists] think that history is the product of material forces acting through the processes of evolution. I think, with Marx, that man makes history, but within the conditions, and with the materials, given by the corresponding period of civilization. And man can be a tremendous social force!"[4]

If there were any doubt remaining, the "Marxist" character of Lenin's formulations would be unmistakably confirmed by the comments in Marx's generally ignored preface to the previously cited essay on Louis Napoleon.[5] For here Marx makes clear his view, that the conditioning circumstances which are external to the individual wills of historical agents determine only the *possibilities* of the historical situation, not the details of its future development.

In the Preface, Marx criticizes two contemporary studies of the coup d'état for falling into the twin pitfalls of "subjectivism" (or "voluntarism") on the one side, and "objectivism" on the other. In Victor Hugo's book *Napoleon the Little,* writes Marx, the coup d'etat appears "like a bolt from the blue." Hugo sees in it "only the violent act of a single individual. He does not notice that he makes this individual great instead of little by ascribing to him a personal power of initiative such as would be without parallel in world history." Proudhon, on the other hand, "seeks to represent the coup d'état as the result of an antecedent historical development," i.e., as an inevitable outcome of preceding events. In the end, "his historical construction of the coup d'état becomes a historical apologia for its hero." (Precisely this charge was leveled at those Marxists who, by demonstrating what they took to be the necessity of the course pursued by the Stalin faction in Russia, also sought to absolve the historical agents of their responsibility for that course.) In this, observes Marx, Proudhon "falls into the error of our so-called *objective* historians." As for his own position, Marx writes: "I, on the contrary, demonstrate how the class struggle in France created the circumstances and relationships that made it *possible* for a grotesque mediocrity to play a hero's part."

In his writings on revolution, Marx includes, among the conditioning elements which determine a particular historical turning point, past tradition,

[2] *The Eighteenth Brumaire of Louis Bonaparte* (1852). Cf. Sartre's treatment of a similar remark (by Engels) in his critique of "orthodox" Marxisms, *Search for a Method* (New York: Knopf, 1964), Part III.

[3] "What the 'Friends of the People Are' and How They Fight the Social Democrats" in *Collected Works* (London: Lawrence and Wishart, 1960-1968), Vol. I. Also printed as a pamphlet.

[4] M. Beer, *Fifty Years of International Socialism* (London: 1935), p. 158. This is also the underlying perspective behind Lenin's critique of the doctrine of "spontaneity" in the seminal pamphlet *What Is to Be Done?*

[5] The preface was written by Marx for the second edition in 1869.

ideology and even the historical situation of a strategically placed class (such as the Prussian bourgeoisie in 1848). But for Marx the most critical determinants of the options available to a given social order are to be found in the economic framework of society and the position of the main social classes within that framework. Indeed, many of the ambiguities surrounding Marx's determinism disappear once it is recognized that the range of options in a historical situation is dependent to a large extent on the degree of development of the technological-economic framework. The more rigid and pervasive the economic framework, the more its parts are interlocking and interdependent through advances in technology, and the more subjected in their coordination and organization to the unplanned rule of a worldwide economic market, the fewer, naturally, the options available to the human agents within it,[6] while the material tendencies of its development assume a correspondingly greater role. Conversely, a more primitive technological and economic development, particularly if it exists within a generally more advanced international framework, would raise certain historical possibilities otherwise denied. It is not surprising, therefore, that Marx should have regarded backward Russia as possessing more than one historical option, among which was "the finest chance ever offered" to a people to pass directly from a feudal to a communist development.[7]

A second "orthodox" misrepresentation of Marxism identifies it with a theory of history in which social development is seen as proceeding inexorably through discrete stages, from primitive communism to feudalism, capitalism and socialism. It is extremely doubtful whether Marx, himself, adhered to any such supra-historical theory,[8] and it is certain that the Bolsheviks did not.[9] For acceptance of the doctrine of inevitable historical stages would not only have entailed the acceptance of an inexorable emergence and long-term growth of capitalism in Russia, but more important, it would have denied the possibility of an immediate proletarian conquest of power.

Such a historical theory was indeed held, however, by one school of Marxism in Russia at the time, which regarded Russia's semifeudal, absolutist society

[6] "The capitalistic economy of the present day is an immense cosmos into which the individual is born, and which presents itself to him, at least as an individual, as an unalterable order of things in which he must live. It forces the individual insofar as he is involved in the system of market relationships, to conform to capitalistic rules of action. The manufacturer who in the long run acts counter to these norms will just as inevitably be eliminated from the economic scene as the worker who cannot or will not adapt himself to them will be thrown into the streets without a job."—Max Weber, *The Protestant Ethic and the Spirit of Capitalism* (New York: Scribner, 1948).

[7] Cf. Marx's letter to the editorial board of the *Otechestvenniye Zapiski*, in *Selected Correspondence*, pp. 376 ff., and the Preface to the Russian edition (1882) of the *Communist Manifesto*, in *Selected Works*, I, 24.

[8] Marx's explicit repudiation of any intent to formulate a general theory of historical development is expressed in the famous letter to the editorial board of *Otechestvenniye Zapiski* (see preceding note) on Mikhailovsky's review of *Capital*. The obvious incompatibility of such an abstract general theory with Marx's basic methodological outlook ought to have prevented confusion on this question. However, many writers, Marxist and otherwise, have insisted on treating Marx's comments in the Preface to *A Contribution to the Critique of Political Economy* as such a general theoretical statement, and so long as this is done, the confusion will persist.

[9] Cf. Lenin's reply to Mikhailovsky in "What the 'Friends of the People' Are." Lenin specifically attacks Mikhailovsky's suggestion that Marx laid claim to having formulated a general theory of history.

 through the prism of what has since become virtually identified as *the* Marxian perspective. In this "orthodox" view, the next stage of the Russian Revolution was to be dominated by the nascent bourgeoisie, which would lead the struggle to overthrow Czarist absolutism, to establish democracy and to develop an industrial capitalist economy. Then and only then, as a consequence of the growing contradiction between the forces and relations of production generated by capitalist development, would a new stage of revolution be ushered in—a *socialist* revolution, led by the industrial proletariat. This was the unwavering perspective at the time of the Menshevik Marxists, the true doctrinaires of the Russian Revolution.

Careful consideration of Marx's own writings shows that he himself had more than one scheme of social revolution.[10] The most famous of these, usually associated with "orthodox" Marxism and adopted by the Russian Mensheviks, was based on Marx's view of the historical tendencies of development in France and England, both of which had already entered the epoch of industrial capitalism. But Marx's attention had also been drawn to the class struggle in his native and more backward Germany, both during his "early" period and also at the time of the revolutionary defeats of 1848-49, and it was on this Marxian analysis and its lessons, rather than the other, that the Bolsheviks concentrated.

Thus, in an extremely important pamphlet assessing the 1905 Revolution in Russia, and drawing appropriate lessons for the future, Lenin cited Marx's analysis of the 1848 events and wrote: "With the proper allowances for concrete national peculiarities and with serfdom substituted for feudalism, all these propositions are fully applicable to the Russia of 1905." Moreover, "there is no doubt that by learning from the experience of Germany as elucidated by Marx," the Russian Bolsheviks could arrive at the correct revolutionary line.[11]

Like Czarist Russia, imperial Germany had experienced no bourgeois revolution, but within its feudal framework the new industrial technologies were already being introduced and a proletariat was in the process of formation. Moreover, because of the peculiar features of the *belated* bourgeois revolution developing in the womb of German society, Marx suggested a dramatically different course for Germany from that taken by her predecessors. "The Communists turn their attention chiefly to Germany," declared the *Communist Manifesto,* "because that country is on the eve of a bourgeois revolution that is bound to be carried out under the more advanced conditions of European civilization, and with a much more developed proletariat, than that of England was in the seventeenth, and of France in the eighteenth century, and because the bourgeois revolution in Germany will be but the prelude to an *immediately following* proletarian revolution." (Emphasis added.)

This prediction of a proletarian revolution following immediately on the heels of the bourgeois revolution, i.e., of an uninterrupted development of the capitalist "stage" toward its socialist completion—wrong as it turned out to be for Germany, where the bourgeois revolution was not only compromised but defeated, and prescient as it turned out to be for Russia in 1917—had been anticipated by Marx four years earlier. "Germany," he had written, "will

[10] Cf. Oscar Berland, "Radical Chains: The Marxian Concept of Proletarian Mission," *Studies on the Left,* Vol. 6, No. 5 (1966).

[11] "Two Tactics of Social-Democracy in the Democratic Revolution" (1905), in *Collected Works,* IX, 135-36. Cf. also "The Russian Revolution and the Tasks of the Proletariat" (1906), in *Collected Works,* Vol. X.

not be able to emancipate itself from the Middle Ages, unless it emancipates itself at the same time from the partial[12] victories over the Middle Ages," i.e., from the bourgeois revolution as well. "Germany . . . can only make a revolution which upsets the whole order of things."[13]

For the Bolsheviks, the seminal analyses on the subject of belated bourgeois revolution were Marx's articles and addresses on the class struggles in Germany between 1848 and 1850. In these, Marx once again stressed the difference between the English and French revolutions of the seventeenth and eighteenth centuries and the Prussian revolution of March 1848. In both the former, wrote Marx, "the bourgeoisie was the class that *really* formed the van of the movement," and "the victory of the bourgeoisie was . . . the victory of a new order of society."[14]

By contrast, the German bourgeoisie, as a result of the belated development of German society, was neither psychologically fitted, nor socially situated to play a truly revolutionary role: the German bourgeoisie had developed so "slothfully" and "cravenly" that "the moment when it menacingly faced feudalism and absolutism, it saw itself menacingly faced by the proletariat . . ." Unlike the French bourgeoisie which, as a class, represented the whole of modern society against the old, the Prussian bourgeoisie "saw inimically arrayed not only a class behind it, but all of Europe before it." In this situation, the Prussian bourgeoisie was not capable of becoming the vanguard, but played instead a vacillating role. It wanted change, but by bargain and compromise; its interests initially allied it with the proletariat and the peasantry against the feudal reaction, but it perpetually sought to come to terms with the conservative forces of the old order, the monarchy and the army, and to forestall the proletariat's own revolution against itself:

> *Irresolute against each of its opponents . . . because it always saw both of them before or behind it; inclined from the very beginning to betray the people and compromise with the crowned representative of the old society because it itself already belonged to the old society; representing not the interests of a new society against an old but renewed interests within a superannuated society; at the steering wheel of the revolution not because the people stood behind it but because the people prodded it on before it; . . . revolutionary in relation to the conservatives and conservative in relation to the revolutionists; . . . dickering with its own desires, without initiative, without faith in itself, without faith in the people, without a world-historical calling; . . . such was the Prussian bourgeoisie that found itself at the helm of the Prussian state after the March Revolution.*

This Prussian class, far from being unique, was to become the archetype of the bourgeoisie of belated capitalist development. For in all post-1789 bourgeois revolutions the moderate liberals were to pull back, or transfer into the conservative camp at an early stage.[15] It was a peculiarity of the French Revolution that a section of the middle class had been "prepared to remain revolutionary up to and indeed beyond the brink of anti-bourgeois revolution." For

[12] "Partial," because while establishing legal equality, the bourgeois revolution preserved economic servitude and inequality.

[13] "Introduction to the Critique of Hegel's Philosophy of Right" (1844), cited in Berland.

[14] "The Bourgeoisie and the Counter-Revolution," *Selected Works*, I, 67-68.

[15] The exception is the American Civil War.

 the French bourgeoisie had not yet, like subsequent liberals, the instructive memory of the French Revolution itself to take to heart. After 1794, it was clear to moderates that "the Jacobin regime had driven the Revolution too far for bourgeois comfort and prospects, just as it [was] clear to revolutionaries that 'the sun of 1793,' if it were to rise again, would have to shine on a non-bourgeois society." [16]

So vivid and terrifying was the prospect of the "next" revolution to the propertied classes that the theoretical attack on liberalism itself more and more came to be based on the proposition that democratic ideology and reform would pave the way to this new upheaval. Thus, in 1862, the conservative German legal historian Sohm denounced liberal doctrine in the following vein: "From the third estate itself there have arisen the ideas which now . . . incite the masses of the fourth estate against the third. . . . The education that dominates our society is the one that preaches its destruction. Like the education of the eighteenth century, the present-day education carries the revolution beneath its heart. When it gives birth, the child it has nourished with its blood will kill its own mother." [17]

Marx's portrait of the stunted, wavering and compromising bourgeoisie of belated German development—so unlike its Jacobin forebears and so typical of its successors—reappears at the center of Lenin's analysis of class forces in Russia. In Lenin's view the bourgeoisie in Russia is not consistently revolutionary, and like its Prussian counterpart cannot be trusted to carry through the bourgeois-democratic revolution, but to ally itself, in crisis, with the feudal reaction. On the basis of this subsequently confirmed analysis, Lenin evolved the Bolshevik program: a conquest of power by the proletariat and the peasantry "to crush by force the opposition of the autocracy and to paralyze the instability of the bourgeoisie." Then having seized the initiative and the power from the bourgeoisie *within the bourgeois revolution* (a feat made possible by the failure of the bourgeoisie to carry through its revolution, by its betrayal of its own democratic program and of its allies, especially the peasants) the proletariat would be well placed for its struggle for socialism, against the remaining property-owning classes.[18]

Not only was Lenin's appraisal of the role of the bourgeoisie and its relation to the peasantry based squarely on Marx's analysis of the revolution of 1848,[19] but his general strategy for the proletariat was drawn from it as well. With the victory of the new bourgeois government, Marx had written, the workers must simultaneously establish their own "revolutionary workers" governments, in the form of councils (such councils or soviets had already appeared in Russia spontaneously in 1905). They must organize *independently* and *centralize* their organization, and "from the moment of victory, mistrust must be directed no longer against the conquered reactionary party, but against the workers' previous allies, against the party that wishes to exploit the common victory for itself alone." [20] (For no sooner had the liberal bourgeoisie made its peace with feudal-military power in Prussia, than the whole weight of that power had been used to force the workers "into their former oppressed position.")[21]

[16] E. J. Hobsbawm, *The Age of Revolution 1789-1848* (New York: Mentor Books, 1962), p. 85.

[17] Cited in Franz L. Neumann, *Behemoth* (London: Gollancz, 1942).

[18] "Two Tactics," *Collected Works,* IX, 100.

[19] Understood, of course, in the light of the Russian events of 1905. *Ibid.*

[20] "Address of the Central Committee to the Communist League," *Selected Works,* Vol. I.

[21] *Ibid.*

None of the bourgeois parties, in fact, had any desire to revolutionize all of society, observed Marx, but only wanted to make their own position in society more comfortable, and to consolidate the conditions of bourgeois rule. Such "revolutionary" demands as they put forward, therefore, could in no way suffice for the party of the proletariat. In characterizing the demands which *were* to embody the proletarian program to be advanced against the bourgeoisie during its aborted revolution, Marx employed a concept which was to reverberate throughout the history of the later Russian development:

"While the democratic petty bourgeois wish to bring the revolution to a conclusion as quickly as possible, and with the achievement, at most, of [their own demands], it is our interest and our task to make the revolution permanent, until all more or less possessing classes have been forced out of their position of dominance, until the proletariat has conquered state power, and the association of proletarians, not only in one country but in all the dominant countries of the world, has advanced so far that competition among the proletarians of these countries has ceased and that at least the decisive productive forces are concentrated in the hands of the proletarians. For us the issue cannot be the alteration of private property but only its annihilation, not the smoothing over of class antagonisms but the abolition of classes, not the improvement of existing society but the foundation of a new one." [22]

In the concept of "permanent revolution," even as expressed by Marx in this rudimentary form, are adumbrated all of the major elements of Bolshevik theory [23]—the uninterrupted progress of the revolutionary development; the program of completing the merely partial emancipation of the bourgeois stage, and making "permanent" its reforms; the recognition of the international scope of the revolutionary process. This last element, in particular, was to be developed by later Marxists, and especially the Bolsheviks, in conjunction with the theory of imperialism, the interaction of uneven levels of capitalist development and the interdependence of revolutionary and counterrevolutionary dynamics on a trans-national scale.

Just as Marx had recognized the interconnectedness of revolutionary developments in France and Germany, and had speculated on the one providing a spark for the other, or on the intervention of the Holy Alliance itself igniting a revolutionary explosion, so Lenin regarded the Russian Revolution as a catalyst for the European Revolution. So, too, Trotsky very early had anticipated international intervention against the domestic upheaval and Russia's own reciprocal international impact. Even as Marx, however, had been more confident of an initial triumph of the proletariat in advanced Paris accelerating the then retarded German development, so the Bolsheviks had counted on the triumph of revolution in industrial Germany to consolidate and carry forward the "premature" Russian gains.

ii.

> . . . *they themselves must do the utmost for their final victory by clarifying their minds as to what their class interests are, by taking up their*

[22] "Address . . . ," *Selected Works,* I, 110.

[23] Lenin referred to "uninterrupted" or "continuous" revolution rather than "permanent revolution," which had been revived as a term by Parvus and Trotsky. But as E. H. Carr, *The Bolshevik Revolution 1917-1923* (Baltimore, Md.: Pelican Books), I, 56*n*, and others have pointed out, there is no substantive difference between the two concepts.

position as an independent party as soon as possible and by not allowing themselves to be seduced for a single moment by the hypocritical phrases of the democratic petty bourgeois into refraining from the independent organization of the party of the proletariat. Their battle cry must be: Permanent Revolution.

—*Marx and Engels, 1850*

A permanent revolution versus a permanent slaughter: that is the struggle in which the future is man.

—*Trotsky in Pravda, Sept. 7, 1917*

The fate of the bourgeois revolution in the cold war period (and during the entire era following the nineteenth-century colonial expansion) adhered very much to the course indicated in the original Bolshevik perspective. Despite the massive official attention paid to the problems of underdevelopment and the so-called "aid" programs of the developed capitalist powers, and moreover despite the proclaimed commitment of the most important of these powers to promote and defend the "democratic revolution," not a single underdeveloped country remaining within the framework of international capitalism was able to achieve a stabilized bourgeois-democratic revolution and development in the manner of Western Europe and the United States. [1]

As a result, these countries were all beset by a complex of "insoluble" problems, including those of social backwardness, economic stagnation, industrial and agricultural underdevelopment, hence "overpopulation," and, as a surface expression of these deeper currents, chronic political instability. Virtually everywhere in the backward and exploited regions the democratic gains that were made proved superficial and impermanent; in their very impermanence they seemed to confirm Marx's warning after the revolutionary defeats of 1848: "Every revolutionary upheaval, however remote from the class struggle its goal may appear to be, must fail until the revolutionary working class is victorious, . . . every social reform remains a utopia until the proletarian revolution and the feudalistic counter-revolution measure swords in a *world war*." (Emphasis in original.) [2]

The proper starting point for an analysis of the contemporary framework of revolution in the underdeveloped world is, inevitably, the first proletarian conquest of power to take place in a backward environment—the Russian Revolution of 1917. The question that such an analysis must answer is why this revolution, which began in February 1917 as a bourgeois-democratic

[1] Cf. Barrington Moore, Jr., *Social Origins of Dictatorship and Democracy* (Boston: Beacon Press, 1967). He regards the U.S. Civil War as the last capitalist revolution and the Radical Republicans as the last true capitalist revolutionaries: "From the perspective of a hundred years later, they appear as the last revolutionary flicker that is strictly bourgeois and strictly capitalist, the last successors to medieval townsmen beginning the revolt against their feudal overlords. Revolutionary movements since the Civil War have been either anticapitalist, or fascist and counterrevolutionary if in support of capitalism."—p. 142.

[2] Introduction, *Wage Labour and Capital* (1849). Marx, of course, was thinking of Europe and in a sense this war was and yet was not fought in 1914-1918 and again in 1939-1945. See below, pp. 174 ff. The "feudalistic" counterrevolution has since been subordinated to the counterrevolution organized by the metropolitan bourgeois capitalist powers who attained undisputed supremacy in 1945. But the incompletion of the bourgeois revolution and the impermanence of its reforms remain valid notions.

revolution against Czarist autocracy and feudal backwardness, was unable to stabilize itself, and instead was compelled to develop into a proletarian revolution against the capitalist status quo. In other words, what were the sources of the Bolshevik October?

We have already outlined a perspective on belated bourgeois revolutions generally, and the Russian Revolution in particular, which provides an answer to this question. In order to arrive at an intelligible theory of contemporary revolutionary developments, however, it is necessary to take the analysis somewhat further and to examine, in closer detail, the social forces and conditions forming the framework of those events.

The earliest and still most adequate explanation of the peculiarities of the Russian 1917, was given by Trotsky, who, with Lenin, was the most important theoretician of the Bolshevik revolution,[3] as well as being the actual organizer and leader of the October insurrection.[4]

The framework of Trotsky's analysis was provided by the so-called laws of "uneven" and "combined" development. World historical evolution, he observed, was characterized by great inequalities in its levels of development. For while in some regions very advanced stages of social and technical achievement were attained, in others the most primitive forms of backwardness continued to exist. Under the "whip" of the capitalist world market, however, which "prepares and in a certain sense realizes the universality and permanence of man's development," backward countries are compelled to assimilate the material and intellectual conquests of the advanced areas. This does not mean that the backward countries follow the advanced ones "slavishly," reproducing all the stages of their past. On the contrary, late-emerging societies do not take their steps in the same order as their forerunners but are forced to make leaps in their progress: "The privilege of historic backwardness—and such a privilege exists—permits, or rather compels, the adoption of whatever is ready in advance . . . skipping a whole series of intermediate stages. Savages throw away their bows and arrows for rifles all at once, without traveling the road which lay between those two weapons in the past." Thus, in the real world, development takes a course very different from that suggested in the *schema* of discrete and progressive historical stages. Instead, everywhere more advanced social elements combine with those that are retrograde to produce mixed rather than "pure" social forms, and "the development of historically backward nations leads necessarily to a peculiar *combination* of different stages in the historic process."[5]

In Czarist Russia, as Trotsky pointed out, elements of the bourgeois "future" were already grafted directly onto the feudal present, and it was the resultant hybrid development (or, in his terminology, *combined* development) that gave birth to the hybrid revolutions of 1917. Russian industry, for example,

[3] Prior to Trotsky's split with the party's leadership, this view would not have seemed heterodox. Thus, during the first five years of the Communist International, before Stalin imposed his own orthodoxy on party theory, Trotsky's book *Results and Prospects* (1905) was published widely (and in foreign languages) as an official theoretical interpretation of the forces of the Russian Revolution.

[4] "All the work of practical organization of the [October] insurrection was conducted under the immediate leadership of the president of the Petrograd Soviet, Comrade Trotsky."—J. V. Stalin, *Pravda,* November 6, 1918.

[5] Trotsky, *The History of the Russian Revolution,* Chap. 1. See also especially Volume III, Appendix II.

 while small in relation to the economy as a whole, was technically very advanced and highly concentrated, as well as being greatly subordinated to foreign capital. The confluence of such factors peculiar to Russian development (which meant, for example, the absence of large middle sectors of small businessmen) rendered the Russian bourgeoisie weak and isolated. By contrast, the Russian proletariat had developed "abnormal" strength for this "stage" of the historical process. In fact, the strength of the proletariat rested on the same advanced factors of technical and social organization (the concentration of workers in huge modern enterprises, for example) that produced the relative isolation and weakness of the bourgeoisie. In addition, the proletariat was armed with an advanced revolutionary ideology developed by the much older and politically more mature working classes of Western Europe. Thus, as in Germany before, the revolutionary stage was set very differently in Russia in 1917 from the way it had been for the great bourgeois-democratic revolution in France.

The French bourgeoisie had been in a strong and independent position to lead both the democratic and agrarian revolutions against the feudal nobility and to withstand the unfocused left challenge of the *sans-culotte* and laboring masses; but the Russian bourgeoisie, because of the peculiarities of its *combined* development—its lack of independence, its entanglement with the landed aristocracy, its very fear of the socialism of the relatively advanced proletariat—proved inadequate to its historic tasks, and fell to an organized and mature working-class revolt. "Russia was so late in accomplishing her bourgeois revolution," as Trotsky summarized the difference, "that she found herself compelled to turn it into a proletarian revolution." [6]

Lenin was already convinced in 1905, that only the proletariat and the peasantry would stand consistently behind the democratic revolution and form its real vanguard. Hence, he had put forward the program of distrust of the bourgeoisie in its "own" revolution and struggle for the *revolutionary-democratic dictatorship of the proletariat and peasantry.* Trotsky, in the same period, and from the same perspective, had gone even further. He did not believe that such a revolutionary power could or would stop at the stage of bourgeois reforms. To defend its gains, "to safeguard its political supremacy," the proletariat, once in power would be compelled to push the revolution forward, to put *socialist* problems on the revolutionary agenda.[7]

Twelve years later, when the February Revolution of 1917 deposed Czar Nicholas and established the "dual power" of the provisional (bourgeois) government, on the one hand, and the soviets of workers and peasants, on the other, Lenin responded with a new program, the famous "April Theses," which reflected a perspective similar to that of Trotsky's 1905 analysis. In the existence of the soviets, which exercised effective power in the revolution, Lenin saw the revolutionary-democratic dictatorship of the proletariat and the

[6] *The History of the Russian Revolution,* Introduction to Volumes II and III.

[7] Cf. Rosa Luxemburg, *The Russian Revolution, 1917* (Ann Arbor: University of Michigan Press, 1962): ". . . the Russian Revolution has but confirmed the basic lesson of every great revolution, the law of its being, which decrees: either the revolution must advance at a rapid, stormy and resolute tempo, break down all barriers with an iron hand and place its goals ever farther ahead, or it is quite soon thrown backward behind its feeble point of departure and suppressed by counterrevolution."—p. 36. To a large extent, Trotsky, in his forecast, was merely extrapolating from the revolutionary experience of 1905.

peasantry "already accomplished in reality." The formula was, therefore, "already antiquated."[8] The new task facing the Bolsheviks was "to effect a split *within* this dictatorship between the proletarian elements . . . and the small-proprietor or petty-bourgeois elements," while calling for a transfer of all state power to the Soviets—in other words, to organize for a proletarian, i.e., a *socialist* conquest of power.

While recognizing the extreme difficulties besetting any attempt to put into effect "socialist changes" in "one of the most backward countries of Europe amidst a vast population of small peasants," Lenin stressed that "it would be a grave error, and *in effect even a complete desertion to the bourgeoisie* to infer from this that the working class must support the bourgeoisie, or that it must keep its activities within limits acceptable to the petty bourgeoisie, or that the proletariat must renounce its leading role [in promoting] practical steps towards socialism," including nationalization of the land and of the banks, "for which the time is now ripe."[9] (Emphasis added.)

In fact, Lenin's 1917 program of going beyond the bourgeois-democratic revolution had been inherent in his 1905 perspective. "From the democratic revolution," he had written, "we shall begin immediately and within the measure of our strength—the strength of the conscious and organized proletariat—to make the transition to the socialist revolution. We stand for uninterrupted revolution. We shall not stop half way."[10]

What divided Trotsky, who had been alone in actually *predicting* an uninterrupted transition or permanent revolution in Russia, and Lenin, who advocated it,[11] was their differing analyses before April 1917 (when the adoption of Lenin's famous theses eliminated any programmatic differences between them)[12] of the strength and dynamism of the bourgeois revolution in Russia. In Lenin's perspective prior to 1917, the bourgeois revolution itself could be successfully challenged only with the support of a European socialist revolution because the Russian proletariat could not hold power without the backing of the basically nonsocialist peasantry. In Trotsky's view, owing to the peculiarities of Russian backwardness, the "democratic dictatorship" would not be able to stabilize itself; the Russian bourgeois revolution would prove powerless to fulfill its historic tasks, and therefore the Russian proletariat would *necessarily* come to power and set in motion a *socialist* revolution, with or *without* the aid of the proletariat of Europe.[13] "The essence of the dispute about the question of permanent revolution from 1905 till 1917,"

[8] "Letters on Tactics," in *Collected Works,* XXIV, 45. Cf. also "The Tasks of the Proletariat in the Present Revolution," in the "April Theses," *ibid.*, p. 21.

[9] "Resolution on the Current Situation," adopted by the Seventh (April 1917) All-Russia Conference of the Bolsheviks, *Collected Works,* XXIV, 311-12.

[10] "Social Democracy's Attitude toward the Peasant Movement," *Collected Works* IX, 236-37. The above translation is from Carr, *The Bolshevik Revolution,* I, 68.

[11] Lenin regarded the victory of the democratic revolution consistently from the point of view of establishing an advanced position for the proletariat in its struggle for a *socialist* revolution. Cf. "Two Tactics of Social Democracy in the Democratic Revolution," *Collected Works,* Vol. IX.

[12] The chief differences between Lenin and Trotsky had been over party organization. These were resolved when Trotsky joined the Bolsheviks in July 1917, taking the position that Lenin had been right.

[13] For the *construction* of socialism in Russia, however, as opposed merely to the establishment of collective ownership—its "legal premise"—Trotsky agreed with Lenin on the necessity of international revolution.

 Trotsky later wrote, "reduces itself . . . to the question whether a bourgeois revolution really capable of solving the agrarian problem [14] was still possible in Russia, or whether for the accomplishment of this work a dictatorship of the proletariat would be needed." [15]

As events actually turned out, the February Revolution in Russia was unable to distribute land to the peasants, and therefore proved unstable. To "solve" the agrarian problem—which had been one of the historic tasks of the bourgeois revolution in France, but which the Russian bourgeoisie had not the will to solve, and the peasantry had not the independence or organization to solve for itself—the peasant classes of rural Russia were obliged to support the October Revolution, the *proletarian* conquest of power.

What was true in regard to the question of land was also true in regard to the other great and intimately related social question of the revolution—the question of peace. For the major classes and their parties divided on the distribution of the land in the same way as they divided on the issue of ending the imperialist war. The coalition of bourgeois "revolutionary" parties, for example, opposed the immediate distribution of the land and the consequent up-ending of the social structure while supporting the war. They supported the war not only because they wished to preserve their alliance with the other bourgeois powers and to obtain control over the Dardanelles and the territory in the Balkans promised under the secret London Treaty of 1915, but because they saw in the war—with its military controls and patriotic fervor—a profoundly conservative force. As the Russian historian and liberal foreign minister of the first Provisional Government commented in early April 1917: "Perhaps something will be preserved as a result of the War; without the War everything would break up more quickly." [16]

Predictably, the moderate parties, socialist and nonsocialist alike, vacillated hopelessly over the main questions of the day. While opposing the annexationist war aims of the Czarist government, they were prepared to continue the war, without the Czar but under the social, economic and political regime of the old ruling classes, as a "war for democracy." Similarly, while sympathizing with the peasants' desire for land, which was leading to insurgency in the countryside and sapping the morale of the army, they were not ready to break with the bourgeoisie (or the aristocracy) or to jeopardize the war effort by promoting domestic upheaval. So momentous a decision as land reform, they held, should be decided by a constituent assembly. But when the bourgeois ministers insisted on delaying the assembly, fearing that such a body convened at the height of the revolution would be too radical, the socialist ministers "sacrificed the assembly to save the coalition." [17]

Of all the organized *parties,* therefore, only the Bolsheviks were ready to break decisively with the bourgeoisie and the landowners on the questions of land and peace, while among the consistently revolutionary *classes* only the urban proletariat was willing and able to seize *state* power.

To what extent this pattern of dynamic revolutionary forces is repeated in subsequent upheavals in the underdeveloped world can be suggested by comparing the Russian experience with the other great and, in many ways, even

[14] That is, as a problem of distribution.
[15] Trotsky, *History of the Russian Revolution,* Vol. III, Appendix II.
[16] Milyukov, cited in Chamberlin, *op. cit.,* I, 107.
[17] Isaac Deutscher, "The Russian Revolution," in *The New Cambridge Modern History,* XII, 401.

more characteristic revolution of the age, the revolution in China. One immediate difference between the two events was that the Bolsheviks had to struggle against nationalist sentiment on the war question, whereas the Chinese Communists were able to take the lead in a national struggle against Japanese imperialism. It is extremely significant, therefore, that despite this difference in the situations, the line-up of class forces on the basic issues of the belated bourgeois-democratic revolution remained the same. In China, as in Russia, it was not the party of the bourgeois that led, or consistently supported, the popular revolutionary struggle on the agrarian, democratic and national questions, but the armed and independently organized Communist Party, which mobilized the revolutionary-nationalist ferment among the lower classes. In Russia the Bolsheviks supported the demands of the non-Russian nationalities for self-determination. In China the bourgeois party was itself a nationalist party, but when confronted by an independent force mobilizing and leading the agrarian revolution, it subordinated national interests to class interests—a policy which eventually led to its defeat.[18] "Except for the Communist Party," wrote Mao at the end of the thirties, "no political party (bourgeois or petty bourgeois) is equal to the task of leading China's two great revolutions, the democratic and the socialist revolutions, to complete fulfillment." [19]

In one respect, however, the Chinese Revolution did represent a major departure from the Russian. In contrast to the Russian Marxists, the Maoists based their revolutionary party on the peasantry and carried their revolutionary struggle from the countryside to the towns. The Russian experience had seemed to confirm both Lenin's and Trotsky's stress on the proletariat as providing the only viable class basis for a revolutionary conquest of power.[20] However, many different circumstances in China (not least the prolonged national war of liberation) altered the social assumptions on which Lenin's and Trotsky's analysis had been based, and therefore vitiated its conclusions.[21]

Unlike the Bolsheviks, the Chinese Communists arrived at the conception of their own role, as leaders in the *bourgeois* "stage" of the revolution, only after bitter experience and tragic defeats.[22] The pragmatic nature of the Chinese gravitation toward a "Leninist" strategy of permanent revolution seems to confirm the rootedness of that strategy in the social realities of belated bourgeois development. "The bourgeois-democratic revolution in present-day China," wrote Mao in 1939, "is no longer of the general, old type, which is now

[18] Cf. Chalmers A. Johnson, *Peasant Nationalism and Communist Power* (Stanford, Calif.: Stanford University Press, 1962). Johnson's thesis is that the national struggle takes primacy over the class struggle in determining the Communists' success. In fact, what his material shows is that in China and Yugoslavia (the countries studied) the class character of the contending parties determined their national orientation (in the way outlined above) and their ability to take the lead in the nationalist struggle.

[19] *Selected Works,* II, 331. In Cuba, the revolutionary experience provided a similar conclusion: "In the present historical conditions of Latin America the national bourgeoisie cannot lead the anti-feudal and anti-imperialist struggle. Experience demonstrates that in our nations this class—even when its interests clash with those of Yankee imperialism—has been incapable of confronting imperialism, paralyzed by fear of social revolution and frightened by the clamor of the exploited masses."—*Second Declaration of Havana*, February 4, 1962.

[20] Cf. Chamberlin, *op. cit.,* II, 458.

[21] For an appraisal of the Chinese Revolution in terms of the classical framework and these altered assumptions, see Isaac Deutscher, "Maoism—Its Origins and Outlook," in *Ironies of History* (New York: Oxford University Press, 1966).

[22] Cf. Harold R. Isaacs, *The Tragedy of the Chinese Revolution* (London: 1938) for the authoritative account of these defeats.

 obsolete, but of the special, new type. This kind of revolution is developing in China as well as in all other colonial and semi-colonial countries, and we call it the new-democratic revolution."[23] This "new-democratic" revolution, according to Mao, embraces the stages of both the bourgeois and socialist revolution; the first providing the conditions for the second,[24] and the two taking place consecutively, i.e., "*without allowing any intervening stage of bourgeois* dictatorship."[25] (Emphasis added.) A 1958 resolution of the Central Committee of the Chinese Communist Party expressed this theoretical position: "We are partisans of the Marxist-Leninist theory of permanent revolution. We hold that there is not and cannot be a great wall between the democratic revolution and the socialist revolution . . ."[26]

This formulation by the Chinese, in classical Marxist terms, owed its parentage not to Trotsky, whom the Chinese in their neo-Stalinist vein, still reviled,[27] but to Lenin. "Beginning in *April* 1917," Lenin had explained in his postrevolution polemic against Kautsky, "long before the October Revolution, that is, long before we assumed power, we publicly declared and explained to the people: the revolution cannot now stop at this stage, for the country has marched forward, capitalism has advanced, ruin has reached unprecedented dimensions, which (whether one likes it or not) will *demand* steps forward, to *Socialism*. For there is *no* other way of advancing [than by this path] . . . To attempt to raise an artificial Chinese Wall between the first and second [stages], to separate them by anything else than the degree of preparedness of the proletariat and the degree of its unity with the poor peasants, means monstrously to distort Marxism, to vulgarize it, to substitute liberalism in its place. It means smuggling in a reactionary defense of the bourgeoisie against the socialist proletariat by means of quasi-scientific reference to the progressive character of the bourgeoisie as compared with medievalism."[28] (Emphasis added.)

[23] "The Chinese Revolution and the Chinese Communist Party" (n.d., 1939?), in Stuart Schram, ed., *The Political Thought of Mao Tse-tung* (New York: Praeger, 1964), p. 161; also in *Selected Works* (Peking, 1965), Vol. II.

[24] Cf. Lenin, "Two Tactics of the Social-Democrats in the Democratic Revolution," in *Collected Works*, IX, 84-86, 95, 112.

[25] "On New Democracy" (1940), in *Selected Works* (Peking: 1965), II, 360.

[26] *Jen-min Jih-pao*, December 19, 1958, cited in Schram, *op. cit.*, p. 53. This perspective was also pragmatic in origin. The "radicalization" of the Chinese Revolution toward a socialist program having taken place only under the impact of an imperialist offensive in Asia.

[27] The term "permanent revolution," which in the Stalinist and neo-Stalinist canon is the technical term for Trotskyite heresy, was first "rehabilitated" by Liu Shao-ch'i in a speech on May 5, 1958 (Schram, *op. cit.*).

[28] Lenin, *The Proletarian Revolution and the Renegade Kautsky* (Peking: 1965), pp. 97-98.

CAN AMERICAN WORKERS MAKE A SOCIALIST REVOLUTION?

● *george novack*

The capitalist rulers of the United States have choirs of troubadours, voluntary and hired, to chant their praises nowadays. Intellectuals of all categories exalt their own functions in the fields of culture and communications. Countless books, movies, and TV series depict the joys and cares of suburban middle-class families. The press features the doings of youth, from the antics of hippies and yippies to the demonstrations of the campus rebels.

For a long time the Afro-American was, in the phrase of novelist Ralph Ellison, "the invisible man." But first the civil-rights movement and now the deeply felt black nationalist demands, exploding in ghetto uprisings, have pushed the black masses into view. Their grievances may be unsatisfied and their tactics deplored, but their forceful presence can no longer be ignored.

The least attention is being paid to the largest part of the American people. The white workers have almost fallen from public sight. Their social prestige is at the lowest point in this century. The wageworker has the fewest friends, admirers, and defenders among the intellectuals and in politically articulate circles. Who cares if the wealth-producers of the world's richest country have no Homer or even Walt Whitman to celebrate them?

The current devaluation of the social significance of the workers as a class, and the white workers in particular, stands in contrast with the latter half of the nineteen-thirties, when the mass production workers were invading the open-shop strongholds of big business and installing powerful unions in them. At that time they were widely believed to possess the potential energy, not only to change relations within industry, which they did, but to overthrow American capitalism. This esteem for labor's progressive capacities persisted in radical and even liberal quarters until after the postwar strike wave of 1945-46. (See *The New Men of Power*, written around that time by C. Wright Mills.)

In the two decades since, as a result of the prolonged prosperity, political reaction, union bureaucratism, and labor conservatism, the wageworking class has dropped to the bottom of the rating scale. Today there is "none so poor as to do them reverence." How pointless it seems to ask: Do the American workers have any revolutionary potential? Can they break loose from established institutions, develop an anticapitalist consciousness, engage in a struggle for power, and go on to build a socialist society?

Run through the hierarchy of American society and every level of it will come up with negative answers to these questions. The corporate chiefs, their political agents, and the comfortable middle classes would agree that, except for a few disgruntled "subversives," the workers in the United States are content with their lot and station, have few deep grudges against the existing system, and will never look forward to changing it. Most professors and intellectuals look askance at the notion that ordinary workers have what it takes to organize themselves and lead a mass movement that can challenge and displace the monopolist and militarist masters of their fate.

Skepticism about such qualifications among the workers extends beyond the well-to-do. The union bureaucrats, who do not permit the ranks to lead their own unions, hardly expect them to run the whole of American society. Afro-Americans view privileged and prejudiced white workers as indifferent and hostile to black emancipation, and they are to a certain extent correct.

In their quest for forces that can bring about revolutionary change in the contemporary world, some young radicals look toward the "poor," the unemployed, the lumpenproletariat, student rebels, and the peoples of the Third World. They turn in every direction but one: the millions of industrial workers in their own land. Although the Socialist and Communist parties preserve some ritual rhetoric, inherited from their Marxist pretensions, that links the prospects of socialism with the working class, in practical politics they display a lack of faith in its independent power by supporting capitalist parties and liberal politicians and refusing to propagandize for a labor party based on the unions.

This attitude has been formulated in philosophical terms by Prof. Herbert Marcuse in his popular book, *One-Dimensional Man*. In a symposium at the University of Notre Dame in April 1966, he argued that Marxism has broken down in its central contention that the working class is the predestined gravedigger of capitalism. "In the advanced industrial countries where the transition to socialism was to take place, and precisely in those countries, the laboring classes are in no sense a revolutionary potential," he asserted. More recently, in an interview published in the October 28, 1968, *New York Times,* Marcuse flatly ruled out any possibility of revolution in the United States. Revolution is inconceivable without the working class and that class is integrated in the affluent society and "shares in large measure the needs and aspirations of the dominant classes," he stated.

In a reassessment of Marx's theory of the revolutionary role of the industrial proletariat at the 1967 Socialist Scholars Conference in New York, *Monthly Review* editor Paul Sweezy propounded the proposition that, in sharp contrast with the peasant masses in the Third World, the advances of modern technology and its prodigious productivity in a developed democratic capitalist framework tend to shape a proletariat which is less and less revolutionary.

These write-offs of the workers by the Left have been matched by liberals who proceed on non-Marxist premises. Thus, after announcing that Marx erred in expecting the working class to be the prime agency of revolutionary change, David Bazelon in *Power in America: The Problem of the New Class* assigns that function to the managers and technocratic intellectuals who he thinks are about to supplant the capitalists as the future ruling class.

To round out this record of disparagement, most American workers would hardly give positive answers to a pollster who asked whether they had the need, right, or prospect of taking control of the economic and political system from the present possessors of power and property.

Hardly anyone but revolutionary Marxists nowadays retain faith in the anticapitalist strivings and sentiments of the working people or believe that they can in time participate in a mighty movement oriented toward socialist objectives. For adhering to these convictions and being guided by them, we are looked upon as ideological freaks and political fossils, ridiculous relics of a bygone era, dogmatists who cling to outworn views and cannot understand what is going on in front of our own eyes.

Indeed, it may seem quixotic to put up countervailing arguments against such an overwhelming preponderance of public opinion and dulled class consciousness among the workers themselves. Why not go along with the crowd?

Unfashionable as it may be, Marxists have substantial reasons for their adamant resistance on this point. Their convictions are not an affirmation of religious-like faith. They are derived from a scientific conception of the course and motor forces of world history, a reasoned analysis of the decisive trends of our time, and an understanding of the mainsprings and the necessities of capitalist development. Marxism has clarified many perplexing problems in philosophy, sociology, history, economics, and politics. Its supreme achievement is the explanation it offers of the key role of the working class in history.

This is far too serious an issue to be treated in an offhand way. Nothing less is at stake than the destiny of American civilization and with it the future of mankind.

So grave a question cannot be definitively disposed of by reference to the present mood, mentality, and lack of political organization of the workers themselves. Nor can it be permanently suppressed. It keeps reasserting itself at each new turn of events. No sooner has the revolutionism of the working class been dismissed for the hundredth time than it returns from exile to haunt its banishers.

The year 1967, for example, marked the fiftieth anniversary of the October revolution, when the workers did conquer power for the first time in history, opening a breach in the structure of world capitalism which has been widened and deepened by a series of subsequent socialist revolutions. Will this process never be extended to the United States when it has already come within ninety miles of its shores?

The general strike of ten million French workers in May-June 1968 disclosed an unsuspected readiness for anticapitalist action in the advanced industrial West. Cannot the American workers become imbued at some point with a similar militancy?

There is another side to this problem. Those who deny any latent radicalism in the industrial workers seldom appreciate what consequences logically flow from this negative position in the areas of most concern to them.

If the working masses cannot be counted on to dislodge the capitalists, who else within the country can do that job? It would be exceedingly difficult to point out another social force or find a combination of components that could effectively act as a surrogate for the industrial workers. The struggle against capitalist domination then looms as a lost cause and socialist America becomes a Utopia.

Recognition of this difficulty gives rise to pessimistic forecasts of America's future. Some see the iron heel of fascism already poised above the nation; others emphasize the powerlessness of the Left. People who seriously envisage such a perspective must logically reconcile themselves to the eventual unloosing of a nuclear holocaust by the American imperialists at bay.

A typical instance of such prostration was provided by the historian Gabriel Kolko of the University of Pennsylvania in an article on "The Decline of American Radicalism in the Twentieth Century," published in the September-October 1966 issue of the now defunct *Studies on the Left*. After pronouncing Marxism obsolescent, he concluded: "Given the consensual basis of American politics and society in the 20th century, and the will of the beneficiaries of consensus to apply sufficient force and power at home and abroad when resistance to consensus and its hegemony arises, the new left must confront the prospect of failure as an option for radical, democratic politics in America. Rational hopes for the 20th century now rest outside America and in spite of it. . . ."

In view of the omnipotence of the ruling class and the weakness of its internal opposition, all that radicals can do is "to define a new intellectual creed at home which permits honest men to save their consciences and integrity even when they cannot save or transform politics." As though to verify these arguments, *Studies on the Left* shut up shop shortly thereafter, and its editors have scattered in search of a new critique of "post-industrial society" to save (or should we say "salve") their scholarly consciences.

Before succumbing to such sentiments of hopelessness, it would seem advisable at least to reexamine the problem in a more rounded way. It might then be seen that the Marxist analysis and inferences on the prospects of the American working class are not so unfounded as the critics make out.

the present situation of american labor

The potential of any class is derived from the place it occupies in the dynamics of economic development. Is it advancing or receding, rising or declining in the system of production? From all statistical indices it is plain that the small family farmer falls into the second category. Is the industrial worker shriveling as well?

All over the world—regardless of the social form of production—industrialization and urbanization is causing the proletariat to grow in size and gain in economic, social, and political importance. The wage-working class, defined as those who sell their own labor power to the owners of capital, is no exception to that rule in the most advanced of all the industrial countries. Between 1880 and 1957 the ratio of wage earners of all sorts in the gainfully employed population of the United States rose steadily from 62 percent to 84 percent, with a corresponding decline for entrepreneurs of all kinds (from 37 percent to 14 percent).

The number of jobs in American industry has more than doubled since 1940, rising from 33 to well over 70 million. This army of wage earners operates the most complex and up-to-date productive facilities and produces the most abundant and diversified output of goods. The product of their energies and skills provides the riches of the owners of industry and supports their gigantic armed forces.

Thanks to the prodigious capacities of the productive apparatus, this working class has the highest wage rates and living standards, even though it receives a diminishing share of the annual wealth it creates. Eighteen millions or so have organized strong unions and engaged in many of the biggest and bitterest strikes in labor's history.

At the same time most members of this class are extremely retarded in political and social outlook, the least aware of their class status and responsibilities, racist-minded, privileged, and conservatized. They remain the only working class of the highly industrialized countries which has not cut loose from subservience to the capitalist parties and established a mass political organization of their own, whether of a Laborite, Socialist, or Communist type. Although they may be steady union-dues payers, they are by and large uneducated in Marxist ideas and the socialist program.

Many of today's young radicals are far more impressed by the undeniable shortcomings of the labor movement than by any of its positive accomplishments. Sometimes they appear to deny it any progressive features. They slight the significance of the sheer existence of powerful union organizations which act as a shield against lowering wages and working conditions and check the aggressions of capitalist reaction. They leave out of consideration the working conditions of a century ago, before unionization, the fourteen- to sixteen-hour day, the exploitation of child labor, the early mortality rate for all workers; and they neglect to study what happens when unions are exceptionally weak and fragmented—or destroyed—in the epoch of imperialism, for instance in Mussolini's Italy or Hitler's Germany.

According to the anti-Marxist ideologues, whatever else happens, the workers will never become a force ready, willing, and able to transform the United States. Their ranks are so smugly and snugly integrated into the mass "consumer society" that they can have no compelling reasons to turn against it. It is out of the question for them to attain the political or ideological level of their European counterparts and certainly not the revolutionary temper of the Cuban workers.

Such a long-term prognosis rests upon two suppositions. One, that American capitalism has been immunized against severe crises and will maintain its domestic stability indefinitely. Two, that the present characteristics, attitudes, and relations of the working force are essentially unalterable by any foreseeable change in circumstances. Much hinges then on the prospects of U.S. monopoly capitalism in the last third of the twentieth century. What are these likely to be?

the outlook for american capitalism

Despite the elimination of private property elsewhere, the capitalist rulers of America today have an arrogant faith in the longevity of their system. They firmly believe that the empire of the almighty dollar is assured of perpetual dominion at home and abroad.

From an offhand glance at developments since the Civil War, the case for their continued supremacy would appear unassailable. Over the past century the magnates of capital have succeeded in concentrating economic, political, military, and cultural power in their hands. They have emerged from two world wars stronger and richer than before. They hold the commanding heights within the country and over two-thirds of the globe.

While peoples on other continents have become more and more cognizant of the revolutionary nature of our epoch, Americans consider themselves completely detached from it because of the contradictory effects the international upheavals since 1917 have had on the fortunes of American capitalism.

While the system that it is committed to defend to the death has been losing ground step by step to the socialist forces on a world scale, U.S. capitalism has been gaining enormously at the expense of its rivals. Today it towers above them all.

This country has been the prime capitalist beneficiary of the cataclysmic changes that have marked the first period of the transition from capitalism to socialism. The main beneficiary of the capitalist past, it has flourished more than ever during the first phase of capitalism's decline. As it holds the fort for the rest of the capitalist camp, the United States has drawn into itself most of the residual vitality of the disintegrating capitalist order.

This temporarily favorable aspect of the world situation for America's ruling class accounts for the unexampled strength of monopolist domination, the stability of its social alignments, the complacency of its political outlook. The eminence that so pleases the rich and the very rich and deludes the rest of the American people is viewed as a fitting culmination and reward of the entire career of American civilization.

The basic reasons for the political backwardness which appears so insuperable and everlasting are not to be found in any irremovable psychology of the American people and its working class but rather in the exceptionally auspicious circumstances of the development of American bourgeois society. It was the offspring of a lusty young capitalism which swept everything before it from the time the New World was opened up for settlement and exploitation half a millennium ago.

The population of the United States has been the most favored, pampered, and even spoiled child in the family of capitalist nations. Capitalism has attained the most luxuriant growth here in almost every respect. This consummate development of capitalism, which is the outstanding peculiarity of our history, has set its stamp upon the thinking, values, and outlook of almost every American. That is why the worship of the golden calf, the frantic chase after the fast and not so elusive buck, and confidence in the eternity of this system are so deep-rooted and widespread. Any suggestion that world capitalism in general, and its American segment in particular, has reached its zenith seems incredible to the ordinary citizen who expects that the system as he knows it will, like old man river, just keep rolling along.

These devout believers in the perpetuity of U.S. capitalism fail to take into consideration the impact of five mighty tendencies upon its further development.

First is the fact that America's wealth and preponderance have been gained, and are being sustained, at the expense of the poverty and weakness of less fortunate countries in other parts of the world. Their blood and flesh fatten the vulture of imperalism. The gap between rich and poor keeps widening on a global scale. American citizens make up one-fifteenth of the world's population and consume one-half of its total output.

Second, this unequal and oppressive relationship has its consequences. Those underdeveloped—or, more accurately, overexploited—countries which have been shut off from almost all the benefits of capitalist expansion, while suffering from imperialist depredation and domination, are increasingly resorting to anticapitalist actions to achieve their liberation. They are determined to get access to a rightful share of the conquests of modern civilization. This is the motivation and meaning of the irrepressible revolutionary movements in Asia, the Near East, Africa, and Latin America.

Third, the predominant trend of history since 1917 has not been the building up but the breaking down of world capitalism. This process of socialist expansion has already established workers' states all the way from the Adriatic in Europe to the Pacific Ocean; in Cuba it has come within hailing distance of the United States. This international anticapitalist struggle, which is the ascending social and political trend of the twentieth century, celebrated the first half-century of its conquests in October 1967. The next half-century does not promise fewer advances toward socialism than the first.

Fourth, the spread of world revolution has already administered stiff jolts to American imperalism and continually confronts its strategists with grave problems on the foreign field. Their disastrous setback in Vietnam is only a down payment on the enormous costs they must incur in undertaking the overambitious design of policing the world for the preservation of the profiteering way of life.

Finally, the cumulative effects of all the problems growing out of the convulsions of a chronically sick capitalism are sooner or later bound to have sizable and serious repercussions within the United States itself. They will tend to undermine its stability, upset its conservatism, and give rise to new forms of mass radicalism. These have already announced themselves in the strivings of black America for national self-determination, the disaffection among the youth, and the antiwar movement that changed the face of American politics in 1968.

It should be noted that these expressions of discontent emerged amidst the longest boom of the twentieth century and virtually full employment. A slump in economic activity would intensify the growing dissidence in the unions and add a sizable amount of labor unrest to the array of opposition to the monopolist regime.

Is it reasonable to expect that the United States alone will remain indefinitely separated from the world historical movement toward socialism when it is already up to its ears in every other international development? It is more likely that its reckless and far-ranging activities in attempting to safeguard its system from decline and destruction, combined with the fluctuations in its economy, will bring about an eventual radicalization of its own working class.

Japanese seismologists monitor micro-earthquakes every day to detect signs of impending tremors that portend major upheavals. So the recurrent strikes at the lowest ebb of the class struggle in the United States serve as reminders that its workers cannot be completely counted out as a factor in the calculations of American radicalism.

possible precipitants of labor radicalism

The skeptics who repose unlimited confidence in the longevity of capitalism rule out the possibility that the workers will be any more insurgent in the next twenty years than the last. What will incite them to change from being a prop to a peril to capitalism, they ask. Won't they become more and more like the housebroken "cheerful idiots" depicted by C. Wright Mills?

Surprisingly, it may turn out that the past two decades of inertia were not a totally dead loss. They may have enabled the working class to rejuvenate its ranks and accumulate energies which await a suitable occasion for discharge. Thus the French workers, who appeared to be disarmed under de Gaulle, seized the tenth anniversary of his assumption of authoritarian power to launch the greatest of all general strikes and make an aborted bid for power.

The United States has hardly been a model of social peace since Johnson started bombing North Vietnam in 1965—and the rising tide of radicalism is far from its crest. The workers will not join it solely as a result of verbal exhortations. But they can get moving again in reaction to some whiplash of the capitalist regime. Here the subsequent course of international economic development will be the decisive factor.

 Throughout the postwar expansion the exceptionally high productivity of the American economy has enabled its capitalists to dominate the world market despite the higher wage scale of our industrial workers. Now the unbeatable international advantages enjoyed by U.S. corporations for two decades are fast diminishing as other industrialized countries have reequipped, rationalized, and modernized their productive systems. Although West European and Japanese industries continue to trail behind the American giants in the computer and aircraft fields, they are today fully capable of challenging them in auto, steel, chemicals, shipbuilding, and many lines of consumer goods.

Under intensified foreign competition, U.S. corporations will be increasingly pressed to shave their costs, beginning with the cost of labor. The average wage of the American worker has been two and a half times that of the West European and five times greater than the Japanese. Big business will have to try to reduce this immense wage differential through direct or indirect moves against the earnings and living standards of the industrial work force. As the unions engage in defensive actions against such attacks, sharp tension can quickly replace the prevailing toleration between the bosses and the workers.

The resurgence of labor radicalism may come from the flagging of the long-term postwar capitalist expansion and an extended downturn in the industrial cycle—or it may be precipitated by intensified inflation. It could be provoked by anger against antilabor legislation or by resistance to another military venture and debacle of U.S. imperialism. It could be hastened by the impact of a black insurrection, student clashes with the authorities, as in France, or by the penetration of these forces into the unions through black caucuses and radicalized young workers. The possibilities are so diverse that it is impossible to foretell where or how the break in the dike will come.

the irregular development of american radicalism from 1928 to 1968

The widespread underrating of the working class comes from reliance on short-range criteria. Marxism has other standards of judgment. Its general strategy in the struggle for socialism is based upon a long-term, many-sided and dialectical approach to the development of the proletariat.

It is important to note that from 1928 to 1968 the struggles of the three main anticapitalist elements have unfolded in a disparate manner and at an uneven tempo. The industrial workers, the black masses, and the students have manifested fluctuating degrees of radicalism over those forty years which have brought them into differing relations with one another as well as with the ruling class.

The American workers of the nineteen-twenties were far more passive, helpless, and poorly organized than today. Many experts at that time could not figure out how these weaknesses might be overcome, and it was not easy to do so. The touchstone of labor's impotence in their eyes was its inability to introduce unionism into basic industry where most low-paid workers were located.

They marshaled imposing reasons why the workers were unlikely to emerge from disorganization. The workers were divided against themselves: native against foreign-born, white against black, craft workers against mass production workers. The anti-union forces were rich, crafty, and powerful. The magnates of capital had the workers at their mercy. They controlled the courts, legislatures, Congress, and the press. They used the blacklist, their private police, labor spies, and reserves of strikebreakers to crush and victimize organizers in the shops.

Moreover, the AFL officialdom was uninterested in bringing unionism to the unorganized. How, then, were the mass production workers to organize themselves? They were considered too unintelligent and unaware of their own interest and bereft of the necessary resources, national connections, and experience.

The most telling argument advanced by the empiricists was the failure of every effort that militants and radicals had made for forty years to organize basic industry. The campaigns undertaken by Eugene Debs in the early eighteen-nineties; by the De Leonists, Wobblies, and left Socialists before the first world war; and, finally, by the Communists in the nineteen-twenties had all come to nothing.

The gloomy prognosis drawn from these empirical facts had one flaw: it assumed that previous conditions would prevail with undiminished effect from one decade to the next. However, the 1929 crash intervened and upset many things. Once the workers recovered from the paralyzing onset of the depression, and industry picked up in 1933, their morale and fighting spirit revived with it. Before the end of the decade, they broke down the open shop and unionized basic industry.

Such swings tell a great deal about the mutability in the disposition of social forces. Consider the contrasting positions of the white workers and the black people in the nineteen-thirties and the nineteen-sixties. This is as instructive as the reversals that took place in the state of the working class from the nineteen-twenties to the nineteen-thirties and from the thirties to the sixties.

Labor was on the offensive against corporate capital in the nineteen-thirties, with the white workers in the lead. Once the black workers became convinced that they were really welcome in the new industrial unions, they joined wholeheartedly with the white workers in the organizing struggles of the CIO. In fact, pro-union sentiment was stronger in the black community as a whole than in the white community in the late thirties and early forties.

Black militancy and black radicalism were expressed mainly through general labor struggles in the thirties, rather than as a specifically black movement. There were scattered pockets of black nationalist organization, and black nationalist sentiment was undoubtedly more widespread than most whites realized, but the strength and potential of Afro-Americans as an autonomous force had not yet been expressed in any significant organizational form. It was not until 1941, with the emergence of the short-lived March on Washington movement, that there appeared the first signs of a nationwide nationalist awakening, or reawakening, since the heyday of Garveyism in the nineteen-twenties. Its development was slow and erratic during the forties and early fifties, but by the sixties it had become one of the central features of the present epoch.

So the relative roles of the white workers and the black people became reversed. While the white workers were by and large quiescent, millions of black Americans were now pounding against the status quo. The initiative in struggle, held by the working class in the nineteen-thirties, had now passed into the hands of blacks as a people.

Suppose that learned sociologists, projecting from the state of affairs in the thirties, had concluded that the black people never would or could rise up on their own and take the lead in social protest. Would such an extrapolation be better grounded than the current presumption that apathetic white workers, now in the rearguard, must be disqualified as a fighting force for the rest of the century, or even the coming decade?

What about students? Throughout the nineteen-thirties they played a small part in the surge of radicalism dominated by labor. During the great strike wave from 1945 to 1947 they were not heard from. At that point could they not have been written off for all time as a ferment for revolution? Indeed, they remained "the silent generation" through the nineteen-fifties and did not pass over to radicalism until they were animated by the civil-rights movement, the Cuban Revolution, and the anti-H bomb demonstrations in the early sixties.

Such pronounced irregularities in the radical activities of diverse sectors of society speak against making hasty categorical judgments about their respective capacities for combat from their postures over a limited time. The prophets of gloom may easily mistake the recharging of the energies of the American working class for their exhaustion.

proposed alternatives to the working class

Once the workers have been canceled out as the chief bearer of social progress, the question is insistently posed, Who will take their place? Obviously, the peasantry, which has been the most massive revolutionary battering ram in the colonial countries, cannot serve as a substitute in the United States.

One answer is that the twenty-two million Afro-Americans will fill the vacancy because they occupy a comparable status as an oppressed colonial people inside the imperialist monster. At the present stage the battlers for black liberation unquestionably stand in the front line against the capitalist power structure. They have not waited for anyone else to launch a vigorous attack upon the caste system that victimizes them in so many ways. And they have begun to form their own leadership and create their own organizations in pursuing that struggle.

However, these facts do not exhaust the problem of their place in the overall development of the American revolution. Black Americans have need of powerful allies at home as well as abroad in order to overcome "the man" and win liberation from the oppression of Uncle "Sham." They can count on sympathetic support from radical students and intellectuals. But that is hardly enough. Remote and improbable as it seems in the prevailing situation, the principal source of internal reinforcement for their liberation movement can come only from the white end of the labor force.

The long-term strategical formula for throwing off the rule of the rich is an anticapitalist alliance in action between insurgent Afro-Americans and militant white industrial workers. No other coalition of forces can carry through that task. Like the workers and peasants in colonial lands, the two will triumph together or not at all.

Some non-Marxists rebut this strategical orientation by counterposing the aggressiveness of black America to the docility of the white workers. They thereby lose sight of significant similarities in the socio-economic positions of the two parts of the proletariat which can acquire great importance at a later time.

The black liberation movement itself has a dual character. It combines the democratic struggle for self-determination of a national minority with a drive for proletarian demands and objectives. This is because the black masses are not peasants in the countryside who aspire to change agrarian relations. They are largely wageworkers penned in city slums who are up in arms against intolerable conditions of life and labor.

In 1957-58, for example, almost 90 percent of the half-million blacks in Detroit were blue-collar workers. Most were in the auto, steel, and chemical plants and belonged to the industrial unions. Many participated in the 1967 uprising. According to John C. Leggett's study, *Class, Race and Labor* (1968), they are not only highly race conscious but "more class conscious than whites." That is, they are more outraged by the privations imposed on them by "the big-money class" and readier to resist it. The same holds true for Chicago and other centers of industry, as the black caucuses springing up in unions from the East to the West Coast indicate.

The composite character of the superexploited wage slaves in the cities makes their struggles doubly explosive. The democratic demands of the black people for an end to discriminatory treatment and racism are fused with their proletarian demands for jobs, rank-and-file control of the unions, more welfare, and other essentials. Although many nationalist black militants do not yet see the matter in this light, they act as the anticapitalist vanguard of the entire American working class.

However much the black masses are now estranged from the white workers, both are objectively yoked together through their joint subordination to the profiteers. They constitute two distinct segments of a single labor force. They are, to be sure, diametrically different in certain respects, since black and white are unequally subjected to the pressures of capitalist exploitation. Nevertheless, their common economic positions vis-a-vis the ruling economic and political power tend to draw them closer together, despite the width of their divergences.

* * *

Apart from the national minorities or along with them, anarchistically inclined thinkers imagine that such elements as the chronically unemployed, the lumpenproletariat, the hippies or other temporary dropouts from bourgeois society can be alternative gravediggers of capitalism. But they cannot explain how these outcast groupings can organize themselves or others for sustained economic or political activity of any kind, whatever spasmodic and despairing outbursts they may indulge in.

C. Wright Mills looked to the dissidents among the "intellectual apparatus" as "a possible immediate, radical agency of change." The wageworkers, he theorized, acted as a decisive political force only in the early stages of industrialization. Now these workers had become coopted into the bureaucratized "mass consumption" United States and the "cultural workers" would have to lead the struggle against "the power elite."

The general experience of the past decade has not confirmed this conclusion of the empirical sociologist, or rather, it has certified its limitations. Dissident intellectuals can play significant roles in starting and stimulating oppositional currents against authoritarian regimes and unpopular policies, as Czechoslovakia in the East and the anti-Vietnam-war teach-ins in the West have indicated. But however great their political impact, nowhere have their initiatives or activities in and of themselves overturned an established social or political regime and put a new one in its place.

Students have likewise demonstrated the world over that they can play a vanguard role in opposing official and unofficial reaction and detonating struggles of broader scope by setting an example of resistance for other forces to imitate. But in the dynamics of the revolutionary process as a whole, their intervention is auxiliary to the decisive power of the working masses. Once the ten million French strikers returned to work in June 1968, the student rebels, who had touched off the workers' offensive, could not sustain their confrontation with the de Gaulle government.

The perspectives of a triumphant fight to the finish against capitalist domination and imperalism are inseparably connected with the entry of the workers onto the arena. Who else can organize and mobilize a counterpower strong enough to challenge and crush the powers-that-be? Who else is in a position to take control of the means of production, socialize them, and plan their operation? Who else can become the directors of the new social order? To understand this and act upon it distinguishes the vanguard students who become Bolsheviks from all others.

* * *

There is a further consideration. The non-Marxist rebels want greater democracy. Yet, paradoxically, the reputation of the workers as the central agency of social reconstruction leads to extremely undemocratic options.

The white and black workers and their families compose the vast majority of the American people. Suppose some other agency is delegated or destined to lead the way to the abolition of capitalism. What relation is the savior-force to have to the working masses during this process? If the workers are not self-active, it could at best be paternalistic. In that event, the revolutionary movement would fall under the auspices of a benevolent elite or a maleficent bureaucracy.

How does such a mode of development square with the insistence of these young rebels that they are more devoted to democratic methods than the Marxists and opposed to all forms of elitism or bureaucratism? How are they, or anyone else, going to promote a revolution along democratic lines without the conscious consent and active participation of the wageworking majority? And what happens if that majority remains antipathetic and resistant to the ongoing revolution—as they should, according to certain preconceptions? If the workers cannot be revolutionized under any conceivable circumstances, then the prospects for expanding American democracy are no brighter than those for achieving socialism.

depreciating the working class

It is ironical that young rebels who reject conformism to big business mimic its low opinion of the working class. One reason for this attitude is a limited historical vision. Contemporary Americans are divided, according to University of Michigan sociologists, into the "depression" and the "prosperity" generations.

The new radicals belong to the latter group. Cradled in the prosperity and domestic stability of the postwar Western world, they are acquainted only with a nonmobilized union movement. They have never witnessed combative legions of labor at first hand nor seen what they can accomplish. They regard the union structure as an unbreakable solid block and make no distinction between the membership and the officialdom that sits upon it. Consequently, they feel as alienated from the ranks of labor as the ranks do from them.

Many unwittingly share the disdain of middle-class intellectuals for less formally educated people. They visualize the mass of workers as contented cattle who cannot look beyond their bellies or ever be inspired by a call to struggle for broad social causes and political aims.

Although they may have taken courses in economics or sociology, they fail to perceive how the psychology of the better-paid workers has been debased by middle-class values. The worst aspect is not, as some think, an artificially stimulated craving for meretricious goods and the latest gadgets.

Far more vicious and pernicious are the feelings of inferiority induced in the popular masses through systematic indoctrination in the standards of the master class which underrate their real worth to society. The self-reliance of the workers is so weakened that they do not realize they can say "no" to capitalist domination or escape from the status quo.

By echoing the pervasive disparagement of the workers, supercilious students involuntarily help to reinforce such class mistrust. The revolt of the Afro-Americans shows that the techniques of submissiveness practiced by bourgeois miseducators have limited effectiveness. The new radicals accept the fact that the black masses, so long depicted as menials, can reject their degradation, heighten their racial pride, resist their oppressors. Yet it has still to dawn on these new radicals that, at some later date, white workers too can pass through similar processes of remoralization. If black can become beautiful, so can labor in its most energetic and creative periods.

Not a few young radicals come from working-class families. Although they have come to comprehend how and why Afro-Americans have been taught to hold themselves in contempt and bend the knee to the master race and class, they fail to recognize that they can fall victim to similar pressures. Cut off from their own roots, they have been tricked into accepting the disdain for the capacities of working people inculcated by the bourgeois system.

They acquire so one-sided a view of the wageworkers by conceiving of them, not as the chief agents of production, but primarily as consumers motivated by suburbanite standards. However, the functions of the workers as purchasers of commodities are not equal in social importance to their role as the creators of wealth in the productive process. Nor do these different sides of their activities have the same weight in shaping their conduct. The reactions of the workers are primarily and ultimately determined by what happens to them in the labor market and at the point of production. That is where they encounter speedups, short time, layoffs, discrimination, insecurity, wage reductions, and other evils of exploitation. That is why any drastic fluctuation in their economic welfare can quickly alter their tolerance of the existing state of affairs.

* * *

The more sociologically inclined among the new radicals have elaborated some theoretical justifications for their disqualification of the industrial workers. They base their arguments, not on the narcotizing effects of capitalist consumption and culture, but upon changes in the productive process. They point out that white-collar workers are growing faster than blue-collar workers and conclude that this relative reduction has qualitatively diminished the economic, social, and political power of the latter. Is this the case?

It is true that the labor force is undergoing marked changes in all industrial countries. Two such shifts have special significance. Because of its high capital intensity, the number of workers engaged in modern industry tends to decrease relative to the personnel employed in transport and communications, the educational system, research, government jobs, and the service trades. Further, as a result of mechanization, the percentage of technical and highly skilled workers tends to grow at the expense of the unskilled.

The implications of these structural changes in the work force do not signify that the working class as such has less importance since, in fact, the sellers of labor power grow relative to the farm population, independent small proprietors, and other sectors of society.

The declining role of such social strata in production and distribution enhances the weight of others. Thus the decrease of the small farmer with the growth of large-scale mechanized enterprises in agriculture is accompanied by increases in the numbers of agricultural workers; the obsolescence of the small retailer with the expansion of chain stores creates scores of thousands of commercial employees; mechanization and automation industrialize many departments of economic activity previously unaffected by wage labor. These interrelated developments extend the scope of wage-labor relations on a scale unknown in the nineteenth century.

The main meaning of these changes is that education and skill become ever more vital in the competition for jobs and the scramble for social survival and economic advancement. On the one hand, the low-paid, unskilled segments of the laboring population become more miserable, insecure, ground down. On the other hand, the growing numbers of white-collar, professional, and technical personnel become more subjected to capitalist exploitation and alienation, more and more proletarianized, more responsive to unionization and its methods of action, more and more detached from loyalty to their corporate employers. These trends pile up combustible materials which can flare into massive anticapitalist movements.

The relative reduction in the directly producing force does not nullify the key role of the proletarians within industry. In the relations of production, quality is more decisive than quantity. Ten thousand transport workers are far more crucial in social struggle than ten thousand office workers. When 35,000 transport workers shut down the New York City subways and buses several years ago, everything ground to a halt in the hub of U.S. capitalism.

The strategic position that the mass production, transport, and communications workers occupy in the operations of capitalism invests their actions with a power exceeding their actual numbers. As direct producers, they alone can start or stop the most vital sectors of the economy. The capitalist régime is well aware of the latent power of the strike weapon wielded by blue-collar workers and constantly seeks to hamper its use. In practice, the rulers have little doubt about its revolutionary potential.

Thus one million industrial workers command incomparably more revolutionary power than seven million college students. Although the three million teachers constitute the largest single occupational group in the country, their collective economic power is less than that of the half-million blue-collar workers in the steel mills.

* * *

Some envisage the imminent ejection of almost all workers from industry through the swift spread and consummation of automation. Under capitalism, mechanization and cybernation do threaten the jobs of skilled and unskilled alike, in one industry after another. The dislocations and job instability caused by these processes have to be guarded against by both the economic action and political organization of the working class.

Capitalist production cannot do without an ample laboring force, no matter how many are unemployed, because profit-making and the accumulation of capital depend upon the consumption of large quantities of labor power which creates value in the form of commodities. Although this or that segment or individual may be squeezed out of jobs temporarily or permanently, the industrial work force as such is not expendable, no matter how fast or how far automation proceeds under capitalist auspices.

Indeed, the inherent limitations upon its introduction and extension under capitalism, the inability of the profiteers fully to utilize the immense potential of the new science and technology for reducing the working day and rationalizing production, provide further reasons for breaking their hold upon industry. Socialism envisages the elimination from industry of the capitalist proprietors and coupon-clippers, rather than the workers.

In any event, the industrial workers are far from obsolescent and cannot be conjured away by abstract extrapolations. They will be on hand from now until the socialist revolution—and quite a while thereafter, because they provide the minds and the muscles for the production of all material wealth.

marxism and the "labor metaphysic"

Two authoritative periodicals of the plutocracy, the *London Times Literary Supplement* and the *New York Times,* paid high tributes to the genius of Karl Marx on the centennial of the publication of *Capital* in 1967. It is "the most influential single work of economics ever written," said the *New York Times* editors. In the same breath they hastened to expose what in their eyes were the basic errors of Marx's teachings. Prominent among them, they insisted, was his false prediction about "the role of the working class as the gravedigger of capitalism."

"New Left" theorists play on this same theme from a different standpoint. Orthodox Marxists glorify the working class, they claim. Instead of facing up to the realities of contemporary capitalism and appraising its assimilation of the industrial workers in a dispassionate scientific manner, the disciples of Marx fall prey to what C. Wright Mills has called "the labor metaphysic." To be effective reformers of society, they ought to give up doctrinaire fascination with the leading role of the working class and look elsewhere for more suitable candidates.

They dismiss the fact that, despite the vicissitudes of the class struggle, every so often since 1917 the revolt of the workers and their allies has been victorious. Over the long run, the sum total of their successes has outweighed the reverses; the overall movement of the world working class keeps advancing toward its social goals.

The surest index to the validity of Marxism is the balance sheet of world history in this age of permanent revolution. International experience demonstrates that Marx's ideas have been vindicated over the past half-century, though only in a partial way. Like shipwrecked sailors hanging onto an overturned lifeboat in a stormy sea, all sorts of anti-Marxists cling to the fact that not all of Marx's prognoses have yet been verified, above all, in the United States. The impregnability of American capitalism constitutes their rock of salvation.

Yet they are not wholly secure even here. A not unimportant part of Marx's theory on the evolution of capitalism has already been confirmed in the United States. His forecast of the inherent tendencies of a matured capitalism to pass from competition to monopoly through the concentration and centralization of capital is epitomized by contemporary America.

What remains to be verified are the logical *political and ideological* consequences of these economic trends, namely, the transition of the workers from union to class consciousness, from bourgeois and petty bourgeois to socialist ideology, from subservience to capitalist parties to independent and militant political organization and action. The fact that these developments have been considerably retarded does not bar them from ever being realized. This very delay sets the tasks that will have to be tackled and solved in the next stage of radicalism.

The dispute between the "New Lefts" and Marxists over the role of the working class is less concerned with divergent appraisals of the facts in the present situation than with their methods of reasoning. The two proceed along different lines in analyzing the dynamics of contemporary social development. The anti-Marxists of the New Left are provincial-minded empiricists. They reject the ideas and perspectives of Marxism, not so much because these have been rendered invalid by irrefutable argument or overwhelming evidence, but because these are not yet accomplished facts.

Although they fancy themselves ahead of their contemporaries, they remain captive to the ideological and political backwardness of American life. They are swayed by the prevailing prejudices against dialectical materialism which can go unchallenged because of the absence of solid Marxist traditions and a strong socialist movement in the United States. They are hardly aware of the extent to which they have been swept along by the pragmatic habits of thought so deeply embedded in our national culture.

the hidden capacities of the oppressed

In determining whether the American working class is a dead volcano or whether explosive energies still simmer in its depths, it should be kept in mind that neither revolutionary situations nor revolutionized classes are normal occurrences. They mature at rare intervals when the slow growth of the preconditions for a showdown between contending social forces comes to a head. During the intervening lulls in mass activity, people come to believe that the social contradictions of capitalism will never generate insurrectionary moods and movements in their time.

Such a conviction became fixed in the minds of the reformists when no direct confrontation between capitalists and workers took place for fifty years from the Paris Commune of 1871 to the Russian Revolution of 1917. A like conclusion has come to the fore whenever the working class has suffered grave setbacks or passed through a protracted quiescence over the past half-century.

It has taken a new upsurge or victory of the workers to dispel that defeatism.

Over the past half-century the close association of oscillations of confidence in the capacities of the working class with alternations in the intensity of the class struggle can be charted in three major waves. The pessimism produced by the collapse of the European Social Democracy in 1914 was counteracted by the triumph of the Russian workers in 1917; the catastrophic defeats of the nineteen-thirties leading to the second world war were succeeded by the revolutionary upsurge after 1943, which culminated in the Yugoslav, Chinese, Vietnamese, and Cuban victories; and the torpor of the Western working class from 1948 on was unexpectedly upset by the French general strike of May-June 1968.

Cuba shows how the urge to power can break out in the most unscheduled ways and places. Nobody in 1958 expected that a few years later the workers of that island would become uplifted by the ideals of socialist internationalism which the organizers of the July 26th Movement themselves did not then consciously hold.

Time and again funeral ceremonies performed over the revolutionism of a particular national section of the working class, or the class in general, have turned out to be premature. Such shortsightedness has resulted from an overestimation of the "reasonableness" of capitalism on the one hand and an underestimation of the latent capacities of the toilers on the other. Sudden shocks can cause the rebelliousness of the oppressed to spring to life with a celerity that confounds the skeptics and amazes the participants themselves.

Beaten down in so many ways, workers seldom suspect what they are capable of achieving under the extraordinary stimulus of a revolutionary crisis. That genius of propaganda, Tom Paine, once testified how his plunge into the First American Revolution brought forth talents hidden in him. "I happened to come to America a few months before the breaking out of hostilities . . ." he wrote some years after the Battle of Lexington. "I had no thoughts of Independence or of arms. The world could not then have persuaded me that I should be either a soldier or an author. If I had any talents for either, they were buried in me, and might ever have continued so, had not the necessity of the times dragged and driven them into action." *(Political Writings,* vol. I, 169-170).

The "necessity of the times" forces groupings, classes, and whole peoples, as well as individuals, to perform prodigious feats. The colonial rebels displayed a tenacity of purpose, unity, and skill at warfare that astonished their foe and their contemporaries, much as the Vietnamese liberation fighters have in our own day.

In a speech he made in 1968 on the fifteenth anniversary of the attack on the Moncada army garrison, Fidel Castro emphasized the immense untapped resources, lodged in the masses, that a revolution can draw upon. "The history of this Revolution has furnished us with many examples, repeated examples, of the fact that those who were in error were those who did not believe in man, that those who made the mistake and failed were those who had no confidence in the peoples, who had no confidence in man's ability to attain and develop a revolutionary awareness.

"In the past, those of us who proclaimed the revolutionary struggle, who proclaimed the need for a revolution, were told the same thing: that we were mistaken, that we were a bunch of dreamers and that we would fail.

"This was what the politicians, the 'savants' of politics, the 'professors of politics,' the 'brains' of politics, the leaders of the traditional, bourgeois parties, had to say. They did not believe in the people; they underestimated the people. They thought the people incapable of accomplishing anything. They thought of the people as an ignorant herd to be manipulated at their will. Those of you who are here today—especially those who are here as guests—and can take a good look at this enormous congregation of people which is the living expression of our Revolution's power, should not forget that only fifteen years ago we were a small group of youngsters whom many considered dreamers, who had been told they would fail because it was impossible to make a revolution in a country of illiterate, ignorant people. And yet, what is it that we see today? What has been the result of the effort begun fifteen years ago by a small group of youngsters here at that stage of our revolutionary history? How much has been accomplished by this people? How much has this unarmed people accomplished? How much has this people that they called ignorant, that they underestimated, that they considered lacking in every virtue, accomplished?"

Such historical precedents suggest that the American workers ought to be sized up, not simply for what they are at a given moment, but for what they may be compelled to become under changed circumstances.

The historical judgment of the skeptics is at fault. With all its appurtenances of power, it is the corporate plutocracy rather than the proletariat that is a decaying class heading toward its demise. The American working class is fresh, vigorous, undefeated, undemoralized. It has displayed considerable fighting spirit, initiative, and stamina in the past—and its career as a creative social force has barely begun.

When republican and democratic movements first emerged in the bourgeois era, spokesmen for royalism, aristocracy, and clerical domination argued that common people were unfit to be entrusted with affairs of state. The same sort of elitist prejudice motivates some of those who today permanently preclude the workers from sovereignty in society.

On what grounds are they justified in setting arbitrary and insurmountable limits to the creative capacities of American labor? If the workers can produce airplanes and precision instruments for the industrialists and militarists and all kinds of commodities for the market, if they can build and maintain powerful industrial unions for themselves, why can't they go beyond all that?

What prevents them from organizing a mass political party of their own, being won over to socialist ideas, and eventually manning a revolutionary movement which can challenge the existing order and lead the way to a new society? Why can't these workers, who make such a plenitude of other things, also make history and remake society and, in the process, remake themselves? If they perform all kinds of jobs for the profiteers, why can't they do their own jobs? If they wage and win wars for the imperialist rulers, why can't they conduct a civil war in defense of their own interests, as their predecessors did in the nineteenth century?

The wageworkers are no more fated to remain servants in their own house than the American colonists were condemned to remain subjects of the British Crown, or the slaves to remain the property of the Southern planters. If a few million workers and a mass of illiterate peasants in less developed lands have succeeded in revolutionizing themselves along socialist lines, what inherent qualifications did they possess that the better-equipped American workers cannot acquire? The class struggle within the United States should give an answer to these questions before this century is over.

the problem of leadership

The capacities and conduct of a class at any given time depend in no slight degree on the character of its leadership. If the American workers have such a poor record over the recent past, the responsibility rests more with the men at their head than with their own inadequacies. The potentially most dynamic body of workers in the world has the most corrupt, servile, and obtuse official union leadership.

These leaders kowtow to the corporations and the government while lushly living on munificent salaries and expense accounts. They think more like big businessmen than representatives of a progressive social force. They cannot inspire the members of their organizations to higher levels of achievement in industry or politics or teach them anything new. They are rightly despised by young rebels on the campuses and distrusted and held in contempt by young workers in the plants.

Many mistakenly believe that this breed of leaders faithfully and fully represents the caliber of their ranks, that it is the only kind they can produce or follow. Actually, these officials are the product and the promoter of a prolonged period of stagnation. A resurgent labor movement would thrust forward a new type of leadership from below, and even prod some susceptible bureaucrats, as it proved capable of doing during the industrial union drive of the nineteen-thirties. Under a comparable radicalization, labor can both reenergize itself and renew its leadership.

And one thing may be anticipated. Once their militancy revives on a large scale, the American workers will travel at jet-plane speed. They will take off from the point where their march was halted and thrown back several decades ago. The mass production workers did not go ahead to form an independent political organization after they created the industrial unions in the nineteen-thirties. They were prevented from taking this next step by the John L. Lewis-Communist Party coalition in the CIO. They have suffered heavily ever since from this failure to disengage from the two big capitalist political machines.

When they again rise up, the fighting vanguard of the union movement will have to seek the road of independent political action to promote their objectives, as workers elsewhere have already done. However, they will not duplicate the precise course of political development taken by their predecessors. They will follow an exceptional line of march because their thrust toward independence comes so late on the scene, is directed against the most formidable and ruthless adversary, will be objectively intertwined with the revolutionary struggle for Afro-American liberation, and will have been preceded by a new, radicalized generation of college and high school students and young workers. The most advanced workers will be inclined to adopt the best methods of militant action and revolutionary organization available to them.

The sharpness of their break with the old ties can impel this vanguard to make a big leap in their ideas and activity in relatively short order. Whereas the workers who were radicalized at earlier dates in other countries were attracted to Social Democratic, Fabian, or Stalinist programs and parties, these movements have today become largely discredited and decrepit. They cannot provide a new generation of rebellious workers with the leadership, organization, and program they need in the harsh struggle against the monopolists, militarists, and union bureaucracy. These militants will be open to the acceptance of the ideas of authentic Marxism, which the Trotskyist movement alone presents in the United States.

The American working class has colossal tasks ahead of it. It confronts the most formidable and ferocious of adversaries in the monopolist-militarist combine that controls American capitalism. Yet it possesses the potential of a giant. Like Gulliver, it has been pinned down by lilliputians while it has fallen into a drugged sleep.

This class will be roused from its slumber by events beyond anyone's control. Marxists do not believe that the popular masses can be summoned into battle on anyone's command. The class struggle unfolds with a rhythm of its own, according to internal laws determined by weighty objective historical conditions.

On the other hand, Marxists are neither fatalists nor anarchists. They recognize that the working masses can launch mighty offensives on their own initiative once capitalism goads them into action. It occurred to no one that February 23, 1917, would be the first day of the Russian Revolution or that May 13, 1968, in France would see the start of the greatest general strike in working-class history.

The revolutionary program and perspectives of Marxism are predicated upon fusing such autonomous actions of the masses with the conscious intervention of its socialist vanguard. The correct combination of these factors is the only guarantee of success in the combat against capitalism.

If it is not correctly oriented in time, the most powerful spontaneous upsurge can fall short of its mark, dribble away, be turned back and crushed. This misfortune has befallen the workers' movement many times over the past century.

The revolutionary party helps workers take full advantage of their opportunities in good times or bad. That is its reason for existence. Just as every army has its training camps, officer corps, and a high command, so every serious revolutionary movement needs experienced cadres of militants and a dependable general staff. Such a leadership cannot be created overnight. It should be assembled, tested, and tempered in the preparatory period of a revolutionary process. Otherwise, it may be too late. Default on this score has ruined many promising openings for the conquest of power.

The American workers will have to be morally and ideologically rearmed in order to conduct an effective struggle to the end against their exploiters. As every teacher and student knows, self-confidence is necessary to learn new skills and perform greater tasks. Any vanguard that aspires to prepare a revolutionary change in the United States will have to impart assurance to the working people that they have what it takes to meet and beat the ruling rich and liberate themselves.

This is a reciprocal process. The revolutionary socialist party enhances its own confidence to the extent that the masses it proposes to assist elevate their reliance on themselves.

The will to win is an indispensable factor in the way to win. The decisive sections of the working class, black and white, can go forward to victory only as they become convinced that the profiteers are not born to command, that they are misruling the nation and leading the world to catastrophe, that they are not omnipotent and unbeatable, that their system of exploitation is not everlasting but has to go and can be abolished. This is the essential message of Marxism. It teaches that the workers are qualified and mandated by historical progress to supplant the plutocrats as the directors and organizers of economic and political life and become the pioneers of the first truly human society.

It is obvious from these considerations that the continuing controversy over the capacities of the American working class does not involve minor issues. Nothing less than the course and outcome of the struggle for socialism and self-determination in the United States, if not the very survival of society, depend upon whether an affirmative or negative answer is given to it, first in principle, then in practice.

* * *

LONG LIVE THE VICTORY OF PEOPLE'S WAR: MAO TSE-TUNG'S THEORY OF PEOPLE'S WAR

● *lin piao*

correctly apply the line and policy of the united front

In order to win a people's war, it is imperative to build the broadest possible united front and formulate a series of policies which will ensure the fullest mobilization of the basic masses as well as the unity of all the forces that can be united.

The Anti-Japanese National United Front embraced all the anti-Japanese classes and strata. These classes and strata shared a common interest in fighting Japan, an interest which formed the basis of their unity. But they differed in the degree of their firmness in resisting Japan, and there were class contradictions and conflicts of interest among them. Hence the inevitable class struggle within the united front.

In formulating the Party's line of the Anti-Japanese National United Front, Comrade Mao Tse-tung made the following class analysis of Chinese society.

The workers, the peasants and the urban petty bourgeoisie firmly demanded that the War of Resistance should be carried through to the end; they were the main force in the fight against Japanese aggression and constituted the basic masses who demanded unity and progress.

The bourgeoisie was divided into the national and the comprador bourgeoisie. The national bourgeoisie formed the majority of the bourgeoisie; it was rather flabby, often vacillated and had contradictions with the workers, but it also had a certain degree of readiness to oppose imperialism and was one of our allies in the War of Resistance. The comprador bourgeoisie was the bureaucrat-capitalist class, which was very small in number but occupied the ruling position in China. Its members attached themselves to different imperialist powers, some of them being pro-Japanese and others pro-British and pro-American. The pro-Japanese section of the comprador bourgeoisie were the capitulators, the overt and covert traitors. The pro-British and pro-American section of this class favoured resistance to Japan to a certain extent, but they were not firm in their resistance and very much wished to compromise with Japan, and by their nature they were opposed to the Communist Party and the people.

The landlords fell into different categories; there were the big, the middle and the small landlords. Some of the big landlords became traitors, while others favoured resistance but vacillated a great deal. Many of the middle and small landlords had the desire to resist, but there were contradictions between them and the peasants.

In the face of these complicated class relationships, our Party's policy regarding work within the united front was one of both alliance and struggle. That is to say, its policy was to unite with all the anti-Japanese classes and strata, try to win over even those who could be only vacillating and temporary allies, and adopt appropriate policies to adjust the relations among these classes and strata so that they all served the general cause of resisting Japan. At the same time, we had to maintain our Party's principle of independence and initiative, make the bold arousing of the masses and expansion of the people's forces the centre of gravity in our work, and wage the necessary struggles against all activities harmful to resistance, unity and progress.

Our Party's Anti-Japanese National United Front policy was different both from Chen Tu-hsiu's Right opportunist policy of all alliance and no struggle, and from Wang Ming's "Left" opportunist policy of all struggle and no alliance. Our Party summed up the lessons of the Right and "Left" opportunist errors and formulated the policy of both alliance and struggle.

Our Party made a series of adjustments in its policies in order to unite all the anti-Japanese parties and groups, including the Kuomintang, and all the anti-Japanese strata in a joint fight against the foe. We pledged ourselves to fight for the complete realization of Dr. Sun Yat-sen's revolutionary Three People's Principles. The government of the Shensi-Kansu-Ningsia revolutionary base area was renamed the Government of the Shensi-Kansu-Ningsia Special Region of the Republic of China. Our Workers' and Peasants' Red Army was redesignated the Eighth Route Army and the New Fourth Army of the National Revolutionary Army. Our land policy, the policy of confiscating the land of the landlords, was changed to one of reducing rent and interest. In our own base areas we carried out the "three thirds system"[1] in our organs of political power, drawing in those representatives of the petty bourgeoisie, the national bourgeoisie and the enlightened gentry and those members of the Kuomintang who stood for resistance to Japan and did not oppose the Communist Party. In accordance with the principles of the Anti-Japanese National United Front, we also made necessary and appropriate changes in our policies relating to

[1] The "three thirds system" refers to the organs of the political power which were established according to the principle of the Anti-Japanese National United Front and in which the members of the Communist Party, non-Party progressives and the middle elements each occupied one-third of the places.

the economy, taxation, labour and wages, anti-espionage, people's rights, culture and education, etc.

While making these policy adjustments, we maintained the independence of the Communist Party, the people's army and the base areas. We also insisted that the Kuomintang should institute a general mobilization, reform the government apparatus, introduce democracy, improve the people's livelihood, arm the people, and carry out a total war of resistance. We waged a resolute struggle against the Kuomintang's passive resistance to Japan and active opposition to the Communist Party, against its suppression of the people's resistance movement and its treacherous activities for compromise and capitulation.

Past experience had taught us that "Left" errors were liable to crop up after our Party had corrected Right errors, and that Right errors were liable to crop up after it had corrected "Left" errors. "Left" errors were liable to occur when we broke with the Kuomintang ruling clique, and Right errors were liable to occur when we united with it.

After the overcoming of "Left" opportunism and the formation of the Anti-Japanese National United Front, the main danger in our Party was Right opportunism or capitulationism.

Wang Ming, the exponent of "Left" opportunism during the Second Revolutionary Civil War, went to the other extreme in the early days of the War of Resistance Against Japan and became the exponent of Right opportunism, *i.e.*, capitulationism. He countered Comrade Mao Tse-tung's correct line and policies with an out-and-out capitulationist line of his own and a series of ultra-Right policies. He voluntarily abandoned proletarian leadership in the Anti-Japanese National United Front and willingly handed leadership to the Kuomintang. By his advocacy of "everything through the united front" or "everything to be submitted to the united front", he was in effect advocating that everything should go through or be submitted to Chiang Kai-shek and the Kuomintang. He opposed the bold mobilization of the masses, the carrying out of democratic reforms and the improvement of the livelihood of the workers and peasants, and wanted to undermine the worker-peasant alliance which was the foundation of the united front. He did not want the Communist-led base areas of the people's revolutionary forces but wanted to cut off the people's revolutionary forces from their roots. He rejected a people's army led by the Communist Party and wanted to hand over the people's armed forces to Chiang Kai-shek, which would have meant handing over everything the people had. He did not want the leadership of the Party and advocated an alliance between the youth of the Kuomintang and that of the Communist Party to suit Chiang Kai-shek's design of corroding the Communist Party. He decked himself out and presented himself to Chiang Kai-shek, hoping to be given some official appointment. All this was revisionism, pure and simple. If we had acted on Wang Ming's revisionist line and his set of policies, the Chinese people would have been unable to win the War of Resistance Against Japan, still less the subsequent nation-wide victory.

For a time during the War of Resistance, Wang Ming's revisionist line caused harm to the Chinese people's revolutionary cause. But the leading role of Comrade Mao Tse-tung had already been established in the Central Committee of our Party. Under his leadership, all the Marxist-Leninists in the Party carried out a resolute struggle against Wang Ming's errors and rectified them in time. It was this stuggle that prevented Wang Ming's erroneous line from doing greater and more lasting damage to the cause of the Party.

Chiang Kai-shek, our teacher by negative example, helped us to correct Wang Ming's mistakes. He repeatedly lectured us with cannons and machine-guns. The gravest lesson was the Southern Anhwei Incident which took place in January 1941. Because some leaders of the New Fourth Army disobeyed the directives of the Central Committee of the Party and followed Wang Ming's revisionist line, its units in southern Anhwei suffered disastrous losses in the surprise attack launched by Chiang Kai-shek and many heroic revolutionary fighters were slaughtered by the Kuomintang reactionaries. The lessons learned at the cost of blood helped to sober many of our comrades and increase their ability to distinguish the correct from the erroneous line.

Comrade Mao Tse-tung constantly summed up the experience gained by the whole Party in implementing the line of the Anti-Japanese National United Front and worked out a whole set of policies in good time. They were mainly as follows:

1. All people favouring resistance (that is, all the anti-Japanese workers, peasants, soldiers, students and intellectuals, and businessmen) were to unite and form the Anti-Japanese National United Front.
2. Within the united front, our policy was to be one of independence and initiative, *i.e.*, both unity and independence were necessary.
3. As far as military strategy was concerned, our policy was to be guerrilla warfare waged independently and with the initiative in our own hands, within the framework of a unified strategy; guerrilla warfare was to be basic, but no chance of waging mobile warfare was to be lost when the conditions were favourable.
4. In the struggle against the anti-Communist die-hards headed by Chiang Kai-shek, our policy was to make use of contradictions, win over the many, oppose the few and destroy our enemies one by one, and to wage struggles on just grounds, to our advantage, and with restraint.
5. In the Japanese-occupied and Kuomintang areas our policy was, on the one hand, to develop the united front to the greatest possible extent and, on the other, to have selected cadres working underground. With regard to the forms of organization and struggle, our policy was to assign selected cadres to work under cover for a long period, so as to accumulate strength and bide our time.
6. As regards the alignment of the various classes within the country, our basic policy was to develop the progressive forces, win over the middle forces and isolate the anti-Communist die-hard forces.
7. As for the anti-Communist die-hards, we followed a revolutionary dual policy of uniting with them, in so far as they were still capable of bringing themselves to resist Japan, and of struggling against and isolating them, in so far as they were determined to oppose the Communist Party.
8. With respect to the landlords and the bourgeoisie—even the big landlords and big bourgeoisie—it was necessary to analyse each case and draw distinctions. On the basis of these distinctions we were to formulate different policies so as to achieve our aim of uniting with all the forces that could be united.

The line and the various policies of the Anti-Japanese National United Front formulated by Comrade Mao Tse-tung stood the test of the War of Resistance and proved to be entirely correct.

History shows that when confronted by ruthless imperialist aggression, a

Communist Party must hold aloft the national banner and, using the weapon of the united front, rally around itself the masses and the patriotic and anti-imperialist people who form more than 90 per cent of a country's population, so as to mobilize all positive factors, unite with all the forces that can be united and isolate to the maximum the common enemy of the whole nation. If we abandon the national banner, adopt a line of "closed-doorism" and thus isolate ourselves, it is out of the question to exercise leadership and develop the people's revolutionary cause, and this in reality amounts to helping the enemy and bringing defeat on ourselves.

History shows that within the united front the Communist Party must maintain its ideological, political and organizational independence, adhere to the principle of independence and initiative, and insist on its leading role. Since there are class differences among the various classes in the united front, the Party must have a correct policy in order to develop the progressive forces, win over the middle forces and oppose the die-hard forces. The Party's work must centre on developing the progressive forces and expanding the people's revolutionary forces. This is the only way to maintain and strengthen the united front. "If unity is sought through struggle, it will live; if unity is sought through yielding, it will perish." [2] This is the chief experience gained in our struggle against the die-hard forces.

History shows that during the national-democratic revolution there must be two kinds of alliance within this united front, first, the worker-peasant alliance and, second, the alliance of the working people with the bourgeoisie and other non-working people. The worker-peasant alliance is an alliance of the working class with the peasants and all other working people in town and country. It is the foundation of the united front. Whether the working class can gain leadership of the national-democratic revolution depends on whether it can lead the broad masses of the peasants in struggle and rally them around itself. Only when the working class gains leadership of the peasants, and only on the basis of the worker-peasant alliance, is it possible to establish the second alliance, form a broad united front and wage a people's war victoriously. Otherwise, everything that is done is unreliable, like castles in the air or so much empty talk.

rely on the peasants and establish rural base areas

The peasantry constituted more than 80 per cent of the entire population of semi-colonial and semi-feudal China. They were subjected to the threefold oppression and exploitation of imperialism, feudalism and bureaucrat-capitalism, and they were eager for resistance against Japan and for revolution. It was essential to rely mainly on the peasants if the people's war was to be won.

But at the outset not all comrades in our Party saw this point. The history of our Party shows that in the period of the First Revolutionary Civil War, one of the major errors of the Right opportunists, represented by Chen Tu-hsiu, was their failure to recognize the importance of the peasant question and their opposition to arousing and arming the peasants. In the period of the Second Revolutionary Civil War, one of the major errors of the "Left" opportunists, represented by Wang Ming, was likewise their failure to recognize the importance of the peasant question. They did not realize that it was essential to

[2] Mao Tse-tung, "Current Problems of Tactics in the Anti-Japanese United Front", *Selected Works,* Eng. ed., FLP, Peking, 1965, Vol. II, p. 422.

 undertake long-term and painstaking work among the peasants and establish revolutionary base areas in the countryside; they were under the illusion that they could rapidly seize the big cities and quickly win nation-wide victory in the revolution. The errors of both the Right and the "Left" opportunists brought serious setbacks and defeats to the Chinese revolution.

As far back as the period of the First Revolutionary Civil War, Comrade Mao Tse-tung had pointed out that the peasant question occupied an extremely important position in the Chinese revolution, that the bourgeois-democratic revolution against imperialism and feudalism was in essence a peasant revolution and that the basic task of the Chinese proletariat in the bourgeois-democratic revolution was to give leadership to the peasants' struggle.

In the period of the War of Resistance Against Japan, Comrade Mao Tse-tung again stressed that the peasants were the most reliable and the most numerous ally of the proletariat and constituted the main force in the War of Resistance. The peasants were the main source of manpower for China's armies. The funds and the supplies needed for a protracted war came chiefly from the peasants. In the anti-Japanese war it was imperative to rely mainly on the peasants and to arouse them to participate in the war on the broadest scale.

The War of Resistance Against Japan was in essence a peasant revolutionary war led by our Party. By arousing and organizing the peasant masses and integrating them with the proletariat, our Party created a powerful force capable of defeating the strongest enemy.

To rely on the peasants, build rural base areas and use the countryside to encircle and finally capture the cities—such was the way to victory in the Chinese revolution.

Basing himself on the characteristics of the Chinese revolution, Comrade Mao Tse-tung pointed out the importance of building rural revolutionary base areas.

> *Since China's key cities have long been occupied by the powerful imperialists and their reactionary Chinese allies, it is imperative for the revolutionary ranks to turn the backward villages into advanced, consolidated base areas, into great military, political, economic and cultural bastions of the revolution from which to fight their vicious enemies who are using the cities for attacks on the rural districts, and in this way gradually to achieve the complete victory of the revolution through protracted fighting; it is imperative for them to do so if they do not wish to compromise with imperialism and its lackeys but are determined to fight on, and if they intend to build up and temper their forces, and avoid decisive battles with a powerful enemy while their own strength is inadequate.*[3]

Experience in the period of the Second Revolutionary Civil War showed that, when this strategic concept of Comrade Mao Tse-tung's was applied, there was an immense growth in the revolutionary forces and one Red base area after another was built. Conversely, when it was violated and the nonsense of the "Left" opportunists was applied, the revolutionary forces suffered severe damage, with losses of nearly 100 per cent in the cities and 90 per cent in the rural areas.

[3] Mao Tse-tung, "The Chinese Revolution and the Chinese Communist Party", *Selected Works*, Eng. ed., FLP, Peking, 1965, Vol. II pp. 316-17.

During the War of Resistance Against Japan, the Japanese imperialist forces occupied many of China's big cities and the main lines of communication, but owing to the shortage of troops they were unable to occupy the vast countryside, which remained the vulnerable sector of the enemy's rule. Consequently, the possibility of building rural base areas became even greater. Shortly after the beginning of the War of Resistance, when the Japanese forces surged into China's hinterland and the Kuomintang forces crumbled and fled in one defeat after another, the Eighth Route and New Fourth Armies led by our Party followed the wise policy laid down by Comrade Mao Tse-tung and boldly drove into the areas behind the enemy lines in small contingents and established base areas throughout the countryside. During the eight years of the war, we established nineteen anti-Japanese base areas in northern, central and southern China. With the exception of the big cities and the main lines of communication, the vast territory in the enemy's rear was in the hands of the people.

In the anti-Japanese base areas, we carried out democratic reforms, improved the livelihood of the people, and mobilized and organized the peasant masses. Organs of anti-Japanese democratic political power were established on an extensive scale and the masses of the people enjoyed the democratic right to run their own affairs; at the same time we carried out the policies of "a reasonable burden" and "the reduction of rent and interest", which weakened the feudal system of exploitation and improved the people's livelihood. As a result, the enthusiasm of the peasant masses was deeply aroused, while the various anti-Japanese strata were given due consideration and were thus united. In formulating our policies for the base areas, we also took care that these policies should facilitate our work in the enemy-occupied areas.

In the enemy-occupied cities and villages, we combined legal with illegal struggle, united the basic masses and all patriots, and divided and disintegrated the political power of the enemy and his puppets so as to prepare ourselves to attack the enemy from within in co-ordination with operations from without when conditions were ripe.

The base areas established by our Party became the centre of gravity in the Chinese people's struggle to resist Japan and save the country. Relying on these bases, our Party expanded and strengthened the people's revolutionary forces, persevered in the protracted war and eventually won the War of Resistance Against Japan.

Naturally, it was impossible for the development of the revolutionary base areas to be plain sailing all the time. They constituted a tremendous threat to the enemy and were bound to be attacked. Therefore, their development was a tortuous process of expansion, contraction and then renewed expansion. Between 1937 and 1940 the population in the anti-Japanese base areas grew to 100,000,000. But in 1941-42 the Japanese imperialists used the major part of their invading forces to launch frantic attacks on our base areas and wrought havoc. Meanwhile, the Kuomintang, too, encircled these base areas, blockaded them and went so far as to attack them. So by 1942, the anti-Japanese base areas had contracted and their population was down to less than 50,000,000. Placing complete reliance on the masses, our Party resolutely adopted a series of correct policies and measures, with the result that the base areas were able to hold out under extremely difficult circumstances. After this setback, the army and the people in the base areas were tempered and grew stronger. From 1943 onwards, our base areas were gradually restored and expanded, and by 1945 the population had grown to 160,000,000. Taking the entire course of the

 Chinese revolution into account, our revolutionary base areas went through even more ups and downs, and they weathered a great many tests before the small, separate base areas, expanding in a series of waves, gradually developed into extensive and contiguous base areas.

At the same time, the work of building the revolutionary base areas was a grand rehearsal in preparation for nation-wide victory. In these base areas, we built the Party, ran the organs of state power, built the people's armed forces and set up mass organizations; we engaged in industry and agriculture and operated cultural, educational and all other undertakings necessary for the independent existence of a separate region. Our base areas were in fact a state in miniature. And with the steady expansion of our work in the base areas, our Party established a powerful people's army, trained cadres for various kinds of work, accumulated experience in many fields and built up both the material and the moral strength that provided favourable conditions for nation-wide victory.

The revolutionary base areas established in the War of Resistance later became the springboards for the People's War of Liberation, in which the Chinese people defeated the Kuomintang reactionaries. In the War of Liberation we continued the policy of first encircling the cities from the countryside and then capturing the cities, and thus won nation-wide victory.

build a people's army of a new type

"Without a people's army the people have nothing."[4] This is the conclusion drawn by Comrade Mao Tse-tung from the Chinese people's experience in their long years of revolutionary struggle, experience that was bought in blood. This is a universal truth of Marxism-Leninism.

The special feature of the Chinese revolution was armed revolution against armed counter-revolution. The main form of struggle was war and the main form of organization was the army which was under the absolute leadership of the Chinese Communist Party, while all the other forms of organization and struggle led by our Party were co-ordinated, directly or indirectly, with the war.

During the First Revolutionary Civil War, many fine Party comrades took an active part in the armed revolutionary struggle. But our Party was then still in its infancy and did not have a clear understanding of this special feature of the Chinese revolution. It was only after the First Revolutionary Civil War, only after the Kuomintang had betrayed the revolution, massacred large numbers of Communists and destroyed all the revolutionary mass organizations, that our Party reached a clearer understanding of the supreme importance of organizing revolutionary armed forces and of studying the strategy and tactics of revolutionary war, and created the Workers' and Peasants' Red Army, the first people's army under the leadership of the Communist Party of China.

During the Second Revolutionary Civil War, the Workers' and Peasants' Red Army created by Comrade Mao Tse-tung grew considerably and at one time reached a total of 300,000 men. But it later lost nine-tenths of its forces as a result of the wrong political and military lines followed by the "Left" opportunist leadership.

At the start of the War of Resistance Against Japan, the people's army led by

[4] Mao Tse-tung, "On Coalition Government", *Selected Works*, Eng. ed., FLP, Peking, 1965, Vol. III, pp. 296-97.

the Chinese Communist Party had only a little over 40,000 men. The Kuomintang reactionaries attempted to restrict, weaken and destroy this people's army in every conceivable way. Comrade Mao Tse-tung pointed out that, in these circumstances, in order to sustain the War of Resistance and defeat the Japanese aggressors, it was imperative greatly to expand and consolidate the Eighth Route and New Fourth Armies and all the guerrilla units led by our Party. The whole Party should give close attention to war and study military affairs. Every Party member should be ready at all times to take up arms and go to the front.

Comrade Mao Tse-tung also incisively stated that Communists do not fight for personal military power but must fight for military power for the Party and for the people.

Guided by the Party's correct line of expanding the revolutionary armed forces, the Communist-led Eighth Route and New Fourth Armies and anti-Japanese guerrilla units promptly went to the forefront at the very beginning of the war. We spread the seeds of the people's armed forces in the vast areas behind the enemy lines and kindled the flames of guerrilla warfare everywhere. Our people's army steadily expanded in the struggle, so that by the end of the war it was already a million strong, and there was also a militia of over two million. That was why we were able to engage nearly two-thirds of the Japanese forces of aggression and 95 per cent of the puppet troops and to become the main force in the War of Resistance Against Japan. While resisting the Japanese invading forces, we repulsed three large-scale anti-Communist onslaughts launched by the Kuomintang reactionaries in 1939, 1941 and 1943, and smashed their countless "friction-mongering" activities.

Why were the Eighth Route and New Fourth Armies able to grow big and strong from being small and weak and to score such great victories in the War of Resistance Against Japan?

The fundamental reason was that the Eighth Route and New Fourth Armies were founded on Comrade Mao Tse-tung's theory of army building. They were armies of a new type, a people's army which whole-heartedly serves the interests of the people.

Guided by Comrade Mao Tse-tung's theory on building a people's army, our army was under the absolute leadership of the Chinese Communist Party and most loyally carried out the Party's Marxist-Leninist line and policies. It had a high degree of conscious discipline and was heroically inspired to destroy all enemies and conquer all difficulties. Internally there was full unity between cadres and fighters, between those in higher and those in lower positions of responsibility, between the different departments and between the various fraternal army units. Externally, there was similarly full unity between the army and the people and between the army and the local government.

During the anti-Japanese war our army staunchly performed the three tasks set by Comrade Mao Tse-tung, namely, fighting, mass work, and production, and it was at the same time a fighting force, a political work force and a production corps. Everywhere it went, it did propaganda work among the masses, organized and armed them and helped them set up revolutionary political power. Our armymen strictly observed the Three Main Rules of Discipline and the Eight Points for Attention,[5] carried out campaigns to "sup-

[5] The Three Main Rules of Discipline and the Eight Points for Attention were drawn up by Comrade Mao Tse-tung for the Chinese Workers' and Peasants' Red Army during the Agrarian Revolutionary War and were later adopted as rules of discipline by the

 port the government and cherish the people", and did good deeds for the people everywhere. They also made use of every possibility to engage in production themselves so as to overcome economic difficulties, better their own livelihood and lighten the people's burden. By their exemplary conduct they won the whole-hearted support of the masses, who affectionately called them "our own boys".

Our army consisted of local forces as well as of regular forces; moreover, it energetically built and developed the militia, thus practising the system of combining the three military formations, *i.e.*, the regular forces, the local forces and the militia.

Our army also pursued correct policies in winning over enemy officers and men and in giving lenient treatment to prisoners of war. During the anti-Japanese war we not only brought about the revolt and surrender of large numbers of puppet troops, but succeeded in converting not a few Japanese prisoners, who had been badly poisoned by fascist ideology. After they were politically awakened, they organized themselves into anti-war organizations such as the League for the Liberation of the Japanese People, the Anti-War League of the Japanese in China and the League of Awakened Japanese, helped us to disintegrate the Japanese army and co-operated with us in opposing Japanese militarism. Comrade Sanzo Nosaka, the leader of the Japanese Communist Party, who was then in Yenan, gave us great help in this work.

The essence of Comrade Mao Tse-tung's theory of army building is that in building a people's army prominence must be given to politics, *i.e.*, the army must first and foremost be built on a political basis. Politics is the commander, politics is the soul of everything. Political work is the lifeline of our army. True, a people's army must pay attention to the constant improvement of its weapons and equipment and its military technique, but in its fighting it does not rely purely on weapons and technique, it relies mainly on politics, on the proletarian revolutionary consciousness and courage of the commanders and fighters, on the support and backing of the masses.

Owing to the application of Comrade Mao Tse-tung's line on army building, there has prevailed in our army at all times a high level of proletarian political consciousness, an atmosphere of keenness to study the thought of Mao Tse-tung, an excellent morale, a solid unity and a deep hatred for the enemy, and thus a gigantic moral force has been brought into being. In battle it has feared

Eighth Route Army and the New Fourth Army and the present People's Liberation Army. As these rules varied slightly in content in the army units of different areas, the General Headquarters of the Chinese People's Liberation Army in October 1947 issued a standard version as follows:

The Three Main Rules of Discipline:

(1) Obey orders in all your actions.
(2) Do not take a single needle or piece of thread from the masses.
(3) Turn in everything captured.

The Eight Points for Attention:

(1) Speak politely.
(2) Pay fairly for what you buy.
(3) Return everything you borrow.
(4) Pay for anything you damage.
(5) Do not hit or swear at people.
(6) Do not damage crops.
(7) Do not take liberties with women.
(8) Do not ill-treat captives.

neither hardships nor death, it has been able to charge or hold its ground as the conditions require. One man can play the role of several, dozens or even hundreds, and miracles can be performed.

All this makes the people's army led by the Chinese Communist Party fundamentally different from any bourgeois army, and from all the armies of the old type which served the exploiting classes and were driven and utilized by a handful of people. The experience of the people's war in China shows that a people's army created in accordance with Comrade Mao Tse-tung's theory of army building is incomparably strong and invincible.

carry out the strategy and tactics of people's war

Engels said, "The emancipation of the proletariat, in its turn, will have its specific expression in military affairs and create its specific, new military method."[6] Engels' profound prediction has been fulfilled in the revolutionary wars waged by the Chinese people under the leadership of the Chinese Communist Party. In the course of protracted armed struggle, we have created a whole range of strategy and tactics of people's war by which we have been able to utilize our strong points to attack the enemy at his weak points.

During the War of Resistance Against Japan, on the basis of his comprehensive analysis of the enemy and ourselves, Comrade Mao Tse-tung laid down the following strategic principle for the Communist-led Eighth Route and New Fourth Armies: "Guerrilla warfare is basic, but lose no chance for mobile warfare under favourable conditions."[7] He raised guerrilla warfare to the level of strategy, because, if they are to defeat a formidable enemy, revolutionary armed forces should not fight with a reckless disregard for the consequences when there is a great disparity between their own strength and the enemy's. If they do, they will suffer serious losses and bring heavy setbacks to the revolution. Guerrilla warfare is the only way to mobilize and apply the whole strength of the people against the enemy, the only way to expand our forces in the course of the war, deplete and weaken the enemy, gradually change the balance of forces between the enemy and ourselves, switch from guerrilla to mobile warfare, and finally defeat the enemy.

In the initial period of the Second Revolutionary Civil War, Comrade Mao Tse-tung enumerated the basic tactics of guerrilla warfare as follows:

> *The enemy advances, we retreat; the enemy camps, we harass; the enemy tires, we attack; the enemy retreats, we pursue.*[8]

Guerrilla war tactics were further developed during the War of Resistance Against Japan. In the base areas behind the enemy lines, everybody joined in the fighting—the troops and the civilian population, men and women, old and young; every single village fought. Various ingenious methods of fighting

[6] Frederick Engels, "Possibilities and Perspectives of the War of the Holy Alliance Against France in 1852", *Collected Works of Marx and Engels*, Russ. ed., Moscow, 1956, Vol. VII, p. 509.

[7] Mao Tse-tung, "On Protracted War", *Selected Works*, Eng. ed., FLP, Peking, 1965, Vol. II, p. 116.

[8] Mao Tse-tung, "A Single Spark Can Start a Prairie Fire", *Selected Works*, Eng. ed., FLP, Peking, 1965, Vol. I, p. 124.

 were devised, including "sparrow warfare",[9] land-mine warfare, tunnel warfare, sabotage warfare, and guerrilla warfare on lakes and rivers.

In the later period of the War of Resistance Against Japan and during the Third Revolutionary Civil War, we switched our strategy from that of guerrilla warfare as the primary form of fighting to that of mobile warfare in the light of the changes in the balance of forces between the enemy and ourselves. By the middle, and especially the later, period of the Third Revolutionary Civil War, our operations had developed into large-scale mobile warfare, including the storming of big cities.

War of annihilation is the fundamental guiding principle of our military operations. This guiding principle should be put into effect regardless of whether mobile or guerrilla warfare is the primary form of fighting. It is true that in guerrilla warfare much should be done to disrupt and harass the enemy, but it is still necessary actively to advocate and fight battles of annihilation whenever conditions are favourable. In mobile warfare superior forces must be concentrated in every battle so that the enemy forces can be wiped out one by one. Comrade Mao Tse-tung has pointed out:

> *A battle in which the enemy is routed is not basically decisive in a contest with a foe of great strength. A battle of annihilation, on the other hand, produces a great and immediate impact on any enemy. Injuring all of a man's ten fingers is not as effective as chopping off one, and routing ten enemy divisions is not as effective as annihilating one of them.*[10]

Battles of annihilation are the most effective way of hitting the enemy; each time one of his brigades or regiments is wiped out, he will have one brigade or one regiment less, and the enemy forces will be demoralized and will disintegrate. By fighting battles of annihilation, our army is able to take prisoners of war or capture weapons from the enemy in every battle, and the morale of our army rises, our army units get bigger, our weapons become better, and our combat effectiveness continually increases.

In his celebrated ten cardinal military principles Comrade Mao Tse-tung pointed out:

> *In every battle, concentrate an absolutely superior force (two, three, four sometimes even five or six times the enemy's strength), encircle the enemy forces completely, strive to wipe them out thoroughly and do not let any escape from the net. In special circumstances, use the method of dealing crushing blows to the enemy, that is, concentrate all our strength to make a frontal attack and also to attack one or both of his flanks, with the aim of wiping out one part and routing another so that our army can swiftly move its troops to smash other enemy forces. Strive to avoid battles of attrition in which we lose more than we gain or only break even. In this way, although we are inferior as a whole (in terms of numbers), we are absolutely superior in every part and every specific campaign, and this*

[9] Sparrow warfare is a popular method of fighting created by the Communist-led anti-Japanese guerrilla units and militia behind the enemy lines. It was called sparrow warfare because, first, it was used diffusely, like the flight sparrows in the sky; and because, second, it was used flexibly by guerrillas or militiamen, operating in threes or fives, appearing and disappearing unexpectedly and wounding, killing, depleting and wearing out the enemy forces.

[10] Mao Tse-tung, "Problems of Strategy in China's Revolutionary War", *Selected Works*, Eng. ed., FLP, Peking, 1965, Vol. I, p. 248.

ensures victory in the campaign. As time goes on, we shall become superior as a whole and eventually wipe out all the enemy.[11]

At the same time, he said that we should first attack dispersed or isolated enemy forces and only attack concentrated and strong enemy forces later; that we should strive to wipe out the enemy through mobile warfare; that we should fight no battle unprepared and fight no battle we are not sure of winning; and that in any battle we fight we should develop our army's strong points and its excellent style of fighting. These are the major principles of fighting a war of annihilation.

In order to annihilate the enemy, we must adopt the policy of luring him in deep and abandon some cities and districts of our own accord in a planned way, so as to let him in. It is only after letting the enemy in that the people can take part in the war in various ways and that the power of a people's war can be fully exerted. It is only after letting the enemy in that he can be compelled to divide up his forces, take on heavy burdens and commit mistakes. In other words, we must let the enemy become elated, stretch out all his ten fingers and become hopelessly bogged down. Thus, we can concentrate superior forces to destroy the enemy forces one by one, to eat them up mouthful by mouthful. Only by wiping out the enemy's effective strength can cities and localities be finally held or seized. We are firmly against dividing up our forces to defend all positions and putting up resistance at every place for fear that our territory might be lost and our pots and pans smashed, since this can neither wipe out the enemy forces nor hold cities or localities.

Comrade Mao Tse-tung has provided a masterly summary of the strategy and tactics of people's war: You fight in your way and we fight in ours; we fight when we can win and move away when we can't.

In other words, you rely on modern weapons and we rely on highly conscious revolutionary people; you give full play to your superiority and we give full play to ours; you have your way of fighting and we have ours. When you want to fight us, we don't let you and you can't even find us. But when we want to fight you, we make sure that you can't get away and we hit you squarely on the chin and wipe you out. When we are able to wipe you out, we do so with a vengeance; when we can't, we see to it that you don't wipe us out. It is opportunism if one won't fight when one can win. It is adventurism if one insists on fighting when one can't win. Fighting is the pivot of all our strategy and tactics. It is because of the necessity of fighting that we admit the necessity of moving away. The sole purpose of moving away is to fight and bring about the final complete destruction of the enemy. This strategy and these tactics can be applied only when one relies on the broad masses of the people, and such application brings the superiority of people's war into full play. However superior he may be in technical equipment and whatever tricks he may resort to, the enemy will find himself in the passive position of having to receive blows, and the initiative will always be in our hands.

We grew from a small and weak to a large and strong force and finally defeated formidable enemies at home and abroad because we carried out the strategy and tactics of people's war. During the eight years of War of Resistance Against Japan, the people's army led by the Chinese Communist Party fought more than 125,000 engagements with the enemy and put out of action more

[11] Mao Tse-tung, "The Present Situation and Our Tasks", *Selected Works*, Eng. ed., FLP, Peking, 1961, Vol. IV, p. 161.

 than 1,700,000 Japanese and puppet troops. In the three years of the War of Liberation, we put eight million of the Kuomintang's reactionary troops out of action and won the great victory of the people's revolution.

adhere to the policy of self-reliance

The Chinese people's War of Resistance Against Japan was an important part of the Anti-Fascist World War. The victory of the Anti-Fascist War as a whole was the result of the common struggle of the people of the world. By its participation in the war against Japan at the final stage, the Soviet army under the leadership of the Communist Party of the Soviet Union headed by Stalin played a significant part in bringing about the defeat of Japanese imperialism. Great contributions were made by the peoples of Korea, Vietnam, Mongolia, Laos, Cambodia, Indonesia, Burma, India, Pakistan, Malaya, the Philippines, Thailand and certain other Asian countries. The people of the Americas, Oceania, Europe and Africa also made their contribution.

Under extremely difficult circumstances, the Communist Party of Japan and the revolutionary forces of the Japanese people kept up their valiant and staunch struggle, and played their part in the defeat of Japanese fascism.

The common victory was won by all the peoples, who gave one another support and encouragement. Yet each country was, above all, liberated as a result of its own people's efforts.

The Chinese people enjoyed the support of other peoples in winning both the War of Resistance Against Japan and the People's Liberation War, and yet victory was mainly the result of the Chinese people's own efforts. Certain people assert that China's victory in the War of Resistance was due entirely to foreign assistance. This absurd assertion is in tune with that of the Japanese militarists.

The liberation of the masses is accomplished by the masses themselves—this is a basic principle of Marxism-Leninism. Revolution or people's war in any country is the business of the masses in that country and should be carried out primarily by their own efforts; there is no other way.

During the War of Resistance Against Japan, our Party maintained that China should rely mainly on her own strength while at the same time trying to get as much foreign assistance as possible. We firmly opposed the Kuomintang ruling clique's policy of exclusive reliance on foreign aid. In the eyes of the Kuomintang and Chiang Kai-shek, China's industry and agriculture were no good, her weapons and equipment were no good, nothing in China was any good, so that if she wanted to defeat Japan, she had to depend on other countries, and particularly on the U.S.-British imperialists. This was completely slavish thinking. Our policy was diametrically opposed to that of the Kuomintang. Our Party held that it was possible to exploit the contradictions between U.S-British imperialism and Japanese imperialism, but that no reliance could be placed on the former. In fact, the U.S.-British imperialists repeatedly plotted to bring about a "Far Eastern Munich" in order to arrive at a compromise with Japanese imperialism at China's expense, and for a considerable period of time they provided the Japanese aggressors with war *materiel*. In helping China during that period, the U.S. imperialists harboured the sinister design of turning China into a colony of their own.

Comrade Mao Tse-tung said: "China has to rely mainly on her own efforts in the War of Resistance."[12] He added, "We hope for foreign aid but cannot be dependent on it; we depend on our own efforts, on the creative power of the whole army and the entire people."[13]

Self-reliance was especially important for the people's armed forces and the Liberated Areas led by our Party.

The Kuomintang government gave the Eighth Route and New Fourth Armies some small allowances in the initial stage of the anti-Japanese war, but gave them not a single penny later. The Liberated Areas faced great difficulties as a result of the Japanese imperialists' savage attacks and brutal "mopping-up" campaigns, of the Kuomintang's military encirclement and economic blockade and of natural calamities. The difficulties were particularly great in the years 1941 and 1942, when we were very short of food and clothing.

What were we to do? Comrade Mao Tse-tung asked: How has mankind managed to keep alive from time immemorial? Has it not been by men using their hands to provide for themselves? Why should we, their latter-day descendants, be devoid of this tiny bit of wisdom? Why can't we use our own hands?

The Central Committee of the Party and Comrade Mao Tse-tung put forward the policies of "ample food and clothing through self-reliance" and "develop the economy and ensure supplies", and the army and the people of the Liberated Areas accordingly launched an extensive production campaign, with the main emphasis on agriculture.

Difficulties are not invincible monsters. If everyone co-operates and fights them, they will be overcome. The Kuomintang reactionaries thought that it could starve us to death by cutting off allowances and imposing an economic blockade, but in fact it helped us by stimulating us to rely on our own efforts to surmount our difficulties. While launching the great campaign for production, we applied the policy of "better troops and simpler administration" and economized in the use of manpower and material resources; thus we not only surmounted the severe material difficulties and successfully met the crisis, but lightened the people's burden, improved their livelihood and laid the material foundations for victory in the anti-Japanese war.

The problem of military equipment was solved mainly by relying on the capture of arms from the enemy, though we did turn out some weapons too. Chiang Kai-shek, the Japanese imperialists and the U.S. imperialists have all been our "chiefs of transportation corps". The arsenals of the imperialists always provide the oppressed peoples and nations with arms.

The people's armed forces led by our Party independently waged people's war on a large scale and won great victories without any material aid from outside, both during the more than eight years of the anti-Japanese war and during the more than three years of the People's War of Liberation.

Comrade Mao Tse-tung has said that our fundamental policy should rest on the foundation of our own strength. Only by relying on our own efforts can we in all circumstances remain invincible.

The peoples of the world invariably support each other in their struggles against imperialism and its lackeys. Those countries which have won victory

[12] Mao Tse-tung, "Interview with Three Correspondents from the Central News Agency, the *Sao Tang Pao* and the *Hsin Min Pao*", *Selected Works,* Eng. ed., FLP, Peking, 1965, Vol. II, p. 270.

[13] Mao Tse-tung, "We Must Learn to Do Economic Work", *Selected Works,* Eng. ed., FLP, Peking, 1965, Vol. III, p. 241.

 are duty bound to support and aid the peoples who have not yet done so. Nevertheless, foreign aid can only play a supplementary role.

In order to make a revolution and to fight a people's war and be victorious, it is imperative to adhere to the policy of self-reliance, rely on the strength of the masses in one's own country and prepare to carry on the fight independently even when all material aid from outside is cut off. If one does not operate by one's own efforts, does not independently ponder and solve the problems of the revolution in one's own country and does not rely on the strength of the masses, but leans wholly on foreign aid—even though this be aid from socialist countries which persist in revolution—no victory can be won, or be consolidated even if it is won.

the international significance of comrade mao tse-tung's theory of people's war

The Chinese revolution is a continuation of the great October Revolution. The road of the October Revolution is the common road for all people's revolutions. The Chinese revolution and the October Revolution have in common the following basic characteristics: (1) Both were led by the working class with a Marxist-Leninist party as its nucleus. (2) Both were based on the worker-peasant alliance. (3) In both cases state power was seized through violent revolution and the dictatorship of the proletariat was established. (4) In both cases the socialist system was built after victory in the revolution. (5) Both were component parts of the proletarian world revolution.

Naturally, the Chinese revolution had its own peculiar characteristics. The October Revolution took place in imperialist Russia, but the Chinese revolution broke out in a semi-colonial and semi-feudal country. The former was a proletarian socialist revolution, while the latter developed into a socialist revolution after the complete victory of the new-democratic revolution. The October Revolution began with armed uprisings in the cities and then spread to the countryside, while the Chinese revolution won nation-wide victory through the encirclement of the cities from the rural areas and the final capture of the cities.

Comrade Mao Tse-tung's great merit lies in the fact that he has succeeded in integrating the universal truth of Marxism-Leninism with the concrete practice of the Chinese revolution and has enriched and developed Marxism-Leninism by his masterly generalization and summation of the experience gained during the Chinese people's protracted revolutionary struggle.

Comrade Mao Tse-tung's theory of people's war has been proved by the long practice of the Chinese revolution to be in accord with the objective laws of such wars and to be invincible. It has not only been valid for China, it is a great contribution to the revolutionary struggles of the oppressed nations and peoples throughout the world.

The people's war led by the Chinese Communist Party, comprising the War of Resistance and the Revolutionary Civil Wars, lasted for twenty-two years. It constitutes the most drawn-out and most complex people's war led by the proletariat in modern history, and it has been the richest in experience.

In the last analysis, the Marxist-Leninist theory of proletarian revolution is the theory of the seizure of state power by revolutionary violence, the theory of countering war against the people by people's war. As Marx so aptly put it, "Force is the midwife of every old society pregnant with a new one."[14]

It was on the basis of the lessons derived from the people's wars in China that Comrade Mao Tse-tung, using the simplest and the most vivid language, advanced the famous thesis that "political power grows out of the barrel of a gun".[15]

He clearly pointed out:

> *The seizure of power by armed force, the settlement of the issue by war, is the central task and the highest form of revolution. This Marxist-Leninist principle of revolution holds good universally, for China and for all other countries.*[16]

War is the product of imperialism and the system of exploitation of man by man. Lenin said that "war is always and everywhere begun by the exploiters themselves, by the ruling and oppressing classes."[17] So long as imperialism and the system of exploitation of man by man exist, the imperialists and reactionaries will invariably rely on armed force to maintain their reactionary rule and impose war on the oppressed nations and peoples. This is an objective law independent of man's will.

In the world today, all the imperialists headed by the United States and their lackeys, without exception, are strengthening their state machinery, and especially their armed forces. U.S. imperialism, in particular, is carrying out armed aggression and suppression everywhere.

What should the oppressed nations and the oppressed people do in the face of wars of aggression and armed suppression by the imperialists and their lackeys? Should they submit and remain slaves in perpetuity? Or should they rise in resistance and fight for their liberation?

Comrade Mao Tse-tung answered this question in vivid terms. He said that after long investigation and study the Chinese people discovered that all the imperialists and their lackeys "have swords in their hands and are out to kill. The people have come to understand this and so act after the same fashion".[18] This is called doing unto them what they do unto us.

In the last analysis, whether one dares to wage a tit-for-tat struggle against armed aggression and suppression by the imperialists and their lackeys, whether one dares to fight a people's war against them, means whether one dares to embark on revolution. This is the most effective touchstone for distinguishing genuine from fake revolutionaries and Marxist-Leninists.

In view of the fact that some people were afflicted with the fear of the imperialists and reactionaries, Comrade Mao Tse-tung put forward his famous thesis that "the imperialists and all reactionaries are paper tigers". He said,

[14] Karl Marx, *Capital*, Eng. ed., Foreign Languages Publishing House, Moscow, 1954, Vol. I, p. 751.

[15] Mao Tse-tung, "Problems of War and Strategy", *Selected Works*, Eng. ed., FLP, Peking, 1965, Vol. II, p. 224.

[16] *Ibid.*, p. 219.

[17] V. I. Lenin, "The Revolutionary Army and the Revolutionary Government", *Collected Works*, Eng. ed., FLPH, Moscow, 1962, Vol. VIII, p. 565.

[18] Mao Tse-tung, "The Situation and Our Policy After the Victory in the War of Resistance Against Japan", *Selected Works*, Eng. ed., FLP, Peking, 1961, Vol. IV, pp. 14-15.

All reactionaries are paper tigers. In appearence, the reactionaries are terrifying, but in reality they are not so powerful. From a long-term point of view, it is not the reactionaries but the people who are really powerful.[19]

The history of people's war in China and other countries provides conclusive evidence that the growth of the people's revolutionary forces from weak and small beginnings into strong and large forces is a universal law of development of class struggle, a universal law of development of people's war. A people's war inevitably meets with many difficulties, with ups and downs and setbacks in the course of its development, but no force can alter its general trend towards inevitable triumph.

Comrade Mao Tse-tung points out that we must despise the enemy strategically and take full account of him tactically.

To despise the enemy strategically is an elementary requirement for a revolutionary. Without the courage to despise the enemy and without daring to win, it will be simply impossible to make revolution and wage a people's war, let alone to achieve victory.

It is also very important for revolutionaries to take full account of the enemy tactically. It is likewise impossible to win victory in a people's war without taking full account of the enemy tactically, and without examining the concrete conditions, without being prudent and giving great attention to the study of the art of struggle, and without adopting appropriate forms of struggle in the concrete practice of the revolution in each country and with regard to each concrete problem of struggle.

Dialectical and historical materialism teaches us that what is important primarily is not that which at the given moment seems to be durable and yet is already beginning to die away, but that which is arising and developing, even though at the given moment it may not appear to be durable, for only that which is arising and developing is invincible.

Why can the apparently weak new-born forces always triumph over the decadent forces which appear so powerful? The reason is that truth is on their side and that the masses are on their side, while the reactionary classes are always divorced from the masses and set themselves against the masses.

This has been borne out by the victory of the Chinese revolution, by the history of all revolutions, the whole history of class struggle and the entire history of mankind.

The imperialists are extremely afraid of Comrade Mao Tse-tung's thesis that "imperialism and all reactionaries are paper tigers", and the revisionists are extremely hostile to it. They all oppose and attack this thesis and the philistines follow suit by ridiculing it. But all this cannot in the least diminish its importance. The light of truth cannot be dimmed by anybody.

Comrade Mao Tse-tung's theory of people's war solves not only the problem of daring to fight a people's war, but also that of how to wage it.

Comrade Mao Tse-tung is a great statesman and military scientist, proficient at directing war in accordance with its laws. By the line and policies, the strategy and tactics he formulated for the people's war, he led the Chinese people in steering the ship of the people's war past all hidden reefs to the shores of victory in most complicated and difficult conditions.

It must be emphasized that Comrade Mao Tse-tung's theory of the establishment of rural revolutionary base areas and the encirclement of the cities

[19] Mao Tse-tung, "Talk with the American Correspondent Anna Louise Strong", *Selected Works,* Eng. ed., FLP, Peking, 1961, Vol. IV, p. 100.

from the countryside is of outstanding and universal practical importance for the present revolutionary struggles of all the oppressed nations and peoples, and particularly for the revolutionary struggles of the oppressed nations and peoples in Asia, Africa and Latin America against imperialism and its lackeys.

Many countries and peoples in Asia, Africa and Latin America are now being subjected to aggression and enslavement on a serious scale by the imperialists headed by the United States and their lackeys. The basic political and economic conditions in many of these countries have many similarities to those that prevailed in old China. As in China, the peasant question is extremely important in these regions. The peasants constitute the main force of the national-democratic revolution against the imperialists and their lackeys. In committing aggression against these countries, the imperialists usually begin by seizing the big cities and the main lines of communication, but they are unable to bring the vast countryside completely under their control. The countryside, and the countryside alone, can provide the broad areas in which the revolutionaries can manoeuvre freely. The countryside, and the countryside alone, can provide the revolutionary bases from which the revolutionaries can go forward to final victory. Precisely for this reason, Comrade Mao Tse-tung's theory of establishing revolutionary base areas in the rural districts and encircling the cities from the countryside is attracting more and more attention among the people in these regions.

Taking the entire globe, if North America and Western Europe can be called "the cities of the world", then Asia, Africa and Latin America constitute "the rural areas of the world". Since World War II, the proletarian revolutionary movement has for various reasons been temporarily held back in the North American and West European capitalist countries, while the people's revolutionary movement in Asia, Africa and Latin America has been growing vigorously. In a sense, the contemporary world revolution also presents a picture of the encirclement of cities by the rural areas. In the final analysis, the whole cause of world revolution hinges on the revolutionary struggles of the Asian, African and Latin American peoples who make up the overwhelming majority of the world's population. The socialist countries should regard it as their internationalist duty to support the people's revolutionary struggles in Asia, Africa and Latin America.

The October Revolution opened up a new era in the revolution of the oppressed nations. The victory of the October Revolution built a bridge between the socialist revolution of the proletariat of the West and the national-democratic revolution of the colonial and semi-colonial countries of the East. The Chinese revolution has successfully solved the problem of how to link up the national-democratic with the socialist revolution in the colonial and semi-colonial countries.

Comrade Mao Tse-tung has pointed out that, in the epoch since the October Revolution, anti-imperialist revolution in any colonial or semi-colonial country is no longer part of the old bourgeois, or capitalist world revolution, but is part of the new world revolution, the proletarian-socialist world revolution.

Comrade Mao Tse-tung has formulated a complete theory of the new-democratic revolution. He indicated that this revolution, which is different from all others, can only be, nay must be, a revolution against imperialism, feudalism and bureaucrat-capitalism waged by the broad masses of the people under the leadership of the proletariat.

 This means that the revolution can only be, nay must be, led by the proletariat and the genuinely revolutionary party armed with Marxism-Leninism, and by no other class or party.

This means that the revolution embraces in its ranks not only the workers, peasants and the urban petty bourgeoisie, but also the national bourgeoisie and other patriotic and anti-imperialist democrats.

This means, finally, that the revolution is directed against imperialism, feudalism and bureaucrat-capitalism.

The new-democratic revolution leads to socialism, and not to capitalism.

Comrade Mao Tse-tung's theory of the new-democratic revolution is the Marxist-Leninist theory of revolution by stages as well as the Marxist-Leninist theory of uninterrupted revolution.

Comrade Mao Tse-tung made a correct distinction between the two revolutionary stages, *i.e.*, the national-democratic and the socialist revolutions; at the same time he correctly and closely linked the two. The national-democratic revolution is the necessary preparation for the socialist revolution, and the socialist revolution is the inevitable sequel to the national-democratic revolution. There is no Great Wall between the two revolutionary stages. But the socialist revolution is only possible after the completion of the national-democratic revolution. The more thorough the national-democratic revolution, the better the conditions for the socialist revolution.

The experience of the Chinese revolution shows that the tasks of the national-democratic revolution can be fulfilled only through long and tortuous struggles. In this stage of revolution, imperialism and its lackeys are the principal enemy. In the struggle against imperialism and its lackeys, it is necessary to rally all anti-imperialist patriotic forces, including the national bourgeoisie and all patriotic personages. All those patriotic personages from among the bourgeoisie and other exploiting classes who join the anti-imperialist struggle play a progressive historical role; they are not tolerated by imperialism but welcomed by the proletariat.

It is very harmful to confuse the two stages, that is, the national-democratic and the socialist revolutions. Comrade Mao Tse-tung criticized the wrong idea of "accomplishing both at one stroke", and pointed out that this utopian idea could only weaken the struggle against imperialism and its lackeys, the most urgent task at that time. The Kuomintang reactionaries and the Trotskyites they hired during the War of Resistance deliberately confused these two stages of the Chinese revolution, proclaiming the "theory of a single revolution" and preaching so-called "socialism" without any Communist Party. With this preposterous theory they attempted to swallow up the Communist Party, wipe out any revolution and prevent the advance of the national-democratic revolution, and they used it as a pretext for their non-resistance and capitulation to imperialism. This reactionary theory was buried long ago by the history of the Chinese revolution.

The Khrushchev revisionists are now actively preaching that socialism can be built without the proletariat and without a genuinely revolutionary party armed with the advanced proletarian ideology, and they have cast the fundamental tenets of Marxism-Leninism to the four winds. The revisionists' purpose is solely to divert the oppressed nations from their struggle against imperialism and sabotage their national-democratic revolution, all in the service of imperialism.

The Chinese revolution provides a successful lesson for making a thoroughgoing national-democratic revolution under the leadership of the proletariat; it likewise provides a successful lesson for the timely transition from the national-democratic revolution to the socialist revolution under the leadership of the proletariat.

Mao Tse-tung's thought has been the guide to the victory of the Chinese revolution. It has integrated the universal truth of Marxism-Leninism with the concrete practice of the Chinese revolution and creatively developed Marxism-Leninism, thus adding new weapons to the arsenal of Marxism-Leninism.

Ours is the epoch in which world capitalism and imperialism are heading for their doom and socialism and communism are marching to victory. Comrade Mao Tse-tung's theory of people's war is not only a product of the Chinese revolution, but has also the characteristics of our epoch. The new experience gained in the people's revolutionary struggles in various countries since World War II has provided continuous evidence that Mao Tse-tung's thought is a common asset of the revolutionary people of the whole world. This is the great international significance of the thought of Mao Tse-tung.

SOCIALISM IN ONE COUNTRY – PROGRAM OF THE COMMUNIST INTERNATIONAL'S SIXTH CONGRESS: SELECTIONS

introduction

The epoch of imperialism is the epoch of dying capitalism. The world war of 1914-18 and the general crisis of capitalism which it unleashed, being the direct outcome of the profound contradiction between the growing productive forces of world economy and national barriers, prove that the material prerequisites for socialism have already matured in the womb of capitalist society; they prove that the capitalist shell has become an intolerable restraint on the further development of mankind, and that history has put on the order of the day the revolutionary overthrow of the capitalist yoke.

From the centres of capitalist power to the most remote corners of the colonial world, imperialism subjects the great mass of proletarians in all countries to the dictatorship of the finance-capitalist plutocracy. With elemental force it exposes and deepens all the contradictions of capitalist society, intensifies to the utmost the oppression of the exploited classes, and brings to a head the struggle between capitalist States. In so doing it gives rise to inexorable world-wide imperialist wars which shake the entire prevailing regime to its foundations, and leads with iron necessity to the proletarian world revolution.

Imperialism binds the whole world in the chains of finance capitalism, forces its yoke on the proletarians of all countries, peoples, and races, by starvation, blood, and iron, and intensifies in an immeasurable degree the exploitation, oppression, and enslavement of the proletariat. In so doing, imperialism directly confronts the proletariat with the task of seizing power, and compels the workers to unite closely in a single international army of the proletariat of all countries, irrespective of frontiers and of all differences of nationality, culture, language, race, sex, or occupation. Thus, while developing and completing the process of creating the material prerequisites of socialism, imperialism at the same time mobilizes the army of its own grave-diggers by compelling the proletariat to organize in a militant international workers' association.

On the other hand, imperialism detaches from the great mass of the working class that section whose material circumstances are the most secure. This upper stratum of the working class, bribed and corrupted by imperialism, which constitutes the leading cadres of the social-democratic parties, has an interest in the imperialist exploitation of the colonies, is loyal to 'its' bourgeoisie and 'its' imperialist State, and at decisive moments in the class struggle is to be found in the camp of the class enemies of the proletariat. The split in the socialist movement in 1914 caused by this treachery, and the subsequent treachery of the social-democratic parties, which became bourgeois labour parties, demonstrated clearly that the international proletariat can accomplish its historical mission of smashing the imperialist yoke and establishing the proletarian dictatorship only in relentless struggle against social-democracy. Hence it is only on the communist platform that the forces of world revolution can be organized. In opposition to the opportunist Second International of social-democracy, which had become an agency of imperialism within the working class, there arose inevitably the Third, Communist International, the international organization of the working class, the embodiment of the true unity of the revolutionary workers of the entire world.

The war of 1914–18 gave rise to the first attempts to found a new, revolutionary international as a counterpoise to the Second, social-chauvinist International, and as a weapon of resistance to belligerent imperialism (Zimmerwald, Kienthal). The triumph of the proletarian revolution in Russia provided the impetus to the formation of communist parties in capitalist centres and in the colonies. In 1919 the Communist International was founded, which, for the first time in history, closely unites in the practical revolutionary struggle the vanguard of the European and American proletariat with the proletarians of China and India and the coloured labour slaves of Africa and America.

The Communist International, the united and centralized international party of the proletariat, is the only organization which upholds the principles of the First International in the new context of the revolutionary proletarian mass movement. The lessons of the first imperialist war and of the subsequent period of the revolutionary crisis of capitalism—the series of revolutions in Europe and the colonial countries, the lessons of the proletarian dictatorship and the construction of socialism in the Soviet Union, the lessons of all sections of the Communist International as recorded in the resolutions of its congresses, and finally the increasingly international character assumed by the struggle between the imperialist bourgeoisie and the proletariat—all this makes it essential to have a single programme of the Communist International that is common to all its sections. As the most comprehensive critical generalization of the entire historical experience of the international revolutionary movement of the proletariat, the programme of the Communist International is the programme of the fight for the world proletarian dictatorship, the programme of the struggle for world communism.

Assembling under its banner the revolutionary workers who lead the millions of the enslaved and the exploited against the bourgeoisie and their 'socialist' agents, the Communist International considers itself the executor of the historical legacy of the Communist League and the First International, both led directly by Marx, and as the inheritor of the traditions of the pre-war Second International. The First International established the intellectual premises of the international proletarian struggle for socialism. In its best days the Second International prepared the ground for the broad expansion of the labour movement among the masses. The Third, the Communist International, is continuing the work of the First, it is gathering the fruits of the work of the Second, while resolutely discarding its opportunism and social-chauvinism and its bourgeois distortion of socialism; it has begun to make a reality of the proletarian dictatorship. The Communist International carries on all the glorious and heroic traditions of the international labour movement: the traditions of the English Chartists and the French insurgents of 1831; of the revolutionary workers of Germany and France in 1848; of the immortal fighters and martyrs of the Paris Commune; of the valiant soldiers of the German, Hungarian, and Finnish revolutions, of the workers of the former Tsarist autocracy, the victorious bearers of the proletarian dictatorship; of the traditions of the Chinese proletarians, the heroes of Canton and Shanghai.

In its theoretical and practical work the Communist International, relying on the historical experience of the revolutionary labour movement in all continents and among all peoples, stands unreservedly on the platform of revolutionary Marxism and of the form it took later, Leninism, which is nothing but the Marxism of the epoch of imperialism and the proletarian revolution.

The Communist International champions and propagates the dialectical materialism of Marx and Engels, and employs it as a revolutionary method of perceiving reality, in order to accomplish the revolutionary transformation of that reality; it fights actively against every variety of bourgeois philosophy, and against opportunism in theory and practice. With its platform of consistent proletarian class struggle, it subordinates the temporary, sectional, national, and partial interests of the proletariat to its enduring, general, international interests. It mercilessly exposes the doctrine, borrowed by the reformists from the bourgeoisie, of 'class peace', in all its forms. In meeting the historical demand for an international organization of revolutionary proletarians, the gravedigger of the capitalist system, the Communist International is the only international force that has as its programme the dictatorship of the proletariat and communism, and that comes out openly as the organizer of the international proletarian revolution.

the capitalist world system, its development, and its inevitable destruction

the laws of capitalist dynamics and the epoch of industrial capital

Capitalist society, which arose on the basis of commodity production, is distinguished by the monopoly held by the class of capitalists and large landowners in the most important and decisive means of production, by the exploitation of the wage-labour of the class of proletarians who, deprived of the means of production, are compelled to sell their labour power; it is distinguished by commodity production for profit; and by the planlessness and anarchy of the production process as a whole which this involves. The exploitation relationship and the economic domination of the bourgeoisie are expressed politically in the State, the capitalist organization serving as instrument for the suppression of the proletariat.

The history of capitalism has completely confirmed the Marxist theory of the laws of development of capitalist society and of its contradictions, leading to the destruction of the entire capitalist system.

In their search for profits the bourgeoisie were compelled to expand productive forces on an ever-increasing scale, and to consolidate and extend the dominion of capitalist relations of production. Thus as capitalism developed it constantly reproduced at a higher level all the inherent contradictions of the capitalist system, above all the fundamental contradiction between the social character of labour and the private character of appropriation, between the growth of productive forces and property relations under capitalism. The rule of private property in the means of production and the anarchic course of production combined with the development of the contradiction between the tendency towards the unlimited expansion of production and the restricted consumption of the proletarian masses (general over-production) to disturb the economic equilibrium between the different branches of production; this brought in its train periodically recurring and devastating crises and mass unemployment. The rule of private property was expressed also in competition within each capitalist country and on the steadily expanding world market. This form of capitalist rivalry resulted in a series of wars, the inseparable corollaries of capitalist development.

In the competitive struggle, large-scale production, because of its technical and economic superiority, supplanted and destroyed precapitalist economic forms; capital became more and more concentrated and centralized. In industry the law of concentration and centralization was manifested primarily in the outright ruin of small enterprises, and partly in their degradation to the position of auxiliary units of large enterprises. In agriculture, which, because of the monopoly in land and of absolute rent, necessarily lagged behind the rate of general development, this law of concentration and centralization was manifested not only in the differentiation of the peasantry and the proletarianization of broad peasant strata, but also and above all in the subordination, open and concealed, of small peasant farms to the dictatorship of large capital. The small farm could maintain an appearance of independence only at the price of the most extreme exertion of labour and of systematic underconsumption.

The increasing use of machines, steady technical improvement, and the consequent uninterrupted rise in the organic composition of capital were accompanied by a further division of labour, and by an increase in its productivity and intensity. This resulted in the wider employment of the labour of women and children, and in the creation of enormous industrial reserve armies which were constantly replenished by proletarianized peasants forced out of their villages and by the impoverished petty and middle bourgeoisie of the towns. The division of society into two camps, with a small handful of capitalist magnates at one pole and vast masses of proletarians at the other; the steady rise in the rate of exploitation of the working class; the reproduction on a higher scale of the fundamental contradictions of capitalism and their consequences (crises, wars, etc.); the uninterrupted growth of social inequality; the rising discontent of the proletariat, drawn together and schooled by the process of capitalist production itself—all this undermined the foundations of capitalism and brought the hour of its collapse nearer.

At the same time a profound change occurred in the social and cultural life of capitalist society: the parasitic degeneration of the bourgeois rentier; the general decay of the family as a result of the growing contradictions between the widespread employment of women in social production and the forms of domestic and family life inherited in large part from earlier economic epochs; the growing shallowness and degeneration of intellectual and cultural life as a result of the minute specialization of labour, of the distortions of urban life and the narrowness of rural life; the inability of the bourgeoisie, notwithstanding immense progress in the natural sciences, to achieve the synthesis of a scientific philosophy; the growth of idealistic, mystical, and religious superstitions—all these phenomena proclaimed the approaching historical end of the capitalist system.

the epoch of finance capital (imperialism)

The period when industrial capital was dominant was in the main one of 'free competition', of the relatively steady development and expansion of capitalism over the whole earth, as the colonies that were still free were divided up and occupied by arms. As this happened the inherent contradictions of capitalism grew steadily; their weight bore most heavily on the colonial periphery which was methodically plundered, intimidated, and enslaved.

At the beginning of the twentieth century this period gave place to the period of imperialism, one in which capitalism developed in a series of conflict-ridden leaps and free competition began rapidly to give way to monopoly. In this period, when all formerly 'free' colonies were already appropriated, the disputes concerning a redistribution of colonies and spheres of influence assumed more and more the character of armed struggle.

Thus capitalist contradictions, embracing the whole world, were manifested most clearly in the epoch of imperialism (of finance-capital). Imperialism is a historically new form of capitalism, a new relationship between the various parts of capitalist world economy, a changed form of relations between the primary classes of capitalist society.

This new historical period was the outcome of the operation of the most important laws of motion of capitalist society. It arose out of the development of industrial capitalism and as its historical sequel. In imperialism the basic trends and laws of motion of capitalism, all its fundamental contradictions and antagonisms, stand out more clearly. The law of capital concentration and centralization led to the formation of powerful monopolist associations (cartels, syndicates, trusts) and to a new form of giant undertaking combining several enterprises linked together by the banks. The fusion of industrial and banking capital, the absorption of large landownership into the general system of capitalist organization, and the monopolistic character of this form of capitalism transformed the epoch of industrial capitalism into the epoch of finance-capital. The 'free competition' of the earlier period which had replaced feudal monopoly and the monopoly of trading capital, was now changed into the monopoly of finance-capital. Capitalist monopolies, however, do not eliminate the free competition from which they arose, but exist above and alongside it; this produces a series of exceptionally grave and profound contradictions, frictions, and conflicts.

The growing use of complicated machinery, chemical processes, and electrical power, the higher organic composition of capital on this basis, and the consequent fall in the rate of profit, which can be only temporarily halted by a policy of higher cartel prices favouring the largest monopolist associations, stimulate the quest for colonial super-profits and make the struggle for a new division of the world more acute. Standardized mass production requires new external markets. A feverish search is set on foot for new sources of raw materials and fuel to meet the growing demand. A further impulse is given to the export of capital by the system of high protective tariffs, which makes the export of goods more difficult and ensures super-profits for exported capital. In this way the export of capital becomes the essential and specific form of economic association linking the various parts of capitalist world economy. Lastly, the monopolistic domination of colonial markets, of raw material sources, and of spheres for capitalist investment accentuates the general unevenness of capitalist development to an extreme degree and brings to a head the conflicts among the 'Great Powers' of finance-capital for a redivision of colonies and spheres of influence.

Thus the growth of the productive forces of world economy leads both to a further internationalization of economic life and to a struggle for the re-division of a world already divided up among the most powerful finance-capitalist States. The methods used in this struggle change and grow sharper, price-cutting being replaced more and more by coercive pressure (boycotts, high tariffs, tariff wars, wars in the real meaning of the word, etc). Thus the monopolistic form of capitalism is necessarily accompanied by imperialist wars, which in their scope and the destructive power of their technique are without parallel in history.

the forces of imperialism and the forces of revolution

The imperialist form of capitalism has a tendency to unite the various factions of the ruling class and to bring the broad mass of the proletariat into opposition, not to the individual employer, but more and more to the entire class of capitalists and their State This form of capitalism breaks down the barriers of the national State, which have become too cramping, and expands the domain where the ruling nation among the large capitalist States exercises power. It brings the millions suffering national oppression, the so-called small nations, and the colonial peoples into opposition to this State. Finally, it accentuates to the utmost the contradictions among the imperialist States.

This being the case the State power, as it becomes the dictatorship of the finance-capitalist oligarchy and the expression of its concentrated strength, acquires special importance for the bourgeoisie. The functions of this multinational imperialist State expand in all directions; it develops agencies which facilitate both the struggle for external markets (mobilization of the economy for war) and the struggle against the working class; militarism (land, sea, and air forces, chemical and bacteriological weapons) grows to gigantic proportions; the pressure of the imperialist State on the working class (greater exploitation and outright suppression coupled with a systematic policy of bribing the bureaucratic-reformist upper strata) is heightened. These developments reflect the tremendous growth of the specific weight of State power. In these conditions every more or less important action by the proletariat becomes an action against the power of the State, i.e. it becomes a political act.

In this fashion capitalist development, particularly in its imperialist phase, reproduces the fundamental contradictions of capitalism on an ever-widening scale. Competition among small capitalists ceases only to give way to competition among large capitalists; where this dies down, competition flares up between powerful associations of capitalist magnates and their States; from being local and national, crises spread over several countries and finally become world crises; local wars are succeeded by wars between coalitions of powers and then by world wars; the class struggle loses its character of isolated actions by small groups of workers and takes on national dimensions, turning finally into the international struggle of the world proletariat against the world bourgeoisie. Lastly, the two main revolutionary forces gather in opposition to the powerful concentrated forces of finance-capital—the workers of the capitalist countries and the popular masses of the colonies, held under by foreign capital, who are advancing under the leadership and hegemony of the international revolutionary proletarian movement.

This basic revolutionary tendency is, however, temporarily crippled by the bribery of certain sections of the European, North American, and Japanese proletariat by the imperialist bourgeoisie, and by the treachery of the national bourgeoisie in the colonial and semi-colonial countries who are frightened by the revolutionary movement. Because of their position on the world market (greater technical development, the export of capital to countries with a higher rate of profit, etc.) and their plundering of the colonies and semi-colonies, the bourgeoisie of the imperialist Powers secure additional profits; these they use to raise the wages of a section of 'their' workers, who thus have an interest in the development of capitalism in 'their' fatherland, in the plunder of the colonies, and in loyalty to the imperialist State. This systematic bribery was and is practised in the strongest imperialist countries on an extremely wide scale; it is reflected most strikingly in the ideology and practice of the labour aristocracy and the bureaucratic strata of the working class; that is, the leading cadres of social-democracy and the trades unions, who have shown themselves to be the direct channels for bourgeois influence in the proletariat and the most stalwart pillars of the capitalist system.

While imperialism stimulates the growth of a corrupt upper stratum in the working class, in the long run it undermines their influence in the working class. For the heightening of imperialist contradictions, the worsening of the position of large masses of workers and mass unemployment, the enormous costs of military conflicts, the loss by certain Powers of their monopoly position on world markets, and finally the loss of colonies, etc., undermine the foundations of social-imperialism among the masses. Similarly, the systematic bribery of various strata of the bourgeoisie in the colonies and semi-colonies, their treachery to the national-revolutionary movement, their rapprochement with the imperialist Powers, can only for a time halt the development of the revolutionary crisis. In the long run this brings about more intense imperalist oppression, a decline in the influence of the national bourgeoisie over the popular masses, a more acute revolutionary crisis, the unleashing of a mass peasant agrarian revolution, creating the prerequisites for proletarian hegemony in the struggle of the masses in the colonies and dependent countries for independence and complete national emancipation.

imperialism and the downfall of capitalism

Imperialism has developed the productive forces of world capitalism to a very high degree. It has completed the creation of all the material prerequisites for the socialist organization of society. Imperialist wars show that the productive forces of world economy have outgrown the limits of the imperialist State and require the economy to be organized on an international scale embracing the whole world. Imperialism seeks to resolve this contradiction by paving the way with fire and sword for a single state-capitalist world trust which will organize the entire world economy. The social-democratic ideologues extol this bloody utopia as a peaceful method of the new, 'organized' capitalism. In reality, however, this utopia comes up against such great and insuperable objective obstacles that capitalism must with iron necessity break down under the weight of its own contradictions. The law of the unequal development of capitalism, which operates still more powerfully in the imperialist epoch, makes lasting and firm international combinations of imperialist Powers impossible. Imperialist wars, on the other hand, growing into world wars and marking the road by which capital centralization strives to reach its limit in the single world trust, are accompanied by such devastation, impose such burdens on the working class and on the millions of proletarians and peasants in the colonies, that capitalism must collapse under the blows of the proletarian revolution long before that goal is reached.

Imperialism, the highest phase of capitalist development, immensely increases the productive forces of world economy, shapes the entire world in its own image, and drags all colonies, all races, all peoples into the sphere of finance-capitalist exploitation. At the same time the monopolist form of capital increasingly develops elements of parasitic degeneration and decay, of the decline of capitalism. To a certain extent monopoly capital eliminates the driving force of competition, pursues a policy of high cartel prices and obtains unrestricted control of markets, and thus tends to obstruct the further expansion of productive forces. Imperialism piles up untold wealth from the immense super-profits it squeezes out of the millions of colonial workers and peasants. In this process imperialism creates the type of the decaying, parasitically degenerating rentier State and entire strata of parasites who live by coupon-clipping. The epoch of imperialism, which completes the process of creating the material prerequisites of socialism (concentration of the means of production, socialization of labour on a gigantic scale, the strengthening of workers' organizations) at the same time makes the contradictions between the 'Great Powers' sharper, and provokes wars which result in the breakdown of the single world economy. Thus imperialism is decaying, dying, capitalism. It is the last stage of capitalist development as a whole; it is the onset of the socialist world revolution.

Thus the international proletarian revolution arises from the conditions of capitalist development generally, and specifically from its imperialist phase. The capitalist system as a whole is approaching its final collapse. The dictatorship of finance-capital breaks down and yields to the dictatorship of the proletariat.

the ultimate aim of the communist international—world communism

The ultimate aim of the Communist International is to replace capitalist world economy by a world communist system. Communist society, towards which the entire course of historical development is leading, is the only hope for mankind, for it alone can eliminate the fundamental contradictions of the capitalist system which threaten mankind with degeneration and ruin.

The communist régime will eliminate the division of society into classes; that is to say, by abolishing the anarchy of production it will abolish every kind and form of oppression and of man's exploitation of man. Warring classes will be replaced by a single world commonwealth of labour. For the first time in history mankind will take its fate into its own hands. Instead of destroying countless lives and untold wealth in class wars and national wars, mankind will use all its energies in the struggle with the forces of nature, in developing and raising its own collective strength.

Once having abolished private property in the means of production and made them public property, world communism will replace the spontaneous forces of the world market, the planless sway of competition, the blind operation of social production, by the socially planned regulation of production in accordance with the rapidly growing needs of society. With the anarchy of production and competition abolished, devastating crises and still more devastating wars will disappear. The immense waste of productive forces, the convulsive development of society will be replaced by the ordered disposition of all material wealth and the economy will develop without friction through the unrestricted, harmonious, and rapid development of productive forces.

The abolition of private property, the withering away of classes will put an end to the exploitation of man by man. To work will no longer mean to work for the class enemy. From being nothing more than making a living, it will become the first necessity of life. Poverty will vanish, economic inequality among men will vanish, along with the poverty of the oppressed classes and the wretchedness of material life in general; the hierarchy established by the division of labour will disappear and with it the antagonism between mental and manual labour; lastly, all traces of social inequality between the sexes will disappear. Together with all these, the agencies of class rule will disappear, above all the State. As the embodiment of class rule, it will wither away as classes themselves disappear. Gradually every kind of coercion will die out.

The disappearance of classes will do away with every kind of monopoly in education. Culture will become a common good for all and the class ideologies of the past will be replaced by the scientific-materialist world outlook. This will make the domination of man by man, in whatever form, impossible; undreamed of possibilities of social selection and of the harmonious development of all the capacities dormant in mankind will be opened up.

The expansion of productive forces will not be hampered by any social restrictions. In communist society there will be no place for private property in the means of production, no selfish striving for profit; the masses will not be kept in the poverty and artificial ignorance which obstruct technical progress in capitalist society; the enormous unproductive expenditure characteristic of capitalism will cease. The maximum productivity of social labour will be secured, and incalculable human energies set free for a tremendous development of art and science, by the most expedient utilization of natural forces and natural conditions of production in the different parts of the world, by eliminating the contradiction between town and country which results from the backwardness of agriculture and its low technical level; by the most comprehensive collaboration between science and technology and research, the results being applied for the benefit of society; by the planned organization of scientific work, the introduction of the most up-to-date methods for the statistical analysis and planned regulation of the economy, and, finally, by the rapid growth of social needs, which is the most powerful driving force in the whole system.

By developing the forces of production, communist world society will make it possible to raise the well-being of all mankind and to cut down to the minimum the amount of time devoted to material production; a golden age of culture unparalleled in history will open. In contrast to capitalism, this new culture, of a humanity united for the first time in history, between whom all State frontiers have fallen, will rest upon clear and transparent human relationships. It will bury for ever mysticism and religion, prejudices and superstitions, and so give a powerful impulse to the development of triumphant scientific knowledge.

This highest stage of communism, when communist society has already developed on its own foundations, when, together with the all-round development of man, the social forces of production have made a mighty advance, and society has inscribed on its banner: 'From each according to his abilities, to each according to his needs', presupposes a lower historical stage of development, the socialist stage. At this stage communist society is only beginning to cast off the capitalist shell; it still bears, economically, morally, and intellectually, the birthmarks of the old society from whose womb it emerged. Under socialism productive forces are not developed far enough to enable the products of labour to be distributed according to need. Distribution proceeds rather in accordance with performance. The division of labour, that is, the allocation of certain labour functions to certain groups of people, has not yet been eliminated; in particular, the contradiction between mental and manual labour still persists. Despite the abolition of classes, traces of the old class division of society still survive, and consequently survivals of proletarian State power, of coercion, of law. Some remnants of inequality therefore still exist. The contradiction between town and country remains. But none of these survivals of the old society is any longer protected and defended by any social force. Since they are linked with a definite stage in the development of productive forces, they will disappear as mankind, liberated from the shackles of the capitalist system, rapidly gains control over the forces of nature, educates itself anew in the spirit of communism, and advances from socialism to complete communism.

the period of transition from capitalism to socialism and the proletarian dictatorship

the transition period and the conquest of power by the proletariat

Between capitalist and communist society lies the period of the revolutionary transformation of the one into the other. To it there corresponds a period of political transition, in which the State can be nothing but the revolutionary dictatorship of the proletariat. The transition from the world dictatorship of imperialism to the world dictatorship of the proletariat covers a long period of proletarian struggles, defeats, and victories, a period of the continuing general crisis of capitalism and the maturing of socialist revolutions, that is, of civil wars of the proletariat against the bourgeoisie, a period of national wars and colonial revolts which, while not in themselves socialist movements of the revolutionary proletariat, objectively become a consistent part of the proletarian world revolution to the extent that they shake imperialist rule; a period when capitalist and socialist socio-economic systems exist side by side within world economy, in 'peaceful' relationships as well as in armed conflict; a period of the formation of a union of Socialist Soviet States, a period of the wars of imperialist States against them, a period when the union between these States and the colonial peoples becomes closer and closer, etc.

Unevenness of economic and political development is an absolute law of capitalism, and is even more marked in the imperialist epoch. Hence the international proletarian revolution cannot be conceived as a single act taking place everywhere simultaneously. The victory of socialism is therefore possible at first only in a few capitalist countries, or even in one, but every such victory enlarges the basis of world revolution and makes the general capitalist crisis still more acute. In this way the capitalist system approaches its final breakdown. The dictatorship of finance–capital collapses and yields to the proletarian dictatorship.

While bourgeois revolutions signify no more than political emancipation of a system of production relationships that is already established and economically dominant, and the transfer of power from the hands of one exploiting class to another, the proletarian revolution signifies the violent irruption of the proletariat into the property relations of bourgeois society, the expropriation of the exploiting classes, and the transfer of power into the hands of that class whose mission it is to reshape radically the economic basis of society and to abolish all exploitation of man by man. While bourgeois revolutions took centuries to put an end throughout the world to the political domination of the feudal nobility, which could be destroyed only by a series of separate revolutions, the international proletarian revolution can accomplish its task in a shorter time, because of the closer interdependence of countries, although it is by no means a single event, but extends over an entire epoch. Only with the complete victory of the proletariat throughout the world and the consolidation of its power will the prolonged epoch of the intensive construction of a socialist world economy open.

The conquest of power by the proletariat is the necessary prerequisite for the development of socialist forms of economy and the cultural growth of the proletariat, which will reshape its own nature, become mature enough to guide society in all spheres of human activity, draw the other classes into this process of transformation, and thus create the basis for the abolition of classes altogether.

In the course of the struggle for the proletarian dictatorship and the subsequent refashioning of society, the basis for that dictatorship is created by the alliance of workers and peasants, under the intellectual and political hegemony of the working class, in opposition to the bloc of landowners and capitalists.

The transition period as a whole is characterized by the relentless suppression of the resistance of the exploiters, the organization of socialist construction, the mass retraining of the people in the spirit of socialism, and the gradual elimination of class divisions. Only to the degree in which the society of the transition period fulfils these great historical tasks will it change into communist society.

The dictatorship of the world proletariat is thus the most essential and decisive prerequisite for the transition from capitalist to socialist world economy. This dictatorship can, however, be established only by the victory of socialism in individual countries or groups of countries. The newly arisen proletarian republics will ally themselves with those already in existence, and these federations, drawing in the colonies as they throw off the imperialist yoke, will increase steadily in number and will finally become the World Union of Socialist Soviet Republics, uniting the whole of mankind under the hegemony of the international proletariat organized as a State.

The conquest of power by the proletariat does not mean the peaceful 'capture' of the ready-made bourgeois State machine by means of a parliamentary majority. The bourgeoisie make use of every kind of force and terror to maintain their stolen property and strengthen their political mastery. Like the feudal nobility before them, the bourgeoisie will not give up their place in history to the new class without the most bitter and desperate struggle. The violence of the bourgeoisie can be broken only by the most resolute use of violence by the proletariat. The conquest of power by the proletariat means the violent annihilation of bourgeois power, the destruction of the capitalist State machine (the bourgeois army, police, civil – service hierarchy, courts, parliament, etc.) and its replacement by new agencies of proletarian power, which serve primarily as instruments for the suppression of the exploiters.

the struggle for the world proletarian dictatorship and the principal types of revolution

The international proletarian revolution consists of a series of processes, differing in character and in time: purely proletarian revolutions; revolutions of a bourgeois-democratic type which turn into proletarian revolutions; wars of national liberation, or colonial revolutions. It is only when this development reaches its conclusion that the revolutionary process emerges as the world proletarian dictatorship.

The unequal development of capitalism, accentuated in the epoch of imperialism, has given rise to a great variety of types of capitalism with differing degrees of maturity in different countries, and to a great variety of conditions of the revolutionary process peculiar to each. It follows with historical inevitability that the proletariat will seize power in a variety of ways and with varying degrees of rapidity, and that in a number of countries it will be necessary to pass through a transitional stage to the proletarian dictatorship. It follows further from this that the construction of socialism will assume different forms in different countries.

The varied conditions and roads of the transition to the proletarian dictatorship in different countries may be reduced schematically to the following three types: in highly developed capitalist countries (the United States, Germany, England, etc.), with powerful productive forces, a high degree of centralization of production, relatively insignificant small-scale enterprise, and an old and well-established bourgeois-democratic political régime, the principal political demand of the programme is the direct transition to the proletarian dictatorship. In the economic domain the essential demands are the expropriation of all large concerns, the establishment of a substantial number of Soviet State farms, the transfer of only a relatively small proportion of the land to the peasants, comparatively small scope for the operation of spontaneous market relationships, rapid socialist development in general and very rapid collectivization of peasant farms.

Countries at a medium level of capitalist development (Spain, Portugal, Poland, Hungary, the Balkans, etc.), where semi-feudal relationships largely survive in agriculture, although the material prerequisites for the construction of socialism are present in some degree, the bourgeois-democratic revolution not having been completed: in some of these countries it is possible that the bourgeois-democratic revolution will develop more or less rapidly into the socialist revolution, while in others there may be types of proletarian revolution which will have many tasks of the bourgeois-democratic revolution to accomplish. In the first case it is possible that the proletarian dictatorship will be established not immediately, but only in the course of the transition from the democratic dictatorship of the proletariat and peasantry to the socialist dictatorship of the proletariat, while the second, where the revolution develops as a directly proletarian one, presupposes a broad agrarian and peasant movement led by the proletariat; the agrarian revolution plays a tremendous, sometimes a decisive part. With the expropriation of large estates, a considerable part of the confiscated land is handed over to the peasantry; after the victory of the proletariat market relations prevail over a large area; the task of organizing the peasantry into co-operatives and into large production units is one of the most important of the many tasks of socialist construction. The rate of that construction is relatively slow.

Colonial and semi-colonial countries (China, India, etc.) and independent countries (Argentina, Brazil, etc.): in some of these countries industry is only rudimentary, in others it is fairly well developed, but for the most part insufficient to provide a basis for independent socialist construction; both in the economy as in the political superstructure, medieval feudal relationships prevail, or the 'Asiatic mode of production'; the key industries, the dominant trading, banking, and transportation concerns, as well as plantations, etc., are concentrated in the hands of foreign imperialist groups. In these countries the struggle against feudalism, against pre-capitalist forms of exploitation, the consistent pursuit of the peasant agrarian revolution, and the struggle against foreign imperialism and for national independence are of decisive importance. Here the transition to the proletarian dictatorship is as a rule possible only through a series of preparatory stages, only as the outcome of an entire period of transformation of the bourgeois-democratic into the socialist revolution. In most of these countries the successful construction of socialism is possible only with the direct help of the countries where the proletarian dictatorship is already established.

In still more backward countries (for example in parts of Africa) where there are virtually no industrial wage earners, where the majority of the population live in tribal conditions and traces of the old clan society still survive, where there is practically no national bourgeoisie and foreign imperialism appears primarily as armed conquest and seizure of the land—in these countries the struggle for national liberation is the central task. Here victorious national uprisings may open the road to socialism while by-passing the capitalist stage, if sufficiently powerful help is given by the countries with a proletarian dictatorship.

At a time when, in the advanced capitalist countries, the seizure of power by the proletariat is on the order of the day, while in the Soviet Union the proletarian dictatorship already exists and is a factor of world importance, the liberation movements provoked by the penetration of world capital into the colonial and semi-colonial countries can lead—despite the immaturity of social conditions there if they are regarded in isolation—to socialist development, provided they receive the help and support of the proletarian dictatorship and the international proletarian movement generally.

the struggle for the world proletarian dictatorship and colonial revolutions

The peculiar conditions of the revolutionary struggle in colonial and semi-colonial countries, the inevitability of a prolonged period of struggle for the democratic dictatorship of the proletariat and peasantry and for its development into a proletarian dictatorship, and the decisive importance of the national factor in this contest impose a number of special tasks on the communist parties of these countries; the general tasks of the proletarian dictatorship cannot be mastered before these special tasks are accomplished. The Communist International considers that the most important among them are the following:

1. The overthrow of foreign imperialism, of feudalism, and of the landlord bureaucracy.
2. Establishment of the democratic dictatorship of the proletariat and peasantry on the basis of Soviets.
3. Complete national independence and political unification.
4. Cancellation of State debts.
5. Nationalization of large undertakings (in industry, transport, banking, etc.) belonging to the imperialists.
6. Expropriation of large landowners, of church and monastery estates, nationalization of all land.
7. Introduction of the eight-hour day.
8. Establishment of a revolutionary workers' and peasants' army.

As the struggle continues to develop and to become more acute (sabotage by the bourgeoisie, confiscation of enterprises belonging to the sabotaging sections of the bourgeoisie, which is bound to develop into the nationalization of large-scale industry), the bourgeois-democratic revolution, consistently pursued, will be transformed into the proletarian revolution in those colonies and semi-colonies where the proletariat acts as leader and exercises hegemony over the movement. In colonies without a proletariat the overthrow of imperialist power must be accompanied by the organization of a popular (peasant) Soviet régime, the confiscation of businesses and land owned by foreigners, and the transfer of this property to the State.

Colonial revolutions and national liberation movements play an extremely important part in the struggle against imperialism and the conquest of power by the working class. In the transition period colonies and semi-colonies are also important because they represent the village on a world scale *vis-à-vis* the industrial countries, which represent the town in the context of world economy. Hence the problem of organizing a socialist world economy, of the correct combination of industry and agriculture, resolves itself to a large extent into the question of relations with the former colonies of imperialism. To establish a fraternal militant alliance with the working masses of the colonies is therefore one of the principal tasks of the industrial world proletariat as leader and hegemon in the fight against imperialism.

The course of the world revolution drives the workers of the imperialist States into the fight for the proletarian dictatorship, and at the same time rouses hundreds of millions of colonial workers and peasants to the struggle against foreign imperialism. Once centres of socialism exist, in the form of socialist Soviet republics with steadily growing economic power, the colonies which have broken away from imperialism draw nearer, economically, to the industrial centres of world socialism and gradually unite with them. Drawn in this way into the path of socialist construction, and by-passing the stages of development when capitalism is the dominant system, they can make rapid economic and cultural progress. Peasant Soviets in the backward ex-colonies, and workers' and peasant' Soviets in the more advanced, will gravitate politically towards the centres of proletarian dictatorship and will in this way be drawn into the general system of the ever-expanding federation of Soviet republics and the world dictatorship of the proletariat.

Socialism, as the new mode of production, will thus develop on a world scale.

the colonial countries and the chinese revolution

The general crisis of the international capitalist system is most clearly expressed today in the revolts and revolutions of the colonial and semi-colonial countries. . . .

The most important of these, an event of epochal importance, is the Chinese revolution. In its immediate scope it covers tens of millions, and indirectly hundreds of millions, a gigantic mass which for the first time is taking up in such strength the battle against imperialism. China's close links with Indochina and India immensely increase the significance of the revolution there. The entire course of this revolution, its democratic character, its inevitable transformation into a proletarian revolution, are bound to make clear to the entire world proletariat its international importance in all its immensity.

As an anti-imperialist movement for national liberation, the Chinese revolution is at the present stage, according to its objective content, a bourgeois-democratic revolution which will inevitably become a proletarian revolution. As it developed . . . the national bourgeoisie (the Kuomintang) in a series of upheavals at last landed in the counter-revolutionary camp, and made an alliance with the feudalists and an agreement with the imperialists. Therefore the struggle against imperialism is inseparably bound up with the struggle for the land and the fight against the counter-revolutionary bourgeoisie. . . .

These tasks can be accomplished only if the broad peasant masses, under the leadership and hegemony of the Chinese proletariat, carry through a successful insurrection. The main features of the Chinese revolution at its present stage are that the bloc of imperialists, feudalists, and bourgeoisie has, despite its internal contradictions, inflicted severe defeats on the proletariat and the peasantry and physically destroyed a large part of the communist party cadres. The labor movement has not yet fully recovered from its defeats. On the other hand the peasant movement is advancing in a number of areas. Where peasant insurrections were victorious, organs of peasant power have been set up, in some cases peasant Soviets. The communist party is growing and consolidating; its authority and influence among the masses are growing. . . .

The Chinese Communist Party has suffered a number of severe defeats, which are to be attributed to a series of grave opportunist errors in the past, to the lack of independence and freedom to criticize *vis-à-vis* the Kuomintang, to the failure to understand the transition from one stage of the revolution to the next and the need for prompt preparations for defence, and, finally, to the braking of the agrarian revolution. Under the blows of defeat the heroic party corrected these mistakes and declared a relentless war on opportunism. Its leaders, however, fell into another error and did not put up enough resistance to openly putschist, adventurist sentiments which led to abortive revolts in Hunan, Hupeh, &c. . . .

THE PROGRAM OF THE INTERNATIONAL REVOLUTION OR A PROGRAM OF SOCIALISM IN ONE COUNTRY? – SELECTIONS

● *leon trotsky*

The most important question on the agenda of the Sixth Congress is the adoption of a program. The nature of the latter may for a long time determine and fix the physiognomy of the International. The importance of a program does not lie so much in the manner in which it formulates general theoretical conceptions (in the last analysis, this boils down to a question of "codification," i.e., a concise exposition of the truths and generalizations which have been firmly and decisively acquired); it is to a much greater degree a question of drawing up the balance of the world economic and political experiences of the last period, particularly of the revolutionary struggles of the last five years—so rich in events and mistakes. For the next few years, the fate of the Communist International—in the literal sense of the word—depends upon the manner in which these events, mistakes, and controversies are interpreted and judged in the program.

the general structure of the program

In our epoch, which is the epoch of imperialism, i.e., of *world* economy and *world* politics under the hegemony of finance capital, not a single communist party can establish its program by proceeding solely or mainly from conditions and tendencies of developments in its own country. This also holds entirely for the party that wields the state power within the boundaries of the U.S.S.R. On August 4, 1914, the death knell sounded for national programs for all time. The revolutionary party of the proletariat can base itself only upon an international program corresponding to the character of the present epoch, the epoch of the highest development and collapse of capitalism. An international communist program is in no case the sum total of national programs or an amalgam of their common features. The international program must proceed directly from an analysis of the conditions and tendencies of world economy and of the world political system taken as a whole in all its connections and contradictions, that is, with the mutually antagonistic interdependence of its separate parts. In the present epoch, to a much larger extent than in the past, the national orientation of the proletariat must and can flow only from a world orientation and not *vice versa*. Herein lies the basic and primary difference between communist internationalism and all varieties of national socialism. . . .

the criterion of internationalism

The draft, as we already know, seeks to proceed in its construction from the standpoint of world economy and its internal tendencies—an attempt which merits recognition. *Pravda* is absolutely correct in saying that herein lies the basic difference in principle between us and the national-patriotic social democracy. A program of the international party of the proletariat can be built only if world economy, which dominates its separate parts, is taken as the point of departure. But precisely in analyzing the main tendencies of world development, the draft not only reveals inadequacies which depreciate its value . . . but it also is grossly one-sided, which leads it to commit grave blunders.

The draft refers time and again, and not always in the proper place, to the law of uneven development of capitalism as the main and almost all-determining law of that development. A number of mistakes in the draft, including one fundamental error, are theoretically based on the one-sided and false non-Marxian and non-Leninist interpretation of the law of uneven development.

In its first chapter the draft states that "the unevenness of economic and political development is an unconditional law of capitalism. This unevenness becomes still more accentuated and aggravated in the epoch of imperialism."

This is correct. This formulation in part condemns Stalin's recent formulation of the question, according to which both Marx and Engels were ignorant of the law of uneven development which was allegedly first discovered by Lenin. On September 15, 1925, Stalin wrote that Trotsky has no reason whatever to refer to Engels because the latter wrote at a time "when there could be *no talk* [!!] about the knowledge of the law of uneven development of capitalist countries." Unbelievable as these words may be, Stalin, one of the authors of the draft, has nevertheless repeated them more than once. The text of the draft, as we have seen, has taken a step forward in this respect. However, if we leave aside the correction of this elementary mistake, what the draft says about the law of uneven development remains in essence one-sided and inadequate.

In the first place, it would have been more correct to say that the entire history of mankind is governed by the law of uneven development. Capitalism finds various sections of mankind at different stages of development, each with its profound internal contradictions. The extreme diversity in the levels attained, and the extraordinary unevenness in the rate of development of the different sections of mankind during the various epochs, serve as the *starting point* of capitalism. Capitalism gains mastery only gradually over the inherited unevenness, breaking and altering it, employing therein its own means and methods. In contrast to the economic systems which preceded it, capitalism inherently and constantly aims at economic expansion, at the penetration of new territories, the surmounting of economic differences, the conversion of self-sufficient provincial and national economies into a system of financial interrelationships. Thereby it brings about their *rapprochement* and equalizes the economic and cultural levels of the most progressive and the most backward countries. Without this main process, it would be impossible to conceive of the relative leveling out, first, of Europe with Great Britain, and then, of America with Europe; the industrialization of the colonies, the diminishing gap between India and Great Britain, and all the consequences arising from the enumerated processes upon which is based not only the program of the Communist International but also its very existence.

By drawing the countries economically closer to one another and leveling out their stages of development, capitalism, however, operates by methods of *its own,* that is to say, by anarchistic methods which constantly undermine its own work, set one country against another, and one branch of industry against another, developing some parts of world economy while hampering and throwing back the development of others. Only the correlation of these two fundamental tendencies—both of which arise from the nature of capitalism—explains to us the living texture of the historical process.

Imperialism, thanks to the universality, penetrability, and mobility and the break-neck speed of the formation of finance capital as the driving force of imperialism, lends vigor to *both these tendencies.* Imperialism links up incomparably more rapidly and more deeply the individual national and continental units into a single entity, bringing them into the closest and most vital dependence upon each other and rendering their economic methods, social forms, and levels of development more identical. At the same time, it attains this "goal" by such antagonistic methods, such tiger-leaps, and such raids upon backward countries and areas that the unification and leveling of world economy which it has effected, is upset by it even more violently and convulsively than in the preceding epochs. Only such a dialectical and not purely mechanical understanding of the law of uneven development can make possible the avoidance of the fundamental error which the draft program, submitted to the Sixth Congress, has failed to avoid.

Immediately after its one-sided characterization of the law of uneven development pointed out by us, the draft program says:

"Hence it follows that the international proletarian revolution must not be regarded as a single, simultaneous, and universal act. Hence it follows that the victory of socialism is at first possible in a few, or even in one isolated capitalist country."

That the international revolution of the proletariat cannot be a simultaneous act, of this there can of course be no dispute at all among grown-up people after the experience of the October Revolution, achieved by the proletariat of a backward country under pressure of historical necessity, without waiting in the least for the proletariat of the advanced countries "to even out the front." Within these limits, the reference to the law of uneven development is absolutely correct and quite in place. But it is entirely otherwise with the second half of the conclusion—namely, the hollow assertion that the victory of socialism is possible "in one isolated capitalist country." To prove its point the draft program simply says: "Hence it follows. . . ." One gets the impression that this follows from the law of uneven development. But this does not follow at all. "Hence follows" something quite the contrary. If the historical process were such that some countries developed not only unevenly but even *independently of each other,* isolated from each other, then from the law of uneven development would indubitably follow the possibility of building socialism in one capitalist country—at first in the most advanced country and then, as they mature, in the more backward ones. Such was the customary and, so to speak, average idea of the transition to socialism within the ranks of the pre-war social democracy. This is precisely the idea that formed the theoretical basis of social-patriotism. Of course, the draft program does not hold this view. But it inclines towards it. . . .

The theoretical error of the draft lies in the fact that it seeks to deduce from the law of uneven development something which the law does not and cannot imply. Uneven or sporadic development of various countries acts constantly to *upset* but in no case to *eliminate* the growing economic bonds and interdependence between those countries which the very next day, after four years of hellish slaughter, were compelled to exchange coal, bread, oil, powder, and suspenders with each other. On this point, the draft posits the question as if historical development proceeds only on the basis of sporadic leaps, while the economic basis which gives rise to these leaps, and upon which they occur, is either left entirely out of sight by the authors of the draft, or is forcibly eliminated by them. This they do with the sole object of defending the indefensible theory of socialism in one country.

After what has been said it is not difficult to understand that the only correct formulation of the question should read that Marx and Engels, even prior to the imperialist epoch, had arrived at the conclusion that on the one hand, unevenness, i.e., sporadic historical development, stretches the proletarian revolution through an entire epoch in the course of which nations will enter the revolutionary flood one after another; while on the other hand, the organic interdependence of the several countries, developing toward an international division of labor, excludes the possibility of building socialism in one country. This means that the Marxian doctrine, which posits that the socialist revolution can begin only on a national basis, while the building of socialism in one country is impossible, has been rendered *doubly and trebly true,* all the more so now, in the modern epoch when imperialism has developed, deepened, and sharpened *both* of these antagonistic tendencies. On this point, Lenin merely developed and concretized Marx's own formulation and Marx's own answer to this question.

Our party program is based entirely upon the international conditions underlying the October Revolution and the socialist construction. . . .

the contradiction between the productive forces and the national boundaries as the cause of the reactionary utopian theory of "socialism in one country"

The basis for the theory of socialism in one country, as we have seen, sums up to sophistic interpretations of several lines from Lenin on the one hand, and to a scholastic interpretation of the "law of uneven development" on the other. By giving a correct interpretation of the historic law as well as of the quotations in question we arrive at a directly opposite conclusion, that is, the conclusion that was reached by Marx, Engels, Lenin, and all of us, including Stalin and Bukharin, up to 1925.

From the uneven sporadic development of capitalism flows the non-simultaneous, uneven, and sporadic character of the socialist revolution; from the extreme tensity of the interdependence of the various countries upon each other flows not only the political but also the economic impossibility of building socialism in one country.

Let us examine once again from this angle the text of the program a little closer. We have already read in the introduction that:

"Imperialism . . . aggravates to an exceptional degree the contradiction between the growth of the national productive forces of world economy and national state barriers."

We have already stated that this proposition is, or rather was meant to be, the keystone of the international program. But it is precisely this proposition which excludes, rejects, and sweeps away *a priori* the theory of socialism in one country as a reactionary theory because it is irreconcilably opposed not only to the fundamental *tendency* of development of the productive forces but also to the *material results* which have already been attained by this development. The productive forces are incompatible with national boundaries. Hence flow not only foreign trade, the export of men and capital, the seizure of territories, the colonial policy, and the last imperialist war, but also the economic impossibility of a self-sufficient socialist society. The productive forces of *capitalist* countries have long since broken through the national boundaries. Socialist society, however, can be built only on the most advanced productive forces, on the application of electricity and chemistry to the processes of production including agriculture; on combining, generalizing, and bringing to maximum development the highest elements of modern technology. From Marx on, we have been constantly repeating that capitalism cannot cope with the spirit of new technology to which it has given rise and which tears asunder not only the integument of bourgeois private property rights but, as the war of 1914 has shown, also the national hoops of the bourgeois state. Socialism, however, must not only take over from capitalism the most highly developed productive forces but must immediately carry them onward, raise them to a higher level and give them a state of development such as has been unknown under capitalism. The question arises: how then can socialism drive the productive forces back into the boundaries of a national state which they have violently sought to break through under capitalism? Or, perhaps, we ought to abandon the idea of "unbridled" productive forces for which the national boundaries, *and consequently also the boundaries of the theory of socialism in one country,* are too narrow, and limit ourselves, let us say, to the curbed and domesticated productive forces, that is, to the technology of economic backwardness? If this is the case, then in many branches of industry we should stop making progress right now and decline to a level even lower than our present pitiful technical level which managed to link up bourgeois Russia with world economy in an inseparable bond and to bring it into the vortex of the imperialist war for an *expansion of its territory for the productive forces* that had outgrown the state boundaries.

Having inherited and restored these productive forces the workers' state is *compelled* to import and export.

The trouble is that the draft program injects mechanically into its text the thesis of the incompatibility of modern capitalist technology with the national boundaries, and then the argument proceeds as if there were no question at all of this incompatibility. Essentially the whole draft is a combination of ready-made revolutionary theses taken from Marx and Lenin and of opportunist or centrist conclusions which are absolutely incompatible with these revolutionary theses. That is why it is necessary *without becoming allured by the isolated revolutionary formulas contained in the draft* to watch closely *whither its main tendencies lead.*

the question can be solved only on the arena of world revolution

The new doctrine proclaims that socialism can be built on the basis of a national state *if only there is no intervention.* From this there can and must follow (notwithstanding all pompous declarations in the draft program) a collaborationist policy towards the foreign bourgeoisie with the object of averting intervention, as this will guarantee the construction of socialism, that is to say, will solve the main historical question. The task of the parties in the Comintern assumes, therefore, an auxiliary character; their mission is to protect the U.S.S.R. from intervention and not to fight for the conquest of power. It is, of course, not a question of the subjective intentions but of the objective logic of political thought.

"The difference in views lies in the fact," says Stalin, "that the party considers that these [internal] contradictions and possible *conflicts can be entirely overcome* on the basis of the inner forces of our revolution, whereas comrade Trotsky and the Opposition think that these contradictions and conflicts can be overcome 'only on an international scale, on the arena of the world-wide proletarian revolution.' " (*Pravda,* No. 262, Nov. 12, 1926.)

Yes, this is precisely the difference. One could not express better and more correctly the difference between national reformism and revolutionary internationalism. If our internal difficulties, obstacles, and contradictions, which are fundamentally a reflection of world contradictions, can be settled merely by "the inner forces of our revolution" without entering "the arena of the world-wide proletarian revolution" then the International is partly a subsidiary and partly a decorative institution, the Congress of which can be convoked once every four years, once every ten years, or perhaps not at all. Even if we were to add that the proletariat of the other countries must protect our construction from military interventions, the International according to this schema must play the role of a *pacifist* instrument. Its main role, the role of an instrument of world revolution, is then inevitably relegated to the background.

 And this, we repeat, does not flow from anyone's deliberate intentions (on the contrary, a number of points in the program testify to the very best intentions of its authors), but it does flow from the internal logic of the new theoretical position which is a thousand times more dangerous than the worst subjective intentions. . . .

the theory of socialism in one country as a series of social patriotic blunders

The theory of socialism in one country inexorably leads to an underestimation of the difficulties which must be overcome and to an exaggeration of the achievements gained. One could not find a more anti-socialist and anti-revolutionary assertion than Stalin's statement to the effect that "socialism has already been 90 percent realized in the U.S.S.R." This statement seems to be especially meant for a smug bureaucrat. In this way one can hopelessly discredit the idea of a socialist society in the eyes of the toiling masses. The Soviet proletariat has achieved grandiose successes, if we take into consideration the conditions under which they have been attained and the low cultural level inherited from the past. But these achievements constitute an extremely small magnitude on the scales of the socialist ideal. Harsh truth and not sugary falsehood is needed to fortify the worker, the agricultural laborer, and the poor peasant, who see that in the eleventh year of the revolution, poverty, misery, unemployment, bread lines, illiteracy, homeless children, drunkenness, and prostitution have not abated around them. Instead of telling them fibs about having realized 90% socialism, we must say to them that our economic level, our social and cultural conditions, approximate today much closer to capitalism, and a backward and uncultured capitalism at that, than to socialism. We must tell them that we will enter on the path of *real* socialist construction only when the proletariat of the most advanced countries will have captured power; that it is necessary to work unremittingly for this, using both levers—the short lever of our internal economic efforts and the long lever of the international proletarian struggle. . . .

To be sure, this perspective does not harmonize with the pedantic and schematic conceptions concerning the interrelations between economics and politics. But the responsibility for this disharmony so disturbing to the prejudices which have newly taken root and which were already dealt a not inconsiderable blow by the October Revolution must be placed not on "Trotskyism" but on the *law of uneven development*. In this particular case this law is especially applicable.

It would be unwise pedantry to maintain that, had a Bolshevik policy been applied in the revolution of 1925–1927, the Chinese Communist Party would *unfailingly* have come to power. But it is contemptible philistinism to assert that such a possibility was entirely out of the question. The mass movement of workers and peasants was on a scale entirely adequate for this, as was also the disintegration of the ruling classes. The national bourgeoisie sent its Chiang Kai-sheks and Wang Ching-weis as envoys to Moscow, and through its Hu Han-mins knocked at the door of the Comintern, precisely because it was hopelessly weak in face of the revolutionary masses; it realized its weakness and sought to insure itself. Neither the workers nor the peasants would have followed the national bourgeoisie if we ourselves had not dragged them by a rope. Had the Comintern pursued any sort of correct policy, the outcome of the struggle of the communist party for the masses would have been predetermined—the Chinese proletariat would have supported the communists, while the peasant war would have supported the revolutionary proletariat. . . .

PERMANENT REVOLUTION

● *leon trotsky*

basic postulates

1. The theory of the permanent revolution now demands the greatest attention from every Marxist, for the course of the class and ideological struggle has fully and finally raised this question from the realm of reminiscences over old differences of opinion among Russian Marxists, and converted it into a question of the character, the inner connexions and methods of the international revolution in general.

2. With regard to countries with a belated bourgeois development, especially the colonial and semi-colonial countries, the theory of the permanent revolution signifies that the complete and genuine solution of their tasks of achieving *democracy and national emancipation* is conceivable only through the dictatorship of the proletariat as the leader of the subjugated nation, above all of its peasant masses.

3. Not only the agrarian, but also the national question assigns to the peasantry—the overwhelming majority of the population in backward countries—an exceptional place in the democratic revolution. Without an alliance of the proletariat with the peasantry the tasks of the democratic revolution cannot be solved, nor even seriously posed. But the alliance of these two classes can be realized in no other way than through an irreconcilable struggle against the influence of the national-liberal bourgeoisie.

4. No matter what the first episodic stages of the revolution may be in the individual countries, the realization of the revolutionary alliance between the proletariat and the peasantry is conceivable only under the political leadership of the proletarian vanguard, organized in the Communist Party. This in turn means that the victory of the democratic revolution is conceivable only through the dictatorship of the proletariat which bases itself upon the alliance with the peasantry and solves first of all the tasks of the democratic revolution.

5. Assessed historically, the old slogan of Bolshevism—'the democratic dictatorship of the proletariat and peasantry'—expressed precisely the above-characterized relationship of the proletariat, the peasantry and the liberal bourgeoisie. This has been confirmed by the experience of October. But Lenin's

 old formula did not settle in advance the problem of what the reciprocal relations would be between the proletariat and the peasantry within the revolutionary bloc. In other words, the formula deliberately retained a certain algebraic quality, which had to make way for more precise arithmetical quantities in the process of historical experience. However, the latter showed, and under circumstances that exclude any kind of misinterpretation, that no matter how great the revolutionary rôle of the peasantry may be, it nevertheless cannot be an independent rôle and even less a leading one. The peasant follows either the worker or the bourgeois. This means that the 'democratic dictatorship of the proletariat and peasantry' is only conceivable as a *dictatorship of the proletariat that leads the peasant masses behind it.*

6. A democratic dictatorship of the proletariat and peasantry, as a régime that is distinguished from the dictatorship of the proletariat by its class content, might be realized only in a case where an *independent* revolutionary party could be constituted, expressing the interests of the peasants and in general of petty-bourgeois democracy—a party capable of conquering power with this or that degree of aid from the proletariat, and of determining its revolutionary programme. As all modern history attests—especially the Russian experience of the last twenty-five years—an insurmountable obstacle on the road to the creation of a peasants' party is the petty-bourgeoisie's lack of economic and political independence and its deep internal differentiation. By reason of this the upper sections of the petty-bourgeoisie (of the peasantry) go along with the big bourgeoisie in all decisive cases, especially in war and in revolution; the lower sections go along with the proletariat; the intermediate section being thus compelled to choose between the two extreme poles. Between Kerenskyism and the Bolshevik power, between the Kuomintang and the dictatorship of the proletariat, there is not and cannot be any intermediate stage, that is, no democratic dictatorship of the workers and peasants.

7. The Comintern's endeavour to foist upon the Eastern countries the slogan of the democratic dictatorship of the proletariat and peasantry, finally and long ago exhausted by history, can have only a reactionary effect. Insofar as this slogan is counterposed to the slogan of the dictatorship of the proletariat, it contributes politically to the dissolution of the proletariat in the petty-bourgeois masses and thus creates the most favourable conditions for the hegemony of the national bourgeoisie and consequently for the collapse of the democratic revolution. The introduction of this slogan into the programme of the Comintern is a direct betrayal of Marxism and the October tradition of Bolshevism.

8. The dictatorship of the proletariat which has risen to power as the leader of the democratic revolution is inevitably and very quickly confronted with tasks, the fulfilment of which is bound up with deep inroads into the rights of bourgeois property. The democratic revolution grows over directly into the socialist revolution and thereby becomes a *permanent* revolution.

9. The conquest of power by the proletariat does not complete the revolution, but only opens it. Socialist construction is conceivable only on the foundation of the class struggle, on a national and international scale. This struggle, under the conditions of an overwhelming predominance of capitalist relationships on the world arena, must inevitably lead to explosions, that is, internally to civil wars and externally to revolutionary wars. Therein lies the permanent character of the socialist revolution as such, regardless of whether it is a backward country that is involved, which only yesterday accomplished its dem-

ocratic revolution, or an old capitalist country which already has behind it a long epoch of democracy and parliamentarism.

10. The completion of the socialist revolution within national limits is unthinkable. One of the basic reasons for the crisis in bourgeois society is the fact that the productive forces created by it can no longer be reconciled with the framework of the national state. From this follow, on the one hand, imperialists wars, on the other, the utopia of a bourgeois United States of Europe. The socialist revolution begins on the national arena, it unfolds on the international arena, and it completed on the world arena. Thus, the socialist revolution becomes a permanent revolution in a newer and broader sense of the word; it attains completion only in the final victory of the new society on our entire planet.

11. The above-outlined sketch of the development of the world revolution eliminates the question of countries that are 'mature' and 'immature' for socialism in the spirit of that pedantic, lifeless classification given by the present programme of the Comintern. Insofar as capitalism has created a world market, a world division of labour and world productive forces, it has also prepared world economy as a whole for socialist transformation.

Different countries will go through this process at different tempos. Backward countries may, under certain conditions, arrive at the dictatorship of the proletariat sooner than advanced countries, but they will come later than the latter to socialism.

A backward colonial or semi-colonial country, the proletariat of which is insufficiently prepared to unite the peasantry and take power, is thereby incapable of bringing the democratic revolution to its conclusion. Contrariwise, in a country where the proletariat has power in its hands as the result of the democratic revolution, the subsequent fate of the dictatorship and socialism depends in the last analysis not only and not so much upon the national productive forces as upon the development of the international socialist revolution.

12. The theory of socialism in one country, which rose on the yeast of the reaction against October, is the only theory that consistently and to the very end opposes the theory of the permanent revolution.

The attempt of the epigones, under the lash of our criticism, to confine the application of the theory of socialism in one country exclusively to Russia, because of its specific characteristics (its vastness and its natural resources), does not improve matters but only makes them worse. The break with the internationalist position always and invariably leads to national *messianism*, that is, to attributing special superiorities and qualities to one's own country, which allegedly permit it to play a rôle to which other countries cannot attain.

The world division of labour, the dependence of Soviet industry upon foreign technology, the dependence of the productive forces of the advanced countries of Europe upon Asiatic raw materials, etc., etc., make the construction of an independent socialist society in any single country in the world impossible.

13. The theory of Stalin and Bukharin, running counter to the entire experience of the Russian revolution, not only sets up the democratic revolution mechanically in contrast to the socialist revolution, but also makes a breach between the national revolution and the international revolution.

This theory imposes upon revolutions in backward countries the task of establishing an unrealizable régime of democratic dictatorship, which it counterposes to the dictatorship of the proletariat. Thereby this theory introduces illusions and fictions into politics, paralyses the struggle for power of the proletariat in the East, and hampers the victory of the colonial revolution.

The very seizure of power by the proletariat signifies, from the standpoint of the epigones' theory, the completion of the revolution ('to the extent of nine-tenths', according to Stalin's formula) and the opening of the epoch of national reforms. The theory of the kulak growing into socialism and the theory of the 'neutralization' of the world bourgeoisie are consequently inseparable from the theory of socialism in one country. They stand or fall together.

By the theory of national socialism, the Communist International is downgraded to an auxiliary weapon useful only for the struggle against military intervention. The present policy of the Comintern, its régime and the selection of its leading personnel correspond entirely to the demotion of the Communist International to the rôle of an auxiliary unit which is not destined to solve independent tasks.

14. The programme of the Comintern created by Bukharin is eclectic through and through. It makes the hopeless attempt to reconcile the theory of socialism in one country with Marxist internationalism, which is, however, inseparable from the permanent character of the world revolution. The struggle of the Communist Left Opposition for a correct policy and a healthy régime in the Communist International is inseparably bound up with the struggle for the Marxist programme. The question of the programme is in turn inseparable from the question of the two mutually exclusive theories: the theory of permanent revolution and the theory of socialism in one country. The problem of the permanent revolution has long ago outgrown the episodic differences of opinion between Lenin and Trotsky, which were completely exhausted by history. The struggle is between the basic ideas of Marx and Lenin on the one side and the eclecticism of the centrists on the other.

REVOLUTIONARY PRACTICE

Saint Augustine held that one could properly be a theologian only by first being a devout Christian. So, too, throughout history, revolutionaries have defined their faith by putting it into practice, seeking to separate those revolutionary principles which have universal applicability from those which can be profitably employed only in specific places at specific times. In "The Science of Revolutions and the Art of Making Them," George Novak illustrates how the Russian revolution of 1917 tested Marx's theory of revolution and found that it worked. Peter Camejo, like Novack a Trotskyist, argues in "How to Make a Revolution in the United States" that despite differences in place and time, the Bolshevik experience remains essentially the best practical model for changing the basic structure of the United States and hence the world. Eldridge Cleaver, in an interview from exile, relates world revolution to repression in America's Black community. In "How to Commit Revolution in Corporate America," G. William Domhoff contends that within whatever plans revolutionaries make—and they must have a plan—they must take into account certain psychological foundations of modern life. They must employ "psychic guerrilla warfare" to convince all manner of people from New Left to New Right that the establishment of a socialist society is in their best psychological and material interests. Vo Nguyen Giap, a consummate practitioner of real physical guerrilla warfare, explains in "Our People Will Certainly Defeat the U. S. Imperialist Aggressors" why he thinks that the fighting tactics of the National Liberation Front of South Vietnam and of the Army of the Democratic Republic of Vietnam will necessarily lead toward victory for socialist forces within his country. Giap points out that the struggle for Vietnamese national liberation, already in progress for over a quarter of a century, has slowly achieved victory after victory, has consolidated those victories, and is sure to win once again, whatever the odds. The defeat of Che Guevara's guerrilla *foco* in Bolivia has cast some doubt upon the general efficacy of using guerrilla warfare as a prime instrument in revolution, and few revolutionary theoreticians would call for guerrilla actions as a central overall revolutionary tactic (for the major exception see the essay by Régis Debray in Section IV). But in the final selection, Inti Peredo, successor to Che in Bolivia, argues that guerrilla type activity is necessary to some significant degree for the success of the revolution.

THE SCIENCE OF REVOLUTIONS AND THE ART OF MAKING THEM

● *george novack*

The tremendous tasks of combating the colossus of imperialism on its home grounds and promoting the socialist transformation of society require a revolutionary party equipped with a Marxist policy. Revolutionary policy has to do with the practical aspects of carrying forward the class struggle. It seeks the most effective ways and means of speeding up the processes of revolutionary change and conducting them to a victorious conclusion on a national- and world-historical scale.

The solution of such problems depends upon another equally important side of the revolutionary movement—the theory of the class struggle which has been most correctly and comprehensively formulated by Marxism. The whole art of working-class leadership consists in harmonizing scientific inquiry into the social and political conditions of our time with revolutionary practice.

Even though existentialists, irrationalists, spontaneists and empiricists would deny its existence or efficacy, such a branch of knowledge as the science of revolution does exist. This sort of learning does not bear a special name, like biology, the science of life, or sociology, the science of social development. Very few if any courses on this subject are given by the faculties of the universities and I have yet to hear of a professor with a PhD in this specialty.

Fortunately for the emancipation of mankind, not all the knowledge about social and political phenomena is confined to or concentrated in official institutions of learning. There have been and there are today experts in this line of endeavor, people who have devoted a lifetime of study to its intricacies and applied themselves to putting into effect what they found out.

Some have met with conspicuous success. Few on either side of the contending class camps would dispute the judgment that Marx and Engels, Lenin and Trotsky, Castro and Guevara—to name only three of the top teams—exercised considerable influence upon the thought and action of their time and have all shaped the destiny of modern society. These men were preeminent practitioners of the science of revolution, proletarian-style. Before the October 1917 revolution the Mensheviks used to deride the Bolsheviks as mere "technicians of revolution" because their leadership insisted that the cadres persistently prepare for a decisive confrontation with the régime. However, when that showdown came, Lenin's school of Bolshevism demonstrated that constant study, acquisition of skills and organizational preadaptation to the demands of revolutionary struggle pay off.

The December 6, 1969, *New Yorker* magazine carried a two-page advertisement by Olin, one of the huge multinational corporations that control the United States and a large part of this planet. One page featured a bust of Karl Marx; the headline on the opposite page read: "If Africa, Asia and South America go communist, don't blame him."

The copywriter went on to say: "Karl Marx is not responsible for famines in Asia or epidemics in Africa. It's not his fault that the average South American earns 75 cents a day.

"All he did was predict the consequences.

 "That a population living in misery will turn to communism as a way out. Unless something is done to alleviate these conditions.

"But the countries themselves don't have the economic resources to make these changes. The U. N. doesn't. Even the United States doesn't.

"They need the help of world industry. Particularly U. S. industry."

This advertisement explicitly counterposes the gospel of monopolist domination and capitalist counter-revolution to the socialist science of revolutionary mass struggle. However, in the injunction to leave the job of defusing the colonial revolution to the corporate profiteers, this arms manufacturer neglects to mention that big business could not carry on the "good deeds of industry" Olin boasts of without the constant surveillance and occasional military interventions in Africa, Asia and Latin America of its chief consumer, the Pentagon.

The science of revolution is a branch of the science of politics. I need hardly say that this has very faint resemblance to the political science courses taught in the colleges. Real politics deals with the class struggle and the power of the state, not with efforts to deny and obfuscate these crucial factors. Theoretical reflection on this important activity of civilized humanity is fairly old as social sciences go, dating back to the ancient Greeks of the sixth to the fourth centuries B. C.

Nowadays the science of politics pivots around the making—or the breaking—of the proletarian struggle for supremacy which is aimed at the overthrow of capitalism and the construction of a new social order. This epoch of socialist revolutions, which began with the Russian revolution of October 1917 and has already passed the half-century mark, is still in its early stages. Its decisive battles on a global scale have yet to be fought and won.

Those who are going to participate in the most crucial of these battles, which will take place on North American soil, need a deeper understanding of the job ahead of them. In order to counter and beat the most powerful and cunning of all the adversaries of socialism, American revolutionists have to be armed with the very best methods of thought and action. This means among other things that they must become more historical-minded, more aware of what they have to do and more expert in doing it.

In an anthology of Trotsky's writings, Isaac Deutscher and I designated the century which began with the first world war and the Russian revolution as "The Age of Permanent Revolution." But it is essential to point out that the twentieth century round of revolutions was preceded by another series of revolutions which stretched over four centuries. That was the historical period of the bourgeois democratic revolutions which was inaugurated with the successful struggle for the Dutch Republic against Spanish dominion in the sixteenth century.

There are many dissimilarities between these two eras of revolution. They differ in their historical tasks and in the class agencies delegated to accomplish them. The first promoted the development of capitalist society and was led by bourgeois forces. The second seeks the abolition of capitalist relations and the creation of socialist ones and is being led by the working class and its allies.

The contrast between these two periods and kinds of revolutionary activity is no less pronounced on the subjective than on the objective side. This is especially true in the field of ideology. From its origin the socialist movement has been far more conscious, far more theoretically motivated than its democratic predecessor. A close study of the development of the bourgeois revolutions in Holland, England, France and North America makes it clear why empiricism was the appropriate method and favored philosophy of so many of its foremost figures. All these revolutions ran their course in a most empirical manner. Almost without exception their principal proponents did not foresee their outbreak, anticipate or mark out their main line of march, formulate their chief objectives in advance, and work out a program and course of action to attain them in the most expeditious way.

On the contrary, the participants were usually taken by surprise by the eruption of the showdown with the old régime, improvised measures to organize their forces for the revolutionary combat, and were reluctant to state openly and unequivocally what alternatives they proposed to the established institutions being defended by the counterrevolution. In most cases the leaders of the revolution did not before its outbreak build any organized party with well-defined principles which expressed the interests of their constituents. They had to form their grouping, or re-form and redirect it, in the very midst and heat of the conflict.

The empiricism of the bourgeois radicals in the confrontation with the feudalists was evidenced, for example, in their vacillations over the key political question, What kind of government should replace the monarchy? The only consistent and principled answer from the standpoint of a revolutionary democracy was a republic.

However, the bourgeois oppositionists, especially those speaking for the upper crust, were extremely hesitant about openly proclaiming this political goal or going ahead to set it up. They preferred a remodeled and domesticated monarchy with a new figurehead to the daring and untried innovation of a republic and did everything to forestall the abolition of the throne in Holland, England and France. Even when, at the peak of revolutionary intensity, the bourgeois revolutionists were forced to behead the king and illegalize the monarchy, they did so with a very heavy heart and, as soon as the class commotions subsided and their immediate aims were secured, they restored it.

England is the classic example. After the Cromwellians cut off King Charles' head in 1649 and established a republic, the Restoration put Charles II on the throne in 1660. The triumphant bourgeoisie and their aristocratic associates substituted a more compliant dynasty in 1688. Following its successful bourgeois revolution, Holland got along without a king or queen for one hundred and fifty years or so—and then the monarchy, which is still reigning there, was installed at the beginning of the nineteenth century.

By contrast, the revolutionary socialist movement occupied from its birth a far wider vantage point of insight and foresight into social and political developments. It was placed on an incomparably higher level of scientific theory by its founders, Marx and Engels. They explained, as early as the *Communist Manifesto* of 1848, the necessity and inevitability of the proletarian revolution as a deduction from the whole historical development of the productive forces at the disposal of mankind, the structure and operation of capitalism, the intensification of its contradictions, the insuperable antagonism of interests between the capitalist exploiters and the industrial wage workers, and the increasing organization and understanding of the proletariat. This document has been the most important and influential of all political pronouncements ever written.

Leon Trotsky emphasized the qualitatively greater role played by preparation and planning in the socialist revolution as compared with the presocialist political struggles in the *Lessons of October*. This essay on how to prepare for revolutionary mass action leading to the conquest of power originally appeared in 1924 as an introduction to two volumes of his *Collected Works* dealing with 1917. Here is what he said:

> *Consciousness, premeditation, and planning played a far smaller part in bourgeois revolutions than they are destined to play, and already do play in proletarian revolution. In the former instance the motive force of the revolution was also furnished by the masses, but the latter were much less organized and much less conscious than at the present time. The leadership remained in the hands of different sections of the bourgeoisie, and the latter had at its disposal wealth, education, and all the organizational advantages connected with them (the cities, the universities, the press, etc.). The bureaucratic monarchy defended itself in a hand-to-mouth manner, probing in the dark and then acting. The bourgeoisie would bide its time to seize a favorable moment when it could profit from the movement of the lower classes and throw its whole social weight into the scale, and so seize the state power. The proletarian revolution is precisely distinguished by the fact that the proletariat—in the person of its vanguard—acts in it not only as the main offensive force, but also as the guiding force. The part played in bourgeois revolutions by the economic power of the bourgeoisie, by its education, by its municipalities and universities, is a part which can be filled in a proletarian revolution only by the party of the proletariat. The role of the party has become all the more important in view of the fact that the enemy has also become far more conscious. (See "Lessons of October," in* The Essential Trotsky. *Unwin Books, Barnes and Noble, New York, 1963, p. 170.).*

The latter point has acquired far greater force since Trotsky made that observation. World imperialism has become better organized and more sensitized to the threat to its rulership emanating from the working class and its revolutionary allies. Washington, for example, was taken off guard by the victory of the anti-capitalist revolution in Cuba. It is determined to forestall its repetition elsewhere in Latin America and is taking the most extensive measures to insure that, as the tragic outcome of Che Guevara's last stand in Bolivia illustrated. The revolutionary vanguard there now has to take that development into account in working out its strategy and tactics.

The greater degree of clarity and foresight attending the struggle for socialism has two main sociological sources. One is the special nature of the prime social force at the head of the anticapitalist camp. The working class is situated in the center of modern economy, acts as its principal productive force, and is indeed its most important product. It is a highly socialized, centralized, compactly organized, technically skilled and educated class. The achievements of science and the applications of technology are integral elements of its culture and familiar instruments of its everyday labor activity. They make autos and drive them; they make TV sets and watch them. All these factors give the working class an outlook which is worldwide, and even cosmic in scope, since we have observed the first flights to the moon over TV.

The theoretical principles and ideological outlook which express the social position, historical functions and destiny of this class must be correspondingly far-ranging and penetrating. In order to arrive at their dialectical materialist philosophy and socialist views, Marx and Engels had to go through the entire inventory of prior human knowledge, subject it to critical review, sift out what was valid from what was incorrect and obsolete, and fuse their findings with the new ideas they had arrived at. They applied this process of creative criticism or critical creativity first and most of all to earlier discoveries about history, sociology, economics and politics.

Their epoch-making achievement, as Engels explained, consisted in converting socialism from a utopia into a science. What did this mean? Up to their time socialism had been a dream, an aspiration, an ideal of many people discontented with class society and bourgeois life. While these critics and idealistic pioneers recognized the desirability of a fundamental reorganization of the existing social system, even the most perspicacious among them were unable to see how humanity had arrived at its impasse, how it could get out of it, and pass over from bourgeois to socialist relations. They did not know what social force could liberate humanity from oppression and exploitation and along what lines the job could be done.

Marx's theory of historical materialism demonstrated that the mainspring of social progress was the development of the productive forces; that social revolutions and their associated political changes were engendered by the growing conflict between expanding forces of production and obsolete relations of production; that capitalism was rendering itself parasitic and reactionary by its feverish expansion of the productive forces; and along with it producing and provoking the antagonistic social and political power of the proletariat that was destined to supersede its system. By exposing to full view the nature, course and inevitable outcome of the confrontation between the capitalists and wage workers, Marx blew away the mists enshrouding the next necessary stage of human evolution and made apparent the road leading to it. The new social order could be brought into being, the founders of scientific socialism asserted, only through the anticapitalist movement of the working masses which would culminate in a revolutionary showdown with the upholders of the old order.

Until 1917 these conclusions set forth in *The Communist Manifesto* and further writings of the Marxists were still only working hypotheses which served to guide the most advanced elements of the proletarian cause but had yet to be realized. The overthrow of czarism and capitalism by the Russian workers and peasants led by the Bolsheviks converted the propositions of scientific socialism regarding the transition from capitalism to socialism from well-founded speculations into *verified laws* of the contemporary class struggle. The victory of 1917 effected a qualitative transformation in the status of Marxism as a theory of social transformation and a guide to revolutionary practice.

It placed Marxism in an altogether different category from all other theories of social and political development either in the labor movement or in bourgeois academic circles. Marxism had demonstrated in real life its capacity to predict, prepare, direct and bring forth the most profound changes ever known in social relations and political institutions. These changes denoted a new chapter in human history.

This is something which none of the rival theories have been able to do. These adversary schools may outbid the Marxists here and there and for a time, in their pretensions, their claims, even in their popularity. What they have failed to do is match Marxism in performance. That difference is all-important because all ideas, all theories must prove their worth and their truth by passing the decisive tests of experiment and practice. In the last analysis, that is what counts the most in all departments of science.

In transforming revolutionary politics from a utopia into a science, Marxism followed the path taken by other branches of knowledge. In all fields of science the period of conscious theorizing and of ascertaining definitive laws, has been preceded by an earlier, more primitive, more groping phase of a more or less protracted character. That is the time of blind experimentation, of hit and miss methods, of fumbling around for the right line of investigation and the key to the situation. Such a period of looking for the right road and determining what it is is inescapably dominated by empiricism. This pioneering lays the basis and paves the way for the next and higher phase where theoretical insight, foresight and control, based upon the correct concepts corresponding to the essential objective facts, play a larger and ultimately a dominant role.

Every science has passed through such a development. The alchemists, for example, tried many ways to convert baser metals into gold and silver. They didn't succeed, although today chemists can turn carbon into diamonds. But the kinds of apparatus they devised, like retorts and filters, the techniques they developed, the properties of the chemical reactions they studied, and even certain ideas they advanced, contributed to the creation and advancement of the present genuine science of chemistry.

The science of politics has gone through comparable phases. Before it acquired a solid scientific foundation and methods of procedure through Marxism, it was largely empirical and descriptive in nature. This will become clearer if we trace some of the steps it took along the way.

The ancient Greeks were the first to study politics in a systematic way. Aristotle's *Politics* is still a valuable handbook of information on the subject. He and his school collected historical data about 158 city-states and analyzed their institutions to find out which had the best features and could provide the maximum stability.

These philosophers, and others such as the Sophists, were impelled to inquire into the causes, characteristics and consequences of political changes and the different forms of sovereignty, because of the turbulent character of the class conflicts which shook the Greek city-states. Unlike the Oriental societies based upon agriculture, where despotisms and dynasties continued to rule for centuries without being challenged or superseded, the commercial Greek cities were subjected to tremendous changes, disorders and upheavals whereby one form of rulership would rapidly and convulsively be replaced by another. In addition, out of excess of population and commercial enterprises, the Greeks had to set up colonies which posed to them the practical problem of what pattern the constitutions of these outposts should have.

These Greek thinkers were the first probing investigators of revolutions and counterrevolutions. They endeavored to find out why they happened, what social forces were involved and benefited from them, and what constitutional changes issued from them. As spokesmen for the aristocracy, Plato and Aristotle did not favor democratic régimes nor desire to promote popular revolutions. To the contrary, they wanted to find out and teach how to prevent these from occurring and recurring, or at least to limit their consequences by restraining the democratic forces from doing too much damage to the property and power of the patricians.

In the fifth book of his *Politics* Aristotle discusses many aspects of the problems of revolution and counterrevolution. He takes up the causes of dissensions and revolutions in both the democracies and the oligarchies. He quite correctly asserts that inequality was a main source of revolutionary feeling among the lower classes. That is still true in the class societies of today.

He then goes on to consider how constitutional stability can be preserved. Revolution, he says, breaks out wherever there is a disturbance of the established balance of power between the aristocrats and the democrats, the patricians and the plebians. His formula for avoiding revolutions and for the best political community is a golden mean between the rule of the rich and the poor in which the middle class, the possessors of moderate and sufficient property, holds the balance of power and can mediate between the oligarchs and the lower orders. This part of Aristotle's treatise is a most instructive account of how one of the greatest intellects of the Greek aristocracy looked at the political overturns occasioned by the class conflicts of his time.

Numerous other astute individuals studied revolutions and the recoils against them over the two and a half millennia separating Aristotle from Marx. Prominent among them were: Polybius, the Greek historian of the rise of the Roman empire; Ibn Kahldun, the eminent Arab founder of sociology in the fourteenth century; the Italian, Machiavelli (it has been said that *The Prince* is a commentary on the last chapters of Aristotle's work dealing with the theory of revolutions); the seventeenth century English political theorists, Hobbes, Harrington and Locke; the Frenchmen, Montesquieu and Condorcet in the eighteenth century; Jefferson and Tom Paine (the international revolutionary who participated in both the American and French revolutions and tried to promote one in England as well); and finally, the French historians of the Restoration period in the early decades of the nineteenth century.

Through the commentaries of these writers and others Western mankind amassed a considerable fund of information and ideas about the phenomena of social and political revolution. Yet, for all their observations and insights, the most profound motive forces of revolutionary change remained hidden from these theorists. The explanations they offered and the books they wrote were more descriptive than deeply analytical. They dealt largely with the superstructural factors and features of revolutionary movements and failed to reach down to bedrock to uncover the fundamental causes of structural changes in society. These were lodged in the domain of the productive relations and property forms which were then studied by the economists rather than by the historians and political theorists.

The unsurpassed merit of Marxism as a method, as a system of principles and a body of knowledge, is its success in exploring and explaining the reasons for the motion, the progress and the stagnation of societies. It has most profoundly elucidated those qualitative leaps in history when peoples have passed from one level of development to a higher, more productive and efficient one. Marxism is a doctrine of social evolution which gives a set of directives for class struggle, political revolution and the reconstruction of human relations.

This is not always understood. Ever since Marxism became the predominant ideology in advanced political and intellectual circles, a profession known as "trimming Marx's beard" has come into vogue. This is a chore comparable to what Delilah, the Philistine, did to Samson. An assortment of literary, professorial and reformist tendencies have tried to make Marx over into an image conforming to their particular antirevolutionary predilections. They have made him into a philanthropic spiritual humanist (see Erich Fromm), a red professor, an academic economist, a nationalist, a reformed revolutionary, even in two bizarre cases, into an anti-Semite and a male chauvinist. In a recent collection of his essays entitled *Marxism and the Intellectuals* (Doubleday, New York, 1969) Professor Lewis Feuer depicts Marx as an individual who hated his mother, the Jews and capitalism, in that order, but did worthy work as an empirical research sociologist much like Feuer himself.

Marx and Engels were many-sided personalities. They were philosophers, economists, historians, sociologists, cultural critics and military strategists. But they were above all practicing socialist revolutionaries. They were the original and foremost representatives of a new breed of specialists who, throughout their careers, have integrated the theory and practice of making the proletarian revolution in the happiest combination.

Unlike the anarchists, spontaneists and New Lefts, Marx and Engels not only believed in the necessity of building a vanguard political organization but worked tirelessly at it until their dying days. They were not national-minded like the labor and Stalinist bureaucrats, but internationalists to the core who devoted their energies to launching and strengthening a flesh-and-blood international, uniting the national revolutionary leaderships of the world working class and all the oppressed. Here is the true Marx and Engels, the quintessential Marx and Engels who served as the mentors and models for Lenin, Luxemburg, Trotsky and lesser figures, including ourselves.

These founders of our movement and their best disciples were primarily concerned with developing the strategy and tactics of the class struggle which could lead the workers to the conquest of power in their country and in the rest of the world. They asked, they kept asking, What kind of methods, what system of measures could insure success in that task? All the rest of their activities, their studies and their writings, were designed to clarify and answer the problems of making a socialist revolution.

For them the science of revolution incessantly passes over and merges with the techniques for promoting revolution. Antiquity knew quite a few illustrious makers of popular revolutions such as the Gracchi, the leaders of the Roman plebians, and Spartacus, the hero of the Roman slave insurgents. The bourgeois democratic movements brought forth such figures as Cromwell and Lilburne, Marat, Robespierre, Saint-Just, Jacques Roux, Gracchus Babeuf, Toussaint L'Ouverture and Nat Turner. Sam Adams was regarded by his contemporaries on both sides of the battlefield as the foremost organizer of the American war of independence. In London he was acclaimed as "the foremost politician in the world," who was without a peer in the business of "forwarding a rebellion." He fully deserved that reputation.

These bourgeois democratic revolutionists edited journals, served in legislatures, mobilized and inspired masses, led armies, overturned governments and created new republics. What they did not have was a well-grounded scientific understanding of social development and political strategy nor a revolutionary party organized beforehand and based on a principled program directed toward explicit objectives. They had to sink or swim as best they could when they were lifted up and carried along with the revolutionary torrent.

When the New Lefts and spontaneists inveigh against Marxism or Leninism because it advocates preparing and organizing in advance for the revolutionary struggle, they are unknowingly trying to pull the most advanced and enlightened elements back into a bypassed and benighted prescientific state and onto a level of understanding—or lack of it—proper to a bourgeois but not to a socialist revolution—and they are doing so in advanced capitalist countries at that!

The purpose of science is to know what reality is in order to foresee its operations and development correctly and thus to act to realize human aims most effectively and opportunely. That is its irreplaceable value in practice. Man has recently gone to the moon, not "by guess and by God," but by learning among other things the rules of mathematics and telecommunications, applying the laws of aerodynamics, conforming to the properties of the atmosphere and of space, utilizing the characteristics of metals and checking the capacities of the human organism under unusual stress. The entire project was planned to the finest detail and pretested by computer simulation.

Marxism holds that scientific methods which have produced such triumphs can be put to work, with due regard to the differences between coping with physical and social phenomena, in the politics of revolutionary change. The paramount objective of our age is not to go from the earth to the moon or to Mars but from capitalism to socialism. And all the knowledge accumulated by mankind in its past struggles, which Marxism puts at our disposal, is required to accomplish that difficult transition.

Only part of the conditions necessary for creating a revolutionary situation or opening are subject to conscious direction and control by the vanguard. Such major factors of development as the state of the productive forces, the interrelations of the contending classes, the functioning of the economy and the world-historical context in which the class struggle unfolds have their own path and pace of development under capitalism.

The subjective elements of the movement are, however, in a quite different category from these more objective ones. They are amenable to a degree of foresight, to a measure of control and calculation. They can be prepared for and strengthened by deliberated action. The central subjective factor in the making of a proletarian revolution is the party which embodies the historical memory and highest collective consciousness of the working class. This is codified in its program and exemplified in its methods of organization and action.

The foremost school of revolutionary strategy in our century was provided by the Bolsheviks whose leadership demonstrated what to do and how to do it from 1917 to 1921. The lessons of that experience are contained in the writings of Lenin, Trotsky and their associates. They are set forth in a masterful manner in Trotsky's *History of the Russian Revolution*. An objective measure of how much the scientific understanding of revolutions progressed from ancient Greece to the modern Marxists can be obtained by comparing what Aristotle and Thucydides wrote about the processes of revolution in their works with Trotsky's treatment of the problems of the first socialist victory.

After Lenin's death in 1924 and the ensuing recession of the Russian and world revolutions over the next two decades, Trotsky more than anyone else carried forward and enriched the theory and traditions of Marxist policy. His crowning contribution to the strategy of the world revolution was the *Transitional Program* which he drafted for adoption by the founding congress of the Fourth International in 1938, two years before his death. It summarizes his maturest thinking on the ways and means of promoting the struggle for working-class power and socialism in the epoch of the decline of capitalism and the flourishing of labor bureaucratism, in all its variants from social democratic reformism to Stalinism.

For the Marxist, foresight and planning are not methods which are reserved for running the economy after capitalism has been abolished; they are equally indispensable for preparing and furthering the forces and movement for its overthrow. Through the *Transitional Program* of the Fourth International the revolutionary party can introduce elements of conscious planning which give direction to the unconscious and spontaneous movements of the insurgent masses.

The masses act and react in response to weighty objective conditions produced by the development and crises of the capitalist-colonialist system which are beyond the control of any party or leadership. A sensitive and alert vanguard can sometimes perceive premonitory signs of changes in the moods and movements of the masses and adjust to them in time. But the reflexes of the masses are in most cases ungovernable and unpredictable because they are not planned or anticipated by those who initiate or participate in them. The general strike of the French workers, which took everyone by surprise in May-June 1968, is a fresh case in point.

However, if any specific upsurge or outburst of the masses is unforeseen and confronts the revolutionary vanguard as a given fact, the possibility, the probability, even the inevitability of such large-scale anti-capitalist offensives can be anticipated and prepared for thanks to the precedents already at hand and an understanding of the convulsive nature of our epoch.

The spontaneists and anarchists bank everything on the independent and unplanned actions of the rebellious masses. Marxists not only foresee and welcome these occurrences but go much beyond that to take the necessary steps to intervene in their development, organize them, and direct them toward the desired goals. Otherwise, without adequate guidance and direction, the energy of the upsurge can become exhausted, permitting the class enemy to rally its forces, counterattack and push back the masses. This syndrome has happened many times since 1917.

The May-June events in France likewise demonstrated how the most promising and powerful insurgence of the masses can be derailed by the opportunism of the Communist parties and aborted by the absence of an adequate alternative leadership firmly rooted in the working class.

Lest these generalizations appear too far removed from everyday politics, let me indicate how the theory and practice of a revolutionary Marxist strategy have been combined and applied to the antiwar movement of the United States since 1965. The organization of the fight against American intervention in Vietnam has been an acid test of the character and capacities of all groups on the left. Here is how the American Trotskyists met this formidable challenge of contending with the warmakers on their home grounds.

First, we characterized and condemned Washington's war as imperialist and counterrevolutionary and supported the cause of the Vietnamese freedom fighters as just. On the basis of this analysis we worked out the following line of opposition to the aggressors: 1) We sought to bring together the broadest masses in large-scale antiwar demonstrations. 2) These protests were to be initiated and organized by a coalition of forces whose sole required ground of agreement was a willingness to oppose the warmakers in action. 3) The masses were to be mobilized under the central demand "Withdraw the American troops now" which could unify the biggest forces, while recognizing the democratic right of self-determination of the Vietnamese.

Nowadays, these three points of policy are evident and acceptable to most antiwar activists. Yet all along the way since 1965 every one of them has been resisted and rejected by one or all of the other political tendencies who put forward alternative courses of antiwar action and fought for them against us. Some counterposed individual and isolated deeds to mass action; others tried to narrow down the movement and its appeal by exclusionist regulations and maneuvers or by trying to impose multi-issue programs or opportunist electoral moves on the coalition. The moderates advocated negotiations instead of withdrawal while the ultralefts and sectarians have insisted on acceptance of the National Liberation Front program and positions as a precondition for participation. We have had to combat all these incorrect proposals and procedures unremittingly in order to sustain the antiwar movement and make it grow as it has.

The controversy over military policy was equally arduous and instructive. At first many pacifists, members of the Students for a Democratic Society and other New Lefts stigmatized the conscript soldiers as mercenaries and murderers, turned their backs upon them and advised individual draft resistance, conscientious objection or moving to Canada. We Marxists pointed out that every mass army reflects, sometimes in more intense forms, the features of its society, and that the reluctant draftees were not immunized from the antiwar feelings and ideas agitating the civilian population from which they had so recently come and to which they were still tied. It was therefore preferable for socialist opponents of the war to enter the armed forces, if drafted, and to fight there to exercise the right to express their opinions on this and related political issues among their fellow GIs.

There was nothing original in this line of conduct; it accorded with the doctrines of Lenin and the Bolsheviks. It was not an individualist, pacifist, neutralist, petty-bourgeois, anarchist policy but an activist, militant, proletarian and revolutionary course. Today the antiwar movement not only in the United States but elsewhere recognizes the results and rightness of this orientation followed by the Socialist Workers Party and Young Socialist Alliance and so ably carried out by the antiwar GIs under their inspiration in the army bases.

The achievements registered in these campaigns were ratified by the majority of the 4,000 antiwar activists at the Student Mobilization Committee Conference in Cleveland, February 14-15, 1970. They are a tribute to scientific analysis and foresight as against the methods of improvisation, impressionism and guesswork encouraged by empiricism and emotionalism. They testify to the value of Marxist principles and methods compared with the inconsistent hit-or-miss notions propounded by other political currents who are opposed to them or depart from them.

The poster announcing the successful Young Socialist National Convention held in Minneapolis in December 1969 rightly proclaimed that "it takes revolutionaries to make a revolution." I would propose a few amending adjectives. It takes *informed* and *experienced* revolutionaries to make a *successful* revolution. And that's what our movement is all about.

HOW TO COMMIT REVOLUTION IN CORPORATE AMERICA

● *g. william domhoff*

I appear here today by courtesy of the Legal Staff of the Regents of the University of California. Now I know that they didn't invite me, that the Student Mobilization Committee invited me, but I also know that the Regents put out a ruling that faculty members will be fired for participating in any strike. Thus, being a good and faithful employee, and much enjoying the sunshine and redwoods of Santa Cruz, I thought I'd better get clearance from university experts on the matter of this student strike before I did anything rash and compromising. And, thank goodness, these good and true, legal men assured me that I wouldn't be fired for appearing here today—just as long as I didn't advocate anything illegal.

Since the title of my little talk is "How to Commit Revolution in Corporate America," and since committing revolution might be construed by some people as being somewhat illegal, I certainly wouldn't want to appear to be advocating it. No, I don't advocate anything. I consider myself as acting in one of the many capacities of a well-rounded professor in the modern multiversity—as a consultant, just a consultant, to some group of citizens within the community that feels a need to call upon its tax-supported knowledge factory to give advice on a particular activity or undertaking. As a consultant, then, I'm not being illegal. In fact, I am doing what every good professor does, although for a tremendously reduced fee, and I expect to get credit for it when I am considered for promotion and tenure.

I am well aware that most of you aren't revolutionaries—that you are mostly upper-middle-class people cutting loose from home by temporarily growing beards or indulging in exotic potions or getting all caught up in doing good things for your less fortunate brethren from the other side of the tracks. I know that most of you think it is just a matter of a little more time, a little more education, and a little more good will before most of this country's social and economic problems are straightened out, and I suspect that many of you who are currently among the earnest and concerned are going to be somewhere else in a few years, as is that idealistic student group of past years, your parents. But maybe someday some of you will be looking around for a revolutionary consulting service. Maybe someday you will wise up to the Square Deals, New Deals, Fair Deals, New Frontiers, and other quasi-liberal gimmicks used to shore up and justify an overdeveloped, inhuman, and wasteful corporate capitalism as it gradually rose to power in the 20th century. Maybe someday some significant number of people, Left and Right, will really learn that courage, integrity, and a casual style aren't enough to bring about meaningful, substantial changes, that moral anguish has to be translated into changes in the social structure to do more than make you feel all warm and good and guilt-free inside. Maybe some day those of you, who are already on the right road, will learn that no matter how militant or violent or critical you may be, you are still not your own person or a revolutionary as long as you merely try to get your leaders to pay attention and better understand, whether it be through letters or sit-ins or time bombs. Maybe you will learn to ignore the leaders you are harassing and decide to replace them and their system—with yourselves and your own system, and on that day you will become revolutionaries instead of militant supplicants appealing to the stuffy Father Figures for a little more welfare and social justice, and a little less war.

At any rate, if and when you give up on these futile attempts at minor social improvements, and turn to the really exhilarating experience of freeing your own self by committing revolution, then perhaps these observations may be of some use. I offer them in a tentative fashion, fully expecting them to be reworked, challenged, developed. Since I am only a consultant, no hard feelings if you reject them. We academics are very philosophical about such matters. It's part of being professional, of being a good consultant.

There are three aspects, I think, to any good revolutionary program for corporate America. These aspects are closely intertwined, and all three must be developed alongside each other, but there is nonetheless a certain logic, a certain order of priorities, in the manner in which I present them. First, you need a comprehensive, overall analysis of the present-day American system. You've got to realize that the corporate capitalism of today is not the 19th-century individual capitalism that conservatives yearn for. Nor is it the pluralistic paradise that liberals rave about and try to patch up. Nor is it the finance capitalism of the American Communists who are frozen in their analyses of another day.

Second, you need relatively-detailed blueprints for a post-industrial America. You've got to show people concrete plans that improve their lot either spiritually or materially. There's no use scaring them with shouts of socialism, which used to be enough of a plan however general, but which today only calls to mind images of Russia, deadening bureaucracy, and 1984. And there's no use boring them with vague slogans about participation and vague abstractions about dehumanization. You've got to get down to where people live, and you've got to get them thinking in terms of a better America without the spectre of Russia, rightly or wrongly, driving any thought of risking social change out of their heads.

Third, and finally, you need a plan of attack, a program for taking power. For make no mistake about it—before most people get involved in revolutionary activity they take a mental look way down the road. Maybe not all the way down the road, but a long way down. They want to know what they are getting into, and what the chances are, and whether there is really anything positive in sight that is worth the gamble. In short, I suspect that most people just don't fit the formula that seems to be prevalent in America: get people involved in anything—rent strikes, anti-nuclear testing demonstrations, rat strikes, draft demonstrations, whatever, and gradually they will develop a revolutionary mentality. According to this theory, apparently, people will realize their power and want more if they win the rat strike, or they will wise up if they are hit on the head by a police officer at the draft demonstration. Well, maybe that works for some people, but I wouldn't count on it, and I wouldn't rely on it to the exclusion of all else. Actually, most people seem to sink back into lethargy when the rats are gone, or nuclear testing in the atmosphere is abandoned. And I know of no convincing evidence that getting people hit on the head or thrown in jail makes them into revolutionaries—certainly many of those who believed this didn't become revolutionaries by this route. So, ponder carefully about this activity for activity's sake. You need a plan of attack, not just some issues like peace or rats. And one thing more on this point: that plan has to come out of your analysis of the present socioeconomic system and out of your own life experience, that is, out of the American experience, and not out of the experiences of Russia, or China, or Cuba, all of which have been different from each other, and are different from the U.S.A. The world moves, even in America, and as it moves new realities arise and old theories become irrelevant. New methods become necessary. If you expect to be listened to, you will have to look around you afresh and build your own plan, abandoning all the sacred texts on "What Is To Be Done."

An analysis of the system, a set of blueprints, and a program for gaining power. That is the general framework. Let me now say something more concrete about each, admitting in advance that some points will be touched on only lightly and that others, which should be read as friendly criticisms of past and present efforts of American revolutionaries, may be too cryptic for those who have not observed these movements or read about their beliefs and strategies.

As to the analysis, here I will be the most cryptic. The name of the system is corporate capitalism. Huge corporations have come to dominate the economy, reaping fabulous, unheard-of profits and avoiding their share of the taxes, and their owners and managers—the corporate rich—are more and more coming to dominate all aspects of American life, including government. Corporate rich foundations like Ford, Rockefeller, and Carnegie finance and direct cultural and intellectual innovations, corporate rich institutes and associations like the Council on Foreign Relations, the Committee for Economic Development and the Rand Corporation do most of the economic, political, and military research and provide most of the necessary government experts and consultants. As for the future, well, Bell Telephone is undertaking a pilot project in which it will run a high school in the Detroit ghetto, and Larry Rockefeller has suggested that every corporation in New York "adopt" a city block and help make sure that its residents are healthy, happy, and nonriotous. Adopt-a-block may never happen, and corporations may not run many high schools any time soon, but such instances are symbolic of where we are probably headed—corporate feudalism, cradle to the grave dependency on some aspect or another of a corporate structure run by a privileged few who use its enormous rewards to finance their own private schools, maintain their own exclusive clubs, and ride to the hounds on their vast farm lands. Even agriculture is being corporatized at an amazing rate. Family farmers are in a state of panic as the corporate rich and their corporations use tax loopholes to gobble up this last remaining bastion of 19th-century America.

Much work on this necessary analysis of corporate capitalism, or feudalism, has been done, but much more needs to be done. It is a scandal, or, rather, a sign of corporate rich dominance of the universities, that so little social stratification research concerns the social upper class of big businessmen; that so little political sociology research concerns the power elite that is the operating arm of the corporate rich, indeed, that so much of the social sciences in general concern themselves with the workers, the poor, and other countries—that is, with things that are of interest to the corporate rich. If you want to know anything interesting about the American power structure you have to piece together the hints of journalists, read the few books by a handful of Leftists who are academic outcasts, follow the research reports of two excellent student groups, and listen to and read Dan Smoot. Dan Smoot? Yes, Dan Smoot. Properly translated, he has a better view of the American power structure than most American political scientists, who of course merely laugh at him. He may not use the same labels I would for the men in charge (he thinks David Rockefeller & Co. are communists or dupes!), but at least he knows who's running the show. It is truly a commentary on American academia that he and one journalist—Establishment journalist Joseph Kraft—have done the only work on the all-important Council on Foreign Relations, one of the most influential policy-forming associations of the corporate rich. While the professors are laughing at Dan Smoot and equating the business community with the National Association of Manufacturers and the U.S. Chamber of Commerce, Smoot is keeping up with the activities of the richest, most powerful, and most internationally oriented of American big businessmen, the vanguard of corporate feudalism.

This really brings you to your first revolutionary act. Research one thing and one thing only—the American power structure. . . . Just turning the spotlight on the power elite is a revolutionary act, although only Act One. Ideas and analyses are powerful, and they shake people up. The problem of would-be American revolutionaries has not been an overemphasis on ideas, but the use of old ones, wrong ones, and transplanted ones. That is why C. Wright Mills grabbed American students and parts of American academia. He had new, relevant ideas and facts about the here and now—he exploded old clichés and slogans. And, I might add without being autobiographical—for Lincoln Steffens and Bertrand Russell had already done the job on me—I think he created more radicals with his work than any hundred Oakland and Los Angeles policemen with their billy clubs.

But analysis is not only important so that you can better criticize the system, it is necessary as well as for developing blueprints and plans of attack. As for the developing of blueprints, to go beyond mere devastating criticism of the system you have to understand it so that you can figure out what kind of a better system you can build on it. The most important and obvious point here is that you will be building on a fully industrialized, non-farming system. This means that your post-industrial society can look very different from systems built on pre-industrial, agricultural bases such as was the case in Russia, China, and Cuba.

As to the importance of a good analysis in developing a program for taking power, this is essential because it tells you what you can and cannot expect, what you can and cannot do, and what you should and should not advocate. Let me give four examples:

1. Corporate capitalism, if it can continue to corporatize the "underdeveloped" world and displace small businessmen and realtors in the cities, may have a lot more room for reform. In fact, if creature comfort is enough, it may come to satisfy most of its members. Be that as it may, and I doubt if it can solve its problems in a humanly tolerable way, the important point is that no American revolutionary should feel shocked or irrelevant because the corporate rich agree to nationwide health insurance or guaranteed annual incomes, or agree to pull out of one of their military adventures. And don't get your hopes up for any immediate collapse. Better to be surprised by a sudden turn that hastens your time schedule than to be disappointed once again by the flexibility of the corporate rich. This means that you should rely on your own program, and not on depression or war, to challenge the system and bring about change. It means that you should have a flexible, hang-loose attitude toward the future. Predictions of the inevitability of anything, whether collapse or socialism, fall a little flat and leave us jaded after

 comparing earlier predictions with the experience of the 20th century. We need a political philosophy that is a little more humble than those which currently entrap most of the world's Leftists.

2. Corporate capitalism seems to be very much dependent on overseas sales and investments, probably much more so than it is on the military spending necessary to defend and extend that Free World empire. And even if some economists would dispute that, I think it is 100% safe to say that most members of the corporate rich are convinced that this overseas economic empire is essential—and that is what affects their political, economic and military behavior. Thus, the corporate rich fear, nay, more than that, have utter horror of isolationism, and that suggests that you revolutionaries should agree with conservatives about the need for isolationism.

3. The American corporate rich have at their command unprecedented, almost unbelievable firepower and snooping power. This makes it questionable whether or not a violent revolutionary movement has a chance of getting off the ground. It also makes it doubtful whether or not a secret little Leninist-type party can remain secret and unpenetrated for very long. In short, a non-violent and open party may be dictated to you as your only choice by the given fact of the corporate leaders' military and surveillance capability, just as a violent and closed party was dictated by the Russian situation.

4. The differences between present-day corporate capitalism and 19th-century individual capitalism must be emphasized again and again if you are to reach those currently making up the New Right. Those people protest corporate capitalism and its need for big government and overseas spending in the name of small business, small government, competition, the market place—all those things destroyed or distorted by the corporate system. You must agree with the New Right that these things have happened and then be able to explain to them how and why they have happened, not due to the communists or labor, or liberal professors, but due to the growing corporatization of the society and the needs of these corporations. You can't give up on these New Rightists—they know the Rockefellers, the J. J. McCloys, the Averell Harrimans, the Paul Hoffmans, the Adlai Stevensons, and the John V. Lindsays run American society. (Here I am just naming some of the relatively few multi-millionaire businessmen and corporation lawyers known to the American public.) And, like the New Left, they don't like it. It is your job to teach them that the new corporate system is the problem, not the motives and good faith of the corporate rich they call communists and dupes of liberal academics.

Now, as to your second general need, blueprints for a post-industrial America. Blueprints are first of all necessary to go beyond mere criticism. Any half-way moral idiot can criticize corporate capitalism, anyone can point to slums, unemployment, waste, phony advertising, inflation, shoddy goods, and so on. To be revolutionary, you have got to go beyond the militantly liberal act of offering some criticism and then asking people to write their congressman or to "sit in" somewhere so that the authorities will do something about the problem. And it is necessary for you to self-consciously begin to develop this plan because it is not going to miraculously appear after a holocaust or emanate mystically from the collective mind of that heterogeneous generalization called "The Movement." Individuals are going to have to develop aspects of these blueprints, wild, yea-saying blueprints that you can present with excitement and glee to Mr. and Mrs. Fed-up America. It is not enough to be for peace and freedom, which is really only to be against war and racism. It is not positive enough. As a smug little man from the Rand Corporation—a consultant for the other side—once reminded me, everyone, even him, is for peace and justice—the differences begin when you get to specifics.

Blueprints are also necessary to break the Russian logjam in everyone's thinking, revolutionary and non-revolutionary alike. Only by talking about concrete plans, thus getting people reacting to them and thereby developing their own plans, will people forget about Russia, a centralized, bureaucratic, industrialized country that is neither here nor there as far as you are concerned, and has no relevance to either your criticisms or your plans. In short, you have got to show people that your concern is America, that you love America, and that your moral concern is based upon what America could be, as compared with what it is. No one should out-Americanize you. You, as revolutionaries, have a right to that flag. And if you don't feel like grabbing the present American flag right at this juncture, then reach back into American revolutionary history, to the unfinished revolution, for your flags. Like that great snake flag, that great phallic message, of the Gadsden Rebellion, with its prideful warning hissing out across the centuries: DON'T TREAD ON ME.

The point is that you are Americans and that you want to build a better, a post-industrial America, that you want to use the base your forefathers gave you to realize the American dream. Forget all this internationalism talk. The foreign revolutions some of you often hope to copy were fought by men who were fervent nationalists, not bigoted ethnocentrics who believed that no other nationalism was as good or moral as theirs, but nationalists who were of their people, who loved their country and its culture, and who really lived and developed their own heritage. They talked internationalism, they read widely, they were appreciative and tolerant of many other cultures, but they were heart and soul products of their land and its traditions. To throw away the potent psychological force of nationalism because it has been identified in this country with an Americanism that is often parochial and ethnocentric, and especially anti-Semitic, is to ignore, ironically enough, one of the few things you can learn from studying other 20th-century revolutions. A feeling for your country and its little nuances is an intimate and potent part of Western man. If that sounds too narrow and unemotional for some of you, I would add that it is probably wrong anyhow to think your internationalism somehow supports foreign revolutionaries. Do you really think the Viet Cong derive any strength from telegrams of support from or demonstrations by little New York-based committees on This and That? That's Dean Rusk's mentality. Don't you think the Cong and the Russians and the Chinese are big enough to take care of themselves? Isn't it perhaps a little bit paternalistic to think you are in any way helping those indigenous movements? Your task is here at home, and the way to get to this task is to develop a set of blueprints to go with your critique.

Now, I don't make these statements, and this distinction between nationalism and ethnocentrism, as one who has not considered the problem long and hard. As a Freudian-oriented psychologist, I believe more than anyone, certainly more than you who subscribe to one or other of the environmentalisms (liberalism and Marxism in their various guises) that predominate in American social science, that people everywhere have the same basic psyche, the same wishes and fears. I believe that the transition rites, myths, and rituals from tribes all over the world show that all men and women suffer from fears of separation from mother and group, that all men come to feel rivalry toward father and brother, that all men must go to the desert or the mountain to struggle for independence from their parents, and that all men have a strange sweet ambivalence toward death. In short, I know that all people have the same problems, but I also know that there are such things as personality and culture, that is, that we all have slightly different ways of handling our wishes and fears. And since I know that these personality and cultural differences are in good part, if not totally, defenses against anxiety and wishes that cause anxiety, I recognize that to attack them, or to ask people to discard them without offering them a new set of defenses, is to invite resistance, is to invite fear and distrust. We are faced with the seeming paradox that men who share the same problems can easily come to mistrust or hate each other if one person's defenses threaten those of the other. So I am saying that you should bypass these resistances, that as theoretical psychologists you should of course recognize the psychic universality of mankind, but that as revolutionaries you should also recognize that such a general truism is of no use to you in your day-to-day dealings with people if you are not sensitive to and sympathetic toward those individual and group defenses called personality and culture. In short, you have got to recognize that we are all nationalists in the sense of our identity, and work with this fact, trying to bring out the best in your own national tradition. If this sounds risky to you somehow, as something that might lead to outcomes you don't advocate, or to a narrow parochialism, then you have underestimated the importance of blueprints in your revolutionary program. For it is the blueprints that are the key to transcending narrow outlooks and ensuring that only the best in the American national character is more fully manifested. It is the explicitly stated blueprints which ensure that some implicit retrogressive program does not come to tacitly guide your actions as a revolutionary movement.

What could this post-industrial society look like? Naturally, as you might suspect of someone trying to be a respectable consultant, I have a few suggestions, all tentative, and I will mention some of them to give you an idea of what I mean, but I want to emphasize that it is on this project that so many more people could become totally involved in the revolutionary process. If it would be by and large intellectuals, academics, and students who would work on the analysis and critique of the growing corporate feudalism, it would be people from all walks of life who would be essential to this second necessity. You need men and women with years of experience in farming, small business, teaching, city planning, recreation, medicine, and so on, to start discussing and writing about ways to organize that part of society they know best for a post-industrial America. You need to provide outlets via forums, discussions, papers, and magazines for the pent-up plans and ideals of literally millions of well-trained, experienced, frustrated Americans who see stupidity and greed all around them but can't do a thing about it. You need to say, for example, "Look Mr. and Mrs. City Planning Expert trapped in this deadly bureaucracy controlled by big businessmen, draw up a sensible plan for street development, or park development, in your town of 30,000 people." "Look, Mr. Blue-Collar Worker, working for this big corporation, how should this particular plant be run in a sensible society?"

And, you need not only to discuss and to develop these programs, you need to make them clear to every American, not only to the ones you might win to your side because the present systems disgusts them morally, or exploits them, or ignores them, or rejects them. No, even more, you need to reach the many millions more who, once they did not fear you or distrust you, would be willing to live under either the new or old system. And make no mistake about their importance. When people talk about the small percentage of Bolsheviks who took over Russia, they often forget the overwhelming numbers who passively accepted them. They did so out of disgust with war, despair, and the lack of a plan of their own that they really believed in.

Let me repeat to make its importance clear that the neutralization of large masses should be a prime goal for a program to develop and present blueprints for a post-industrial America. To this end it should be personally handed by some revolutionary to every person in America. Each person should receive a short, simple, one-page handbill especially relevant to his situation or occupation. It would begin, for example, "Policeman, standing here protecting us from Evil at this demonstration, Where Will You Be After The Revolution?" And then, in a few short sentences you will tell this bewildered soul, whom you embraced after handing him his message, that there will still be a great need for policemen after the revolution, but that policemen will tend to do more of the things that they like to do—helping, assisting, guiding—rather than the things that get them a bad name, that is, faithfully carrying out the repressive dictates of their power elite masters. You will tell him that you know that some policemen are prejudiced or authoritarian, but that you know that is neither here nor there because orders on whether to shoot ("to do whatever is necessary to keep 'law and order' in this ghetto") or not to shoot come from officials higher up who are intimately intertwined in the corporate system.

Similar handbills should be prepared for every person. Some would hear good things, like more money and better health. Some would hear things that would surprise them or make them wonder, like "You won't be socialized, Mr. Small Businessman producing a novelty or retailing pets on a local level, because the socialized corporations can produce more than enough; and furthermore, keep in mind that government in a post-industrial America couldn't possibly harass you as much as the big bankers who won't lend you money, the big corporations who undercut you, and the corporate-oriented politicians who overtax you." Others, for whom there is no good news, would get such cheery messages as "Stock Broker—we hope you have other skills, like gardening or typing"; "Corporate Manager—we hope you like working for the anonymous public good as much as you liked working for anonymous millionaire coupon clippers"; "CIA man—we hope you are as good at hiding as you are supposed to be at seeking".

Perhaps most of all, there has to be a consideration of the role of Mr. John Bircher, Mr. Physician, Mr. Dentist, and others now on the New Right. Those who are put off or ignored by the increasing corporatization have to be shown that their major values—individuality, freedom, local determination—are also the values of a post-industrial America. This does not mean that they will suddenly become revolutionaries, but it is important to start them wondering as to whether or not they would find things as bad in the new social system as they do in this system which increasingly annoys them, exasperates them, and ignores them. They must be weaned from the handful of large corporations and multi-millionaires who use them for their own ends by talking competition while practicing monopoly, by screaming about taxes while paying very little, and by talking individuality while practicing collectivism.

What would a post-industrial America look like? First of all, it would be certain large American institutions—like the Berkeley food co-op that is locally controlled by consumers, like the Pasadena water and electric systems that are publicly owned, like the Tennessee Valley Authority which has allowed the beginnings of the sane, productive, and beautiful development of at least one river region in our country. In short, the system would start from local controls and work up, like it used to be before all power and taxes were swept to the national level by war and the big corporations. And, as you can see, it would be a mixed system, sometimes with control by consumers, sometimes with control by local government, sometimes with control by regional authorities, and sometimes, as should be made clear in the handbill to certain small businessmen, with control in private hands. For many retail franchises, for many novelty productions, and, I suspect, for many types of farms and farmers, depending on region, crop and other considerations, private enterprise may be the best method of control.

The question will be raised—is this promise of some private ownership pandering to a voting bloc? Is it like the old Communist trick of the United Front? The answer is a resounding NO. Any post-industrial society that does not maximize chances for freedom, flexibility, and individuality is not worth fighting for. Given the enormous capabilities of corporate production, the economic and cultural insignificance of most small businessmen, and the very small number of family farmers, there is simply no economic or political or cultural reason to socialize everything. . . .

I have left the most obvious for last. Of course the corporations would be socialized. Their profits would go to the people in the form of lower prices (and thus higher real wages) and/or repair to local, state, and national treasuries in the amounts necessary to have a park on every corner (replacing one of the four gas stations), and medical, dental, educational, recreational, or arts facilities on the other corners (replacing the other three gas stations—there being no need for any but a few gas stations due to the ease of introducing electric cars when a few hundred thousand rich people are not in a position to interfere). But how to man this huge corporate enterprise? First, with blue-collar workers, who would be with you all the way in any showdown no matter how nice some members of the corporate rich have been to them lately. Second, with men from lower-level management positions who have long ago given up the rat race, wised up, and tacitly awaited your revolution. Fantasy? Perhaps, but don't underestimate the cynicism at minor levels of the technostructure. I have spoken with and to these groups, and there is hope. They are not all taken in, any more than most Americans are fooled by the mass media about domestic matters. They are just trapped, with no place to go but out if they think too much or make a wave. Now, "out" is easy enough if you're young and single, but it's a little sticky if you didn't wake up to the whole corporate absurdity until you were long out of college and had a wife and two kids. Cultivate these well-educated men and women whose talents are wasted and ill-used. Remind them that the most revolutionary thing they can do—aside from feeding you information and money so you can further expose the system and aside from helping to plan the post-industrial society—is to be in a key position in the technostructure when the revolution comes. You may not win many of them percentagewise, but then it wouldn't take many to help you through a transition.

Then too, part of the corporate system would disappear—one computerized system of banking and insurance would eliminate the incredible duplication, paperwork, and nonsense now existent in those two "highly profitable" but worthless areas of the corporate economy. Corporate retails would be broken up and given to local consumer co-ops, or integrated into nationalized producer-retailer units in some cases. Corporate transports (air, rails, buses) would be given in different cases to state, local, and national government, as well as to, on occasion, the retailers or producers they primarily serve. The public utilities, as earlier hinted, would finally be given to the public, mostly on the local and regional level, probably on the national level in the case of telephones. The only real problem, I think, is manufacturing, where you have to hold the loyalty of technicians and workers to survive a transition. Blue-collar control—syndicalism—may be the answer in some cases, regional or national government control in others. Here, obviously, is one of those questions that needs much study, with blue-collar and white-collar workers in the various industries being the key informants and idea men.

I have not here presented a final, detailed set of blueprints for a post-industrial America, but I hope I have suggested how important the development of such blueprints is, that I have tossed out a few ideas that might have merit or start you thinking, and that I have made you wonder as to how much energy and enthusiasm might possibly be released by taking such a project to Americans in all walks of life. The "false consciousness" of Americans is not primarily in their misperceptions of the "power structure." Many are already wise to liberal baloney on that score, especially blue-collar workers. The "false consciousness" is in a lack of vision, a resigned cynicism, a hopeless despair. "Struggle" without vision will never achieve success in America.

I come, then, finally to the third necessity, a program for taking the reins of government from the power elite in order to carry out the plan developed by revolutionary visionaries. It is on this point that there is likely to be found the most disagreement, the most confusion, the most uncertainty, and the most fear. But I think you do have something very important to go on—the ideas and experiences and successes of the Civil Rights and New Left and Hippie movements of the past several years. If they have not given you an analysis of corporate capitalism or a set of blueprints, which is their weakness, they have given you the incredibly-precious gift of new forms of struggle and new methods of reaching people, and these gifts must be generalized, articulated, and more fully developed.

I have a general term, borrowed from a radical hippy, that I like to use because I think it so beautifully encompasses what these movements have given to you—psychic guerrilla warfare—the "psychic" part appealing to my psychologist instincts and summarizing all hard-hitting non-violent methods, the "guerrilla warfare" part hopefully giving to those who want to take to the hills enough measure of satisfaction to allow them to stick around and participate in the only type of guerrilla warfare likely to work in corporate America. For make no mistake about it, psychic guerrilla warfare is a powerful weapon in a well-educated, highly-industrialized country that has a tradition of liberal values and democratic political processes. And it is the kind of guerrilla warfare that America's great new acting-out girls can indulge in on an equal basis with any male anywhere. It is the confrontation politics of the New Left—teach-ins, marches, walk-ins, sit-ins, push-ins, love-ins, folk rocks, and be-ins. It is the non-violent, religiously-based, democratically-inspired confrontation morality of Martin Luther King, and it is the unfailing good humor, psychological analysis, and flower power of the Hippie. Together they are dynamite—what politician or labor leader can fault confrontation, what true Christian or Jew can react violently to non-violence, and what disgruntled middle-classer can fail to smile or admit begrudging admiration for the best in American hippiedom?

Before I suggest how and where to lay this psychological dynamite, I know I must force myself to say a few words concerning what you are wondering about the most, the role of violence. The words aren't easy for me to say, a look at history makes the ground shaky under me, and many will secretly or openly assume that this is cowardly rationalization by an academic. Despite all this, I reject the lesson of history by claiming that the situation is different in this over-industrialized country: I don't think violence will work in corporate America, 1968. I don't believe in non-violence as a way of life as some people do, so I don't argue from any philosophic base. . . . No, I'm just afraid violence is not a winning strategy in corporate America, and a winning strategy is the primary concern of the revolutionary consultant. There is first of all the brute fact of this country's incredible military hardware. But there is more than that. This democracy is far from perfect, and the corporate rich have buggered its functioning at a zillion different junctures, but it has never been tested to its limits either. You've got to see just how much there is to the claim that values and political institutions would win out in a showdown. There are even liberals who might be willing to die for such a cause. In the meantime, the masses you need are deeply committed to the political process.

Is this doubt about the usefulness of violence in corporate America only the opinion of an academic type? I think not. It was also the opinion of one of the greatest violent revolutionaries of all time. I refer to Che, and my reference to him will be my first and only appeal to authority, to sacred text. Indeed, it is almost a tragedy that those who love and admire Che, and at the same time dream of physical guerrilla warfare in the U.S.A., should overlook his very first premise for it—people take to physical guerrilla warfare only when they have lost all hope of non-violent solutions. Che is said to have laughed long and hard when asked about the possibility of guerrilla warfare in this country. In short, he too apparently believed that what works in the maldeveloped, exploited hinterland of the corporate capitalist empire does not necessarily apply in its overdeveloped affluent center.

Americans have not lost their hope. Furthermore, they are not likely to lose it by any of the means currently being used to escalate physical confrontations, for such confrontations do not "expose" the most fundamental aspects of the political system. The only way people would lose their faith in the political system, if they are capable of losing it at all, is in a full and open and honest test of its promise. The political system has got to be tested totally by completely unarmed men and women, and if that doesn't sound courageous enough for you, then you have need for a more hairy-chested proof of masculinity and integrity than I do. And if you argue that people won't listen, that they haven't listened in the past few years, then I say it's because you haven't yet brought to them an analysis that rings true enough, that you haven't yet hit them with a program that is exciting enough, and that you haven't yet provided them with a plan of attack that is believable enough to be worth trying. I say you really haven't turned on with all your intellectual and libidinal resources, that you haven't given them your best shot. What you have done so far is great, but it is only a prelude. You've got to escalate your incredibleness, your audacity, your cleverness, and your playfulness, not your physical encounters, if you are to break through the American malaise.

Enough admonitions, although I fear no one from the Left is any longer listening. Back to the more manic matter of psychic guerrilla warfare. How do you direct this dynamite to its task of destroying the ideological cover of the corporate rich? First, you start a new political party, a wide-open, locally-based political party dedicated to the development of blueprints for a post-industrial America and to the implementation of them through psychic guerrilla warfare. It should be a party with a minimal, low-key ideology which does not find it necessary to have a position on every age-old question in ontology, epistomology, and Russian and Chinese history. It should be a hang-loose outfit open to anyone prepared to abandon all other political affiliations and beliefs—in other words, it would not be an Anti-This-Or-That coalition of liberal Democrats, Communists, Trotskyists, and Maoists. In fact, ignore these groups. The best members will drop out and join yours. For the rest, they have no constituencies and would soon fall to fighting the Old Fights among themselves anyway—Communist and Anti-Communist, Pro-Soviet and Anti-Soviet, and On and On ad tedium. No, you don't need that—it would destroy you like it destroyed them. And like they destroy the organizations they cowbird with their cocksure, know-it-all metaphysics which ignore the various situations from which these theories derived. In fact, they need you, for if you got something going, the party would be big enough for all of them to work in without seeing each other or having to defend the Old Faiths. You've got to patiently show them how to do it here so they can transcend their romantic ties to the ideas and methods of other countries and other ages.

In addition to declining offers of coalition, and instead seeking converts, such a party should reject as inappropriate the Leninist "democratic centralism" for an American revolutionary party. Not that all the Old Leftists would give it up—some would probably join your party and try to "caucus" or "bore from within," but the open give and take of ideas and the local autonomy of chapters could handle the little organizational games they have become so good at while organizing and reorganizing each other over the past thirty or forty years.

Before I go on, let me pause to make some things clear. For all my despair over certain Old Left ideas, I think many of these people are great and good persons—it's when they start planning that their minds lock into the old patterns. Further, I respect their admiration for their heroes. Lenin was great. So was Trotsky. So were Eugene Debs and Thomas Paine, and so are Mao and Fidel, but they have nothing to teach you except guts and perseverance because your situation is different. Honor them for their courage and their example, but most of all, for their ability to let go of sacred texts and do what was necessary in their given society even when it contradicted received doctrine (as it always did): to take power in a pre-industrial state on a very small base, to march to the countryside instead of waiting for the workers, to rely on peasants. If they could forget the sacred texts of their masters, why can't you go beyond theirs? You need your own Lenins, not theirs, your own Ches, not theirs, and I suspect they will be as different as the first is from the second. Begin this self-reliance by starting your own kind of American revolutionary party, one not open to FBI subversion because an open party depends on ideas, and FBI men, having no ideas, would be unable to maintain their cover.

So what does this party do besides present a constant withering critique of corporate capitalism and build blueprints for a post-industrial America? It practices all forms of psychic guerrilla warfare whenever and wherever there is a possible convert. Eventually, and on the right occasions, it even enters elections, not to win votes, but to win converts. In making its pitch, it doesn't ask men and women to quit their jobs or take to the hills, but rather it asks them to commit their allegiances to new socioeconomic arrangements; to help develop new social and intellectual institutions; to financially support the growth of the party; to read party-oriented newspapers; to convert and neutralize friends and neighbors, and to stand firm if the corporate rich try something funny.

After building chapters in every town or city district in the country by word of mouth and small group contact, you would gradually begin to participate in local elections to gain further attention. Then you would enter legislative elections, both to gain converts and to win seats, for the more legislative seats you hold, state and national, the better for the sudden takeover that will come later. You avoid like the plague winning any executive offices, for to be a mayor or governor when you don't control the whole system is meaningless and a waste of energy. You couldn't do anything liberals won't eventually do until you control the entire system. In other words, I'm not suggesting a gradual takeover, which would wear you down, compromise your program, and perhaps allow you to develop an ameliorist mentality as you got used to a little bit of influence and status. Indeed, the British Labor Party should be as sad a lesson to you as any other recent experience, and you should not repeat their failure to force a total and complete change the minute you have a chance to take power. If they couldn't do it, well, you can, because once you take over the national government in a one-election shot, or general uprising a la France in 1968, there is enough power concentrated there to accomplish drastic changes overnight.

I don't mean to imply that you would only control the Presidency, that you would only move on the national level. Actually, you should move on the whole system at once, for each local chapter would have developed parallel governments that would also go into action for the first time when you decided you had the popular support to take over the system. All members of a given chapter would train themselves to fill some government job at local levels—they would be like the shadow cabinets of British politics only more so. The transition would be sudden—and it would be total in the sense of taking money, power, and status from the corporate rich.

But what about the military, you ask? Everyone knows that any serious revolution must not only isolate the ruling social class and eliminate its economic base, but it must do away with the army that is its ultimate instrument. How is that possible in America? By keeping it a civilian, draftee army and by infiltrating its officer ranks. As long as the American army is not a standing, professional army, as long as it is made up mostly of civilian recruits serving short terms, then you have control of that army to the degree that you have the loyalty of the majority of citizens. However, to ensure leadership, at a certain point it would become necessary for party members to sacrifice themselves, not by avoiding the draft, but by joining the ranks of military officers. If that sounds like a very great sacrifice, I agree, but perhaps it will appeal to those among you who like undercover games. Infiltration is an old trick, but the amazing thing is that most American radicals of the past have been concerned with infiltrating labor unions, the Democratic Party, everything but what needs infiltrating, which is the army.

Let me be sure I am being clear. Now is not the time to begin infiltrating the army, but at some point along the line that would become a prime task. Such infiltrators, at least perhaps in some cases, could be secret members of the party, its only secret members. Their only task would be to make sure that the corporate rich could never turn military firepower on the non-violent revolution. They would do this by advocating one thing and one thing only—the subservience of the military to civilian government, the refusal to take sides in an internal political controversy. In so doing they would be indistinguishable from non-party members within the military who truly accepted this tradition. It may be that there are many of those, but that should not be counted on.

O.K., that's action, even if it doesn't prove to unfold exactly as outlined, but to whom does this party address itself as its agitators and organizers drive around on open-air trucks, complete with folk rock bands, shouting their message and distributing their handbills in every town, county fair, ghetto, and shopping center in the country? What is its potential constituency? The answer is first of all a very general one, but this very generality frees American revolutionaries from trying to duplicate the past or fit into theoretical molds. You should direct yourself to anyone disgusted with the present system and assume that your potential constituency is everyone not wrapped up in the power elite. This even includes many sons and daughters of the corporate rich who have seen enough and want out—they've always been there in small numbers on the American Left and Right anyhow, so why pretend differently? In other words, I'm suggesting that you not immediately begin to pander to blue-collar workers because some theory says they are the key to revolution. They may be necessary or they may not, but do they have to be with the party from day one? I don't think so. Kick the Cult of the Proletariat, accept your origins and those of any converts, and look, for openers, to where the rumble is. I suggest as follows: the initial base is, as C. Wright Mills said, radical intellectuals and students. The intellectuals have got to start talking like Gene Debs and Malcolm X. They have got to blast out of the classroom and clinic like Mills and Ben Spock, carrying their revolutionary consultation services to every group in the country that will send them an airplane fare or bus ticket. What with the protection of tenure and the right of academic freedom, and with lots of universities opening up in Canada, Australia, and New Zealand, professors are the least vulnerable group in American society. They ought to be ashamed of themselves for not raising 100 times more ruckus than they are now—just so they don't advocate anything illegal, of course. These professors and their students also have to continue work on the analysis, and begin involving people in their local community in work on the blueprints. They should form small study-action groups in every university, college, and junior college town in the country, off the campus, of course, because the revolution will not be won by cowing harmless administrators and liberal professors.

These small study-action groups have to prepare themselves for a psychic blitz of their most important constituency. That constituency is simply called youth—blue-collar, white-collar, blue skin, black skin, who cares? They are pouring out of schools like crazy, affluence has made them somewhat independent and hang-loose, many of them don't communicate with their parents, and they're going to be a majority in a very few years. Catch them in those years when they are sociologically part of a unique subculture and psychologically looking for something moral and true and meaningful for their lives, and sock it to them with analyses and programs that will make them as wise to the slick McCarthys, Kennedys, and Rockefellers as they are to the Rusks, Johnsons, and Nixons. If you don't get them the first time around, at least they have something to chew over when they get out there in the boredom of being a probation officer, or paper pusher, or real estate salesman. I know that right now an amazing number of the young are enamored of the long hair and sing-song voice of a Kennedy or the integrity and professorial cool of a McCarthy, but that's all those two birds have got—with no program but a little more of the same, wedded to corporate capitalism, and committed to a party with a reactionary Southern wing and a fistful of New York investment bankers—their time is going to run out if they can't produce. Young people react to the put-on, they hate to be fooled or talked down to or pandered to, and someday they will have had enough—they will remember Humphrey's sell-out, if you are there to remind them; they will remember Johnson's campaign fibs about his plans for Vietnam, if you never let them forget it; and they will start looking around again.

After youth, the early appeals or the party must be to the disaffected teachers, librarians, nurses, and bureaucrats of the white-collar class. They are the ones hit by inflation and hurt by the limitations on government spending, not the unionized blue-collar workers with their built-in cost-of-living raises. And besides, you've got something immediate for them—thanks to the Hippies, you can teach them how to be Happy. Happy? Yes, Happy. Get your Hippy friends out of the woods, put a light trim on their beards and hairdos, and start them to work on the poor, wasted paper pushers and people manipulators. I'm serious. They can be had. They're going nowhere, they're restless, and their rage shows how jealous they really are. Their kids—using flower power and psychic guerrilla warfare, can cajole them over the line. After all, these people raised the turned-on kids. Their emptiness and searching is reflected in their children, who have to resort to modern-day ambrosias and Eastern mystical religions to overcome their boredom. If the kids can be had, the parents can be had—if you handle them with psychological bribery and good-humored taunts rather than threats and insults.

As I've implied throughout, an effort has to be made toward those on the Right. I'm under no illusions about the difficulties of this, but I insist that it is necessary to dismiss talk about racism and Fascism on the Right: all white Americans are racists, and parts of the blue-collar world are probably worse than the Right. As to Fascism, if we get a European-style dictatorship in this country, it will probably be more like France anyway, and it will be instituted by the corporate rich presently in power in order to get around their difficulties with Congress and local governments. So forget all this talk about Fascism, which has scared American revolutionaries into the laps of the liberals almost as well as the cry of Communism has scared the Right into the arms of the corporate rich. Old Left and liberal talk about Fascism amounts to their fear of angering the corporate masters to the point where they call on their supposed Right-wing shock troops. See if you can make contact with those people on the New Right, who really have no place to go because there is no turning back now that the huge corporations have destroyed individual capitalism.

Of course they don't share your program, but they do share your view of the power structure and your desire for more individuality and local autonomy.

I suggest two important points in talking with this potential constituency about your blueprints. First, religion is not an issue in the U.S.A. Revolutionaries of recent times have thought it was, and that is a great tragedy. The fact is that religion was here before capitalism, it will probably be here long after capitalism, it is not a trick of the ruling class, and it is not necessarily opposed to all change in the socioeconomic sphere. True, certain organized, institutionalized aspects of religion may resist, but these aspects are not determinative in any case. They can be safely ignored, and religion can be fully respected by those who prefer transcendentalist, mystic, and humanistic expressions of their life-serving impulses. Even more, as Martin Luther King's example has reminded us once again, the New Testament has a Social Gospel that can be social dynamite; it can be a force for change as well as standpatism, and I predict that a lot of clergymen will be with you.

This point about religion is closely related to my next point in dealing with the New Right—respect for individuality and personality. Neither Left nor Right really does this despite their rhetoric. They are both in part personality cults. The fact that personality types who find different styles appealing tend to concentrate in the two different camps attests to this exclusionary bias. (Here I am relying on my own research as well as that of others who have actually studied the problem.) A revolution must transcend personality and respect individuality if it is to get to its task of reaching large masses of people. In fact, personal diversity will be an asset in getting the attention of all types of people. Different religions, different styles, and different hair arrangements must be de-emphasized (not changed), and consciously subordinated by self-analysis and devotion to common goals through the mechanism of the blueprints. The enemy is corporate capitalism, not religion, personality structure, or type of oral indulgent—pot on the Left, alcohol on the Right—used to lessen anxiety and dispel depression.

Why haven't I mentioned black people till now? Aren't they important? Am I just another Whitey who doesn't care about the black man? Not at all. I suggest that you do what the black man told you to: let him do his own thing and you get to work building a party than can unite with him someday far off down the road after you've overcome your racism and he's made up his mind about where he's going and with whom. Maybe someday your party will have a black wing and a white wing instead of a left wing and a right wing, but for now the black man is right—you've got nothing to tell him, and he's got to go it on his own with himself and "The Man" in order to win his manhood. Nobody has ever been given anything worth having. Finally some black men are learning that freeing fact, and the sooner the brown man and the red man learn it, all the sooner are they going to split on that paternalistic pap and unctuous benevolence called the Democratic Party. Leave the black man alone to find out for himself—there are already plenty of would-be white revolutionaries bugging him to tears, trying to take the seemingly easy way to a small, quick success in terms of lots of militants.

Of course black people should be welcome in your party, as is anyone who shares your beliefs, but I suspect it will be a while before many will be along. One group is going to go a separate and/or violent route. They've had enough and they will have to see some fine action from a revolutionary party before they are going to buy any dreams and hopes again. I don't blame them. I for one will never get uppity or moralistic, as so many of the liberals do, black and white, if some blacks decide to wreck the system. I understand their rage, I feel their rage, and I've always wondered why they didn't bring the whole mess to the ground. But despite my sympathy I don't mistake the catharsis of wrecking the system for changing it. Revolutionary movements grow more slowly and have positive goals. But I hope you can show these black radicals something—the ones I've watched have the juice to turn on masses like nothing I've ever seen. Malcolm X was the finest American agitator since Eugene Debs, and a revolutionary party would need a hundred more like him.

Then there's another group of blacks who are committed to non-violence but who think John F. Kennedy freed them! Imagine. Like the Socialists of the Old Left, their hang-up is a faith in the Democratic Party that knows no bounds, through thick and thin, Raw Deal and Double Deal. Pictures of JFK abound in their homes. The tragic thing about this group is that they don't know they freed themselves—they pushed that smooth-talking young conservative to the wall before he would make a move. These people don't know their own power—they haven't quite achieved the manhood and pride of the black separatists. Nor do they understand the limitations of the present socioeconomic system—they are still hoping it will assimilate them economically. Apparently their faith in God and American democracy even includes corporate capitalism. Many even refuse to talk about the Vietnam war, hoping that their white masters will give them a little more if they keep their traps shut about the repression of other colored peoples.[1]

So, one black group—the separatists—has revolutionary instincts but unlikely methods, while the other black group has great methods but the mentality of everyday members of the Democratic Party (and you can't get much more mundane than that). Perhaps by the time these two groups are done exploring their respective paths they will want to help build a revolutionary party. Your job is to have the semblance of one for them to react to if they run up against the limits of the present system.

What about blue-collar workers? Well, what about them? Don't wait till they're ready to swing. If you can't make it without them, you can't make it without them, but at least have a party they have to react to. And don't waste any time trying to control or shape labor unions, which are conservative bureaucratic institutions these days, rightfully looking out for the working man in day-to-day battles with the corporate leaders. Confront these people at home, at school, and at play, and get them involved in the party and its activities. In short, don't get caught in Old Left fixations.

Now I know there are many thousands of dedicated and far-seeing blue-collar workers who would be with you from the start, heart and soul, sweat and tears, but don't get the idea that any great percentage of organized labor will be willing to risk leaving the Democratic Party. Right now they have it relatively good—as long as they're working, or are insulated against automation, or have cost-of-living raises built into their contracts as checks against inflation. But no matter how nicely some of the corporate rich treat blue-collar workers in wartime, don't worry, because there is no question about where blue-collar masses would be in a showdown if you have done your

[1] Neither Cleaver nor Gregory, great as they are in their separate ways, had much effect on this group according to the indications of the 1968 elections.

homework carefully. And by homework I mean showing them something better and how to achieve it. They already understand about capitalism—their problem is they've resigned themselves to it because they can't see risking a struggle they don't believe will succeed. They don't love the present system, but a lot of them have more to lose than they can see gaining in a vaguely defined "struggle" for abstractions like "freedom" and "justice."

I have said what I think must be done and who will be the most likely to initially respond. Now I want to speculate on what would happen in the shortrun. When the revolutionary party started, one of three things could happen—it might be snuffed out, it might be left alone to grow very rapidly, or, forbid, it might flop. Flopping I won't consider here, because all it means is that it was the wrong time and place for your ideas, and the wrong set of consultants; nothing ventured, nothing gained. As to being snuffed out by the corporate rich at the start, I find that highly unlikely—they are more liable to find the whole thing laughable and unbelievable, giving the new revolutionists as much free mass media coverage as they have given any other good human interest story. Then too, they are not likely to want to react violently to a non-violent party, at least not until they found it a serious threat.

Some of you may ask—wouldn't the snuffing out come from the ultra-right? Aren't they the classical perpetrators of violence against revolutionaries? Well, maybe, but I think not in corporate America. They will find it hard to bring themselves to move against a movement that shares their enemies and general values, if not their specific programs; that is in no way involved in or interested in or tied to a foreign power as most recent American radical groups have been; and that in no way attacks the American political structure or the precious right of religious freedom. Each step of the way, as I hope you realize, I've tried to take account of, react to, neutralize this New Right, this Right which is really different in its situation from all previous Rights. But if I am wrong, if they become violent, that is a job for the police, for you too should support your local police. In fact, place all party headquarters as near as possible to police stations and FBI offices so they can better protect you, and maybe take a few stray hits themselves. In short, if violence comes on early from the Right, you must count on the power elite and the liberals to deal with them physically, thus setting the stage for the later showdown between you and the real enemy. The power elite and the liberals don't like the ultra-right one little bit anyway, and they would, I think, rather defend liberties against the Right than allow the slaughter of a minute revolutionary party which could be dealt with later if things got out of hand.

But I just don't assume violence from the Right or anywhere else. To assume violence is to invite violence in the manner of the "defensive," paranoic aggression that has been the rationalization and cause of much of the violence of history. Break that vicious circle, drop your defenses, and thereby free your opponents to break out of the cycle with you. The first move is yours, and it takes a lot of guts. It requires getting close to your opponents, embracing them, and demythologizing their image of the "dangerous revolutionary," not to mention their image of the "greedy Jew" and the "sexy Negro." In other words, more psychic guerrilla warfare, this time using motivational analyses borrowed from the study of unconscious and not-so-unconscious fantasies. Disarm your opponents by psyching them, by embracing them, and by constantly reminding them of their democratic, non-violent values.

So let's assume that the party is not snuffed out in its early stages and that it grows. Then the power elite is in a bind—they will have to compete with it, which means a move towards the Welfare State, or, failing that, they would have to repress it, which would be the great watershed for American liberals, liberalism, and democracy. If you are non-violent, open, of all religions, and not tied to a foreign power, they would be destroying America to move on you. Liberals would have no course but to join the fight on your side or admit that socioeconomic privileges are more basic than political institutions and values; some might even be annoyed enough to join you in the air-conditioned, music-equipped prison cells that the corporate rich are likely to provide. More generally, at that point the masses of people in America would have to draw their own conclusions about what is to be done. At that point all bets would be off; it would be a new game. Your job is to bring people to the point where they want to choose between democracy and corporate feudalism. And, I repeat, you cannot do this merely with analysis and blueprints and a few helpful brawls by policemen. It can only be done by taking the political system on its promise and testing it to its limits. Either way, you win—a democratic, non-violent takeover or proof to all that when it gets down to the nitty-gritty, even in America, the only way to power is the barrel of the gun. But, I repeat, you have to assume good faith and remain non-violent—to secretly arm, or to try to goad the corporate rich into violence, is to destroy the power of your movement. In short, psychic guerrilla warfare requires as much courage and risk as the physical kind. It is no place for the fainthearted who are unwilling to die for a great cause.

To conclude, let me outline what you should do today and tomorrow if you are revolutionaries. . . . First, start a chapter of a future revolutionary party. Call it, say, the American Revolutionary Party or the 1776 Party so as to make your intention clear from the start. Then, to set the sort of tone you want for the thing, print up a membership card, something like, "I, the undersigned, am a card-carrying member of the American Revolutionary Party, dedicated to replacing corporate capitalism with a post-industrial America through psychic guerrilla warfare." Then start a chapter newsletter in which you invite people to discuss and develop blueprints for your local area—for running its schools, its beaches, its universities, its utilities, and its factories. Send particularly good ideas and articles, especially those relevant to the national level or other cities, to the editorial staff of the nationwide party journal.

At the same time, begin to hold classes in which you teach about the nature of corporate capitalism and discuss blueprints for a post-industrial America. Such educational efforts are a must, one of the best lessons to be learned from the Old Left, and they are the start of the parallel educational structure that each local chapter should strive to develop.

As soon as you have enough people in the chapter who are dedicated and know what it's all about, then you look for opportunities to reach larger numbers of people through confrontation politics—marches, rallies, sit-ins, whatever, but always including explicit mention of the party and its goals. If there is a local bond issue asking for higher property taxes to support the schools, then that's the time to show in detail how the corporate rich distort the tax structure and force the burden on the middle levels, even to the point of bribing the tax assessors in some cities. Agree with the New Right that taxes are killing them and tell them why, agree with the liberals on the need for better schools and show them how they would be in a post-industrial America. If the issue is an increase in the gasoline tax, then maybe that's the time to shock conservatives about the price manipulations and tax dodges by the pious oil companies who help finance the New Right. In short, armed with a real understanding of the present system and the beginnings of plans for a better one, you use every occasion possible to get people's attention and gain converts.

If you bother to go on campus for other than speeches to interested student groups, use picketing not to stop recruiters or Dow Chemical agents but to educate and convert more students and professors. Aside from exposing the complicity of leading universities and research institutes in the machinations of the corporate rich (which ranges from CIA involvement at MIT and Michigan State to overseas economic front men at Stanford Research Institute), your main concern is elsewhere. The university is not the key structure in the system, and just exposing its uglier aspects is enough to get you a careful hearing from most students, and even some professors. In short, this advice about dealing with the universities is part of a larger strategy—ignore the corporate rich and their tag-alongs. You have no criticisms or suggestions to offer them. There is nothing they can do to satisfy you, short of joining your party. Don't try to change them and their policies. Leave that for liberals. Talk to people, don't debate with the power structure.

Now, once the party exists and has a distinct identity, it should of course support just causes. You are for anything that makes people's lives better here and now. Making things worse is not going to speed up any "dialectic." The important thing, however, is to show that you are for these causes without getting so caught up in them that you can't see the forest for the trees. Don't get sidetracked. Support "liberal" causes and speak kindly to and of the liberals who fight for them, but do not become the errand boys for these single-issue and short-run causes. I repeat: don't get sidetracked.

Once you have a good-sized local chapter, then add "politics" to your other activities. This consists of developing parallel governments and councils ready to step in if and when, and ready to run for legislative offices in the hopes of winning and thus gaining a better platform from which to reach people.

But action would not take place only on the local level. All the while, the many locals would be in contact through social (not, ugh, business) meetings at regional and national levels. Then too, they would contribute representatives and ideas and money to a loose national party structure which would consist mostly, at the outset, of the editorial staff of the nationwide journal and the organizers, agitators, and revolutionary consultants who would travel around the country helping to organize and strengthen locals. Every chapter would contribute a few members to this national-level effort each year, thus ensuring that a great many members from all over the country get national-level experience and perspective. This not only cross-fertilizes the locals and helps maintain an overall outlook, but it provides some basis for developing a shadow government for the national level and for the selection of candidates for national offices. During the summer the national organization would also coordinate the Student Organizing Teams who would in groups of 20-30 spend several weeks in every hamlet in the country carrying the message of the party to the hinterlands. The groups would be made up of those with an empathy for and knowledge of rural America, including return-to-the-land type Hippies. Their goal would be to develop a chapter, however small, in any settlement or town where people would listen, and listen they might, for the descendants of those people who became populists in the 1890's and took potshots at local bankers and judges in the 1930's are being had once again by the corporate oligarchy.

What do you do next? What do you do if the infiltration of the army is not very far along and the corporate rich attempt to suppress your fast-growing movement? Well, how should I know? And who cares? You can't expect to anticipate everything. If your analysis is sound, if your blueprints are appealing, and if your psychic guerrilla warfare has blown the minds and ideological cover of the power elite, then you are part of the most exciting, inspiring, and creative thing in human history: an unstoppable mass movement *that can take care of itself.* Power grows not out of a gun, but out of masses in action, masses armed with ideas, a vision, and moral fervor. So armed they cannot be beaten. They will suddenly surge ahead of their so-called "leaders," deciding on the spot the tactical question of "What Is To Be Done."

The real problem for you, then, is not how to end. The real problem is how to begin. And good luck, for the enormity of the task is staggering even in contemplation.

HOW TO MAKE A REVOLUTION IN THE U.S.

● *peter camejo*

Revolutionary socialists have been accused for many years of wanting to overthrow the U.S. government by force and violence. When they accuse us of this, what they are really trying to do is to imply that we want to abolish capitalism with a minority, that we want to force the will of the minority on the majority. The opposite is the truth. We believe we can win a majority of the people in this country to support a change in the system. It will be necessary to make a revolution precisely because the ruling powers will not peacefully accept a majority rule which wants a basic change.

How can a revolution involving a majority of the people actually take place in the United States? This is the question I want to discuss today.

First of all, you have to have clear in your mind the meaning of the word "revolution." Many people have a stereotyped picture of what a revolution is like. They say a revolution is when people come with guns, when they surround a fortress or take over a city. What they do is they confuse revolution with insurrection. Insurrection is just one stage of revolution. Revolution is a lot more. It's a long process.

In a certain way you can make a parallel between revolution and pregnancy. In the very early stages of pregnancy, if just on empirical evidence you ask whether or not someone is pregnant, the answer will be no. However, with the use of science you can determine whether the person is pregnant very early. Later on it becomes evident for everybody to see.

The same thing is true of social revolution. In the early stages most people don't see it. You always begin on the assumption that in every society that needs a revolution, the majority of the people don't think it's possible. This is most certainly true for the period in American history we are in right now. We're in the early stages of the third American revolution. I say the third revolution because we've had two others—the revolution of 1776 and the civil war.

the contradictions

Why is it that we are in the early stages of a developing revolutionary situation? The reason is most basically because of the contradiction between the fantastic potential for solving human needs in this society and the existing reality. Let me explain:

Everything you use, everything you eat or wear, your car, your housing—you didn't make any of these things. We don't produce these things as individuals. We produce socially. We have a division of work in the United States, and in the whole world for that matter. People in one part of the world make things which people in another part of the world use.

But, even though we produce socially, through cooperation, we don't own the means of production socially. And this affects all the basic decisions made in this society about what we produce. These decisions are not made on the basis of what people need, but on the basis of what makes a profit.

Take the question of hunger. There are people going hungry all over the world, and the U.S. government recently reported that there are a lot of people going hungry right here in the United States. And yet, because of the profit system, the U.S. government is now paying some farmers not to farm. Farmers don't make their decisions by saying, "We need a lot of corn in the U.S., so I'm going to plant a lot of corn." They never say that. They say, "How much money am I going to make if I plant corn?" Did you know that if decisions were not made on this basis, then the U.S. alone would have the potential to feed the whole world? The economic potential is there.

Take the question of housing. If you took just the money that's spent on the war in Vietnam, you could build beautiful free homes for every nonwhite family in the U.S. and for 30 million of the poorest whites. They could wipe out every slum in the next four years. The potential exists, not only in the factories and materials for building, but in the potential to build new machines and factories. Yet, they are not going to solve the housing question because it's not profitable to build low cost housing.

Did you know that because of the way the system is structured a large percentage of the people do not do any productive work at all? You have the unemployed who are not hired because it's not profitable to hire them. Then you have the people in the Army, not to mention the police, and others who consume a great deal but don't produce anything. Then you have things like the people in the advertising industry. They don't do anything really useful or necessary. In addition, you have a mammoth, organized effort to create waste. For instance, if you designed a car for the Ford company that would last 50 years, they wouldn't use it. Because that would destroy the purpose of making cars, which is to produce profits.

I'll give you another example of how the potential for meeting human needs is destroyed because of the profit system. Say you are a capitalist, and you're about to build a factory. Do you say, "I'll build it where it's nice, where there are trees and fresh air, and where the workers will have nice homes and will be able to go mountain climbing or hunting or swimming"? No, that's not the way you think. You say, "Well, where's my market, where are my raw materials coming in, how can I make the most profit?" And this means you might build the factory where you will pump even more poison into the air.

Smog is another example of a problem which stems directly from this system. Remember when they first discovered smog. They said, "Hey, look, there's smog." And they warned that if the smog increased to a certain point it would be dangerous. But, when they got past that point, they changed the danger level. And the smog is still getting worse. And now they tell us that all the rivers are polluted. In other words, it's not that they just can't meet the problem that exists. Things are getting worse.

third world

But, it is in the underdeveloped world—in Asia, Africa, Latin America and the Arab countries—where the contradictions of this system are the most clear. To really understand what this system means for third world people, consider this one fact: When a worker finishes working a full day in the colonial world, he produces as much as an average American worker does in 22 minutes. There is no way of solving the tremendous problems, the hunger and the poverty, that exist in the third world unless that figure is raised. In order to raise this figure, you have to industrialize, you have to mechanize, you have to invest.

Well, what happens is that instead of getting help from the industrialized sections of the world, instead of getting capital, third world countries are drained of their wealth by the imperialist countries. More important, the third world countries are blocked from industrializing simply because the advanced capitalist countries will not permit the competition which would result from it. In fact, in terms of the effect such exploitation is having on the world, in terms of people actually dying, starving and suffering, and their whole lives being destroyed by poverty, this is one of capitalism's greatest crimes.

Capitalism doesn't just have general long-range problems like the ones I've just mentioned. It has other contradictions—big crises, like depressions and wars. And specifically in this period, when the colonial world is trying to break out of capitalism, the wars are directed against the colonial world.

How do we go about changing this situation? How do we make it so that we can really fulfill our potential as human beings?

First, it is necessary to realize that in the United States we have a ruling class. And it's very important that everyone should get to know and recognize their ruling class. The ruling class in the United States is very small. In fact, I think, proportionately, it is the smallest ruling class in the history of any society. Even defined broadly, there are only about 30,000 of them. There are a lot of people who think they belong to the ruling class, but only about 30,000 who have the real power.

Now, there are certain ways you can go about finding out just who these people are. One example is when you pick up your local newspaper and you look at the society page. You can see their children. The newspapers go to their parties and take pictures of the sons and daughters of the ruling class.

In some cities, the people in the ruling class register themselves. Of course, some ruling class people don't make the register, and there are some people who will slip in who aren't from the ruling class. But basically the social registers are a good indication of who these people are. In addition you can read the many books put out on this question. Books like *The Rich and the Super-Rich*. They spell it out.

how it's done

Now, how does the ruling class do it? Here, you've got some 30,000 people running a society of 200 million and most of the people in the society don't even know it. In the past, ruling classes were proud of their role. They would walk around with feathers in their hats, or big robes and things, and when they went down the street, people would say, "Hey, there goes one of our ruling class." Nowadays, they don't do that. Now, they can slip on the campus where you are, and somebody in the ruling class could walk right by, and you wouldn't even know it. They dress just like you. They're incognito.

Rockefeller would never come to your campus and say, "Hi, how're you doing? Are you studying hard, getting your degrees so you can come to work for me and make me richer?" No, they don't do that. They go around saying that there aren't classes in America, that everybody's middle-class, only that some are a little more middle-class than others. In other words, they are ashamed of their own existence. They have to hide it. And there are good reasons for that. One of their problems, of course, is that they're so small. Why, there are more than 30,000 people on just one or two campuses.

Now, how do they maintain their rule? To find this out you can try an experiment. Get all dressed up, put on a jacket and tie, and walk into some corporation and say, "Hello, I'm a sociologist, I'm here to do a study. Could I just walk around and talk to people?" And then you walk up to somebody and say, "Who's your supervisor?" And he'll point to someplace, and you find someone with a little name plate, and it's a supervisor. And you ask him, "Who's your supervisor?" And he'll point to a different place, and you walk in and there'll be a rug. And you say to him, "Who's your supervisor?" And he'll point to a different floor, and you'll find it gets harder and harder to get in the doors. There's more and more secretaries, and phones, and the rug gets thicker and thicker. Eventually you have to make appointments. And then you hit the sound barrier. Here is where you switch from the people who carry out decisions to people who make the decisions. And that's your local ruling class.

By the way, if you test out any institution in our society, you'll find they are structured in the same way. A pyramid from the top going down. That's the way all institutions are structured in this democratic country. This goes for government, for the political parties, the Army, the churches, the universities, for every basic institution. And when you get to the very top of these structures, to the most powerful people, you will invariably find people who own big property.

Now, how do they keep the structure going? It's a very subtle thing. In the United States, we have freedom of speech, freedom of assembly and other democratic rights. So, say you go to your job one day and test it. Wear a big button that says, "Vote Socialist." And watch how fast you get promoted. Watch how you are treated. Formally you have the right to have any political view you want. But, the truth is that in all these institutions there is a very worked out, institutionalized way of going up. And on the way up, you sell your individuality, you commit yourself to the values of the system.

And you learn very fast that in return for full commitment to the system—for personal discipline, for showing up every morning wearing the right clothes, keeping your hair short, and the rest—in return, you get privileges. It's done on the basis of privileges. That is what holds the society together.

When was the last time you heard someone say, "Capitalism's a great society"? When did you hear anyone say, "Just think what our 30,000 ruling class has done for us. We should give them our full support." They never say that. They don't try to build up an ideological support for capitalism in the sense of telling you the full truth.

All the institutions under capitalism are ideological institutions in the sense that all of them maintain and demand support for the system. So it should be no surprise to you that the higher you go in a corporation, the higher you go in the university structure, the higher you go in the Army, the people get more and more reactionary. They get more and more consciously pro the system; they are more and more for whatever crimes the system has to commit. They simply wouldn't be there if they weren't. This is why you can never capture the existing apparatus and use it for making a basic change.

workers' power

Today the smallness of the ruling class means that other classes have more power in comparison. We have a working-class army, for example, that has a great deal of actual and potential power. Take the basic production of all goods and services. Have you ever thought what a general strike would be like in New York City? Workers can take over this city in a matter of hours. Because workers run everything—the subways, the trucks that bring food, gas, light, heat—everything.

So you have to ask yourself, why is this power never realized politically? Why don't they just kick the 30,000 out? The reason is simple. The mass of people are under illusions. Now let me repeat this because the whole strategy of making a revolution in the U.S. is crucially dependent on understanding this. The 30,000 can rule only through maintaining illusions.

You see, if tomorrow, President Nixon called a press conference and said, "Okay, I'm going to let you in on it; there's 30,000 of us who are running this country. We're canceling all elections. We're canceling freedom of speech, freedom of assembly, and so on. So go back to work, back to the campus—and if there is any disturbance we'll throw you all into concentration camps." How long do you think the ruling class would stay in power? They couldn't do it. Their power is already limited by a certain consciousness that exists in the mass of the people. Their power is limited by the fact that the mass of the people believe in free speech, in free assembly and in democracy.

And this, by the way, is the thing that is least understood by the student movement. Many students believe that the ruling class has unlimited power. They think fascism and concentration camps are around the corner. Of course, we cannot be naive about the ruling class. They will suppress opposition to them insofar as they can get away with it. And they will use the most brutal means available if it suits their needs. But they will try to keep the repression in the bounds of what they can get away with without waking up the mass of the people, without destroying the illusions. Because, if the mass begins to wake up, that's a big danger.

two-sided

There are two sides to democracy in this country, and if you don't understand both sides, you go wrong. One side is that it's phony. There is no real democracy in the sense that we don't run this country. The elections are totally phony. The ruling class simply gets up and picks two people, or three, and they say, "Okay, everybody, we're having elections. Now you can vote for Humphrey, or for Wallace, or for Nixon."

Then they have their candidates have a debate. But the debate isn't entirely phony. The debate often represents a real living struggle between different positions within the ruling class. The ruling class resolves many of the smaller tactical differences they have among themselves through means of elections.

Obviously, such elections do not in any way mean that the people have a voice in ruling this country. At the same time, the masses of people believe in democracy. And this belief in democracy is something that actually weakens the rulers. And it is something that gives us real power.

There is a power relationship between the masses and the ruling class based on the potential power of the working class. Because of this power relationship, you can do many things. It gives us what we call free speech. It gives us free assembly. It gives us the right to organize the YSA legally. Take for example the underground press. The underground press isn't really underground. These papers are published legally even though they attack the system. They don't suppress these newspapers because they know that the minute they start suppressing papers, it's going to wake people up and bring a reaction.

The only hope the ruling class has is if it can isolate the revolutionaries completely from the rest of the people. That is why the number-one task of all revolutionaries who really want to change the system is to know how to reach the people.

This is one of the biggest problems existing in the student movement at this point. The average student radical does not identify with the American people. In fact, he's hostile to them.

He says, "The American people, ugh, they're against the Vietnamese, they're racist, they're this and that." But you know something? That hate for the American people was taught to the student before he became a radical.

middle-class prejudice

When you go to school, the whole concept you are taught is that anyone that works with his hands is below you. The average Joe Shmoe is a stupid fool. And they justify the fact that some people have more privileges by saying that it's because they're more qualified.

Everything you learn in the university is calculated to give you that superiority feeling. And when you become a radical, you just turn around and invert it in a way. You keep the same prejudice in your mind and you continue to say, "How stupid the average American worker is." He's no stupider than you were before you became a radical.

Black people used to imitate white people, right? But, with the radicalization, one of the first things that started happening was that black people stopped imitating the people who oppressed them. It's the same thing with white workers. The thing that white workers do today is they imitate the people they regard as above them. They try to be like them. They vote for their parties. They support their ideas. But when they wake up this is one of the first things that will change.

Now let me explain something about mass awakening. There's no way that we radicals can by ourselves wake up the American people. Just forget about that. There is no special leaflet that we could write so articulately and carefully that when you hand it to a worker, he will pick it up and say, "That's it—I'm with you." If that were how we could do it, we'd have done it a long time ago.

There is only one way it will happen. Capitalism does it for us. The system creates the situation in which people wake up. Let me give you a few examples. Think about why it is that black people are moving today. Weren't they black in 1920? Weren't they actually worse off, if you want to look at objective conditions, in 1910, 1920 and 1930?

role of africa

You know that at the beginning of the century, and after that, one of the biggest putdowns they had for black people was to call them Africans. Then came the revolutions in Africa and other parts of the third world. And black people started identifying with Africa, saying, "We're all Africans." And the ruling class began to say, "No, you're Americans."

At the same time more and more black people were moving to the cities because of the industrialization of the South. And this concentration of black people living in the cities—this begins to give them a sense of power and is one of the reasons you have the rise of black nationalism today. That is another example of how capitalism creates the basis for radicalization.

I'll give you one other example. For those people who were unemployed in the 1930s during the depression, their goal in life was to have a job, to have some stability. If you took a man who was unemployed or who had a lousy job and you gave him a job with fairly good pay, with the perspective of getting continuous increases—that to him was Nirvana. From what he had experienced in life, that was happiness.

But then what happened? His kids grew up. And many of them didn't have the constant image of the unemployed. There would always be food on the table. They could look forward to going to college. And all of a sudden the perspective of doing what their parents did, getting a job, working 40 hours a week, wasn't so inviting. Consciousness is related to what you have lived. And what you expect.

Anybody would have told you that the many years of prosperity would have completely conservatized the youth. But just the opposite has happened. They grew up totally dissatisfied, to the point that it's becoming a mass rebellion of youth.

The rebellion takes place on all levels. For instance, they start growing their hair long, just because it's supposed to be short. They're trying to do everything that they're not supposed to do, because what they're expressing, unconsciously, is that they're totally aware that there's a potential to have an entirely different kind of life. They become aware of it by the very fact of how they live their first 21 years. They go to the university with other young people. And they want to do something creative. They want to be free. And they realize this is possible. They don't want to just go to work for Standard Oil, which for their parents was a great thing.

radicalizing process

So, all of a sudden, you have an increase in consciousness, an awareness about the problems of society, created by the capitalists. And this awareness can become much more intensified if you have a crisis—if you have a major war, or a downturn in the economic situation. Right now we have opposition, we have a radicalization, but even this is nothing compared to what can develop in the future.

Now you can have all this spontaneous radicalization, you can even have uprisings of sorts, but that will never result in a change of the system, unless it's organized, unless there is a concept of how to struggle. Because, the masses of people, when they first radicalize, they don't understand the general problems. They don't understand how to change society. Very few individuals come to this consciousness completely on their own.

Think about the ideas—some of them very complex ideas—which have been a by-product of the accumulation of thought and experience over the long history of revolutionary struggle. It's this thought, this experience which is embodied in what we call the vanguard—organizations like the Young Socialist Alliance and the Socialist Workers Party.

Now, the ruling class has also had experiences, from which they have gained knowledge. They've been running the United States without even any major political opposition for over 70 years now. They know how, when an opposition develops, to try to repress its vanguard, to knock it down, while at the same time how to maneuver and absorb it and buy it off. Eugene McCarthy's campaign was an excellent example of this.

 Without a conscious vanguard with a revolutionary perspective it is hard to deal effectively with these ruling-class maneuvers. It is difficult to do the right thing.

An example of this was the attitude of the early student antiwar movement toward the GIs. When the antiwar movement first began, the students' immediate reaction was to hate GIs, to think of them as killers. I remember in Berkeley they even put up a picture of a GI portraying him as being the same thing as a cop.

saw ahead

At the same time, the YSA opposed this. We could predict, because of the mass opposition to the war and the fact that young people in general were radicalizing, that the GIs would radicalize. So way ahead, before signs of the GI radicalization could be seen concretely, we urged the antiwar movement to go out and leaflet GIs, and to begin to relate to them.

And that's what Marxism is all about. That's what revolutionary politics is all about. It's what has been learned from 100 years of struggle against the system. During this time there have been plenty of examples of how armies radicalize, and under what conditions they radicalize.

There is something else the YSA sees, which we have learned from experiences in the struggle. And that is that you mustn't be sectarian. You should try to get everybody who is against the war to work together. The YSA understands that the best way to end this war, and to weaken the ruling class, is to get massive consciousness against the war—and to break the concept that the people against the war are a minority.

And we know from experience that you have to use the most carefully thought-out actions in order to produce that result. And in many cases, such actions are the so-called stupid, peaceful, mass antiwar demonstrations that some people are sick of—and of which we've now had eleven. And after each one of these mass demonstrations the YSA has said, "Okay, let's do it again now." And the SDS leaders say, "Are you guys crazy? What do you want to do that again for?" They look at it subjectively. They are tired of demonstrations themselves and they forget that demonstrations help other broader layers of people to radicalize. They forget about the impact which the demonstrations have on the GIs, on the average person. They forget that the demonstrations are what helped the students to radicalize in the first place.

Now, we've got a double problem in the antiwar movement and in the radical movement in general, and both sides of this double problem are closely interrelated. One is that some people think they are going to solve the problems of society by supporting some liberal.

Let me explain what a liberal is. A liberal is someone who doesn't like what capitalism does, but likes capitalism. They try to solve the problems created by the system by supporting the system. Now, many students do that too. When they supported McCarthy they did that. What they were looking for was a shortcut. They were trying to change the system from within. They hoped a McCarthy victory would be a substitute for building an independent political movement of the working people, the black people and the students on a mass level, independently and against the ruling class.

On the other side you have the ultraleftists who do the exact same thing—

try to bypass building a mass movement. In California we have a bad rash: people walking around saying, "Everybody get guns." And there is a lot of applauding about guns at rallies.

And then there are those who believe in confrontation as the only method of struggle. By this I mean that the success of an action for them is not measured by how many people are influenced and won over. Their criterion is "We've got to fight the police in the street. Otherwise we aren't revolutionary."

What they are looking for is a shortcut. Some are naive about what the cops can and will do to them. They think that if the present vanguard arms itself and takes on the power structure, then they can change society. But they're not going to change it by themselves. You can't change it without the American people. And you certainly can't change it against them.

What is happening is that the ultraleftists are merely expressing frustration. Just like those who supported McCarthy, they don't have the patience and the understanding of the need to mobilize the people, to win them over, to involve them in the struggle through mass movements.

This is a working-class country. Black people in their great majority are working class. And there are the other oppressed minorities—Chicanos, Puerto Ricans, etc. What you have is an overwhelming mass of people who have objectively no interest in this system. They have to be won over, and our whole strategy, everything we do, has got to be directed at winning them.

french example

Now, how exactly can the American revolution come about? What kind of movements and strategy will allow us to take power? To make this clear, let me tell you what happened in France in May-June of 1968. I said that you need two things to make a revolution—a vanguard and an objective situation in which there is a crisis and a mass radicalization. Well, in France you had that objective situation—but you had no revolutionary vanguard. Let me show you how, if there had been a strong vanguard, revolutionaries in France would have led a struggle to take power from the ruling class:

In France you had 10 million workers on strike. You had another two million farmers supporting them. Plus the 600,000 students. Now, since the total population of the country is 50 million, this means that the overwhelming majority of families had at least one if not two people involved in the strike. It was clear that the majority of the people in France were out on strike, making certain demands. You had a majority. There was no need to negotiate with anyone.

What would a Marxist vanguard do in such a situation? First of all, we would fight for the formation of a strike council of the whole country which could simply say, "Well, it's clear we have a majority, so we are going to have free elections to decide all the questions under demand here. And these elections are going to be run by the strike council because the government has shown itself to be undemocratic."

Remember, at the time of the crisis, de Gaulle had no real power, except in the sense that there was a vacuum which he filled. Do you know that when de Gaulle wanted to hold a referendum during the strike, it was so unpopular that he couldn't get any workers in all of France to print the ballots? He had to go to Belgium, to ask the Belgian workers to print the ballots, and they refused too! He had no strength. One might ask, what about the army? But he had no army with him. Maybe the officers, but the soldiers—who were the soldiers in France? They were the sons and brothers of the strikers.

The first thing a strike council would do would be to immediately hold elections in the army barracks for new officers, and any officer that didn't accept this would be thrown out. And then you would go to the barracks and ask the soldiers to share their guns. The guns would be used to help form militias of the people. Then you would dissolve the police force and have the workers out on the streets patrolling. That could have been done in a number of days under the conditions that existed in France. Just to start with, you had hundreds of thousands of students who would have been immediately willing to participate in the militias and to arm themselves.

Then elections would be held in the factories, and other institutions, and delegates representing the rank-and-file workers in the factories, the students, the soldiers in the army and people in all the various institutions would come together in a central council. And you would put on the floor of this body, which would be the most democratically chosen body in the history of the country, the motion that all industries are nationalized. We would simply pass that, along with other programs which would meet the people's needs.

When you stop to think about it, what would the ruling class have done? Bombed their own cities?

When you think about it, every step I've outlined, every demand, is based on democratic ideas. The word "socialist" hasn't even been used. Because what socialism means is not simply that socialists come to power, but that a class—the masses of the working people—come to power. That could have happened in France. The objective conditions were there, the radicalization among the masses. What was missing? There was no sufficiently strong Marxist vanguard. The working class in France was led by a party which supports capitalism, called the Communist Party. So the big problem in France, in order to make a revolution, is to depose the Communist Party from the leadership of the working class.

In the United States, things are going to happen in a similar way to what happened in France. Not the same, but similar. Look what's happening on campus—it's spontaneous; on campus after campus you see radical actions. The same thing is going to take place in the working class. It is already happening with the masses of black people. As these movements develop, the vanguard at first is small, and can play only a limited role. But, out of these actions come young people who begin to understand that you need to think out the whole question.

They learn from experience. Maybe they get busted and they start thinking how to be effective. And someone sits down with them and explains how you make a revolution, how you form a vanguard and slowly build up and participate in mass struggles, how you get an interrelationship between the mass movements and the vanguard, and how you reach a situation where a crisis will develop and the vanguard will be able to lead the masses to take power.

The key to victory is moving the masses. Any concept, any struggle that eliminates this will only end in disaster. Unfortunately, the ultraleft idea that you can go around the masses, or make the revolution without them, is one

that is creeping into the thinking of many students and young people today.
But there will be a reaction to this. One of the troubles with ultraleftism is; of course, that when people react against it, they sometimes react against militancy in general, and flip over to become opportunists. In fact, you're going to see people who were opportunists yesterday going over to being ultraleft today, and the ultralefts of today flipping over to become opportunists. Because all of them are looking for the same thing—a shortcut. And there is no shortcut to change the system.

It takes a long time. You have to have a perspective of fighting for 10, 20 or even more years. Just like the Vietnamese say they will fight 10, 20, or 40 years—whatever is necessary. You can't walk into the YSA and say, "I want a guarantee that the revolution will happen in five years because after that I have other plans." The revolution doesn't work that way.

So, to end, I want to say this. The ruling class is never going to solve its problems through the capitalist system. Therefore, the objective conditions for revolution are going to rise up over and again. We don't create these conditions, but there is one thing we can do. That is, we can create the subjective factor—the vanguard. By entering the YSA, by building a revolutionary party, by understanding and participating in the revolutionary process, we can make victory possible.

Are we going to be able to do it? Other generations have failed to do it. Are we going to be able to build a revolutionary socialist vanguard that can lead a mass movement to overthrow the system? That's the great challenge to this young generation. And the answer of the YSA is yes, we're going to do it.

ELDRIDGE CLEAVER DISCUSSES REVOLUTION: AN INTERVIEW FROM EXILE

● *eldridge cleaver*

The exiled Minister of Information of the Black Panther Party, Eldridge Cleaver, surfaced last summer at the Pan-African Festival in Algiers. This interview was done at that time by Stefen Aust, a West German journalist.—Liberation News Service.

Question: What was the situation in America at the time of Stokely Carmichael's split from the Black Panther Party, and how did it contribute to the split?

Eldridge: The whole approach to the problem the government is taking, black capitalism, they're using the slogan of black power to conceal that. This forced Stokely to continue articulating what he started in such a way as to make it clear he's not involved in black capitalism. But by quitting the scene and not defending his position, the whole thing has been coopted by people who are in CORE, the whole organization has gone into black capitalism. The former head of CORE, James Farmer, has become the top man in the Nixon administration to implement that, the man who succeeded Farmer as the head of CORE, Floyd McKissick, he has gotten himself an organization, a business firm which he calls Floyd McKissick Inc., and a lot of funds are funneled through him.

We regard this as the advent of the neo-colonialist phase of our peculiar situation in the United States because it corresponds to the moment the colonial power decides to grant a measure of independence to the colony and replace the colonial régime with a régime of puppets. And this is what they're doing now in the United States by pulling certain levels of the black bourgeoisie into the power structure and developing for them a vested interest in the capitalist system. So these really defiant positions, the people who pretended to be revolutionary, are accepting funds.

The government will give anybody money. They offered money to the Black Panther Party; they offer it to everybody, and they don't care what your line is, they just want to get you involved in their programs, then they begin to put the squeezes on you to get you dependent.

A lot of people are accepting this money and they're using the slogan Black Power by equating black capitalism with power. And this is one of the very bad things that has happened as a result of what Stokely was talking about. We offered him the position of Prime Minister of the Party to give him a base which he no longer has as a result of his problems with SNCC and the decomposition of SNCC itself. But he abandoned the field. Now he's talking about the struggles in Africa. He wants to liberate Ghana; it just doesn't stand up.

The key thing to me, he made a statement that I think is very key. He said, "You guys are on top now, but just watch, I'll be back up there." So that whole type of thinking is an ego trip and constantly making these invidious comparisons. We were talking to him when we first came here because we thought he would realize the mistake he had made and apologize to the Party, and we would then accept him back into the Party because we had long been uptight about where he was functioning. He said he did not know the McClellan Committee was engaged in investigations of the Party at the time he issued his resignation and charges. But the charges he lodged against the Party seemed to echo the charges of these stooges who were mumbling before the McClellan Committee. When this was brought to his attention he said he didn't know the McClellan Committee was involved in an investigation. And in light of not knowing this, he said he was willing to make a statement to clarify the situation and to make it clear that he did not have anything to do with the McClellan Committee's attack, so it boiled down to a question of how to do that, and he was procrastinating, and then he made that final statement, something snapped in me, and I was no longer willing to go along with it.

I had been the one who was trying to salvage the situation and give him a chance to apologize to the Party, and everyone else was perfectly willing to let him go and not go to the expense. So when he took the position he took, we called him up and just told him we were not going to try to arrange that other thing that we were talking about, and that we would accept his resignation as he wrote it and deal with it as he put it forth. And that's the last we've heard of him.

Question: His two most important issues in this letter were first, calling the Party dogmatic, and second, condemning the alliances with white radical movements.

Eldridge: I think these two are very related because when he refers to dogmatism, what he is actually referring to is the fact that we are a Marxist-Leninist Party, and implicit in Marxist-Leninism is proletarian internationalism, and solidarity with all people who are struggling and this, of course, includes white people. So that since his main object is non-alliance with whites, and turning one's back on whites and having no policy towards them at all, just to ignore them, he has to come down heavy on both those points in order to maintain his position. And we consider this position to be racist.

We recognize that we cannot function in this way, particularly these days when nationally and internationally they're using negritude as a way to create divisions amongst people, and the domestic counterpart of this international approach is the use of black capitalism, black consciousness. We call it cultural nationalism in the United States, and it's been made very clear how they finance certain cultural nationalist organizations. They have already exposed themselves as being tools of the power structure by their activities. So that another definition is required to make distinctions between friends and enemies when they are coming in all colors. And we feel that the only safe guides to action are the revolutionary principles of Marxist-Leninism, that they are relevant at this point for that reason and we choose to work on that basis and let the rest of that go because black people have already gained their consciousness, they have a sense of their identity, which was lost in the United States. At the time that this was happening, it was very progressive, it was a very good thing that was coming about. But after people had assimilated that and were reminded of who they were and everything, to maintain that position and not to go any further becomes reactionary.

This is what has happened to Stokely and a lot of other people, a lot of other people get hung up culturally in that sense, but Stokely has gotten hung up politically in that sense. There's a false distinction people make between culture and politics, and then after making this false distinction, he confuses culture with politics again. So that it's like an error compounded with an error, and we can't deal with that.

Question: Being critical of cultural nationalism, how do you see the role of this African cultural festival?

Eldridge: Well I think it brought together all of the experienced ideological lines, it forced certain things into the open, and it really serves to drive home to a lot of people that this negritude and cultural nationalism are stumbling blocks to the people's liberation struggles rather than assistances. I think that a lot of the conversations I have had here have been repeated over and over again, people who are involved in the process of struggle for liberation at this moment, seem to be more keenly aware of the negative aspects of this as opposed to those who have already gotten independence and have some very reactionary régimes in power, because they're using this. The people who are struggling are open to all assistance they can get, and they don't want to foreclose any avenue by some simple-minded ideological positions.

But those who are already in power and have gotten their liberation on this false basis, they're content to keep it going. One very interesting thing that I've heard people talking about is that following World War II when all the colonies were fighting for their liberation on the basis of nationalism rather than building a strong revolutionary party. This has proven to be a mistake historically. It was the easy way out because it is easier to mobilize people on the basis of nationalism than it is to create a strong Marxist-Leninist organization.

 The counter-revolutions that have set in and have put many of these nationalist régimes out of power and saddled the people with these oppressive régimes, again demonstrate the point that the only governments that have really been able to survive this sweep have been those governments who have gotten their liberation and created, or even had before, or created during the struggle or after the struggle, a strong Marxist-Leninist Party. And I think this is borne out by the experience of China, Cuba and the Eastern European Socialist countries, including the Soviet Union. That no matter what you say about some of the revisionist policies that are rampant in that area, still I will always choose those Socialist régimes over capitalist régimes. There is something there that is able to withstand the attempt by the imperialists and capitalists to roll back the tide. They found this easy to do in countries that are held together only by very narrow nationalism.

Question: Do you think the role of nationalism in the movement for liberation is no longer important?

Eldridge: I think it will have a continuing importance and there is a proper way to deal with nationalism. I don't think there is necessarily a distinction between, or should I say a conflict between, nationalism and proletarian internationalism, because it's been shown many times that if you can't love those around you, which is a form of nationalism, relate to those within your own entity, then you can't relate to those beyond you, and by the same token if you can relate to those beyond you, and not be able to relate to those near you, then there's still a problem. I'm talking about this full blown nationalist approach to the problem that completely obscures class contradictions and class problems and unites people over class lines and fitting the whole nation out for problems later on. Because on that basis, the bourgeoisie, which is always better educated at this stage, is able to move into the apparatus of the government because people with skills are required, and when they move in they also get the power, and because things are organized on a nationalist base, there's nothing there to counteract them usurping the power, organizing coups and turning the tide back. I think people are moving away from that, particularly young people, young students who are in these countries, most of them are very conscious and most of them are turning to Marxism-Leninism.

Question: The main issue in the split of the American SDS was the relation to the black movement. What do you think of the split, what do you think is the task of the white mother country radicals in this special situation now?

Eldridge: I think the people who were disrupting SDS were the people who had this faulty analysis of the situation, they were still functioning on the basis of an analysis of what we call the Old Left. They are not recognizing the ethnic struggles that are going on in the United States which often obscure the past struggle. The people in SDS who we work with have related to the analysis we have made and they see that it is functional because in the United States you have Mexican-Americans, Puerto-Ricans, Indians, Eskimos, Chinese-Americans, black Americans, white Americans and many other ethnic groups. These ethnic groups have been divided from each other and they are in such a posture at this time that there's no point in trying to make the mistakes that have been made in the past by trying to pull them all into one homogeneous organization without taking all these peculiarities into consideration. We say that's putting the cart before the horse. What we have to do is take the people as they are right now, pull them together into organizational machinery, and then create other machinery that they can be pulled into once they get that consciousness. This is done through a process of coalition, and it does function, and it's functioning right now, and developing, and we're able to deal with much more of the problems than we were when we were trying to pull poor people into one group and continue depleting a lot of our energies by a lot of in-fighting over that. These people who are in PL and who are very dogmatic, and who did not want to recognize what was happening in the other communities and start to impose their own ideological perspective upon the people, did get rebuffed, I consider them splitting from SDS as a fitting rebuff, to the situation they were trying to perpetuate.

Question: After spending so much time in the Third World, have you changed your views on American policy, can you say anything about experiences you have had since you left the United States?

Eldridge: I've been more confirmed in the position and attitude that the Black Panther Party had. I recognize now that some of the things we were doing and trying to do are even more important than we realized they were, particularly in the directions we struck out in, in trying to get around the obstacles that were created by Stokely Carmichael and SNCC, but which we feel were historically necessary—with black power. We took a different course in the United States, and we did it out of necessity. After coming into contact with other people who are revolutionaries but are not black, you see how important it is in order to work with them. I've been appalled to a greater extent than I ever dreamed that I could have been by the visible results of colonialism and imperialism. We in the United States who are oppressed, in comparison to what I've seen around the world, it seems as though we are oppressed between slices of silk, because there's nothing comparable to the poverty I've seen around the world, there's nothing comparable in the United States, even in the most oppressed areas.

I recognize that the United States government is the number one enemy of mankind and very much involved in perpetuating all these things which I have seen, through their international organizations such as NATO, SEATO and through the United Nations. They are able to perpetuate the stagnation of people and to corrupt their attempts to industrialize their countries. This, I think, has had a great influence on me, also a lot of pure revolutionary fervor that I have encountered amongst people has served to stimulate more dedication within myself.

Question: Don't you think it's very important that the liberation fronts in the Third World work very closely with the Black Panther Party?

Eldridge: Not only with the Black Panther Party, but with all revolutionary forces within the United States. Certainly, I think it has been demonstrated here at this festival in Algiers, which has been held under the auspices of the OAU (Organization of African Unity) but also of the whole government of Algeria, the fact that they had the courage to invite us, the fact that they had the courage to invite myself, considering the situation that existed, I think this has gone a long way toward strengthening solidarity.

It had a very strong impact on the United States, I'm sure, and I think that the important thing about this is that in the past there have been individuals, black People from the United States who have come over to make certain contacts and made certain promises that they were unable to fulfill, and for the first time a strong nationwide organization is making contact with these people, and because our relations do not depend on any one person for its perpetuation, that this will have to strengthen these links and create channels that can be perpetuated in the future. These are some of the very positive aspects that I see in this.

 Question: Are there any concrete plans for cooperation, such as sending delegations to other countries?

Eldridge: Naturally we want to cooperate and aid each other in any way that we possibly can. A lot of this of course cannot be talked about, we can say that the people have expressed great gladness at the development in the United States, the fact that revolutionary vanguards are being created. It gives them great hope to know that even in Babylon, a revolution can be struggled for. And it helps them in their struggle because they say that if those guys can do it over there, then what's wrong with us here!? We all know that we are dealing with the same enemy. Just to know that there is someone in the same fight with you always strengthens your dedication.

Question: Do you think the United States had changed since you left?

Eldridge: I think the repression has increased markedly, and this means that the effectiveness of the Party's attack on the power structure was becoming intolerable to the power structure itself. One of the important things that developed after I left was the Breakfast for Children Program that the Party adopted. This was a way for the Party to strengthen its links with the community and to get thousands and thousands of people across the country involved in the program, exposed to the Party. And these people got very angry when the government started attacking the Breakfast for Children Program. There has been much more acceptance of the Party.

It's very interesting that many of the things that we were advocating, that we had been spearheading while I was there, took on more urgency and more acceptability after I left, because people had to relate to that. It's just like—from talking to brothers in the delegation that came here from the United States, just to hear them talk, there was a long time when the Black Panther Party was shot through with cultural nationalism, and we're trying to get out of that bag. The brothers who are here now are brothers who have been in the Party almost from its beginning and I had a chance to watch them develop, see in them resistance to the direction we were trying to take, in terms of relations with white revolutionaries, so that there has been a complete change in that.

I heard one brother refer to the people of Scandinavia as our Scandinavian brothers and sisters, and this particular cat at one time when we were trying to mobilize people from the community to go out to the courthouse and join in a demonstration at the court for Huey Newton when he went to trial, he refused to get into the sound truck because the sound truck was being driven by a white guy.

It was necessary for this guy to drive the sound truck because he had the license and the permit and it just had to be that way. But he refused to get into the sound truck, and now he is the one who made the statement I referred to. That indicates to me that things have changed and that a lot of things that we were trying to do while I was there have become accepted. That's just one, there are other things, but that's one of the most difficult.

There is a lot of development. The Party is stronger and much larger. I think that the great mushrooming and developing of the Party ideologically is one of the most important things that has happened. We always did relate to Marxism-Leninism, but there was a great difficulty in maintaining Party discipline. It wasn't functional, it wasn't really clear how you could apply democratic centralism in that situation, with the cats we had to deal with.

One thing that's important, a lot of people don't understand why a lot of people were purged from the Party. During the time when Huey Newton was going to trial, we dropped a lot of our programs because of the necessity of mobilizing as many people as possible. We virtually closed the membership, we did not make any public announcement, and we started just pulling people in. We knew who the Panthers were, but in order to maximize the number of people we pulled in, we did not argue with people if they put on a black leather jacket or black berets, or said that they were Panthers. They just walked in and said they support Huey Newton and they wanted to join our organization. We didn't have time to conduct our political education classes on this, which is a very important process in our recruitment, that the brothers maintain. After the trial of Huey Newton was over and the verdict was in, it was a question of going back to our other activities that we had been involved in. At that time, a lot of people who came into the organization in that campaign, to free Huey, they proved to be very undisciplined, and non-functional, and they created a lot of problems for the Party and they were not amenable to political education classes. So we just came down hard.

I wasn't there at the time, I was aware of it, I knew what was happening and why it was happening, and a lot of these people were defined as not being members of the Party. And those who wanted to become members of the Party were required to go through political education classes. So that a lot of people who were purged have been admitted back into the Party, but a lot of them were purged for a cause and it will be a long time—if ever—before they will be readmitted.

Question: What do you plan for yourself for the future: What kind of political work do you want to do?

Eldridge: I think there's a lot I can do making contacts for the Party on the international situation, I have a book that I want to finish, but really, I must return to the United States, that's what I want to do. That's really what I'm working on, getting that ready.

Question: Now that the NLF has almost won the Vietnam war and entered this new stage of fighting imperialism, does this change anything?

Eldridge: I think it will be very positive, if you think back you will remember that the whole approach of U.S. imperialism at the time was that the liberation forces in Vietnam had to be defeated, or else other people will get the idea that they can fight for their freedom too. And I think that this has proven that a tenacious fight in the end will be victorious. This is now happening. The United States will, I think, force people to fight just as hard for their liberation; on the whole I think this will strengthen the determination of people to fight on to victory.

Question: Do you think that the persecution of the Black Panther Party now in the United States demands that you create a new kind of tactic to deal with that?

Eldridge: Those things they've been doing have been frame-ups, and a lot of people think we are not serious when we say that, but what they do and what they have been doing is sending in a few provacateurs who will indulge people in conversations about blowing up bridges, or blowing up supermarkets. And on the basis of a few frivolous words that have been passed, they blow it up into a full scale conspiracy and arrest all these people and put ransom on them as opposed to bail, drain our finances; they know what they're doing and this is the technique they use in the United States to keep the Party on the defensive.

 I made the decision that I was not going to submit to this type of chicanery and go to jail when it's very clear that they are manipulating the situation. And I think this is something we are all going to have to get into, because we cannot come up with $200,000 bail. When you think of 21 people in New York, 16 people in Chicago, it adds up to a king's ransom, and we don't have that kind of money, we have no process for getting that kind of money, so I think the people who are dedicated to functioning in a revolutionary manner will start adopting the attitude that they will not be arrested. And they ought to be ready at all times to defend themselves, so that when the man comes down on them and tries to arrest them, these cats are going to start dealing with it right on the spot, because that's more desirable than laying up in a penitentiary rotting away.

Question: And is the United Front Against Fascism part of this tactic to create solidarity?

Eldridge: It's a very important move in that regard, but there's another front that I think needs to be created, and this is something that I have been working on and which I intend to continue working on, and it's something we've been calling the North American Liberation Front. I think it's very timely, because many people see the situation that we are confronted with as one in which politics have been transformed into war, and there's no point in kidding ourselves anymore; what we have to do is fight. We have the terrain there to fight. Many people think that armed struggle carried out in the mountains in Cuba or in Vietnam is one thing, and that it could not happen in the United States. But the United States has more mountains than all of these other areas, it has the advantage of mountainous areas, and a highly organized situation, and it has rural areas. It's so large that the government forces would be forced to spread out very thinly, at the same time that dissatisfaction in the ranks of the United States Army is at an all-time peak. The stockades and military prisons are overflowing with people who have deserted and don't want to fight in Vietnam. And I think that the contradictions that have arisen within the ranks of the United States Army will continue to increase, more so when they are finally turned against the American people.

—*The Black Panther,* October 11, 1969

OUR PEOPLE WILL CERTAINLY DEFEAT THE U.S. IMPERIALIST AGGRESSORS

● *vo nguyen giap*

The situation created by the American imperialists in frenziedly intensifying their aggression in the whole of our country, has placed our people and nation before *the urgent task of mobilizing and uniting our entire people, stepping up our great patriotic war and resolutely fighting to defeat the aggressors in whatever circumstances in order to defend the North, liberate the South and advance towards the reunification of our Fatherland.* "At this moment the struggle against U.S. aggression for national salvation is the most sacred task of all patriotic Vietnamese," said President Ho Chi Minh.

Through many years of heroic and hard revolutionary struggle, under our Party's leadership our people brought the August Revolution and the anti-French imperialist resistance war to victory, liberated half of our country, and have made the North firmly advance to socialism. This revolutionary struggle is going on, we must mobilize the forces of the whole nation, and so we will certainly defeat the American imperialists and their henchmen to safeguard socialist construction in North Vietnam and achieve the people's national democratic revolution all over the country. To defend the North constitutes the revolutionary task of the whole nation because socialist North Vietnam is our people's great revolutionary achievement and the solid bastion of the Vietnamese revolution. At present, American forces are invading the South of our country; to defeat them on this theatre not only aims at liberating the South but also at defending the North in an active way. That is why the task of our people in both zones are closely related. The Northern population must fight to crush the U.S. sabotage warfare and always stand ready to cope with the enemy and defeat him in the event he would extend the war throughout the country. At the same time they must wholeheartedly support the revolution in the South, fulfil its task as the big rear of the whole country. The Southern population who have been fighting unremittingly and with magnificent heroism during these last twenty years, must now endeavour to speed up their struggle with a view to liberating the South and defending the North, deserving the title of Brass Wall of the Fatherland.

Our people's struggle against U.S. aggression to save our Fatherland is a great cause; it will be *protracted, hard but certainly victorious.* In this long-term resistance war our people must do their utmost to work against time and win ever greater successes. We are perfectly capable to do so because we can correctly appreciate the enemy's forces and intention, their strong and weak points, and also the forces and great capacities of our people in both parts of our country. Basing our judgment on an objective and scientific analysis of the relation of forces between the enemy and ourselves, we feel all the more determined to fight and defeat the aggressors in any circumstances, all the more confident in the prospect of our struggle for national liberation: the enemy will certainly be defeated, we shall certainly win.

U.S. imperialism is the international gendarme, the topmost imperialism, having the most powerful economic and military potential in the imperialist camp. In taking a direct part in the aggressive war it hopes it can rely on its material strength to overcome all difficulties in manpower and in political matters, thereby retrieving its predicament in the South. With a sizable expeditionary force which is to be eventually increased it hopes to wrest new vantage-grounds on the theatre of operations: first, to strengthen its military force in general and its strategic mobile force in particular, thus tilt the balance of forces in its favour; second, to control important strategic areas and set up firm bases as springboards to launch mopping-up operations or attacks against the liberated areas; third, to strengthen its air force, develop its superiority in this arm to thin out our forces and to strike deep into the liberated areas.

The American imperialists' scheme is to prevent the collapse of the puppet army and administration, to launch offensives aimed at wiping out the revolutionary forces in the South, especially the Liberation armed forces, to strive to consolidate the areas still under their control and gradually to carry out pacification by priority sectors, to attack the liberated zones and to wrest back some of the lost areas, to seek every means *to encircle and isolate the Southern theatre*. At the same time, they intend to *intensify sabotage warfare* against the North *and carry on deceptive "peace offensives"*. Banking upon a force of over 700,000 men to be eventually increased they hope to realize the abovementioned scheme by means of more radical and efficacious measures. They reckon that they can gradually win military and political successes, secure a position of strength to end the war with a solution favourable to them, or if need be, to prolong or expand the aggressive war.

The U.S. imperialists' design is very ambitious, their scheme most perfidious, and their military and political manoeuvres extremely cruel and machiavellian. However, beside their limited strong points of a material nature they have *most fundamental weak points,* both political and military, in both strategy and tactics.

First of all, the U.S. imperialists are *the enemy not only of the Vietnamese people but also of the progressive people throughout the world*. In the present situation, whereas the socialist camp is growing, the national liberation movement surging, the workers' movement in the capitalist countries and the movement for peace and democracy developing, the forces of imperialism are continually declining. In the over-all relation of forces in the world the American imperialists are not in a strong but in a weak position and have to scatter their forces to cope with the situation everywhere. That is precisely why they cannot send to South Vietnam whatever number of troops without reckoning with their difficulties in every field in the world, right in the U.S.A., and on the Vietnam theatre.

The dispatch of an expeditionary force for the invasion of our country is itself fraught with most fundamental weak points that they cannot overcome.

First, the sending of American troops to invade our country, *exposes still more clearly the U.S. imperialists as aggressors and their lackeys as traitors, thereby the contradictions between the U.S. imperialists and our people become all the sharper*. Stirred by more hatred for the aggressors our entire people more broadly and more firmly unite in the National United Front against the U.S. imperialists and their stooges. All the patriotic forces become more determined to fight for national salvation. Moreover, many Vietnamese in the enemy-temporarily controlled areas, even in the puppet army and administration, in the parties and organizations under the U.S.-puppets' sway, so far unaware of the real nature and intention of the American imperialists and their minions, now begin to see their true faces and more and more definitely side with the people to oppose them.

Second, the U.S. imperialists introduce their troops to invade our country at a time when *their "special strategy warfare" has fundamentally gone bankrupt, whereas our people's patriotic war has powerfully developed,* the Liberation armed forces have grown up, and the liberated areas have included the major part of the Southern population and territory. This precisely makes it impossible for the aggressors, though they may bring in several hundred thousand men, strategically to avoid losing command of the situation and compels them to scatter their forces in defensive as well as in offensive. It is not easy for them to wrest back the initiative as they wish. Instead, they will face the eventuality of increasing failures and deeper entanglement.

Third, due to the loss of political and military initiative mentioned above *no matter how modern its equipment, the American expeditionary force cannot bring into full play its combativeness* and escape a defeat inevitable for all aggressive armies facing a whole nation resolute to resist them. Owing to the unjust character of the war, the morale of the U.S. expeditionary force which has no ideal to fight for, is low. Moreover, on the South Vietnam theatre, it has to cope with a people's war against which the U.S. strategy and tactics based on the bourgeois military conception proves powerless. The organization as well as the composition and training of the American army, generally speaking, are more or less unfit to help deal efficiently with our entire people's revolutionary war, not to mention great difficulties due to unaccustomed terrain and climate, and to the considerable needs in supply and logistics.

Fourth, the introduction of American troops into the South aims at preventing the collapse of the puppet army and administration, and creating favourable conditions to consolidate and strengthen the puppet forces. But the U.S. imperialists openly invade the South of our country at a moment when the puppet army and administration are seriously weakening. In this juncture, *the more open the U.S. aggression, the more isolated and differentiated the puppet army and administration, and the sharper the contradictions between the U.S. imperialists and their placemen.* Those people in the puppet army and administration who still have some national feeling will become more conscious of the real situation and the number of those who cross over to the people's side will increase. Consequently, the introduction of more U.S. troops far from retrieving the predicament of the puppet army and administration aggravates the mercenary army's destruction and disintegration, and the puppet administration's collapse in face of our people's resistance. When the American imperialists' crack troops are defeated by our people the disintegration and collapse of the puppet army and administration will be all the more inevitable.

Fifth, by starting the war in South Vietnam *the U.S. imperialists are more and more sternly condemned by the peace-loving people in the world.* Now that they openly send their troops for a direct aggression against the South and use their air force to strike at the North, an independent and sovereign socialist State, they are meeting with increasing energetic opposition from the peoples of the socialist countries and the world's progressive people including the American people.

The strong points of the U.S. imperialists are limited whereas their weak points are basic ones. As the aggressive war goes on the latter will become more visible and more serious and will surely lead the American imperialists to ignominious failure.

Above are the American imperialists' strong and weak points after some hundred thousand enemy troops have been introduced into South Vietnam. On our side, we do not enjoy the advantages attached to a country with a wide territory and a large population, but our people are resolved to carry on their just patriotic war to defend our life and wrest back our independence and freedom. In this fierce and protracted revolutionary war against such a cruel enemy as American imperialism our force has unremittingly developed, and has many a time put him into confusion. Weak in equipment and technique, and in economic potential, we have absolute political and moral superiority, a correct leadership, the strength of an entirely united people, the invincible people's war and the sympathy and strong support of the world people. It is certain that as we fight, we will score ever greater victories and become stronger. These are the fundamental factors accounting for our people's final victory in the sacred liberation war against U.S. aggression for national salvation. Whatever the number of expeditionary troops that the aggressors may bring in they can in no way escape the inevitable: they will be defeated, the ultimate victory will be ours.

First, *our Party has a correct revolutionary line*. This line is the condensed expression of the clever and creative combination of Marxist-Leninist general principles with the concrete practice of our revolution. This is the line of the people's national democratic revolution progressing to socialism in a former colonial and semi-feudal country. Our Party's line has been tested in our people's long and heroic revolutionary struggle and led our revolution from victory to victory. In the light of this line, Vietnam has been the first colony to rise up and defeat the mighty army of an imperialist power — France —to liberate itself; the North of our country is also the first State to take the path of socialism in Southeast Asia. Today our people have the honour to be in the forefront of the fight against the chieftain of imperialism – U.S. imperialism. This correct line is also that of the revolutionary armed struggle of a small country which rises up to fight and defeat an enemy many times stronger, the line of people's war developed to a high degree with a creative and substantial content. A correct revolutionary line is the surest guarantee for our people's final victory in their just struggle against the American imperialists.

Second, *our entire people are united in the fight against the aggressors to save our Fatherland*. North and South are one-mindedly determined to defeat the American invaders and their lackeys ready to make every sacrifice rather than lose their independence and be enslaved. This iron will reflects our people's tradition of indomitable resistance against foreign aggression. It has brought our people together; millions like one are resolute to fight to defend our country and win back independence, democracy, unity and peace.

Our compatriots in the South have closed their ranks in the fire of the revolutionary struggle, fighting for twenty years, now overcoming countless difficulties and braving a cruel enemy with a firm resolve to march forward, to fight and to win. Today our people in the South have the National Front for Liberation, a broad organization possessed of a correct line and programme and enjoying high prestige at home and abroad. Starting the fight with spike-boards and mantis-like guns they have built big and heroic Liberation armed forces comprising three categories of troops, having high combativeness, skillful strategy and tactics, versed both in guerrilla warfare and large-unit operations and credited with the wiping out of big units of the puppet and American forces. The heroic liberation armed forces have developed everywhere and have been conducting ever more powerful operations in all the South Vietnam theatre from Benhai River to Camau Cape, from the Western Plateaux to the delta countryside and even in the vicinity of big towns. At present the liberated zone accounts for the major part of the population and territory of the South; the Front's policies are being gradually applied there, a new life under an independent and democratic régime is being built and in fact the liberated zone has become the image of to-morrow's entirely liberated South Vietnam.

Meanwhile, the people in the North are steadily progressing to socialism with an ardent love for the Fatherland and for socialism and with an unprecedented political and moral unity. The North is not only a source of inspiration but also a solid rear for our entire people's struggle against the U.S. imperialists for national salvation thanks to its excellent political system and its strong economic and national defence potential. This is a favourable condition which did not exist in our former resistance against the French colonialists.

Since the extension of the war to the North, the D.R.V. army and people have been resolutely fighting and have initially foiled the enemy's sabotage air warfare. In response to the call of the Party Central Committee, the Government and President Ho Chi Minh, our people in the North have launched a strong movement for national salvation, carrying out production and fighting at the same time to defend the North, give wholehearted and all-out support to the liberation revolution in the South, and make a substantial contribution to the common victory of the whole nation.

The Vietnamese people have a tradition of unity and unbending resistance against foreign invasion, but if we look back to its millenary history as well as to the revolutionary struggle of the past many years, we shall realize that never have they united so firmly and so broadly as today, and never has their will to fight off the aggressors and defend the country been promoted to such a degree.

Third, *our weapon is the invincible people's war* and we have gained experiences in conducting it. If it can be said that in nowaday's military affairs there is a greater invention than atomic weapons, i.e., people's war, then the Vietnamese people have effectually contributed to the perfecting of this new arm and are keeping it firmly in their hands. It has developed in Vietnam's historical, political and social conditions and obtained a very high degree with an original and extremely substantial content.

In our country people's war has developed according to the general laws of all revolutionary wars and also to the specific laws of the Vietnamese society and theatre of operations. Hence it is a revolutionary war waged by a whole people on all planes, a revolutionary war fought by a small nation in a narrow and thinly populated country, having an under-developed economy, relying on the strength of an entire people united in the struggle. With it the people will finally win an enemy originally many times stronger.

Generally speaking, people's war in Vietnam is revolutionary armed struggle developing on the basis of the masses' political struggle brought to a high degree. The revolutionary masses' boundless strength has pervaded the revolutionary armed forces and given them an extraordinary capacity to fight and to win. Moreover, the outstanding characteristic of the people's war in our country at the present stage is that, in its very process, armed struggle and political struggle are very closely coordinated, supporting and stimulating each other. Therefore the slogan *"mobilize the entire people, arm the entire people and fight on all fronts"* has become a most lively and heroic reality. Armed struggle in South Vietnam has budded forth from political struggle carried to its peak, and in guerrilla warfare or in limited[1] regular warfare, the operations of the armed forces have always been carried out in accordance with the principle of closest coordination with political struggle. This principle

[1] This is to translate what the author means forms of warfare approaching regular warfare (Transl.).

 was observed in the scattered insurrections in the countryside as later on in the movement to destroy "strategic hamlets", in the uprising of millions of peasants in Nambo[2] as more recently in that of millions of peasants in South Trungbo.[3] Armed struggle in the South has another characteristic: Whether in the form of guerrilla warfare or limited regular warfare, waged with art it is fully capable of solving the question of getting the better of a modernly equipped enemy like the U.S. army. In the South, not only can the regular army but also the regional army and the people's militia and guerrilla force wipe out American and puppet troops and foil their most modern tactics. This is a new development of the revolutionary military art the main content of which is to rely chiefly on man, on his patriotism and revolutionary spirit, to bring into full play all weapons and technique available to defeat an enemy with up-to-date weapons and equipment.

In the North people's war is also developing in the heroic fight against the U.S. sabotage warfare, in the movement among the army and people to down American planes and to turn our North into a vast battleground to counter and foil the enemy air strikes and inflict heavy losses upon the U.S. modern air force. They may attack more fiercely but they can by no means cut off our main communication lines, stop our people's productive activities, let alone shake their determination to oppose the American aggressors, defend the North, and give unqualified assistance to the South.

People's war in Vietnam is the product of our people's resolute and indomitable revolutionary struggle, and also that of the revolutionary struggle of the world people in our times. People's war has led our nation to splendid victories in the revolutionary struggle against Japanese fascism, in the resistance war against French colonialism, and has brought our people great successes in the past few years both in the South and in the North. The great people's war of the Vietnamese nation will certainly outdo the aggressive war of the American imperialists in the eventuality of U.S. imperialists increasing their expeditionary force up to several hundred thousand men.

Fourth, *we enjoy the warm sympathy and wholehearted support of the people of the brother socialist countries, and the progressive people the world over, including the American people.* Our people's struggle against U.S. aggression for national salvation aims not only at liberating half of our country still under domination but also at defending socialist North Vietnam. This grand struggle is the spearhead of all progressive mankind against American imperialism, a great contribution to the world people's revolutionary struggle for peace, national independence, democracy and socialism. That is why the brother socialist countries have given their unreserved support to the stand and line of struggle of our government and the South Vietnam National Front for Liberation, and provide all-out assistance to our people to defeat the U.S. imperialist aggressors. The working class and toiling people of the capitalist countries, the people of the newly-independent countries also side with us, expressing their sympathy and giving their support. All great international conferences and quite recently the Tri-Continental Conference held in Havana addressed warm feelings and very encouraging words to the fighting Vietnamese people and sternly condemned the American imperialists' aggression. Even in the U.S.A. the struggle of

[2] Former Cochinchina.
[3] Former Annam.

the American people against the Johnson Administration's aggressive policy is involving ever-larger strata, taking on bold forms such as self-burning, burning of draft-cards, holding up of the transport of troops to Vietnam . . . This movement is gaining momentum everywhere on a scale unprecedented in the history of the United States. Never in the history of their revolutionary struggle have our people enjoyed such widespread and strong world sympathy and support as today.

What is the development of the war on the Vietnamese theatre of operations since the U.S. imperialists introduced their expeditionary force on a large scale into South Vietnam and, at the same time, began to intensify their air attacks on North Vietnam?

Our entire people like all progressive mankind have seen that the U.S. imperialists' open invasion of our country unmasks their true face as invaders, and the aggressive and unjust character of the war they have kindled is laid bare before world public opinion. The justness of our patrotic struggle and the absolute political supremacy of our people become all the more evident. Our enemy himself has realized that invading our country with his own troops he has suffered a political failure. Nevertheless he thinks that with the increase of his armed forces and the superority of his equipment and technique, he can defy the protest of the world people and trample underfoot all elementary principles of international law which demand the sovereignty and independence of all nations be respected; he thinks that he can overcome all political difficulties to reach his final goal which is to seize the southern part of our country.

The question is: Who will win in the fight between U.S. imperialist aggressors who pursue an unjust cause and our people who pursue a just one? Throughout the past eleven years, every time the U.S. imperialists launched a new aggressive scheme the same question was raised. The liberation struggle of the heroic South Vietnamese people has supplied an eloquent answer: whatever trick the American imperialists may resort to they will inevitably fail in the end. And the fundamental law of the great patriotic struggle of our fellow-countrymen in the South throughout the various stages is: *the further the U.S. imperialists and their flunkeys engage in their scheme to enslave the South of our country, the deeper they will be bogged down and the greater their defeats, whereas the more determined the Vietnamese people in their struggle the greater their victories.*

Today the question as to who will win in South Vietnam is more pressing than ever for in the present juncture there has emerged a new factor: the introduction by the American imperialists of some hundred thousand troops. Can these massive reinforcements reverse the situation? Can the Vietnamese people who have recorded many great successes in their just struggle, win new victories in face of direct aggression by such a modern army as the U.S. imperialists'? Can they defeat the American expeditionary force?

We have here above analysed the enemy's and our strong and weak points, assessed his and our strength and capabilities and drawn the conclusion that the enemy shall be defeated in the end and we will certainly win. This is the theoretical side of the problem. On the other hand, since the introduction of a big U.S. expeditionary force, *the realities of our people's struggle on the South Vietnam theatre have further enlightened the question and is demonstrating that our foregoing theoretical conclusion is entirely correct.*

If in the past when the American imperialists brought Ngo Dinh Diem to power and began to tackle the Collins plan or later on when they put forth the Staley-Taylor plan and the Johnson-McNamara plan, they were extremely optimistic and reckoned that their dark design would certainly be achieved. Recently when they started sending a large expeditionary force to South Vietnam they believed that they could turn the tide. They were confident that within a short time the face of the aggressive war would change, that with their best divisions and brigades and strategic and tactical air force they would be perfectly capable to change the relation of forces, set up solid defence positions, launch bold offensives, and push ahead their pacification by priority sectors, thereby not only preventing the collapse of the puppet army and administration but also consolidating and strengthening the puppet forces. The Pentagon generals hastily declared that at the very moment when big U.S. combat units were introduced into the South and the war was intensified, there were wide prospects of a quick victory. When their initial military operations did not meet with appreciable counter blows they proved still more optimistic and declared that they had shifted to the offensive and compelled the South Vietnam Liberation troops to switch from large scale actions to small unit operations. They also made feverish preparations for attacks on all fronts in the dry season in order to wrest back the initiative and hold it more and more firmly, and drive the South Vietnamese people into an ever more serious defensive position.

However, reality has fallen short of the U.S. imperialists' expectation and purposes. From the point of view of an over all *strategy* in the Southern theatre of operations, is the enemy's strategy offensive or defensive? Is he following the strategy of lightning attack and lightning victory or that of protracted war? As regards operations on various battlefields is he bending his energies in the coastal theatre where he can bring into full play the power of his technical weapons, or in the hinterland theatre where he dreads most to face defeat? Is he concentrating on the Nambo battlefield where lie great political and economic centres or on the High Plateaux that he considers an important strategic position? As regards co-ordination with the puppet troops, is he concentrating on independent or joint operations? These are strategic questions to which the enemy himself cannot give clearcut answers, for the American expeditionary force is strategically engaged in a "blind tunnel." The most outstanding feature of the military situation over the past several months is that not only the South Vietnam Liberation armed forces have kept on stepping up guerrilla warfare but they have developed large-unit actions. If for the whole year 1965 they wiped out over 200,000 enemy troops, including some 50 battalions completely annihilated, in the last five months, since large U.S. contingents landed in South Vietnam and especially since the beginning of October, enemy casualties ran to more than 100,000 men, among them about 25 battalions entirely put out of action including 5 American infantry battalions and a number of American armoured units. This hard fact shows that despite the introduction of several hundred thousand troops the U.S. imperialists cannot reverse the situation. It shows that, confronted with the widespread and powerful development of the people's war, they have no other alternative than to scatter their forces over all theatres of operations and thus cannot avoid being driven into the defensive, and they cannot easily wrest back the initiative and bring into full play the combativeness of their troops. The outstanding feature of the military situation on the South Vietnam theatre is that not only have the Liberation troops successfully turned to account their offensive position since the Binhgia victory, but right after the introduction of a big U.S. expeditionary force they still hold the initiative and promote their vantage-ground on an ever larger scale. No wonder that in face of the heavy setbacks suffered by the expeditionary force McNamara and the American brass hats have shown dismay and toned down, declaring that the war in Vietnam would be long, or that U.S. troops' present attacks are only for defensive. We did not yet mention the moral crisis of the American troops who fear hand-to-hand fighting, leave behind their casualties on the field when hard pressed, throw away their weapons and munitions when withdrawing, are afraid of the jungle, sun, wind, malaria, especially of the Liberation troops and even of the ordinary Vietnamese including old women and children, so much so an American general, speaking of the U.S. expeditionary force said that "its upkeep was expensive but its fighting skill poor."[4] We did yet mention either their great difficulties in logistics and supply, as admitted by the American press: "Once again the U.S. is fighting a big war on the ground and finding itself far from ready to fight that war: the big bottleneck holding up combat operations in this war is logistical." This growing confusion certainly aggravates the United States' economic and financial difficulties and "gold haemorrhage," and reduces its competitive capacity on the world market.

At present, it is evident that from the point of view of military strategy the American imperialists are at sea. And what about their *tactical position?* Though the trial of strength between the U.S. expeditionary corps and the Liberation armed forces has begun recently the latter have proved perfectly capable of checking all of their enemy's tactics.

The Vantuong battle can be considered to be another Apbac[5] for the American expeditionary force. The U.S. deployed a far superior force, including crack troops supported by armoured units, air force and navy to attack a unit of the South Vietnam Liberation army. The result was that far from being wiped out, the Liberation troops fought most valiantly and put out of action many enemy troops. The Vantuong battle which the American generals think can be likened to the Second World War fiercest hand-to-hand engagements was a great victory of the South Vietnam army and people, foreshadowing the tactical failure of the U.S. expeditionary force.

After Vantuong came Chulai, Danang, Datcuoc, Baubang, Pleime, Dongduong and many other battles in which many American and puppet troops were wiped out.

Those resounding and repeated victories prove that:

—*the U.S.* most solid bases *are not immune from attacks.*

—*the American* crack infantry units *such as those belonging to the First Infantry Division can be wiped out (and wiped out at the rate of one or several battalions in a single battle).*

—*U.S.* crack air cavalry units *such as those of the First Airmobile Cavalry Division so much boasted by the U.S. Defence Secretary can be put out of action.*

[4] Retranslated from French (Tranl.).

[5] A victory of the Liberation troops over an enemy ten times stronger in January 1963. In this battle the U.S.-puppet helicopter tactics and armoured car tactics were foiled for the first time.

—puppet units, *though supported by the U.S. expeditionary force, continue to be cut to pieces, not by the battalion but by the combat group as at Pleime, by whole battalions in a single battle like at Dongduong, or by the regiment as at Dautieng.*

—U.S. troops, whether in the defensive or in the offensive, can be wiped out not only by the Liberation army, but also by regional troops, militiamen and guerrillas.

Those splendid exploits are accomplished at a time when the enemy is actively trying to have the best use of his technical weapons including B.52 strategic planes which have made already more than 100 sorties, while spraying chemicals to destroy vegetation and crops, and savagely resorting to poison gases in a number of operations. They are achieved at the same time as great feats performed by the army and people in North Vietnam deal deadly blows to the modern U.S. Air Force's prestige in their continued efforts to defeat the enemy's sabotage warfare.

The significance of those achievements scored in the annihilation of the American and puppet forces lies in *the Liberation armed forces and people of heroic South Vietnam being perfectly capable of putting out of action crack units of the U.S. expeditionary corps, gaining more initiative, stepping up their attacks on all theatres and winning ever greater victories.* In other words, the strategy and tactics of people's war can and will certainly prevail over the strategy and tactics based on the outmoded bourgeois military conception of the American army; in theory as in practice, *the people's war will certainly prevail over the U.S. imperialists' neo-colonialist war of aggression.*

The great victories of the army and people in both zones since the American imperialists started a direct aggression against the South of our country greatly encourage our entire people and rejoice our friends in all continents. We do not feel at all complacent at these initial successes. We definitely guard against subjectivism and never under-estimate our opponent, for American imperialism is a cruel and perfidious enemy who, moreover, has a considerable military potential, an enemy not only obdurate but also quick in drawing lessons from experience to contrive fiercer and more ruthless fighting methods. However, the lively reality of our struggle for national salvation over the past eleven years has strongly convinced our people and the people's armed forces in both zones that *we will certainly defeat the U.S. aggressors under any circumstances.*

The heavy defeats of the expeditionary corps right in its first operations on the Vietnam theatre have caused the U.S. imperialists and their valets many more difficulties, not only military but also political and economic. Far from being strengthened the puppet army and administration are deteriorating as they have lost faith in their patron's modern army. The anti-war movement in the U.S.A. is developing with every passing day while the internal contradictions in the Washington ruling circles are mounting.

In view of this situation the American imperialists are planning to send more combat units to South Vietnam, increase the U.S. expeditionary force by fifty, one hundred or more per cent. They are plotting to intensify their sabotage air warfare against the North, while threatening to expand the war to Laos and neutral Cambodia. President Johnson has talked about taking "hard steps" in Vietnam. Secretary of State Dean Rusk has also stressed, "We will not withdraw from Vietnam" for the U.S.A. must "keep its commitments." The American imperialists' familiar trick is to couple the intensification of their aggressive war with a ballyhoo about their "will for peace." This time, along with preparations for new adventurist military moves, the U.S. administration opens a fraudulent "peace campaign" on a large scale. The Johnson administration's "peace efforts" are only aimed at placating public opinion at home and abroad which has been energetically protesting against their aggressive policy in Vietnam.

But, whatever honeyed words the American imperialists may use they cannot deceive the Vietnamese people and the peace-loving people throughout the world. There has not been the slightest change in their basic design. They cling on to South Vietnam to keep Vietnam permanently partitioned. They do not want to withdraw their troops from the South and to recognize the South Vietnam National Front for Liberation as the sole authentic representative of the South Vietnamese people; they cynically arrogate to themselves the right to bomb and strafe the territory of the Democratic Republic of Vietnam, an independent and sovereign socialist state, and go to the length of demanding from the Vietnamese people a compensation for the interruption of their bombing of North Vietnam. The essence of the "unconditional discussions" hoax is to compel our people to accept their terms.

We must heighten our vigilance in face of the enemy's perfidious scheme. We must step up our entire people's patriotic war, resolutely fight until victory, no matter how many hundred thousand troops the U.S. imperialists may dispatch to South Vietnam and how far they may escalate their sabotage warfare against North Vietnam. Our people are determined not to shrink from any sacrifice to bring our great struggle against the American aggressors for national salvation to final victory.

GUERRILLA WARFARE IN BOLIVIA IS NOT DEAD! IT HAS JUST BEGUN.

● *inti peredo*

'And if we were all capable of uniting to make our blows more solid and more infallible, so that the effectiveness of every kind of support given to the struggling peoples were increased, how great and how near that future would be!'—Che Guevara

Guerrilla warfare in Bolivia is not dead!

It has just begun.

The Bolivian guerrillas are now fully on their way, and we will unflaggingly carry the struggle through the brilliant victory of the revolutionary forces that will bring socialism to Latin American.

Our country has lived through—in principle—a revolutionary experience of undreamed-of continental proportions. The beginning of our struggle was accompanied by tragic adversity. The irreparable physical death of our friend and comrade Major Ernesto Che Guevara, as well as of many other fighters, has been a rude blow to us. They, who were the purest and noblest of our continent's generations, did not hesitate to offer up the only thing they could—their lives—on the altar of human redemption.

But these painful events, far from frightening us, strengthen our revolutionary awareness; increase our determination to fight for a just cause; make it stauncher; and forge, in the purifying and bloody crucible of war, new fighters and leaders, who will honour and pay homage to those who have already fallen.

We know what we are fighting for. We are not waging war for the sake of war. We are not wishful thinkers. We are not fighting for the sake of personal or party ambition. We have confidence in man as a human being. Our single and final goal is the liberation of Latin America, which is more than our continent; it is rather our homeland, temporarily torn into twenty republics. We are convinced that the dream of Bolivar and Che—that of uniting Latin America both politically and geographically—will be attained through armed struggle, which is the only dignified, honest, glorious and irreversible method that will motivate the people. No other form of struggle is purer. Guerrilla warfare is the most effective and correct method of armed struggle.

For this reason, as long as there is a single honest man in Latin America, guerrilla warfare will not die. Armed struggle will surge ahead vigorously until all of the people gain political awareness and rise up in arms against the common enemy, United States imperialism.

Guerrilla warfare in Bolivia is not dead; it has just begun.

Both enemies and friends of the revolution have analysed, more or less profoundly and from a great variety of viewpoints, the complex phenomenon of the guerrilla activity that went on in our country. Guided by petty reasons, they all reach the narrow and biased conclusion that guerrilla warfare is not the correct method for the seizing of power in Bolivia.

Dishonest documents have been put out; accounts have been given which are most biased and slanted; and thus world public opinion has been, to a certain extent, misled in connection with the events. But one thing has not been accomplished: the dulling of the faith and determination of our country's revolutionary forces. The clearest and most unconditional proof of this is the fact that our National Liberation Army (ELN) has remained and still remains staunchly faithful and firm in the struggle, despite the temporary setbacks we have experienced. Due to circumstances, the duty has fallen upon me to explain to the revolutionaries of this country and to those of the whole continent the reasons why we, even though we have recently lost a battle, insist upon our position in support of guerrilla warfare as the most effective and surest method for the seizing of power.

Any one of the comrades who have participated and fallen as heroes in this struggle would likewise have done his duty in this regard. I do so without in the least considering myself the immediate successor of Che Guevara. Being Che's successor would be an undeservedly high honour for me. I am, rather, acting in my capacity as an accidental heir to the last and most valuable teachings of the greatest revolutionary genius of Latin America. I harbour the hope that this document will be a contribution to the rich storehouse of revolutionary experiences of our peoples in their struggle for national liberation, and at no time do I seek to justify our mistakes.

Nor are these words the lamentations or complaints of an isolated survivor of the guerrilla struggle. On the contrary, they are the full expression of the forces making up the National Liberation Army representing our people and having at present the real, staunch and objective conviction that within the armed struggle guerrilla warfare is the specific method offering the best prospects for achieving our ideals of liberty and social justice.

Specious arguments are being put forth in an effort to prove that the opposite is true. It is adduced that 'the guerrilla forces were crushed' in a relatively short time. For us, guerrilla warfare is a form of struggle utilized by the people to seize power, it being understood that one essential characteristic of this form of struggle is its more or less protracted nature.

The first phase of any guerrilla struggle consists in the guerrillas being able to survive until they have established deep roots among the people, mainly among the peasants. The guerrilla nucleus will thus be in a position to renew its forces indefinitely until a stage of development is reached that will render it invincible. From that moment on the guerrilla forces deal the regular army repeated blows, causing it to become demoralized and progressively weaker until it is finally overcome and destroyed completely, along with the régime it supports.

In our own case, the newly established guerrillas were not able to surmount the first phase; but other guerrilla groups will appear and will attain full development and eventually crush the enemy. Based on this circumstance, our critics have come to the conclusion that our method is the wrong one. They fail to mention and avoid analysing the causes of our partial and temporary defeat. The reason they do not do so is that, in so doing, they would have to judge themselves. They observe our struggle from afar. What is more, isolated they refused to co-operate and carried on anti-guerrilla propaganda against our struggle within the ranks of their own organizations. Later, in order to keep up their 'anti-imperialist' posture, each one of their organizations issued a declaration of 'solidarity' with the guerrilla struggle. But, in fact, that 'solidarity' was mere lip-service in the guise of moral support which they could not avoid giving to a small group of 'romantic dreamers'.

Dreamers! Yes. But those dreamers constituted and still constitute the only force in Bolivia that has set itself the task of seizing power by and for the people. The CPB leadership speaks of the Party's preparations for seizing power by 'all methods.' All of the people should and must take part in the seizing of power. For this reason, the people should be prepared to do so, and it is wrong to talk to the people about 'all' methods at a time when preparations for using one of the methods are being made. When a party or a group sets itself the task of seizing power, that party or group must choose a specific method; not to do so is tantamount to not thinking seriously of seizing power.

In an amusing manner, they want the guerrilla method to be scrapped after the first attempt results in failure, and they insist on the feasibility of the 'democratic' or 'reformist' approach in spite of the permanent failure of the latter method. Let us rule out elections! No serious revolutionary can consider this the road for the taking of power in Bolivia or in any other Latin American country.

How many peaceful demonstrations have been held, in which thousands upon thousands of workers and ordinary people have been violently suppressed—with casualties running into the hundreds—by the Government's repressive apparatus? Still fresh in our minds are the events of May and

 September 1965, during which factory workers and miners were brutally murdered, almost without offering any resistance. We can never forget the bloody 24th June 1967, when humble and defenceless miners were slaughtered in cold blood even as our guerrilla force, made up of scarcely forty men, dealt the murderous army hard blows, inflicting considerable casualties and demoralizing it internally. We are not against the people's struggles for the sake of obtaining economic and social gains. But we feel sure these struggles will be much more fruitful and effective when they are waged against a government frightened and weakened by the actions of a guerrilla *foco*.

It is this guerrilla *foco* that will prove to the people—with facts—that it is possible to face the power of imperialism and its puppets, and that it is not only possible to face that power, but also that it is possible to win victory over it. The people—and especially the peasants—will not support something they do not consider as being real. To expect the peasants' support for armed struggle when this struggle has not yet come into being is to play at insurrection in the same way some 'theorists' of armed struggle do when they demand the prior widespread support of the peasantry. The peasants will only give concrete support to a guerrilla *foco* when the latter can show that it is strong. That is why, in the first phase, the aim is for the guerrilla force to grow in strength, to survive on the field of operations. During this phase it is essential for the guerrilla force to be given aid from the cities. Our guerrilla *foco* was denied this aid by political forces that knew of the existence of our movement.

The political parties that seek to play the vanguard role in our people's anti-imperialist struggle are duty-bound to be honest and to account to the people for their actions. These parties are also duty-bound to admit their mistakes when they feel they have erred and to explain their actions, if they believe these actions to be correct.

How can these parties pay homage to fallen guerrillas when they attacked them as the guerrillas were preparing to fight? How can the fact be explained that Monje sounded the warning among the ranks of his party against a 'factionist group' deviating from the Party 'line' and that Zamora had Comrade Moises Guevara—who led a group of followers to join the guerrillas—expelled, for the same reason, from the pro-Chinese CPB?

The people demand and are awaiting an explanation for this double-dealing.

We do not intend to blame the CP for our temporary failure. We do not blame anybody for the outcome of this first phase. Our object is to establish the historic responsibility of the parties which in our country claim to be anti-imperialist fighters.

Some people think that we are a force in the process of dispersal.

They are wrong. We are at the point of reorganizing our armed command cadres; and we will again take up the struggle in the mountains, because we firmly believe that this is the only road that will lead us to the liberation of our people and of Latin America from the clutches of Yankee imperialism.

We are not seeking the formation of a political party. We shall succeed in the structuring of an armed force capable of facing and defeating the army, the main prop of the present régime in our country. But we are not going to be the 'fighting arm' of any political party.

We are fully convinced that the guerrilla force is not an auxiliary instrument of some other 'higher form of struggle.' On the contrary, we believe—and international experience so proves it—that this form of struggle will lead to the liberation of our peoples.

In the heat of the struggle the different forces that have set themselves the goal of liberating their country will unite, and our National Liberation Army will be joined by militants from the various parties. Then the true alliance of anti-imperialist forces will be a reality.

The forces of the Left will progressively support and join the guerrilla *foco*. Our short experience has already proved this fact.

The leaderships of the various political parties representing the people, whose militancy demands a clear-cut anti-imperialist policy, had to support the guerrilla movement. We know that this support was simply formal, but once the guerrilla force passes beyond its first stage the masses will force the leaders to convert this formal support to *de facto* support, lest they be completely isolated from the masses, without anyone to lead. Only then will the political instrument that the people need for the functioning of their future government emerge.

The liberation of our people can never be the work of one single group or one single political party. In that we agree with the parties of the Left. We need a broad, anti-imperialist front. The question is how to achieve this.

Our short experience has shown us that much more was accomplished in a few months of armed struggle than in many years of sitting around tables. Actually, all the parties that expressed their sympathy were uniting around the guerrilla *foco,* whether or not they want to admit it. We have to ask ourselves how these parties would have acted had the guerrilla struggle continued and become stronger. Positions would have been clearly defined, since in an atmosphere of armed struggle, which demands a clear-cut attitude, there isn't much room for demagogy and deceit.

The title vanguard of the people, or of the working class, is not self-bestowed. It is won by leading the people or the class which should become the vanguard in the struggle towards their objective—in this particular case, towards national liberation—by joining the anti-imperialist struggle everywhere.

The issuing of mere expressions of solidarity with a given form of anti-imperialist struggle—anti-imperialist in essence and in deed—can only place us in a rearguard position as regards the leadership of any revolutionary movement. That is why it is not enough to sympathize with the guerrilla force. One must participate in it and attain its leadership by proving that one is the truest exponent of this form of struggle.

To have pretensions of leading the movement before starting it, or to make one's participation in an anti-imperialist movement conditional on who is leading it, is demonstration of sectarianism, which conflicts with the call to 'anti-imperialist unity.'

It will be the people, and only the people, who will bestow the title of vanguard upon those who lead them to their liberation.

The sectarianism of the so-called vanguard is also made evident in its demands for subordinating the guerrilla leadership to the political leadership. This would lead to the question: to whose political leadership?

Is it, perhaps, a case of dividing the struggle into armed struggle and peaceful struggle, by subordinating armed struggle to peaceful struggle? Or would this be an attempt to use armed struggle as a mere instrument of pressure for the 'political struggle' in the cities?

Why not think, instead, of a sole politico-military leadership, considering that, in a state of war—and guerrilla warfare creates a state of war—the most skilled and able revolutionary cadres are to take care of the war?

The struggle waged in the cities must constitute a support for guerrilla action; therefore, the cities cannot lead the guerrillas. It is the guerrillas, as the armed vanguard of the liberation movement, who should lead the movement. This comes naturally. To try to do the opposite would be tantamount to rendering the guerrillas inoperative, bogging them down. In short, it would lead them to defeat.

The struggle itself will bring forth its leaders. The true leaders of the people will be forged in the struggle, and no one who considers himself a true revolutionary should insist upon leading or fear that his position will be taken from him.

The prolonged nature of the struggle is conducive to a clear awareness of one's goal. The opposing forces become defined, and the principal enemy, Yankee imperialism, shows its true nature. The people are able to see clearly how the imperialist demand that their puppets toe the line more assiduously and that they make clear their intentions. The imperialists are not about to abandon their markets, to surrender their colonies. That is why the people must prepare themselves for a long, hard struggle. To think that we are going to seize power without making sacrifices is to daydream and to create conformism among the people. The struggle will be a cruel and bloody one, and it will be waged throughout the country—even in the most humble huts and isolated regions.

In the face of the constant violence of the Yankee imperialists, we—and the people with us—have chosen the way of revolutionary violence, a violence that punishes the oppressors and that, once it has crushed them, gives way to socialist humanism. In short, we do not preach violence for its own sake, but rather advocate the people's organized retaliation against organized oppression, in order to achieve full freedom. Therefore, it will be the entire people, each and every one of the inhabitants of this country, who will contribute by direct action in the cities and in the countryside towards bringing about the insecurity, fear, panic and final defeat of our enemies.

The national liberation movements all over the world are dealing hard blows at the common enemy, imperialism. The criminal war in Vietnam, despite the fact that it balances the United States economy by converting it into a war economy and thus staving off a crisis, is creating serious problems for the imperialists. All the military power of the Yankee has already been proved ineffective in holding back that glorious people-in-arms. The struggle of our Vietnamese brothers is the struggle of all the revolutionaries of the world. They are fighting for us, and we must fight for them. Their war is our war.

The Yankee imperialists cannot withstand another Vietnam. And it is up to us and our people to create this second Vietnam, faithful to the legacy left to us by our heroic Major Ernesto Che Guevara. The idea of creating several Vietnams is no mere whim of the figment of a warmonger mentality, as our enemies and the pseudo-revolutionaries would have others believe; it is an idea in keeping with reality. The Yankee imperialists will not surrender their positions willingly, and on our continent—through their Ministry of Colonies, the OAS—they will order their lackeys in the various countries to join forces to crush any people that may rise up in arms.

The time for a continental revolution has come. We must respond to the united front of the continent's military against the revolution with the unity of all the national liberation movements of the continent. The frantic squealing of the reactionaries and some pseudo-revolutionaries who oppose the participation of patriots from other countries in our people's liberation struggle is nothing but a reflection of their vain attempts to isolate our movement and collaborate with the enemy by creating feelings of chauvinism among the people.

Our guerrillas were attacked by soldiers of the Bolivian Army advised by Yankee 'instructors' (veterans of the war in Vietnam) and equipped with weapons and rations supplied by the armies of Argentina and Brazil. We are sure that, once the guerrillas become a force to be reckoned with in our country and the regular army feels powerless to destroy them, it will receive immediate aid from the armies of several neighbouring countries, in the form not only of war material but also of soldiers. But then the revolutionary war will extend to those countries, bringing about the same state of insecurity and powerlessness among their respective armies. At this point the Pentagon will be forced to change its policy of 'advising' to one of 'direct', ever-growing participation by its troops, as is happening in Vietnam.

Some pseudo-revolutionaries tremble at such a prospect. They wish to spare the people this 'tragedy.' They do not realize that, by acting as they do, they are not avoiding anything. On the contrary, their attitude only serves to keep the people under the scourge of poverty, hunger and death, sacrificing them on the sacrosanct altar of conformism. This is no 'tragedy', weighed against what the people would have to suffer if they were kept under their present yoke for ever, their only prospect being that it would weigh heavier and heavier upon them. This is no 'tragedy', weighed against the miserable lives that our people are forced to lead.

Mining towns are nothing but concentration camps, where the inhabitants don't have any rights—not even the right to amuse themselves, and even less, of course, the right to protest. The massacres that have been systematically perpetrated are tyranny's answer to the just demands of those who bear upon their shoulders the weight of the economy of the country and the luxury of the military castes. No movement of protest or people's demands is tolerated by the military tyranny, the pillar of the present 'democratic' régime. Such movements are violently repressed, to set an example and maintain the 'principle of authority'. Anyone who rebels against such principles will be made to feel the full weight and brutality of the military régime.

Faced with this brutal reality, should we be held back by the prospect of the sacrifices involved in a just war? Our struggle will not demand any more sacrifices than those made by our people under this tyranny. That is why the creation of a new Vietnam does not constitute a 'tragedy.' It is an honour and a duty we will never refuse.

We have lost a battle, a battle in which the foremost leader of the oppressed people, Major Ernesto Che Guevara, gave his life. But our war continues, and we will never stop, because we who fought at Che's side do not recognize the word 'surrender.' His blood and that of other fighters, spilled on the soil of Bolivia, will give life to the seed of liberation and will turn our continent into a volcano spewing forth fire and destruction on imperialism. We will be the triumphant Vietnam that Che, the romantic and heroic visionary, dreamed of and loved.

We are determined to win or die for these ideals.

Cuban comrades died for these ideals.

Peruvian comrades died for these ideals.

Argentinian comrades died for these ideals.

Bolivian comrades died for these ideals.

Honour and glory for Tania, Joaquin, Juan Pablo Chang, Moises Guevara, Jorge Vazquez, Aniceto Reynaga, Antonio Jimenez and Coco Peredo. Honour and glory for each and every one of those who died with weapons in their hands, because they understood that, as Che said: 'Wherever death may surprise us, it will be welcome, provided that this, our battle-cry, reach some receptive ear, that another hand reach out to take up our weapons, and that other fighting men come forward to intone our funeral dirge with the staccato of machine-guns and new cries of battle and victory.'

Our banners bear crêpe, but will never be lowered.

The ELN considers itself the heir to the teachings and example of Che, the new Bolivar of Latin America. Those who cravenly murdered him will never kill his thought and his example.

Let the imperialists and their lackeys withhold their songs of victory, because the war has not ended; it has just begun.

Bolivia will again resound to our cry, VICTORY OR DEATH!

4

THE REVOLUTIONARY PARTY

V. I. Lenin, the classic revolutionary leader of the twentieth century, held quite unambiguously that a highly disciplined, professional revolutionary party is necessary to the success of any revolution. With equal lack of ambiguity, Daniel Cohn-Bendit, perhaps the most popularly known student spokesman during the May-June, 1968 events in France, argues that such a party gets in the way of the revolution; that professional "leaders" diminish and crush the spontaneous overflow of powerful revolutionary fervor that springs from the masses. Somewhere between these polar positions—it is very arguable just exactly where that somewhere is—Rosa Luxemburg takes the position that the revolutionary party, while a necessary part of the revolution, must behave in such a way as to not fall into the errors which Cohn-Bendit says it necessarily must.

The authors have included the selection from Régis Debray not as the summing up of arguments about the revolutionary party but as a catalyst for discussion about the role of the party in the third world liberation movement. Most observers would probably agree that Debray's subordination of the city, with its potential for general strikes, to the country, with its naturally suitable environment for guerrilla *focos,* is hardly orthodox Marxism-Leninism. Neither is his absolute merging of the political and military apparatus of the revolution. But since Debray's *Revolution in the Revolution,* from which the essay in this section is taken, has provoked a very large response, we believe he should get a fair hearing.

The serious and widespread debate over Debray's theories, moreover, points up the importance many revolutionaries place on the role of a revolutionary party. During the sixties, the New Left derided the need for such a party. It is only recently that the New Left and the new revolutionaries have come to the realization that serious attention must be given to the existence and role of such a party.

WHAT IS TO BE DONE? BURNING QUESTIONS OF OUR MOVEMENT: SELECTIONS

● *v. i. lenin*

the beginning of the spontaneous upsurge

In the previous chapter we pointed out how *universally* absorbed the educated youth of Russia was in the theories of Marxism in the middle of the nineties. In the same period the strikes that followed the famous St. Petersburg industrial war of 1896 assumed a similar general character. Their spread over the whole of Russia clearly showed the depth of the newly awakening popular movement, and if we are to speak of the "spontaneous element" then, of course, it is this strike movement which, first and foremost, must be regarded as spontaneous. But there is spontaneity and spontaneity. Strikes occurred in Russia in the seventies and sixties (and even in the first half of the nineteenth century), and they were accompanied by the "spontaneous" destruction of machinery, etc. Compared with these "revolts," the strikes of the nineties might even be described as "conscious," to such an extent do they mark the progress which the working-class movement made in that period. This shows that the "spontaneous element," in essence, represents nothing more nor less than consciousness in an *embryonic form*. Even the primitive revolts expressed the awakening of consciousness to a certain extent. The workers were losing their age-long faith in the permanence of the system which oppressed them and began . . . I shall not say to understand, but to sense the necessity for collective resistance, definitely abandoning their slavish submission to the authorities. But this was, nevertheless, more in the nature of outbursts of desperation and vengeance than of *struggle*. The strikes of the nineties revealed far greater flashes of consciousness; definite demands were advanced, the strike was carefully timed, known cases and instances in other places were discussed, etc. The revolts were simply the resistance of the oppressed, whereas the systematic strikes represented the class struggle in embryo, but only in embryo. Taken by themselves, these strikes were simply trade-union struggles, not yet Social-Democratic struggles. They marked the awakening antagonisms between workers and employers; but the workers were not, and could not be, conscious of the irreconcilable antagonism of their interests to the whole of the modern political and social system, i.e., theirs was not yet Social-Democratic consciousness. In this sense, the strikes of the nineties, despite the enormous progress they represented as compared with the "revolts," remained a purely spontaneous movement.

We have said that *there could not have been* Social-Democratic consciousness among the workers. It would have to be brought to them from without. The history of all countries shows that the working class, exclusively by its own effort, is able to develop only trade-union consciousness, i.e., the conviction that it is necessary to combine in unions, fight the employers, and strive to compel the government to pass necessary labour legislation, etc. The theory of socialism, however, grew out of the philosophic, historical, and economic theories elaborated by educated representatives of the propertied classes, by intellectuals. By their social status, the founders of modern scientific socialism, Marx and Engels, themselves belonged to the bourgeois intelligentsia. In the very same way, in Russia, the theoretical doctrine of Social-Democracy arose altogether independently of the spontaneous growth of the working-class movement; it arose as a natural and inevitable outcome of the development of thought among the revolutionary socialist intelligentsia. In the period under discussion, the middle nineties, this doctrine not only represented the completely formulated programme of the Emancipation of Labour group, but had already won over to its side the majority of the revolutionary youth in Russia.

Hence, we had both the spontaneous awakening of the working masses, their awakening to conscious life and conscious struggle, and a revolutionary youth, armed with Social-Democratic theory and straining towards the workers. . . .

Since there can be no talk of an independent ideology formulated by the working masses themselves in the process of their movement,[1] the *only* choice is—either bourgeois or socialist ideology. There is no middle course (for mankind has not created a "third" ideology, and, moreover, in a society torn by class antagonisms there can never be a non-class or an above-class ideology). Hence, to belittle the socialist ideology *in any way, to turn aside from it in the slightest degree* means to strengthen bourgeois ideology. There is much talk of spontaneity. But the *spontaneous* development of the working-class movement leads to its subordination to bourgeois ideology, *to its development along the lines of the Credo programme;* for the spontaneous working-class movement is trade-unionism, is *Nur-Gewerkschaftlerei,* and trade-unionism means the ideological enslavement of the workers by the bourgeoisie. Hence, our task, the task of Social-Democracy, is *to combat spontaneity, to divert* the working-class movement from this spontaneous, trade-unionist striving to come under the wing of the bourgeoisie, and to bring it under the wing of revolutionary Social-Democracy. . . .

But why, the reader will ask, does the spontaneous movement, the movement along the line of least resistance, lead to the domination of bourgeois ideology? For the simple reason that bourgeois ideology is far older in origin than socialist ideology, that it is more fully developed, and that it has at its disposal *immeasurably* more means of dissemination.[2] And the younger the

[1] This does not mean, of course, that the workers have no part in creating such an ideology. They take part, however, not as workers, but as socialist theoreticians, as Proudhons and Weitlings; in other words, they take part only when they are able, and to the extent that they are able, more or less, to acquire the knowledge of their age and develop that knowledge. But in order that working men *may succeed in this more often,* every effort must be made to raise the level of the consciousness of the workers in general; it is necessary that the workers do not confine themselves to the artificially restricted limits of *"literature for workers"* but that they learn to an increasing degree to master *general literature*. It would be even truer to say "are not confined", instead of "do not confine themselves", because the workers themselves wish to read and do read all that is written for the intelligentsia, and only a few (bad) intellectuals believe that it is enough "for workers" to be told a few things about factory conditions and to have repeated to them over and over again what has long been known.

[2] It is often said that the working class *spontaneously* gravitates towards socialism. This is perfectly true in the sense that socialist theory reveals the causes of the misery of the working class more profoundly and more correctly than any other theory, and for that reason the workers are able to assimilate it so easily, *provided,* however, this theory does not itself yield to spontaneity, *provided* it subordinates spontaneity to itself. Usually this is taken for granted, but it is precisely this which *Rabocheye Dyelo* forgets or distorts. The working class spontaneously gravitates towards socialism; nevertheless, most widespread (and continuously and diversely revived) bourgeois ideology spontaneously imposes itself upon the working class to a still greater degree.

 socialist movement in any given country, the more vigorously it must struggle against all attempts to entrench non-socialist ideology, and the more resolutely the workers must be warned against the bad counsellors who shout against "overrating the conscious element," etc. . . . Yes, our movement is indeed in its infancy, and in order that it may grow up faster, it must become imbued with intolerance against those who retard its growth by their subservience to spontaneity. Nothing is so ridiculous and harmful as pretending that we are "old hands" who have long ago experienced all the decisive stages of the struggle. . . .

And so, we have become convinced that the fundamental error committed by the "new trend" in Russian Social-Democracy is its bowing to spontaneity and its failure to understand that the spontaneity of the masses demands a high degree of consciousness from us Social-Democrats. The greater the spontaneous upsurge of the masses and the more widespread the movement, the more rapid, incomparably so, the demand for greater consciousness in the theoretical, political, and organisational work of Social-Democracy.

The spontaneous upsurge of the masses in Russia proceeded (and continues) with such rapidity that the young Social-Democrats proved unprepared to meet these gigantic tasks. This unpreparedness is our common misfortune, the misfortune of *all* Russian Social-Democrats. The upsurge of the masses proceeded and spread with uninterrupted continuity; it not only continued in the places where it began, but spread to new localities and to new strata of the population (under the influence of the working-class movement, there was a renewed ferment among the student youth, among the intellectuals generally, and even among the peasantry). Revolutionaries, however, *lagged behind* this upsurge, both in their "theories" and in their activity; they failed to establish a constant and continuous organisation capable of *leading* the whole movement. . . .

political agitation and its restriction by the economists

Everyone knows that the economic[3] struggle of the Russian workers underwent widespread development and consolidation simultaneously with the production of "literature" exposing economic (factory and occupational) conditions. The "leaflets" were devoted mainly to the exposure of the factory system, and very soon a veritable passion for exposures was roused among the workers. As soon as the workers realised that the Social-Democratic study circles desired to, and could, supply them with a new kind of leaflet that told the whole truth about their miserable existence, about their unbearably hard toil, and their lack of rights, they began to send in, actually flood us with, correspondence from the factories and workshops. This "exposure literature" created a tremendous sensation, not only in the particular factory exposed in

[3] To avoid misunderstanding, we must point out that here, and throughout this pamphlet, by economic struggle, we imply (in keeping with the accepted usage among us) the "practical economic struggle", which Engels, . . . described as "resistance to the capitalists", and which in free countries is known as the organised-labour, syndical, or trade-union struggle.

the given leaflet, but in all the factories to which news of the revealed facts spread. And since the poverty and want among the workers in the various enterprises and in the various trades are much the same, the "truth about the life of the workers" stirred *everyone*. Even among the most backward workers, a veritable passion arose to "get into print"—a noble passion for this rudimentary form of war against the whole of the present social system which is based upon robbery and oppression. And in the overwhelming majority of cases these "leaflets" were in truth a declaration of war, because the exposures served greatly to agitate the workers; they evoked among them common demands for the removal of the most glaring outrages and roused in them a readiness to support the demands with strikes. Finally, the employers themselves were compelled to recognise the significance of these leaflets as a declaration of war, so much so that in a large number of cases they did not even wait for the outbreak of hostilities. As is always the case, the mere publication of these exposures made them effective, and they acquired the significance of a strong moral influence. On more than one occasion, the mere appearance of a leaflet proved sufficient to secure the satisfaction of all or part of the demands put forward. In a word, economic (factory) exposures were and remain an important lever in the economic struggle. And they will continue to retain this significance as long as there is capitalism, which makes it necessary for the workers to defend themselves. Even in the most advanced countries of Europe it can still be seen that the exposure of abuses in some backward trade, or in some forgotten branch of domestic industry, serves as a starting-point for the awakening of class-consciousness, for the beginning of a trade-union struggle, and for the spread of socialism.[4]

The overwhelming majority of Russian Social-Democrats have of late been almost entirely absorbed by this work of organising the exposure of factory conditions . . . so much so, indeed, that they have lost sight of the fact that this, *taken by itself*, is in essence still not Social-Democratic work, but merely trade-union work. As a matter of fact, the exposures merely dealt with the relations between the workers *in a given trade* and their employers, and all they achieved was that the sellers of labour-power learned to sell their "commodity" on better terms and to fight the purchasers over a purely commercial deal. These exposures could have served (if properly utilised by an organisation of revolutionaries) as a beginning and a component part of Social-Democratic activity; but they could also have led (and, given a worshipful attitude towards spontaneity, were bound to lead) to a "purely trade-union" struggle and to a non-Social-Democratic working-class movement. Social-Democracy leads the struggle of the working class, not only

[4] In the present chapter we deal only with the *political* struggle, in its broader or narrower meaning. Therefore, we note only in passing, merely as a curiosity, *Rabocheye Dyelo's* charge that *Iskra* is "too restrained" in regard to the economic struggle (*Two Conferences*, p. 27, rehashed by Martynov in his pamphlet, *Social-Democracy and the Working Class*). If the accusers computed by the hundredweights or reams (as they are so fond of doing) any given year's discussion of the economic struggle in the industrial section of *Iskra*, in comparison with the corresponding sections of *Rabocheye Dyelo* and *Rabochaya Mysl* combined, they would easily see that the latter lag behind even in this respect. Apparently, the realisation of this simple truth compels them to resort to arguments that clearly reveal their confusion. "*Iskra*", they write, "willy-nilly [!] is compelled [!] to reckon with the imperative demands of life and to publish at least [!!] correspondence about the working-class movement" (*Two Conferences*, p. 27). Now this is really a crushing argument!

 for better terms for the sale of labour-power, but for the abolition of the social system that compels the propertyless to sell themselves to the rich. Social-Democracy represents the working class, not in its relation to a given group of employers alone, but in its relation to all classes of modern society and to the state as an organised political force. Hence, it follows that not only must Social-Democrats not confine themselves exclusively to the economic struggle, but that they must not allow the organisation of economic exposures to become the predominant part of their activities. We must take up actively the political education of the working class and the development of its political consciousness. . . .

The question arises, what should political education consist in? Can it be confined to the propaganda of working-class hostility to the autocracy? Of course not. It is not enough *to explain* to the workers that they are politically oppressed (any more than it is *to explain* to them that their interests are antagonistic to the interests of the employers). Agitation must be conducted with regard to every concrete example of this oppression (as we have begun to carry on agitation round concrete examples of economic oppression). Inasmuch as *this* oppression affects the most divers classes of society, inasmuch as it manifests itself in the most varied spheres of life and activity—vocational, civic, personal, family, religious, scientific, etc., etc.—is it not evident that *we shall not be fulfilling our task* of developing the political consciousness of the workers if we do not *undertake* the organisation of the *political exposure* of the autocracy *in all its aspects*? In order to carry on agitation round concrete instances of oppression, these instances must be exposed (as it is necessary to expose factory abuses in order to carry on economic agitation). . . . A basic condition for the necessary expansion of political agitation is the organisation of *comprehensive* political exposure. *In no way* except by means of such exposures *can* the masses be trained in political consciousness and revolutionary activity. Hence, activity of this kind is one of the most important functions of international Social-Democracy as a whole, for even political freedom does not in any way eliminate exposures; it merely shifts somewhat their sphere of direction. Thus, the German party is especially strengthening its positions and spreading its influence, thanks particularly to the untiring energy with which it is conducting its campaign of political exposure. Working-class consciousness cannot be genuine political consciousness unless the workers are trained to respond to *all* cases of tyranny, oppression, violence, and abuse, no matter *what class* is affected—unless they are trained, moreover, to respond from a Social-Democratic point of view and no other. The consciousness of the working masses cannot be genuine class-consciousness, unless the workers learn, from concrete, and above all from topical, political facts and events to observe *every* other social class in *all* the manifestations of its intellectual, ethical, and political life; unless they learn to apply in practice the materialist analysis and the materialist estimate of *all* aspects of the life and activity of *all* classes, strata, and groups of the population. Those who concentrate the attention, observation, and consciousness of the working class exclusively, or even mainly, upon itself alone are not Social-Democrats; for the self-knowledge of the working class is indissolubly bound up, not solely with a fully clear theoretical understanding or rather, not so much with the theoretical, as with the practical, understanding—of the relationships between *all* the various classes of modern society, acquired through the experience of political life. For this reason the conception of the economic struggle as the most widely applicable means of drawing the masses into the political movement, which our Economists preach, is so extremely harmful and reactionary in its practical significance. In order to become a Social-Democrat, the worker must have a clear picture in his mind of the economic nature and the social and political features of the landlord and the priest, the high state official and the peasant, the student and the vagabond; he must know their strong and weak points; he must grasp the meaning of all the catchwords and sophisms by which each class and each stratum *camouflages* its selfish strivings and its real "inner workings;" he must understand what interests are reflected by certain institutions and certain laws and how they are reflected. But this "clear picture" cannot be obtained from any book. It can be obtained only from living examples and from exposures that follow close upon what is going on about us at a given moment; upon what is being discussed, in whispers perhaps, by each one in his own way; upon what finds expression in such and such events, in such and such statistics, in such and such court sentences, etc., etc. These comprehensive political exposures are an essential and *fundamental* condition for training the masses in revolutionary activity.

Why do the Russian workers still manifest little revolutionary activity in response to the brutal treatment of the people by the police, the persecution of religious sects, the flogging of peasants, the outrageous censorship, the torture of soldiers, the persecution of the most innocent cultural undertakings, etc.? Is it because the "economic struggle" does not "stimulate" them to this, because such activity does not "promise palpable results," because it produces little that is "positive?" To adopt such an opinion, we repeat, is merely to direct the charge where it does not belong, to blame the working masses for one's own philistinism (or Bernsteinism). We must blame ourselves, our lagging behind the mass movement, for still being unable to organise sufficiently wide, striking, and rapid exposures of all the shameful outrages. When we do that (and we must and can do it), the most backward worker will understand, *or will feel,* that the students and religious sects, the peasants and the authors are being abused and outraged by those same dark forces that are oppressing and crushing him at every step of his life. Feeling that, he himself will be filled with an irresistible desire to react, and he will know how to hoot the censors one day, on another day to demonstrate outside the house of a governor who has brutally suppressed a peasant uprising, on still another day to teach a lesson to the gendarmes in surplices who are doing the work of the Holy Inquisition, etc. As yet we have done very little, almost nothing, *to bring* before the working masses prompt exposures on all possible issues. Many of us as yet do not recognise this as our *bounden duty* but trail spontaneously in the wake of the "drab everyday struggle," in the narrow confines of factory life.

what is there in common between economism and terrorism?

. . . The Economists and the present-day terrorists have one common root, namely, *subservience to spontaneity,* with which we dealt in the preceding chapter as a general phenomenon and which we shall now examine in relation to its effect upon political activity and the political struggle. At first sight, our assertion may appear paradoxical, so great is the difference between those who stress the "drab everyday struggle" and those who call for the most self-sacrificing struggle of individuals. But this is no paradox. The Economists and the terrorists merely bow to different poles of spontaneity; the Economists bow to the spontaneity of "the labour movement pure and simple," while the terrorists bow to the spontaneity of the passionate indignation of intellectuals, who lack the ability or opportunity to connect the revolutionary struggle and the working-class movement into an integral whole. It is difficult indeed for those who have lost their belief, or who have never believed, that this is possible, to find some outlet for their indignation and revolutionary energy other than terror. Thus, both forms of subservience to spontaneity we have mentioned are nothing but *the beginning of the implementation* of the notorious programme: Let the workers wage their "economic struggle against the employers and the government". . . and let the intellectuals conduct the political struggle by their own efforts—with the aid of terror, of course! This is an absolutely logical and inevitable *conclusion* which must be insisted on—*even though those* who are beginning to carry out this programme *do not themselves realise* that it is inevitable. Political activity has its logic quite apart from the consciousness of those who, with the best intentions, call either for terror or for lending the economic struggle itself a political character. The road to hell is paved with good intentions, and, in this case, good intentions cannot save one from being spontaneously drawn "along the line of least resistance," along the line of the *purely bourgeois* programme. Surely it is no accident either that many Russian liberals—avowed liberals and liberals that wear the mask of Marxism—whole-heartedly sympathise with terror and try to foster the terrorist moods that have surged up in the present time. . . .

the working class as vanguard fighter for democracy

Class political consciousness can be brought to the workers *only from without,* that is, only from outside the economic struggle, from outside the sphere of relations between workers and employers. The sphere from which alone it is possible to obtain this knowledge is the sphere of relationships of *all* classes and strata to the state and the government, the sphere of the interrelations between *all* classes. For that reason, the reply to the question as to what must be done to bring political knowledge to the workers cannot be merely the answer with which, in the majority of cases, the practical workers, especially those inclined towards Economism, mostly content themselves, namely: "To go among the workers." To bring political knowledge to the *workers* the Social-Democrats must *go among all classes of the population*; they must dispatch units of their army *in all directions.*

We deliberately select this blunt formula, we deliberately express ourselves in this sharply simplified manner, not because we desire to indulge in paradoxes, but in order to "impel" the Economists to a realisation of their tasks which they unpardonably ignore, to suggest to them strongly the difference between trade-unionist and Social-Democratic politics, which they refuse to understand. We therefore beg the reader not to get wrought up, but to hear us patiently to the end. . . .

We must "go among all classes of the population" as theoreticians, as propagandists, as agitators, and as organisers. No one doubts that the theoretical work of Social-Democrats should aim at studying all the specific features of the social and political condition of the various classes. But extremely little is done in this direction, as compared with the work that is done in studying the specific features of factory life. In the committees and study circles, one can meet people who are immersed in the study even of some special branch of the metal industry; but one can hardly ever find members of organisations (obliged, as often happens, for some reason or other to give up practical work) who are especially engaged in gathering material on some pressing question of social and political life in our country which could serve as a means for conducting Social-Democratic work among other strata of the population. In dwelling upon the fact that the majority of the present-day leaders of the working-class movement lack training, we cannot refrain from mentioning training in this respect also, for it too is bound up with the "Economist" conception of "close organic connection with the proletarian struggle." The principal thing, of course, is *propaganda* and *agitation* among all strata of the people. The work of the West-European Social-Democrat is in this respect facilitated by the public meetings and rallies which *all* are free to attend, and by the fact that in parliament he addresses the representatives of *all* classes. We have neither a parliament nor freedom of assembly; nevertheless, we are able to arrange meetings of workers who desire to listen to *a Social-Democrat.* We must also find ways and means of calling meetings of representatives of all social classes that desire to listen to a *democrat;* for he is no Social-Democrat who forgets in practice that "the Communists support every revolutionary movement," that we are obliged for that reason to expound and emphasise *general democratic tasks before the whole people,* without for a moment concealing our socialist convictions. He is no Social-Democrat who forgets in practice his obligation to be *ahead of all* in raising, accentuating, and solving *every* general democratic question. . . .

. . . It goes without saying that we cannot guide the struggle of the students, liberals, etc., for their "immediate interests;" but this was not the point at issue, most worthy Economist! The point we were discussing was the possible and necessary participation of various social strata in the overthrow of the autocracy; and not only are we *able,* but it is our bounden duty, to guide *these* "activities of the various opposition strata," if we desire to be the "vanguard." Not only will our students and liberals, etc., themselves take care of "the struggle that brings them face to face with our political régime;" the police and the officials of the autocratic government will see to this first and foremost. But if "we" desire to be front-rank democrats, we must make it our concern *to direct* the thoughts of those who are dissatisfied only with conditions at the university, or in the Zemstvo, etc., to the idea that the entire political system is worthless. *We* must take upon ourselves the task of organising an all-round political struggle under the leadership of *our* Party in such a manner as to make it possible for all oppositional strata to render their fullest support to the struggle and to our Party. *We* must train our Social-Democratic practical workers to become political leaders, able to guide all the manifestations of this all-round struggle, able at the right time to "dictate a positive programme of action" for the aroused students, the discontented Zemstvo people, the incensed religious sects, the offended elementary schoolteachers, etc., etc.

We shall try to answer this question by giving a brief description of the activity of a typical Social-Democratic study circle of the period 1894-1901. We have noted that the entire student youth of the period was absorbed in Marxism. Of course, these students were not only, or even not so much, interested in Marxism as a theory; they were interested in it as an answer to the question, "What is to be done?", as a call to take the field against the enemy. These new warriors marched to battle with astonishingly primitive equipment and training. In a vast number of cases they had almost no equipment and absolutely no training. They marched to war like peasants from the plough, armed only with clubs. A students' circle establishes contacts with workers and sets to work, without any connection with the old members of the movement, without any connection with study circles in other districts, or even in other parts of the same city (or in other educational institutions), without any organisation of the various divisions of revolutionary work, without any systematic plan of activity covering any length of time. The circle gradually expands its propaganda and agitation; by its activities it wins the sympathies of fairly large sections of workers and of a certain section of the educated strata, which provide it with money and from among whom the "committee" recruits new groups of young people. The attractive power of the committee (or League of Struggle) grows, its sphere of activity becomes wider, and the committee expands this activity quite spontaneously; the very people who a year or a few months previously spoke at the students' circle gatherings and discussed the question, "Whither?," who established and maintained contacts with the workers and wrote and published leaflets, now establish contacts with other groups of revolutionaries, procure literature, set to work to publish a local newspaper, begin to talk of organising a demonstration, and finally turn to open warfare (which may, according to circumstances, take the form of issuing the first agitational leaflet or the first issue of a newspaper, or of organising the first demonstration). Usually the initiation of such actions ends in an immediate and complete fiasco. Immediate and complete, because this open warfare was not the result of a systematic and carefully thought-out and gradually prepared plan for a prolonged and stubborn struggle, but simply the result of the spontaneous growth of traditional study circle work; because, naturally, the police, in almost every case, knew the principal leaders of the local movement, since they had already "gained a reputation" for themselves in their student days, and the police waited only for the right moment to make their raid. They deliberately allowed the study circle sufficient time to develop its work so that they might obtain a palpable *corpus delicti*, and they always permitted several of the persons known to them to remain at liberty "for breeding" (which, as far as I know, is the technical term used both by our people and by the gendarmes). One cannot help comparing this kind of warfare with that conducted by a mass of peasants, armed with clubs, against modern troops. And one can only wonder at the vitality of the movement which expanded, grew, and scored victories despite the total lack of training on the part of the fighters. True, from the historical point of view, the primitiveness of equipment was not only inevitable at first, but even *legitimate* as one of the conditions for the wide recruiting of fighters, but as soon as serious war operations began (and they began in fact with the strikes in the summer of

1896), the defects in our fighting organisations made themselves felt to an ever-increasing degree. The government, at first thrown into confusion and committing a number of blunders (e.g., its appeal to the public describing the misdeeds of the socialists, or the banishment of workers from the capitals to provincial industrial centres), very soon adapted itself to the new conditions of the struggle and managed to deploy well its perfectly equipped detachments of *agents provocateurs*, spies, and gendarmes. Raids became so frequent, affected such a vast number of people, and cleared out the local study circles so thoroughly that the masses of the workers lost literally all their leaders, the movement assumed an amazingly sporadic character, and it became utterly impossible to establish continuity and coherence in the work. The terrible dispersion of the local leaders; the fortuitous character of the study circle memberships; the lack of training in, and the narrow outlook on, theoretical, political, and organisational questions were all the inevitable result of the conditions described above. Things have reached such a pass that in several places the workers, because of our lack of self-restraint and the ability to maintain secrecy, begin to lose faith in the intellectuals and to avoid them; the intellectuals, they say, are much too careless and cause police raids!

organisation of workers and organisation of revolutionaries

. . . The political struggle of Social-Democracy is far more extensive and complex than the economic struggle of the workers against the employers and the government. Similarly (indeed for that reason), the organisation of the revolutionary Social-Democratic Party must inevitably be of *a kind different* from the organisation of the workers designed for this struggle. The workers' organisation must in the first place be a trade-union organisation; secondly, it must be as broad as possible; and thirdly, it must be as public as conditions will allow (here, and further on, of course, I refer only to absolutist Russia). On the other hand, the organisation of the revolutionaries must consist first and foremost of people who make revolutionary activity their profession (for which reason I speak of the organisation of *revolutionaries,* meaning revolutionary Social-Democrats). In view of this common characteristic of the members of such an organisation, *all distinctions as between workers and intellectuals,* not to speak of distinctions of trade and profession, in both categories, *must be effaced.* Such an organisation must perforce not be very extensive and must be as secret as possible. Let us examine this threefold distinction.

In countries where political liberty exists the distinction between a trade-union and a political organisation is clear enough, as is the distinction between trade unions and Social-Democracy. The relations between the latter and the former will naturally vary in each country according to historical, legal, and other conditions; they may be more or less close, complex, etc.

The workers' organisations for the economic struggle should be trade-union organisations. Every Social-Democratic worker should as far as possible assist and actively work in these organisations. But, while this is true, it is certainly not in our interest to demand that only Social-Democrats should be eligible for membership in the "trade" unions, since that would only narrow the scope of our influence upon the masses. Let every worker who understands the need to unite for the struggle against the employers and the government join the trade unions. The very aim of the trade unions would be impossible of achievement, if they did not unite all who have attained at least this elementary degree of understanding, if they were not very *broad* organisations. The broader these organisations, the broader will be our influence over them—an influence due, not only to the "spontaneous" development of the economic struggle, but to the direct and conscious effort of the socialist trade-union members to influence their comrades. But a broad organisation cannot apply methods of strict secrecy (since this demands far greater training than is required for the economic struggle). How is the contradiction between the need for a large membership and the need for strictly secret methods to be reconciled? How are we to make the trade unions as public as possible? Generally speaking, there can be only two ways to this end: either the trade unions become legalised (in some countries this preceded the legalisation of the socialist and political unions), or the organisation is kept secret, but so "free" and amorphous, *lose*[5] as the Germans say, that the need for secret methods becomes almost negligible as far as the bulk of the members is concerned. . . .

. . . A small, compact core of the most reliable, experienced, and hardened workers, with responsible representatives in the principal districts and connected by all the rules of strict secrecy with the organisation of revolutionaries, can, with the widest support of the masses and without any formal organisation, perform *all* the functions of a trade-union organisation, in a manner, moreover, desirable to Social-Democracy. Only in this way can we secure the *consolidation* and development of a *Social-Democratic* trade-union movement, despite all the gendarmes.

It may be objected that an organisation which is so *lose* that it is not even definitely formed, and which has not even an enrolled and registered membership, cannot be called an organisation at all. Perhaps so. Not the name is important. What is important is that this "organisation without members" shall do everything that is required, and from the very outset ensure a solid connection between our future trade unions and socialism. Only an incorrigible utopian would have a *broad* organisation of workers, with elections, reports, universal suffrage, etc., under the autocracy.

The moral to be drawn from this is simple. If we begin with the solid foundation of a strong organisation of revolutionaries, we can ensure the stability of the movement as a whole and carry out the aims both of Social-Democracy and of trade unions proper. If, however, we begin with a broad workers' organisation, which is supposedly most "accessible" to the masses (but which is actually most accessible to the gendarmes and makes revolutionaries most accessible to the police), we shall achieve neither the one aim nor the other; we shall not eliminate our rule-of-thumb methods, and, because we remain scattered and our forces are constantly broken up by the police, we shall only make trade unions of the type the more accessible to the masses. . . .

"A dozen wise men can be more easily wiped out than a hundred fools." This wonderful truth (for which the hundred fools will always applaud you) appears obvious only because in the very midst of the argument you have skipped from one question to another. You began by talking and continued

[5] *Lose* (German)—loose.—*Ed.*

to talk of the unearthing of a "committee," of the unearthing of an "organisation," and now you skip to the question of unearthing the movement's "roots" in their "depths." The fact is, of course, that our movement cannot be unearthed, for the very reason that it has countless thousands of roots deep down among the masses; but that is not the point at issue. As far as "deep roots" are concerned, we cannot be "unearthed" even now, despite all our amateurism, and yet we all complain, and cannot but complain, that the *"organisations"* are being unearthed and as a result it is impossible to maintain continuity in the movement. But since you raise the question of *organisations* being unearthed and persist in your opinion, I assert that it is far more difficult to unearth a dozen wise men than a hundred fools. This position I will defend, no matter how much you instigate the masses against me for my "anti-democratic" views, etc. As I have stated repeatedly, by "wise men," in connection with organisation, I mean *professional revolutionaries,* irrespective of whether they have developed from among students or working men. I assert: (1) that no revolutionary movement can endure without a stable organisation of leaders maintaining continuity; (2) that the broader the popular mass drawn spontaneously into the struggle, which forms the basis of the movement and participates in it, the more urgent the need for such an organisation, and the more solid this organisation must be (for it is much easier for all sorts of demagogues to side-track the more backward sections of the masses); (3) that such an organisation must consist chiefly of people professionally engaged in revolutionary activity; (4) that in an autocratic state, the more we *confine* the membership of such an organisation to people who are professionally engaged in revolutionary activity and who have been professionally trained in the art of combating the political police, the more difficult will it be to unearth the organisation; and (5) the *greater* will be the number of people from the working class and from the other social classes who will be able to join the movement and perform active work in it.

I invite our Economists, terrorists, and "Economists-terrorists"[6] to confute these propositions. At the moment, I shall deal only with the last two points. The question as to whether it is easier to wipe out "a dozen wise men" or "a hundred fools" reduces itself to the question, above considered, whether it is possible to have a mass *organisation* when the maintenance of strict secrecy is essential. We can never give a mass organisation that degree of secrecy without which there can be no question of persistent and continuous struggle against the government. To concentrate all secret functions in the hands of as small a number of professional revolutionaries as possible does not mean that the latter will "do the thinking for all" and that the rank and file will not take an active part in the *movement.* On the

[6] This term is perhaps more applicable to *Svoboda* than the former, for in an article entitled "The Regeneration of Revolutionism" the publication defends terrorism, while in the article at present under review it defends Economism. One might say of *Svoboda* that "it would if it could, but it can't". Its wishes and intentions are of the very best—but the result is utter confusion; this is chiefly due to the fact that, while *Svoboda* advocates continuity of organisation, it refuses to recognise continuity of revolutionary thought and Social-Democratic theory. It wants to revive the professional revolutionary ("The Regeneration of Revolutionism"), and to that end proposes, first, excitative terrorism, and secondly, "an organisation of average workers" (*Svoboda,* No. 1, p. 66, et seq.), as less likely to be "pushed on from outside". In other words, it proposes to pull the house down to use the timber for heating it.

 contrary, the membership will promote increasing numbers of the professional revolutionaries from its ranks; for it will know that it is not enough for a few students and for a few working men waging the economic struggle to gather in order to form a "committee," but that it takes years to train oneself to be a professional revolutionary; and the rank and file will "think," not only of amateurish methods, but of such training. Centralisation of the secret functions of the *organisation* by no means implies centralisation of all the functions of the *movement.* Active participation of the widest masses in the illegal press will not diminish because a "dozen" professional revolutionaries centralise the secret functions connected with this work; on the contrary, it will *increase* tenfold. In this way, and in this way alone, shall we ensure that reading the illegal press, writing for it, and to some extent even distributing it, will *almost cease to be secret work,* for the police will soon come to realise the folly and impossibility of judicial and administrative red-tape procedure over every copy of a publication that is being distributed in the thousands. This holds not only for the press, but for every function of the movement, even for demonstrations. The active and widespread participation of the masses will not suffer; on the contrary, it will benefit by the fact that a "dozen" experienced revolutionaries, trained professionally no less than the police, will centralise all the secret aspects of the work—the drawing up of leaflets, the working out of approximate plans; and the appointing of bodies of leaders for each urban district, for each factory district, and for each educational institution, etc. (I know that exception will be taken to my "undemocratic" views, but I shall reply below fully to this anything but intelligent objection.) Centralisation of the most secret functions in an organisation of revolutionaries will not diminish, but rather increase the extent and enhance the quality of the activity of a large number of other organisations, that are intended for a broad public and are therefore as loose and as non-secret as possible, such as workers' trade unions; workers' self-education circles and circles for reading illegal literature; and socialist, as well as democratic, circles among *all* other sections of the population; etc., etc. We must have such circles, trade unions, and organisations everywhere in *as large a number as possible* and with the widest variety of functions; but it would be absurd and harmful *to confound* them with the organisation of *revolutionaries,* to efface the border-line between them, to make still more hazy the all too faint recognition of the fact that in order to "serve" the mass movement we must have people who will devote themselves exclusively to Social-Democratic activities, and that such people must *train* themselves patiently and steadfastly to be professional revolutionaries.

"conspiratorial" organisation and "democratism"

Yet there are many people among us who are so sensitive to the "voice of life" that they fear it more than anything in the world and charge the adherents of the views here expounded with following a Narodnaya Volya line, with failing to understand "democratism," etc. These accusations, which, of course, have been echoed by *Rabocheye Dyelo,* need to be dealt with.

The writer of these lines knows very well that the St. Petersburg Economists levelled the charge of Narodnaya Volya tendencies also against *Rabochaya Gazeta* (which is quite understandable when one compares it with *Rabochaya Mysl*). We were not in the least surprised, therefore, when soon after the appearance of *Iskra*, a comrade informed us that the Social-Democrats in the town of X describe *Iskra* as a Narodnaya Volya organ. We, of course, were flattered by this accusation; for what decent Social-Democrat has not been accused by the Economists of being a Narodnaya Volya sympathiser?

These accusations are the result of a twofold misunderstanding. First, the history of the revolutionary movement is so little known among us that the name "Narodnaya Volya" is used to denote any idea of a militant centralised organisation which declares determined war upon tsarism. But the magnificent organisation that the revolutionaries had in the seventies, and that should serve us as a model, was not established by the Narodnaya Volya, but by the *Zemlya i Volya*, which split up into the Chorny Peredel and the Narodnaya Volya. Consequently, to regard a militant revolutionary organisation as something specifically Narodnaya Volya in character is absurd both historically and logically; for *no* revolutionary trend, if it seriously thinks of struggle, can dispense with such an organisation. The mistake the Narodnaya Volya committed was not in striving to enlist *all* the discontented in the organisation and to direct this organisation to resolute struggle against the autocracy; on the contrary, that was its great historical merit. The mistake was in relying on theory which in substance was not a revolutionary theory at all, and the Narodnaya Volya members either did not know how, or were unable, to link their movement inseparably with the class struggle in the developing capitalist society. Only a gross failure to understand Marxism (or an "understanding" of it in the spirit of "Struveism") could prompt the opinion that the rise of a mass, spontaneous working-class movement *relieves* us of the duty of creating as good an organisation of revolutionaries as the Zemlya i Volya had, or, indeed, an incomparably better one. On the contrary, this movement *imposes* the duty upon us; for the spontaneous struggle of the proletariat will not become its genuine "class struggle" until this struggle is led by a strong organisation of revolutionaries.

Secondly, many people, including apparently B. Krichevsky (*Rabocheye Dyelo,* No. 10, p. 18), misunderstand the polemics that Social-Democrats have always waged against the "conspiratorial" view of the political struggle. We have always protested, and will, of course, continue to protest against *confining* the political struggle to conspiracy.[7] But this does not, of course, mean that we deny the need for a strong revolutionary organisation. Thus, in the pamphlet mentioned in the preceding footnote, after the polemics against reducing the political struggle to a conspiracy, a description is given (as a Social-Democratic ideal) of an organisation so strong as to be able to "resort to . . . rebellion" and to every "other form of attack," in order to "deliver a smashing blow against absolutism."[8] In *form* such a strong rev-

[7] Cf. *The Tasks of the Russian Social-Democrats*, p. 21, polemics against P. L. Lavrov. (See *Collected Works*, Vol. 2, pp. 340-41.—*Ed.*)

[8] *The Tasks of the Russian Social-Democrats,* p. 23. (See *Collected Works,* Vol. 2, p. 342.—*Ed.*) Apropos, we shall give another illustration of the fact that *Rabocheye Dyelo* either does not understand what it is talking about or changes its views "with the wind". In No. 1 of *Rabocheye Dyelo,* we find the following passage in italics: *"The substance set forth in the pamphlet accords entirely with the editorial programme of Rabocheye Dyelo"* (p. 142). Really? Does the view that the overthrow of the autocracy must not be set as the first task of the mass movement accord with the views expressed in *The Tasks of the Russian Social-Democrats?* Do the theory of "the economic struggle against the employers and the government" and the stages theory accord with the views expressed in that pamphlet? We leave it to the reader to judge whether a periodical that understands the meaning of "accordance in opinion" in this peculiar manner can have firm principles.

 olutionary organisation in an autocratic country may also be described as a "conspiratorial" organisation, because the French word "conspiration" is the equivalent of the Rusian word "*zagovor*" ("conspiracy"), and such an organisation must have the utmost secrecy. Secrecy is such a necessary condition for this kind of organisation that all the other conditions (number and selection of members, functions, etc.) must be made to conform to it. It would be extremely naïve indeed, therefore, to fear the charge that we Social-Democrats desire to create a conspiratorial organisation. Such a charge should be as flattering to every opponent of Economism as the charge of following a Narodnaya Volya line.

The objection may be raised that such a powerful and strictly secret organisation, which concentrates in its hands all the threads of secret activities, an organisation which of necessity is centralised, may too easily rush into a premature attack, may thoughtlessly intensify the movement before the growth of political discontent, the intensity of the ferment and anger of the working class, etc., have made such an attack possible and necessary. Our reply to this is: Speaking abstractly, it cannot be denied, of course, that a militant organisation *may* thoughtlessly engage in battle, which *may* end in a defeat entirely avoidable under other conditions. But we cannot confine ourselves to abstract reasoning on such a question, because every battle bears within itself the abstract possibility of defeat, and there is no way of *reducing* this possibility except by organised preparation for battle. If, however, we proceed from the concrete conditions at present obtaining in Russia, we must come to the positive conclusion that a strong revolutionary organisation is absolutely necessary precisely for the purpose of giving stability to the movement and of *safeguarding* it against the possibility of making thoughtless attacks. Precisely at the present time, when no such organisation yet exists, and when the revolutionary movement is rapidly and spontaneously growing, we *already observe* two opposite extremes (which, as is to be expected, "meet"). These are: the utterly unsound Economism and the preaching of moderation, and the equally unsound "excitative terror", which strives "artificially to call forth symptoms of the end of the movement, which is developing and strengthening itself, when this movement is as yet nearer to the start than to the end" . . . Only a centralised, militant organisation that consistently carries out a Social-Democratic policy, that satisfies, so to speak, all revolutionary instincts and strivings, can safeguard the movement against making thoughtless attacks and prepare attacks that hold out the promise of success.

A further objection may be raised, that the views on organisation here expounded contradict the "democratic principle". . . . Everyone will probably agree that "the broad democratic principle" presupposes the two following conditions: first, full publicity, and secondly, election to all offices. It would be absurd to speak of democracy without publicity, moreover, without a publicity that is not limited to the membership of the organisation. We call the German Socialist Party a democratic organisation because all its activities are carried out publicly; even its party congresses are held in public. But no one would call an organisation democratic that is hidden from every one but its members by a veil of secrecy. What is the use, then, of advancing "the *broad* democratic principle" when the fundamental condition for this principle *cannot be fulfilled* by a secret organisation? "The broad principle" proves itself simply to be a resounding but hollow phrase. Moreover, it reveals a total lack of understanding of the urgent tasks of the moment in regard to organisation. Everyone knows how great the lack of secrecy is among the "broad" masses of our revolutionaries. . . . Yet, persons who boast a keen "sense of realities" *urge,* in a situation like this, not the strictest secrecy and the strictest (consequently, more restricted) selection of members, but "the *broad* democratic principle"! This is what you call being wide off the mark.

Nor is the situation any better with regard to the second attribute of democracy, the principle of election. In politically free countries, this condition is taken for granted. "They are members of the Party who accept the principles of the Party programme and render the Party all possible support," reads Clause 1 of the Rules of the German Social-Democratic Party. Since the entire political arena is as open to the public view as is a theatre stage to the audience, this acceptance or non-acceptance, support or opposition, is known to all from the press and from public meetings. Everyone knows that a certain political figure began in such and such a way, passed through such and such an evolution, behaved in a trying moment in such and such a manner, and possesses such and such qualities; consequently, *all* party members, knowing all the facts, can elect or refuse to elect this person to a particular party office. The general control (in the literal sense of the term) exercised over every act of a party man in the political field brings into existence an automatically operating mechanism which produces what in biology is called the "survival of the fittest". "Natural selection" by full publicity, abuse upon Plekhanov. All the more valuable, therefore, is this witness in the question at issue. In *Nakanune* for July (No. 7) 1899, in an article entitled "Concerning the Manifesto of the Self-Emancipation of the Workers Group," Serebryakov argued that it was "indecent" to talk about such things as "self-deception, leadership, and the so-called Areopagus in a serious revolutionary movement" and, *inter alia,* wrote:

> *"Myshkin, Rogachov, Zhelyabov, Mikhailov, Perovskaya, Figner, and others never regarded themselves as leaders, and no one ever elected or appointed them as such, although in actuality, they were leaders, because, in the propaganda period, as well as in the period of the struggle against the government, they took the brunt of the work upon themselves, they went into the most dangerous places, and their activities were the most fruitful. They became leaders, not because they wished it, but because the comrades surrounding them had confidence in their wisdom, in their energy, in their loyalty. To be afraid of some kind of Areopagus (if it is not feared, why write about it?) that would arbitrarily govern the movement is far too naïve. Who would pay heed to it?"*

We ask the reader, in what way does the "Areopagus" differ from "anti-democratic tendencies?" And is it not evident that *Rabocheye Dyelo*'s "plausible" organisational principle is equally naïve and indecent; naïve, because no one would pay heed to the "Areopagus," or people with "anti-democratic tendencies," if "the comrades surrounding them had" no "confidence in their wisdom, energy, and loyalty;" indecent, because it is a demagogic sally calculated to play on the conceit of some, on the ignorance of others regarding the actual state of our movement, and on the lack of training and the ignorance of the history of the revolutionary movement on the part of still others. The only serious organisational principle for the active workers of our movement should be the strictest secrecy, the strictest selection of members, and the training of professional revolutionaries. Given these qualities, something even more than "democratism" would be guaranteed to us, namely, complete, comradely, mutual confidence among revolutionaries. This is absolutely essential for us, because there can be no question of replacing it by general democratic control in Russia. It would be a great mistake to believe that the impossibility of establishing real "democratic" control renders the members of the revolutionary organisation beyond control altogether. They have not the time to think about toy forms of democratism (democratism within a close and compact body of comrades in which complete, mutual confidence prevails), but they have a lively sense of their *responsibility,* knowing as they do from experience that an organisation of real revolutionaries will stop at nothing to rid itself of an unworthy member. Moreover, there is a fairly well-developed public opinion in Russian (and international) revolutionary circles which has a long history behind it, and which sternly and ruthlessly punishes every departure from the duties of comradeship (and "democratism," real and not toy democratism, certainly forms a component part of the conception of comradeship). Take all this into consideration and you will realise that this talk and these resolutions about "anti-democratic tendencies" have the musty odour of the playing at generals which is indulged in abroad. . . .

The objections raised against the plan of organisation here outlined on the grounds that it is undemocratic and conspiratorial are totally unsound. Nevertheless, there remains a question which is frequently put and which deserves detailed examination. This is the question of the relations between local work and All-Russian work. Fears are expressed that the formation of a centralised organization may shift the centre of gravity from the former to the latter, damage the movement through weakening our contacts with the working masses and the continuity of local agitation generally. To these fears we reply that our movement in the past few years has suffered precisely from the fact that local workers have been too absorbed in local work; that therefore it is absolutely necessary to shift the centre of gravity somewhat to national work; and that, far from weakening, this would strengthen our ties and the continuity of our local agitation. Let us take the question of central and local newspapers. I would ask the reader not to forget that we cite the publication of newspapers only as *an example* illustrating an immeasurably broader and more varied revolutionary activity in general.

In the first period of the mass movement (1896-98), an attempt was made by local revolutionary workers to publish an All-Russian paper—*Rabochaya Gazeta.* In the next period (1898-1900), the movement made an enormous stride forward, but the attention of the leaders was wholly absorbed by local publications. If we compute the total number of the local papers that were published, we shall find that on the average one issue per month was published.[9] Does this not clearly illustrate our amateurism? Does this not clearly show that our revolutionary organisation lags behind the spontaneous growth of the movement? If *the same number* of issues had been published, not by

[9] See *Report to the Paris Congress,*[58] p. 14. "From that time (1897) to the spring of 1900, thirty issues of various papers were published in various places. . . . On an average, over one issue per month was published."

scattered local groups, but by a single organisation, we would not only have saved an enormous amount of effort, but we would have secured immeasurably greater stability and continuity in our work. This simple point is frequently lost sight of by those practical workers who work *actively* and almost exclusively on local publications (unfortunately this is true even now in the overwhelming majority of cases), as well as by the publicists who display an astonishing quixotism on this question. The practical workers usually rest content with the argument that "it is difficult" [10] for local workers to engage in the organisation of an All-Russian newspaper, and that local newspapers are better than no newspapers at all. This argument is, of course, perfectly just, and we, no less than any practical worker, appreciate the enormous importance and usefulness of local newspapers *in general*. But not this is the point. The point is, can we not overcome the fragmentation and primitiveness that are so glaringly expressed in the thirty issues of local newspapers that have been published throughout Russia in the course of two and a half years? Do not restrict yourselves to the indisputable, but too general, statement about the usefulness of local newspapers generally; have the courage frankly to admit their negative aspects revealed by the experience of two and a half years. This experience has shown that under the conditions in which we work, these local newspapers prove, in the majority of cases, to be unstable in their principles, devoid of political significance, extremely costly in regard to expenditure of revolutionary forces, and totally unsatisfactory from a technical point of view (I have in mind, of course, not the technique of printing, but the frequency and regularity of publication). These defects are not accidental; they are the inevitable outcome of the fragmentation which, on the one hand, explains the predominance of local newspapers in the period under review, and, on the other, is *fostered by* this predominance. It is positively *beyond the strength* of a separate local organisation to raise its newspaper to the level of a political organ maintaining stability of principles; it is *beyond its strength* to collect and utilise sufficient material to shed light on the whole of our political life. . . .

The predominance of the local papers over a central press may be a sign of either poverty or luxury. Of poverty, when the movement has not yet developed the forces for large-scale production, continues to flounder in amateurism, and is all but swamped with "the petty details of factory life." Of luxury, when the movement *has fully mastered* the task of comprehensive exposure and comprehensive agitation, and it becomes necessary to publish numerous local newspapers in addition to the central organ. Let each decide for himself what the predominance of local newspapers implies in present-day Russia. I shall limit myself to a precise formulation of my own conclusion, to leave no grounds for misunderstanding. Hitherto, the majority of our local organisations have thought almost exclusively in terms of local newspapers, and have devoted almost all their activities to this work. This is abnormal; the very opposite should have been the case. The majority of the local organisations should think principally of the publication of an All-Russian newspaper and devote their activities chiefly to it. Until this is done, we shall *not* be able to establish a *single* newspaper capable, to any degree, of serving the move-

[10] This difficulty is more apparent than real. In fact, *there is not* a single local study circle that lacks the opportunity of taking up some function or other in connection with All-Russian work. "Don't say, I can't; say, I won't."

 ment with *comprehensive* press agitation. When this is done, however, normal relations between the necessary central newspaper and the necessary local newspapers will be established automatically.

what type of organisation do we require?

From what has been said the reader will see that our "tactics-as-plan" consists in rejecting an immediate *call* for assault; in demanding "to lay effective siege to the enemy fortress"; or, in other words, in demanding that all efforts be directed towards gathering, organising, and *mobilising* a permanent army. . . . it is stupid and unseemly to shout about an immediate "assault," for assault means attack by regular troops and not a spontaneous mass upsurge. For the very reason that the masses *may* overwhelm and sweep aside the regular troops we must without fail "manage to keep up" with the spontaneous upsurge by our work of "introducing extremely systematic organisation" in the regular troops, for the more we "manage" to introduce such organisation the more probably will the regular troops not be overwhelmed by the masses, but will take their place at their head. . . .

For it is precisely the *Svoboda* group that, by including terror *in its programme,* calls for an organisation of terrorists, and such an organisation would indeed prevent our troops from establishing closer contacts with the masses, which, unfortunately, are still not ours, and which, unfortunately, do not yet ask us, or rarely ask us, when and how to launch their military operations.

Those who make nation-wide political agitation the cornerstone of their programme, *their tactics, and their organisational work,* stand the least risk of missing the revolution. . . . And if they live they will not miss the revolution, which, first and foremost, will demand of us experience in agitation, ability to support (in a Social-Democratic manner) every protest, as well as direct the spontaneous movement, while safeguarding it from the mistakes of friends and the traps of enemies. . . . Picture to yourselves a popular uprising. Probably everyone will now agree that we must think of this and prepare for it. But *how*? Surely the Central Committee cannot appoint agents to all localities for the purpose of preparing the uprising. Even if we had a Central Committee, it could achieve absolutely nothing by such appointments under present-day Russian conditions. But a network of agents[11] that would form in the course of establishing and distributing the common newspaper would not have to "sit about and wait" for the call for an uprising, but could carry on the regular activity that would guarantee the highest probability of success in the event of an uprising. Such activity would strengthen our contacts with the broadest strata of the working masses and with all social strata that are

[11] Alas, alas! Again I have let slip that awful word "agents", which jars so much on the democratic ears of the Martynovs! I wonder why this word did not offend the heroes of the seventies and yet offends the amateurs of the nineties? I like the word, because it clearly and trenchantly indicates *the common cause* to which all the agents bend their thoughts and actions, and if I had to replace this word by another, the only word I might select would be the word "collaborator", if it did not suggest a certain bookishness and vagueness. The thing we need is a military organisation of agents. However, the numerous Martynovs (particularly abroad), whose favourite pastime is "mutual grants of generalships to one another", may instead of saying "passport agent" prefer to say, "Chief of the Special Department for Supplying Revolutionaries with Passports", etc.

discontented with the autocracy, which is of such importance for an uprising. Precisely such activity would serve to cultivate the ability to estimate correctly the general political situation and, consequently, the ability to select the proper moment for an uprising. Precisely such activity would train *all* local organisations to respond simultaneously to the same political questions, incidents, and events that agitate the whole of Russia and to react to such "incidents" in the most vigorous, uniform, and expedient manner possible; for an uprising is in essence the most vigorous, most uniform, and most expedient "answer" of the entire people to the government. Lastly, it is precisely such activity that would train all revolutionary organisations throughout Russia to maintain the most continuous, and at the same time the most secret, contacts with one another, thus creating *real* Party unity; for without such contacts it will be impossible collectively to discuss the plan for the uprising and to take the necessary preparatory measures on the eve, measures that must be kept in the strictest secrecy.

LENINISM OR MARXISM?

● *rosa luxemburg*

I

An unprecedented task in the history of the socialist movement has fallen to the lot of the Russian Social Democracy. It is the task of deciding on what is the best socialist tactical policy in a country where absolute monarchy is still dominant. It is a mistake to draw a rigid parallel between the present Russian situation and that which existed in Germany during the years 1878-90, when Bismarck's antisocialist laws were in force. The two have one thing in common—police rule. Otherwise, they are in no way comparable.

The obstacles offered to the socialist movement by the absence of democratic liberties are of relatively secondary importance. Even in Russia, the people's movement has succeeded in overcoming the barriers set up by the state. The people have found themselves a "constitution" (though a rather precarious one) in street disorders. Persevering in this course, the Russian people will in time attain complete victory over the autocracy.

The principal difficulty faced by socialist activity in Russia results from the fact that in that country the domination of the bourgeoisie is veiled by absolutist force. This gives socialist propaganda an abstract character, while immediate political agitation takes on a democratic-revolutionary guise.

Bismarck's antisocialist laws put our movement out of constitutional bounds in a highly developed bourgeois society, where class antagonisms had already reached their full bloom in parliamentary contests. (Here, by the way, lay the absurdity of Bismarck's scheme.) The situation is quite different in Russia. The problem there is how to create a Social Democratic movement at a time when the state is not yet in the hands of the bourgeoisie.

This circumstance has an influence on agitation, on the manner of transplanting socialist doctrine to Russian soil. It also bears in a peculiar and direct way on the question of *party organization*.

Under ordinary conditions—that is, where the political domination of the bourgeoisie has preceded the socialist movement—the bourgeoisie itself instills in the working class the rudiments of political solidarity. At this stage, declares the Communist Manifesto, the unification of the workers is not yet the result of their own aspiration to unity but comes as a result of the activity of the bourgeoisie, "which, in order to attain its own political ends, is compelled to set the proletariat in motion . . ."

In Russia, however, the Social Democracy must make up by its own efforts an entire historic period. It must lead the Russian proletarians from their present "atomized" condition, which prolongs the autocratic régime, to a class organization that would help them to become aware of their historic objectives and prepare them to struggle to achieve those objectives.

The Russian socialists are obliged to undertake the building of such an organization without the benefit of the formal guarantees commonly found under a bourgeois-democratic setup. They do not dispose of the political raw material that in other countries is supplied by bourgeois society itself. Like God Almighty they must have this organization arise out of the void, so to speak.

How to effect a transition from the type of organization characteristic of the preparatory stage of the socialist movement—usually featured by disconnected local groups and clubs, with propaganda as a principal activity—to the unity of a large, national body, suitable for concerted political action over the entire vast territory ruled by the Russian state? That is the specific problem which the Russian Social Democracy has mulled over for some time.

Autonomy and isolation are the most pronounced characteristics of the old organizational type. It is, therefore, understandable why the slogan of the persons who want to see an inclusive national organization should be "Centralism!"

Centralism was the theme of the campaign that has been carried on by the *Iskra* group for the last three years. This campaign has produced the Congress of August 1903, which has been described as the second congress of the Russian Social Democratic Party but was, in fact, its constituent assembly.

At the Party Congress, it became evident that the term "centralism" does not completely cover the question of organization for the Russian Social Democracy. Once again we have learned that no rigid formula can furnish the solution of any problem in the socialist movement.

One Step Forward, Two Steps Backward, written by Lenin, an outstanding member of the *Iskra* group, is a methodical exposition of the ideas of the ultra-centralist tendency in the Russian movement. The viewpoint presented with incomparable vigor and logic in this book, is that of pitiless centralism. Laid down as principles are: 1. The necessity of selecting, and constituting as a separate corps, all the active revolutionists, as distinguished from the unorganized, though revolutionary, mass surrounding this elite.

Lenin's thesis is that the party Central Committee should have the privilege of naming all the local committees of the party. It should have the right to appoint the effective organs of all local bodies from Geneva to Liege, from Tomsk to Irkutsk. It should also have the right to impose on all of them its own ready-made rules of party conduct. It should have the right to rule without appeal on such questions as the dissolution and reconstitution of local organizations. This way, the Central Committee could determine, to suit itself, the composition of the highest party organs as well as of the party còngress. The Central Committee would be the only thinking element in the party. All other groupings would be its executive limbs.

Lenin reasons that the combination of the socialist mass movement with such a rigorously centralized type of organization is a specific principle of revolutionary Marxism. To support this thesis, he advances a series of arguments, with which we shall deal below.

Generally speaking it is undeniable that a strong tendency toward centralization is inherent in the Social Democratic movement. This tendency springs from the economic makeup of capitalism which is essentially a centralizing factor. The Social Democratic movement carries on its activity inside the large bourgeois city. Its mission is to represent, within the boundaries of the national state, the class interests of the proletariat, and to oppose those common interests to all local and group interests.

Therefore, the Social Democracy is, as a rule, hostile to any manifestations of localism or federalism. It strives to unite all workers and all worker organizations in a single party, no matter what national, religious, or occupational differences may exist among them. The Social Democracy abandons this principle and gives way to federalism only under exceptional conditions, as in the case of the Austro-Hungarian Empire.

It is clear that the Russian Social Democracy should not organize itself as a federative conglomerate of many national groups. It must rather become a single party for the entire empire. However, that is not really the question considered here. What we are considering is the degree of centralization necessary inside the unified, single Russian party in view of the peculiar conditions under which it has to function.

Looking at the matter from the angle of the formal tasks of the Social Democracy in its capacity as a party of class struggle, it appears at first that the power and energy of the party are directly dependent on the possibility of centralizing the party. However, these formal tasks apply to all active parties. In the case of the Social Democracy, they are less important than is the influence of historic conditions.

The Social Democratic movement is the first in the history of class societies which reckons, in all its phases and through its entire course, on the organization and the direct, independent action of the masses.

Because of this, the Social Democracy creates an organizational type that is entirely different from those common to earlier revolutionary movements, such as those of the Jacobins and the adherents of Blanqui.

Lenin seems to slight this fact when he presents in his book (page 140) the opinion that the revolutionary Social Democrat is nothing else than a "Jacobin indissolubly joined to the organization of the proletariat, which has become conscious of its class interests."

For Lenin, the difference between the Social Democracy and Blanquism is reduced to the observation that in place of a handful of conspirators we have a class-conscious proletariat. He forgets that this difference implies a complete revision of our ideas on organization and, therefore, an entirely different conception of centralism and the relations existing between the party and the struggle itself.

Blanquism did not count on the direct action of the working class. It, therefore, did not need to organize the people for the revolution. The people were expected to play their part only at the moment of revolution. Preparation for the revolution concerned only the little group of revolutionists armed for the coup. Indeed, to assure the success of the revolutionary conspiracy, it was considered wiser to keep the mass at some distance from the conspirators. Such a relationship could be conceived by the Blanquists only because there was no close contact between the conspiratorial activity of their organization and the daily struggle of the popular masses.

The tactics and concrete tasks of the Blanquist revolutionists had little connection with the elementary class struggle. They were freely improvised. They could, therefore, be decided on in advance and took the form of a ready-made plan. In consequence of this, ordinary members of the organization became simple executive organs, carrying out the orders of a will fixed beforehand, and outside of their particular sphere of activity. They became the instruments of a Central Committee. Here we have the second peculiarity of conspiratorial centralism—the absolute and blind submission of the party sections to the will of the center, and the extension of this authority to all parts of the organization.

However, Social Democratic activity is carried on under radically different conditions. It arises historically out of the elementary class struggle. It spreads and develops in accordance with the following dialectical contradiction. The proletarian army is recruited and becomes aware of its objectives in the course of the struggle itself. The activity of the party organization, the growth of the proletarians' awareness of the objectives of the struggle and the struggle itself, are not different things separated chronologically and mechanically. They are only different aspects of the same process. Except for the general principles of the struggle, there do not exist for the Social Democracy detailed sets of tactics which a Central Committee can teach the party membership in the same way as troops are instructed in their training camps. Furthermore, the range of influence of the socialist party is constantly fluctuating with the ups and downs of the struggle in the course of which the organization is created and grows.

For this reason Social Democratic centralism cannot be based on the mechanical subordination and blind obedience of the party membership to the leading party center. For this reason, the Social Democratic movement cannot allow the erection of an air-tight partition between the class-conscious nucleus of the proletariat already in the party and its immediate popular environment, the nonparty sections of the proletariat.

Now the two principles on which Lenin's centralism rests are precisely these: 1. The blind subordination, in the smallest detail, of all party organs, to the party center, which alone thinks, guides, and decides for all. 2. The rigorous separation of the organized nucleus of revolutionaries from its social-revolutionary surroundings.

Such centralism is a mechanical transposition of the organizational principles of Blanquism into the mass movement of the socialist working class.

In accordance with this view, Lenin defines his "revolutionary Social Democrat" as a "Jacobin joined to the organization of the proletariat, which has become conscious of its class interests."

The fact is that the Social Democracy is not *joined* to the organization of the proletariat. It is itself the proletariat. And because of this, Social Democratic centralism is essentially different from Blanquist centralism. It can only be the concentrated will of the individuals and groups representative of the most class-conscious, militant, advanced sections of the working class. It is, so to speak, the "self-centralism" of the advanced sectors of the proletariat. It is the rule of the majority within its own party.

The indispensable conditions for the realization of Social-Democratic centralism are: 1. The existence of a large contingent of workers educated in the political struggle. 2. The possibility for the workers to develop their own political activity through direct influence on public life, in a party press, and public congresses, etc.

These conditions are not yet fully formed in Russia. The first—a proletarian vanguard, conscious of its class interests and capable of self-direction in political activity—is only now emerging in Russia. All efforts of socialist agitation and organization should aim to hasten the formation of such a vanguard. The second condition can be had only under a régime of political liberty.

With these conclusions, Lenin disagrees violently. He is convinced that all the conditions necessary for the formation of a powerful and centralized party already exist in Russia. He declares that "it is no longer the proletarians but certain intellectuals in our party who need to be educated in the matters of organization and discipline." He glorifies the educative influence of the factory, which, he says, accustoms the proletariat to "discipline and organization."

Saying all this, Lenin seems to demonstrate again that his conception of socialist organization is quite mechanistic. The discipline Lenin has in mind is being implanted in the working class not only by the factory but also by the military and the existing state bureaucracy—by the entire mechanism of the centralized bourgeois state.

We misuse words and we practice self-deception when we apply the same term—discipline—to such dissimilar notions as: 1, the absence of thought and will in a body with a thousand automatically moving hands and legs, and 2, the spontaneous co-ordination of the conscious, political acts of a body of men. What is there in common between the regulated docility of an oppressed class and the self-discipline and organization of a class struggling for its emancipation?

The self-discipline of the Social Democracy is not merely the replacement of the authority of the bourgeois rulers with the authority of a socialist central committee. The working class will acquire the sense of the new discipline, the freely assumed self-discipline of the Social Democracy, not as a result of the discipline imposed on it by the capitalist state, but by extirpating, to the last root, its old habits of obedience and servility.

Centralism in the socialist sense is not an absolute thing applicable to any phase whatsoever of the labor movement. It is a *tendency*, which becomes real in proportion to the development and political training acquired by the working masses in the course of their struggle.

No doubt, the absence of the conditions necessary for the complete realization of this kind of centralism in the Russian movement presents a formidable obstacle.

It is a mistake to believe that it is possible to substitute "provisionally" the absolute power of a Central Committee (acting somehow by "tacit delegation") for the yet unrealizable rule of the majority of conscious workers in the party, and in this way replace the open control of the working masses over the party organs with the reverse control by the Central Committee over the revolutionary proletariat.

The history of the Russian labor movement suggests the doubtful value of such centralism. An all-powerful center, invested, as Lenin would have it, with the unlimited right to control and intervene, would be an absurdity if its authority applied only to technical questions, such as the administration of funds, the distribution of tasks among propagandists and agitators, the transportation and circulation of printed matter. The political purpose of an organ having such great powers is understandable only if those powers apply to the elaboration of a uniform plan of action, if the central organ assumes the initiative of a vast revolutionary act.

But what has been the experience of the Russian socialist movement up to now? The most important and most fruitful changes in its tactical policy during the last ten years have not been the inventions of several leaders and even less so of any central organizational organs. They have always been the spontaneous product of the movement in ferment. This was true during the first stage of the proletarian movement in Russia, which began with the spontaneous general strike of St. Petersburg in 1896, an event that marks the inception of an epoch of economic struggle by the Russian working people. It was no less true during the following period, introduced by the spontaneous street demonstrations of St. Petersburg students in March 1901. The general strike of Rostov-on-Don, in 1903, marking the next great tactical turn in the Russian proletarian movement, was also a spontaneous act. "All by itself," the strike expanded into political demonstrations, street agitation, great outdoor meetings, which the most optimistic revolutionist would not have dreamed of several years before.

Our cause made great gains in these events. However, the initiative and conscious leadership of the Social Democratic organizations played an insignificant role in this development. It is true that these organizations were not specifically prepared for such happenings. However, the unimportant part played by the revolutionists cannot be explained by this fact. Neither can it be attributed to the absence of an all-powerful central party apparatus similar to what is asked for by Lenin. The existence of such a guiding center would have probably increased the disorder of the local committees by emphasizing the difference between the eager attack of the mass and the prudent position of the Social Democracy. The same phenomenon—the insignificant part played by the initiative of central party organs in the elaboration of actual tactical policy—can be observed today in Germany and other countries. In general, the tactical policy of the Social Democracy is not something that may be "invented." It is the product of a series of great creative acts of the often spontaneous class struggle seeking its way forward.

The unconscious comes before the conscious. The logic of the historic process comes before the subjective logic of the human beings who participate in the historic process. The tendency is for the directing organs of the socialist party to play a conservative role. Experience shows that every time the labor movement wins new terrain those organs work it to the utmost. They transform it at the same time into a kind of bastion, which holds up advance on a wider scale.

The present tactical policy of the German Social Democracy has won universal esteem because it is supple as well as firm. This is a sign of the fine adaptation of the party, in the smallest detail of its everyday activity, to the conditions of a parliamentary régime. The party has made a methodical study of all the resources of this terrain. It knows how to utilize them without modifying its principles.

However, the very perfection of this adaptation is already closing vaster horizons to our party. There is a tendency in the party to regard parliamentary tactics as the immutable and specific tactics of socialist activity. People refuse, for example, to consider the possibility (posed by Parvus) of changing our tactical policy in case general suffrage is abolished in Germany, an eventuality not considered entirely improbable by the leaders of the German Social Democracy.

Such inertia is due, in a large degree, to the fact that it is very inconvenient to define, within the vacuum of abstract hypotheses, the lines and forms of still nonexistent political situations. Evidently, the important thing for the Social Democracy is not the preparation of a set of directives all ready for future policy. It is important: 1, to encourage a correct historic appreciation of the forms of struggle corresponding to the given situations, and 2, to maintain an understanding of the relativity of the current phase and the inevitable increase of revolutionary tension as the final goal of the class struggle is approached.

Granting, as Lenin wants, such absolute powers of a negative character to the top organ of the party, we strengthen, to a dangerous extent, the conservatism inherent in such an organ. If the tactics of the socialist party are not to be the creation of a Central Committee but of the whole party, or, still better, of the whole labor movement, then it is clear that the party sections and federations need the liberty of action which alone will permit them to develop their revolutionary initiative and to utilize all the resources of a situation. The ultra-centralism asked by Lenin is full of the sterile spirit of the overseer. It is not a positive and creative spirit. *Lenin's concern is not so much to make the activity of the party more fruitful as to control the party—to narrow the movement rather than to develop it, to bind rather than to unify it.*

In the present situation, such an experiment would be doubly dangerous to the Russian Social Democracy. It stands on the eve of decisive battles against tsarism. It is about to enter, or has already entered, on a period of intensified creative activity, during which it will broaden (as is usual in a revolutionary period) its sphere of influence and will advance spontaneously by leaps and bounds. To attempt to bind the initiative of the party at this moment, to surround it with a network of barbed wire, is to render it incapable of accomplishing the tremendous tasks of the hour.

The general ideas we have presented on the question of socialist centralism are not by themselves sufficient for the formulation of a constitutional plan suiting the Russian party. In the final instance, a statute of this kind can only be determined by the conditions under which the activity of the organization takes place in a given epoch. The question of the moment in Russia is how to set in motion a large proletarian organization. No constitutional project can claim infallibility. It must prove itself in fire.

But from our general conception of the nature of Social Democratic organization, we feel justified in deducing that its spirit requires—especially at the inception of the mass party—the co-ordination and unification of the movement and not its rigid submission to a set of regulations. If the party possesses the gift of political mobility, complemented by unflinching loyalty to principles and concern for unity, we can rest assured that any defects in the party constitution will be corrected in practice. For us, it is not the letter, but the living spirit carried into the organization by the membership that decides the value of this or that organizational form.

II

So far we have examined the problem of centralism from the viewpoint of the general principles of the Social Democracy, and to some extent, in the light of conditions peculiar to Russia. However, the military ultra-centralism cried up by Lenin and his friends is not the product of accidental differences of opinion. It is said to be related to a campaign against opportunism which Lenin has carried to the smallest organizational detail.

"It is important," says Lenin, "to forge a more or less effective weapon against opportunism." He believes that opportunism springs specifically from the characteristic leaning of intellectuals to decentralization and disorganization, from their aversion for strict discipline and "bureaucracy," which is, however, necessary for the functioning of the party.

Lenin says that intellectuals remain individualists and tend to anarchism even after they have joined the socialist movement. According to him, it is only among intellectuals that we can note a repugnance for the absolute authority of a Central Committee. The authentic proletarian, Lenin suggests, finds by reason of his class instinct a kind of voluptuous pleasure in abandoning himself to the clutch of firm leadership and pitiless discipline. "To oppose bureaucracy to democracy," writes Lenin, "is to contrast the organizational principle of revolutionary Social Democracy to the methods of opportunist organization."

He declares that a similar conflict between centralizing and autonomist tendencies is taking place in all countries where reformism and revolutionary socialism meet face to face. He points in particuliar to the recent controversy in the German Social Democracy on the question of the degree of freedom of action to be allowed by the Party to socialist representatives in legislative assemblies.

Let us examine the parallels drawn by Lenin.

First, it is important to point out that the glorification of the supposed genius of proletarians in the matter of socialist organization and a general distrust of intellectuals as such are not necessarily signs of "revolutionary Marxist" mentality. It is very easy to demonstrate that such arguments are themselves an expression of opportunism.

Antagonism between purely proletarian elements and the nonproletarian intellectuals in the labor movement is raised as an ideological issue by the following trends: the semianarchism of the French syndicalists, whose watchword is "Beware of the politician!"; English trade-unionism, full of mistrust of the "socialist visionaries"; and, if our information is correct, the "pure economism," represented a short while ago within the Russian Social Democracy by *Rabochaya Mysl* ("Labor Thought"), which was printed secretly in St. Petersburg.

In most socialist parties of Western Europe there is undoubtedly a connection between opportunism and the "intellectuals," as well as between opportunism and decentralizing tendencies within the labor movement.

But nothing is more contrary to the historic-dialectic method of Marxist thought than to separate social phenomena from their historic soil and to present these phenomena as abstract formulas having an absolute, general application.

Reasoning abstractly, we may say that the "intellectual," a social element which has emerged out of the bourgeoisie and is therefore alien to the proletariat, enters the socialist movement not because of his natural class inclinations but in spite of them. For this reason, he is more liable to opportunist aberrations than the proletarian. The latter, we say, can be expected to find a definite revolutionary point of support in his class interests as long as he does not leave his original environment, the laboring mass. But the concrete form assumed by this inclination of the intellectual toward opportunism and, above all, the manner in which this tendency expresses itself in organizational questions depend every time on his given social milieu.

Bourgeois parliamentarism is the definite social base of the phenomena observed by Lenin in the German, French, and Italian socialist movements. This parliamentarism is the breeding place of all the opportunist tendencies now existing in the Western Social Democracy.

The kind of parliamentarism we now have in France, Italy, and Germany provides the soil for such illusions of current opportunism as overvaluation of social reforms, class and party collaboration, the hope of pacific development toward socialism, etc. It does so by placing intellectuals, acting in the capacity of parliamentarians, above the proletariat and by separating intellectuals from proletarians inside the socialist party itself. With the growth of the labor movement, parliamentarism becomes a springboard for political careerists. That is why so many ambitious failures from the bourgeoisie flock to the banners of the socialist parties. Another source of contemporary opportunism is the considerable material means and influence of the large Social Democratic organizations.

The party acts as a bulwark protecting the class movement against digressions in the direction of more bourgeois parliamentarism. To triumph, these tendencies must destroy the bulwark. They must dissolve the active, class-conscious sector of the proletariat in the amorphous mass of an "electorate."

That is how the "autonomist" and decentralizing tendencies arise in our Social Democratic parties. We notice that these tendencies suit definite political ends. They cannot be explained, as Lenin attempts, by referring to the intellectual's psychology, to his supposedly innate instability of character. They can only be explained by considering the needs of the bourgeois parliamentary politician, that is, by opportunist politics.

The situation is quite different in tsarist Russia. Opportunism in the Russian labor movement is, generally speaking, not the by-product of Social Democratic strength or of the decomposition of the bourgeoisie. It is the product of the backward political condition of Russian society.

The milieu where intellectuals are recruited for socialism in Russia is much more declassed and by far less bourgeois than in Western Europe. Added to the immaturity of the Russian proletarian movement, this circumstance is an influence for wide theoretic wandering, which ranges from the complete negation of the political aspect of the labor movement to the unqualified belief in the effectiveness of isolated terrorist acts, or even total political indifference sought in the swamps of liberalism and Kantian idealism.

However, the intellectual within the Russian Social Democratic movement can only with difficulty be attracted to any act of disorganization. It is contrary to the general outlook of the Russian intellectual's milieu. There is no bourgeois parliament in Russia to favor this tendency.

The Western intellectual who professes at this moment the "cult of the ego" and colors even his socialist yearnings with an aristocratic morale, is not the representative of the bourgeois intelligentsia "in general." He represents only a certain phase of social development. He is the product of bourgeois decadence.

On the other hand, the utopian or opportunist dreams of the Russian intellectual who has joined the socialist movement tend to nourish themselves on theoretic formulae in which the "ego" is not exalted but humiliated, in which the morality of renunciation, expiation, is the dominant principle.

The *Narodniki* ("Populists") of 1875 called on the Russian intelligentsia to lose themselves in the peasant mass. The ultra-civilized followers of Tolstoi speak today of escape to the life of the "simple folk." Similarly, the partisans of "pure economism" in the Russian Social Democracy want us to bow down before the "calloused hand" of labor.

If instead of mechanically applying to Russia formulae elaborated in Western Europe, we approach the problem of organization from the angle of conditions specific to Russia, we arrive at conclusions that are diametrically opposed to Lenin's.

To attribute to opportunism an invariable preference for a definite form of organization, that is, decentralization, is to miss the essence of opportunism.

On the question of organization, or any other question, opportunism knows only one principle: the absence of principle. Opportunism chooses its means of action with the aim of suiting the given circumstances at hand, provided these means appear to lead toward the ends in view.

If, like Lenin, we define opportunism as the tendency that paralyzes the independent revolutionary movement of the working class and transforms it into an instrument of ambitious bourgeois intellectuals, we must also recognize that in the initial stage of a labor movement this end is more easily attained as a result of rigorous centralization rather than by decentralization. It is by extreme centralization that a young, uneducated proletarian movement can be most completely handed over to the intellectual leaders staffing a Central Committee.

Also in Germany, at the start of the Social Democratic movement, and before the emergence of a solid nucleus of conscious proletarians and a tactical policy based on experience, partisans of the two opposite types of organization faced each other in argument. The "General Association of German Workers," founded by Lassalle, stood for extreme centralization. . . . The principle of autonomism was supported by the party which was organized at the Eisenach Congress with the collaboration of W. Liebknecht and A. Bebel. . . .

The tactical policy of the "Eisenachers" was quite confused. Yet they contributed vastly more to the awakening of class-consciousness of the German masses than the Lassalleans. Very early the workers played a preponderant role in that party (as was demonstrated by the number of worker publications in the provinces), and there was a rapid extension of the range of the movement. At the same time, the Lassalleans, in spite of all their experiments with "dictators," led their faithful from one misadventure to another.

In general, it is rigorous, despotic centralism that is preferred by opportunist intellectuals at a time when the revolutionary elements among the workers still lack cohesion and the movement is groping its way, as is the case now in

Russia. In a later phase, under a parliamentary régime and in connection with a strong labor party, the opportunist tendencies of the intellectuals express themselves in an inclination toward "decentralization."

If we assume the viewpoint claimed as his own by Lenin and we fear the influence of intellectuals in the proletarian movement, we can conceive of no greater danger to the Russian party than Lenin's plan of organization. *Nothing will more surely enslave a young labor movement to an intellectual elite hungry for power than this bureaucratic strait jacket, which will immobilize the movement and turn it into an automaton manipulated by a Central Committee.* On the other hand, there is no more effective guarantee against opportunist intrigue and personal ambition than the independent revolutionary action of the proletariat, as a result of which the workers acquire the sense of political responsibility and self-reliance.

What is today only a phantom haunting Lenin's imagination may become reality tomorrow.

Let us not forget that the revolution soon to break out in Russia will be a bourgeois and not a proletarian revolution. This modifies radically all the conditions of socialist struggle. The Russian intellectuals, too, will rapidly become imbued with bourgeois ideology. The Social Democracy is at present the only guide of the Russian proletariat. But on the day after the revolution, we shall see the bourgeoisie, and above all the bourgeois intellectuals, seek to use the masses as a steppingstone to their domination.

The game of the bourgeois demagogues will be made easier if at the present stage, the spontaneous action, initiative, and political sense of the advanced sections of the working class are hindered in their development and restricted by the protectorate of an authoritarian Central Committee.

More important is the fundamental falseness of the idea underlying the plan of unqualified centralism—the idea that the road to opportunism can be barred by means of clauses in a party constitution.

Impressed by recent happenings in the socialist parties of France, Italy, and Germany, the Russian Social Democrats tend to regard opportunism as an alien ingredient, brought into the labor movement by representatives of bourgeois democracy. If that were so, no penalties provided by a party constitution could stop this intrusion. The afflux of nonproletarian recruits to the party of the proletariat is the effect of profound social causes, such as the economic collapse of the petty bourgeoisie, the bankruptcy of bourgeois liberalism, and the degeneration of bourgeois democracy. It is naïve to hope to stop this current by means of a formula written down in a constitution.

A manual of regulations may master the life of a small sect or a private circle. An historic current, however, will pass through the mesh of the most subtly worded statutory paragraph. It is furthermore untrue that to repel the elements pushed toward the socialist movement by the decomposition of bourgeois society means to defend the interests of the working class. The Social Democracy has always contended that it represents not only the class interests of the proletariat but also the progressive aspirations of the whole of contemporary society. It represents the interests of all who are oppressed by bourgeois domination. This must not be understood merely in the sense that all these interests are ideally contained in the socialist program. Historic evolution translates the given proposition into reality. In its capacity as a political party, the Social Democracy becomes the haven of all discontented elements in our society and thus of the entire people, as contrasted to the tiny minority of the capitalist masters.

But socialists must always know how to subordinate the anguish, rancor, and hope of this motley aggregation to the supreme goal of the working class. The Social Democracy must enclose the tumult of the nonproletarian protestants against existing society within the bounds of the revolutionary action of the proletariat. It must assimilate the elements that come to it.

This is only possible if the Social Democracy already contains a strong, politically educated proletarian nucleus class conscious enough to be able, as up to now in Germany, to pull along in its tow the declassed and petty bourgeois elements that join the party. In that case, greater strictness in the application of the principle of centralization and more severe discipline, specifically formulated in party bylaws, may be an effective safeguard against the opportunist danger. That is how the revolutionary socialist movement in France defended itself against the Jaurèsist confusion. A modification of the constitution of the German Social Democracy in that direction would be a very timely measure.

But even here we should not think of the party constitution as a weapon that is, somehow, self-sufficient. It can be at most a coercive instrument enforcing the will of the proletarian majority in the party. If this majority is lacking, then the most dire sanctions on paper will be of no avail.

However, the influx of bourgeois elements into the party is far from being the only cause of the opportunist trends that are now raising their heads in the Social Democracy. Another cause is the very nature of socialist activity and the contradictions inherent in it.

The international movement of the proletariat toward its complete emancipation is a process peculiar in the following respect. For the first time in the history of civilization, the people are expressing their will consciously and in opposition to all ruling classes. But this will can only be satisfied beyond the limits of the existing system.

Now the mass can only acquire and strengthen this will in the course of the day-to-day struggle against the existing social order—that is, within the limits of capitalist society.

On the one hand, we have the mass; on the other, its historic goal, located outside of existing society. On one hand, we have the day-to-day struggle; on the other, the social revolution. Such are the terms of the dialectical contradiction through which the socialist movement makes its way.

It follows that this movement can best advance by tacking betwixt and between the two dangers by which it is constantly being threatened. One is the loss of its mass character; the other, the abandonment of its goal. One is the danger of sinking back to the condition of a sect; the other, the danger of becoming a movement of bourgeois social reform.

That is why it is illusory, and contrary to historic experience, to hope to fix, once for always, the direction of the revolutionary socialist struggle with the aid of formal means, which are expected to secure the labor movement against all possibilities of opportunist digression.

Marxist theory offers us a reliable instrument enabling us to recognize and combat typical manifestations of opportunism. But the socialist movement is a mass movement. Its perils are not the product of the insidious machinations of individuals and groups. They arise out of unavoidable social conditions. We cannot secure ourselves in advance against all possibilities of opportunist deviation. Such dangers can be overcome only by the movement itself—certainly with the aid of Marxist theory, but only after the dangers in question have taken tangible form in practice.

Looked at from this angle, opportunism appears to be a product and an inevitable phase of the historic development of the labor movement.

The Russian Social Democracy arose a short while ago. The political conditions under which the proletarian movement is developing in Russia are quite abnormal. In that country, opportunism is to a large extent a by-product of the groping and experimentation of socialist activity seeking to advance over a terrain that resembles no other in Europe.

In view of this, we find most astonishing the claim that it is possible to avoid any possibility of opportunism in the Russian movement by writing down certain words, instead of others, in the party constitution. *Such an attempt to exorcise opportunism by means of a scrap of paper may turn out to be extremely harmful—not to opportunism but to the socialist movement.*

Stop the natural pulsation of a living organism, and you weaken it, and you diminish its resistance and combative spirit—in this instance, not only against opportunism but also (and that is certainly of great importance) against the existing social order. The proposed means turn against the end they are supposed to serve.

In Lenin's overanxious desire to establish the guardianship of an omniscient and omnipotent Central Committee in order to protect so promising and vigorous a labor movement against any misstep, we recognize the symptoms of the same subjectivism that has already played more than one trick on socialist thinking in Russia.

It is amusing to note the strange somersaults that the respectable human "ego" has had to perform in recent Russian history. Knocked to the ground, almost reduced to dust, by Russian absolutism, the "ego" takes revenge by turning to revolutionary activity. In the shape of a committee of conspirators, in the name of a nonexistent Will of the People, it seats itself on a kind of throne and proclaims it is all-powerful. [The reference is to the conspiratorial circle which attacked tsarism from 1879 to 1883 by means of terrorist acts and finally assassinated Alexander II.—Translator.] But the "object" proves to be the stronger. The knout is triumphant, for tsarist might seems to be the "legitimate" expression of history.

In time we see appear on the scene an even more "legitimate" child of history—the Russian labor movement. For the first time, bases for the formation of a real "people's will" are laid in Russian soil.

But here is the "ego" of the Russian revolutionary again! Pirouetting on its head, it once more proclaims itself to be the all-powerful director of history—this time with the title of His Excellency the Central Committee of the Social Democratic Party of Russia.

The nimble acrobat fails to perceive that the only "subject" which merits today the role of director is the collective "ego" of the working class. The working class demands the right to make its mistakes and learn in the dialectic of history.

Let us speak plainly. Historically, the errors committed by a truly revolutionary movement are infinitely more fruitful than the infallibility of the cleverest Central Committee.

C'EST POUR TOI QUE TU FAIS LA RÉVOLUTION

● *daniel cohn-bendit*
and
● *gabriel cohn-bendit*

There is no such thing as an isolated revolutionary act. Acts that can transform society take place in association with others, and form part of a general movement that follows its own laws of growth. All revolutionary activity is collective, and hence involves a degree of organization. What we challenge is not the need for this but the need for a revolutionary leadership, the need for a party.

Central to my thesis is an analysis of the bureaucratic phenomenon, which I have examined from various viewpoints. For example, I have looked at the French workers' unions and parties and shown that what is wrong with them is not so much their rigidity and treachery as the fact that they have become integrated into the overall bureaucratic system of the capitalist state.

The emergence of bureaucratic tendencies on a world scale, the continuous concentration of capital, and the increasing intervention of the State in economic and social matters, have produced a new managerial class whose fate is no longer bound up with that of the private ownership of the means of production.

It is in the light of this bureaucratization that the Bolshevik Party has been studied. Although its bureaucratic nature is not, of course, its only characteristic, it is true to say that Communists, and also Trotskyists, Maoists and the rest, no less than the capitalist State, all look upon the proletariat as a mass that needs to be directed from above. As a result, democracy degenerates into the ratification at the bottom of decisions taken at the top, and the class struggle is forgotten while the leaders jockey for power within the political hierarchy.

The objections to Bolshevism are not so much moral as sociological; what we attack is not the evil conduct of some of its leaders but an organizational set-up that has become its one and only justification.

The most forceful champion of a revolutionary party was Lenin, who in his *What is to be done?* argued that the proletariat is unable by itself to reach a 'scientific' understanding of society, that it tends to adopt the prevailing, i.e. the bourgeois, ideology.

Hence it was the essential task of the Party to rid the workers of this ideology by a process of political education which could only come to them *from without*. Moreover, Lenin tried to show that the Party can only overcome the class enemy by turning itself into a professional revolutionary body in which everyone is allocated a fixed task. Certain of its infallibility, a Party appoints itself the natural spokesman and sole defender of the interests of the working class, and as such wields power on their behalf–i.e. acts as a bureaucracy .

We take quite a different view: far from having to teach the masses, the revolutionary's job is to try to understand and express their common aspirations; far from being Lenin's 'tribune of the people who uses every manifestation of tyranny and oppression . . . to explain his Socialist convictions and his Social Democratic demands', the real militant must encourage the workers to struggle on their own behalf, and show how their every struggle can be used to drive a wedge into capitalist society. If he does so, the militant acts as an agent of the people and no longer as their leader.

The setting up of any party inevitably reduces freedom of the people to freedom to agree with the party.

In other words, democracy is not suborned by bad leadership but by the very existence of leadership. Democracy cannot even exist within the Party, because the Party itself is not a democratic organization, i.e. it is based upon authority and not on representation. Lenin realized full well that the Party is an artificial creation, that it was imposed upon the working class 'from without'. Moral scruples have been swept aside: the Party is 'right' if it can impose its views upon the masses and wrong if it fails to do so. For Lenin, the whole matter ends there. In his *State and Revolution,* Lenin did not even raise the problem of the relationship between the people and the Party. Revolutionary power was a matter of fact, based upon people who are prepared to fight for it; the paradox is that the Party's programme, endorsed by these people, was precisely: All power to the Soviets! But whatever its programme, in retrospect we can see that the Party, because of its basic conception, is bound to bring in privilege and bureaucracy, and we must wash our hands of all organizations of this sort. To try and pretend that the Bolshevik Party is truly democratic is to deceive oneself, and this, at least, is an error that Lenin himself never committed.

What then is our conception of the role of the revolutionary? To begin with, we are convinced that the revolutionary cannot and must not be a leader. Revolutionaries are a militant minority drawn from various social strata, people who band together because they share an ideology, and who pledge themselves to struggle against oppression, to dispel the mystification of the ruling classes and the bureaucrats, to proclaim that the workers can only defend themselves and build a socialist society by taking their fate into their own hands, believing that political maturity comes only from revolutionary struggle and direct action.

By their action, militant minorities can do no more than support, encourage, and clarify the struggle. They must always guard against any tendency to become a pressure group outside the revolutionary movement of the masses. When they act, it must always be with the masses, and not as a faction.

For some time, the 22 March Movement was remarkable only for its radical political line, for its methods of attack—often spontaneous—and for its non-bureaucratic structure. Its objectives and the role it could play became clear only during the events of May and June, when it attracted the support of the working class. These militant students whose dynamic theories emerged from their practice, were imitated by others, who developed new forms of action appropriate to their own situation. The result was a mass movement unencumbered by the usual chains of command. By challenging the repressive nature of their own institution—the university—the revolutionary students forced the state to show its hand, and the brutality with which it did so caused a general revulsion and led to the occupation of the factories and the general strike. The mass intervention of the working class was the greatest achievement of our struggle; it was the first step on the path to a better society, a path that, alas, was not followed to the end. The militant minorities failed to get the masses to follow their example: to take collective charge of the running of society. We do not believe for a single moment that the workers are incapable of taking the next logical step beyond occupying the factories—which is to run them on their own. We are sure that they can do what we ourselves have done in the universities. The militant minorities must continue to wage their revolutionary struggle, to show the workers what their trade unions try to make them forget: their own gigantic strength. The distribution of petrol by the workers in the refineries and the local strike committees shows clearly what the working class is capable of doing once it puts its mind to it.

During the recent struggle, many student militants became hero-worshippers of the working class, forgetting that every group has its own part to play in defending its own interests, and that, during a period of total confrontation, these interests converge.

The student movement must follow its own road—only thus can it contribute to the growth of militant minorities in the factories and workshops. We do not pretend that we can be leaders in the struggle, but it is a fact that small revolutionary groups can, at the right time and place, rupture the system decisively and irreversibly.

During May and June, 1968, the emergence of a vast chain of workers' committees and sub-committees by-passed the calcified structure of the trade unions, and tried to call together all workers in a struggle that was their own and not that of the various trade union bureaucracies. It was because of this that the struggle was carried to a higher stage. It is absurd and romantic to speak of revolution with a capital R and to think of it as resulting from a single, decisive action. The revolutionary process grows and is strengthened daily not only in revolt against the boredom of a system that prevents people from seeing the 'beach under the paving stones' but also in our determination to make the beach open to all.

If a revolutionary movement is to succeed, no form of organization whatever must be allowed to dam its spontaneous flow. It must evolve its own forms and structures.

In May and June, many groups with these ideas came into being; here is a pamphlet put out by the ICO, not as a platform or programme for action, but as a basis for discussion by the workers:

'The aim of this group is to unite those workers who have lost confidence in the traditional labour organizations—parties and trade unions.

'Our own experiences have shown us that modern trade unions contribute towards stabilizing and preserving the exploitative system.

'They serve as regulators of the labour market, they use the workers' struggle for political ends, they are the handmaidens of the ruling class in the modern state.

'It is up to the workers to defend their own interests and to struggle for their own emancipation.

'Workers, we must try to understand what is being done to us all, and denounce the trade unions with their spurious claims that they alone can help us to help ourselves.

'In the class struggle we intervene as workers together, and not on the basis of our job, which can only split our ranks. We are in favour of setting up committees in which the greatest number of workers can play an active part. We defend every non-sectarian and non-sectional claim of the working class, every claim that is in the declared interest of all. We support everything that widens the struggle and we oppose everything that tends to weaken it. We are in favour of international contacts, so that we may also get in touch with workers in other parts of the world and discuss our common problems with them.

'We have been led to question all exploitative societies, all organizations, and tackle such general problems as state capitalism, bureaucratic management, the abolition of the state and of wage-slavery, war, racism, "Socialism," etc. Each of us is entitled to present his own point of view and remains entirely free to act in whatever way he thinks best in his own factory. We believe in spontaneous resistance to all forms of domination, not in representation through the trade unions and political parties.

'The workers' movement forms a part of the class struggle because it promotes practical confrontations between workers and exploiters. It is for the workers alone to say how, why and where we are all to struggle. We cannot in any way fight for them; they alone can do the job. All we can do is give them information, and learn from them in return. We can contribute to discussions, so as to clarify our common experience, and we can also help to make their problems and struggle known to others.

'We believe that our struggles are milestones on the road to a society that will be run by the workers themselves.' *(Information et Correspondance Ouvrières).*

From the views expressed by this and other groups, we can get some idea of the form that the movement of the future must take. Every small action committee no less than every mass movement which seeks to improve the lives of all men must resolve:

(1) to respect and guarantee the plurality and diversity of political currents within the revolutionary mainstream. It must accordingly grant minority groups the right of independent action—only if the plurality of ideas is allowed *to express itself in social practice* does this idea have any real meaning;

(2) to ensure that all delegates are accountable to, and subject to immediate recall by, those who have elected them, and to oppose the introduction of specialists and specialization at every step by widening the skill and knowledge of all;

(3) to ensure a continuous exchange of ideas, and to oppose any control of information and knowledge;

(4) to struggle against the formation of any kind of hierarchy;

(5) to abolish all artificial distinctions within labour, in particular between manual and intellectual work, and discrimination on grounds of sex;

(6) to ensure that all factories and businesses are run by those who work in them;

(7) to rid ourselves, in practice, of the Judaeo-Christian ethic, with its call for renunciation and sacrifice. These is only one reason for being a revolutionary—because it is the best way to live.

Reaction, which is bound to become more and more violent as the revolutionary movement increases its impact on society, forces us to look to our defences. But our main task is to keep on challenging the traditional bureaucratic structures both in the government and also in the working-class movements.

How can anyone represent anyone else? All we can do is to involve them. We can try and get a few movements going, inject politics into all the structures of society, into the Youth Clubs, Youth Hostels, the YMCA and the Saturday Night dance, get out on to the streets, out on to all the streets of all the towns. To bring real politics into everyday life is to get rid of the politicians. We must pass from a critique of the university to the anti-university, open to all. Our challenge of the collective control of knowledge by the bourgeoisie must be radical and intransigent.

 The multiplication of nuclei of confrontation decentralizes political life and neutralizes the repressive influence of the radio, television and party politics. Every time we beat back intimidation on the spot, we are striking a blow for freedom. To break out from isolation, we must carry the struggle to every market place and not create Messianic organizations to do the job for us. We reject the policy committee and the editorial board.

In the event, the students were defeated in their own struggle. The weakness of our movement is shown by the fact that we were unable to hold on to a single faculty—the recapture of the factories by the CRS (with the help of the CGT) might well have been halted by the working class, had there been a determined defence of a single 'red base'. But this is mere speculation. What is certain is that the movement must look carefully at its actions in May and June and draw the correct lessons for the future. The type of organization we must build can neither be a vanguard nor a rearguard, but must be right in the thick of the fight. What we need is not organization with a capital O, but a host of insurrectional cells, be they ideological groups, study groups—we can even use street gangs.

Effective revolutionary action does not spring from 'individual' or 'external' needs—it can only occur when the two coincide so that the distinction itself breaks down. Every group must find its own form, take its own action, and speak its own language. When all have learnt to express themselves, in harmony with the rest, we shall have a free society.

Reader, you have come to the end of this book, a book that wants to say only one thing: between us we can change this rotten society. Now, put on your coat and make for the nearest cinema. Look at their deadly love-making on the screen. Isn't it better in real life? Make up your mind to learn to love. Then, during the interval, when the first advertisements come on, pick up your tomatoes or, if you prefer, your eggs, and chuck them. Then get out into the street, and peel off all the latest government proclamations until underneath you discover the message of the days of May and June.

Stay awhile in the street. Look at the passers-by and remind yourself: the last word has not yet been said. Then act. Act with others, not for them. Make the revolution here and now. It is your own. *C'est pour toi que tu fais la révolution.*

THE PRINCIPAL LESSON FOR THE PRESENT

● *régis debray*

1. Which should be strengthened today, the Party or the guerrillas, embryo of the people's army? Which is the decisive link? Where should the principal effort be made?

Such are the questions which divide militants today in those vanguard nations of Latin America where a guerrilla movement exists.

Tomorrow the militants of other nations will confront them.

Today they express a dilemma.

These questions have met with a standard response in the history of Marxism and in history as such. An answer so immutable that the mere asking of it in this form will seem a *heresy* to many. That answer is that the Party must be strengthened first, for it is the creator and the directive nucleus of the people's army. Only the Party of the working class can create a true army of the people—as the guarantor of a scientifically based political line—and win power in the interests of the workers.

Theoretical orthodoxy: It is not a matter of destroying an army but of seizing state power in order to transform the social structure. Bourgeois state power has its own superstructure (political, judicial, constitutional, etc.) which is not to be confused with its repressive apparatus. If it is a matter of breaking the *existing* political power and making of it the instrument of the democratic dictatorship of the exploited, it devolves upon the representatives of the exploited classes and of their vanguard, the working class, to carry on this *political* fight up to and including its armed form, revolutionary civil war. Now then, a class is represented by a political party, not by a military instrumentality. The proletariat is represented by that party which expresses its class ideology, Marxism-Leninism. Only the leadership of this party can scientifically defend its class interests.

To the extent that it is a matter of intervening in the total social structure, it is necessary to have scientific knowledge of society in all its complexity, at all its levels (political, ideological, economic, etc.) and in its development. This is the condition for carrying out a global struggle at all levels; and the military struggle, only one level among others, has meaning only within the context of a comprehensive intervention at all levels by the popular forces against bourgeois society. Only the workers' party, on the basis of a scientific understanding of the social structure and of existing conditions, can decide the slogans, the goals, and the alliances required at a given moment. In brief, the party determines the political content and the goal to be pursued, and the people's army is merely an *instrument* of implementation. To take the popular army for the party would be to take the instrument for the goal, the means for the end: a confusion proper to technocracy—hence the terms "technicism" and "militarism" given to this deviation.

Historical orthodoxy: These principles have been applied up to now in the victorious revolutionary struggles of our epoch, in the form of the separation between the political vanguard and the military instrumentality, with absolute supremacy of the former over the latter. In October, 1917, the Bolshevik Red Guards were subject to the orders of the Military Committee of the Party, which was in turn under the control of the Central Committee, whose directives it applied to the letter. It will be said that the example is not conclusive, since it refers to an urban workers' insurrection, not a people's war. Let us, then, take as examples the socialist countries that have carried on a long people's war starting in the countryside. It is in China and Vietnam that this subordination is thrown into sharpest relief. We know how, in China, the principle of "politics directs the gun" (Mao Tse-tung) is expressed in reality through the vigilant leadership of the army by the Party. In Vietnam, Giap writes:

> *The first fundamental principle in the building of our army is the imperative necessity of placing the army under Party leadership, of constantly strengthening Party leadership. The Party is the founder, the organizer, and the educator of the army. Only its exclusive leadership can permit the army to hew to a class line, to maintain its political orientation, and to fulfil its revolutionary tasks.*[1]

A practical expression of this principle can be found in the system of political commissars and Party committees within the Vietnamese Liberation Army. They are not merely political aides, they are the actual leaders of military units. On the question of authority, unit commanders are responsible to the Party Committee, which gives the directives in accordance with the principles of collective leadership and individual responsibility, to all echelons including the cells. Giap says, "If the cell is weak, the company is weak."

In China the Party committee operates at the regimental level and comprises some seven to nine members, among whom the regimental commander has the same rank as the political commissar. This Party committee orients the subordinate units. Battalions and companies have no Party committees, but they have political instructors, who assign militants to various company squads. The principle applies both at the top and at the bottom. The General Staff is not divided into four or five services, as are capitalist armies, but into two essential branches, logistic and political-military, the political branch having equal rank with the operational.

In the interests of brevity, let us resort to a symbol. The distinction between the political and the military is symbolized by certain names: Mao Tse-tung and Chu Teh during the revolutionary civil war and the Long March, Ho Chi Minh and Giap during the war against the French. Perhaps we could add Lenin and Trotsky during the wars of imperialist intervention in the Soviet Union.

In Cuba, military (operational) and political leadership have been combined in one man: Fidel Castro. Is this the result of mere chance, without significance, or is it an indication of an historically different situation? Is it an exception or does it foreshadow something fundamental? What light does it throw on the current Latin American experience? We must decipher this experience in time, and we must not rush to condemn history in the making because it does not conform to received principles. Fidel Castro said recently:

> *I am accused of heresy. It is said that I am a heretic within the camp of Marxism-Leninism. Hmm! It is amusing that so-called Marxist organizations, which fight like cats and dogs in their dispute over possession of revolutionary truth, accuse us of wanting to apply the Cuban formula mechanically. They reproach us with a lack of understanding of the Party's role; they reproach us as heretics within the camp of Marxism-Leninism.*

The fact is that those who want mechanically to apply formulas to the Latin American reality are precisely these same "Marxists," since it is always in the interest of the man who commits a robbery to be the first to cry thief. But what does Fidel Castro say that causes him to be characterized as "a heretic," "subjective," and "petty bourgeois"? What explosive message of his causes people in the capitals of America and of the socialist countries of Europe and Asia, all those who "want to wage revolutionary war by

[1] *Guerre du peuple, armée du peuple*, p. 123.

telepathy," "the unprincipled ones," to join in the chorus against the Cuban Revolution?

"Who will make the revolution in Latin America? Who? The people, the revolutionaries, with or without a party." (Fidel)

Fidel Castro says simply that there is no revolution without a vanguard; that this vanguard is not necessarily the Marxist-Leninist party; and that those who want to make the revolution have the right and the duty to constitute themselves a vanguard, independently of these parties.

It takes courage to state the facts out loud when these facts contradict a tradition. There is, then, no metaphysical equation in which vanguard = Marxist-Leninist party; there are merely dialectical conjunctions between a given function—that of the vanguard in history—and a given form of organization—that of the Marxist-Leninist party. These conjunctions arise out of prior history and depend on it. Parties exist here on earth and are subject to the rigors of terrestrial dialectics. If they have been born, they can die and be reborn in other forms. How does this rebirth come about? Under what form can the historic vanguard reappear?

Let us proceed systematically.

First question: How can we think or state that under the present circumstances there can be a revolution "with or without a party"? This question must be asked, not in order to revive useless and sterile animosities (of which the chief beneficiary is the counter-revolution everywhere), but because the answer to the second question is contingent on it.

Second question: In what form can the historic vanguard appear?

What is depends on what was, what will be on what is. The question of parties, as they are today, is a question of history. To answer it, we must look to the past.

A party is marked by its conditions of birth, its development, the class or alliance of classes that it represents, and the social milieu in which it has developed. Let us take the same counter-examples in order to discover what historic conditions permit the application of the traditional formula for party and guerrilla relationships: China and Vietnam.

(1) The Chinese and Vietnamese parties were involved from the beginning with the problem of establishing revolutionary power. This link was not theoretical but *practical* and manifested itself very early, in the form of a grievous experience. The Chinese Party was born in 1921, when Sun Yat-sen's bourgeois revolution—in which it participated by reason of its affiliation with the Kuomintang—was in the ascendancy. From its inception it received direct aid from the Soviet mission, including military advisers led by Joffe and later by Borodin. The latter, on his arrival, organized the training of Chinese Communist officers at the Whampoa Military Academy, which soon permitted the Chinese Party, as Mao said in 1938, "to recognize the importance of military matters." Three years after it was organized it underwent the disastrous experience of the first revolutionary civil war (1924-1927), the urban insurrection, and the Canton strike in which it took a leading role. It assimilated this experience and, under the aegis of Mao Tse-tung, transmuted it into self-critical understanding, which led to the adoption of an antithetical line, contrary even to the advice of the Third International, i.e., the withdrawal to the countryside and the rupture with the Kuomintang.

The Vietnamese Party came into being in 1930, immediately organized peasant insurrections in the hinterland which were quickly repressed, and two years later defined its line, under the aegis of Ho Chi Minh, in its first program of action: "The only path to liberation is that of armed mass struggle." "Our party," wrote Giap, "came into being when the Vietnamese revolutionary movement was at its peak. From the beginning it led the peasants, encouraged them to rise up and establish soviet power. Thus, at an early stage, it became aware of the problems of revolutionary power and of armed struggle." In brief, these parties transformed themselves, within a few years of their founding, into vanguard parties, each one with its own political line, elaborated independently of international social forces, and each profoundly linked to its people.

(2) In the course of their subsequent development, international contradictions were to place these parties—like the Bolshevik Party some years earlier—at the head of popular resistance to foreign imperialism: in China, against the Japanese invasion in 1937; in Vietnam also against the Japanese in 1939, and against the French colonialists in 1945. The anti-feudal revolt was thus transformed into an anti-imperialist revolt, the latter giving impetus to the former. The class struggle took the form of a patriotic war, and the establishment of socialism corresponded to the restoration of national independence: the two are linked. These parties, spearheading the war of the people against the foreigners, consolidated themselves as the standard-bearers of the fatherland. They became an integral part of it.

(3) The circumstances of this same war of liberation led certain parties originally composed of students and of the best of the workers' élite to withdraw to the countryside to carry on a guerrilla war against the occupying forces. They then merged with the agricultural workers and small farmers; the Red Army and the Liberation Forces (Vietminh) were transformed into peasant armies under the leadership of the party of the working class. They achieved *in practice* the alliance of the majority class and the vanguard class: the worker-peasant alliance. The Communist Party, in this case, was the result and the generative force of this alliance. So were its leaders, not artificially appointed by a congress or co-opted in traditional fashion, but tested, molded, and tempered by this terrible struggle which they led to victory. Function makes the functionary, but paradoxically only historic individuals "make history."

Without going into detail, historic circumstances have not permitted Latin American Communist Parties, for the most part, to take root or develop in the same way. The conditions of their founding, their growth, their link with the exploited classes are obviously different. Each one may have its own history but they are alike in that they have not, since their founding, lived through the experience of winning power in the way the Chinese and Vietnamese parties have; they have not had the opportunity, existing as they do in countries possessing formal political independence, of leading a war of national liberation; and they have therefore not been able to achieve the worker-peasant alliance—an interrelated aggregation of limitations arising from shared historical conditions.

The natural result of this history is a certain structure of directive bodies and of the parties themselves, adapted to the circumstances in which they were born and grew. But, by definition, historic situations are not immutable. The Cuban Revolution and the processes it has set in motion throughout Latin America have upset the old perspectives. A revolutionary armed struggle, wherever it exists or is in preparation, requires a thoroughgoing transformation of peacetime practices. War, as we know, is an extension of politics, but with specific procedures and methods. The effective leadership of an armed revolutionary struggle requires a new style of leadership, a new method of organization, and new physical and ideological responses on the part of leaders and militants.

A new style of leadership. It has been widely demonstrated that guerrilla warfare is directed not from outside but from within, with the leadership accepting its full share of the risks involved. In a country where such a war is developing, most of the organization's leaders must leave the cities and join the guerrilla army. This is, first of all, a security measure, assuring the survival of the political leaders. One Latin American party has already taken this decision. This same party has likewise transformed its Central Committee, replacing most of the old leaders with young men directly involved in the war or in the underground struggle in the cities. The reconstitution of the party thus goes hand in hand with its rejuvenation.

In Latin America, wherever armed struggle is on the order of the day, there is a close tie between biology and ideology. However absurd or shocking this relationship may seem, it is nonetheless a decisive one. An elderly man, accustomed to city living, molded by other circumstances and goals, will not easily adjust himself to the mountain nor—though this is less so—to underground activity in the cities. In addition to the moral factor—conviction—physical fitness is the most basic of all skills needed for waging guerrilla war; the two factors go hand in hand. A perfect Marxist education is not, at the outset, an imperative condition. That an elderly man should be proven militant —and possess a revolutionary training—is not, alas, sufficient for coping with guerrilla existence, especially in the early stages. Physical aptitude is the prerequisite for all other aptitudes; a minor point of limited theoretical appeal, but the armed struggle appears to have a rationale of which theory knows nothing.

A new organization. The reconstitution of the Party into an effective directive organism, equal to the historic task, requires that an end be put to the plethora of commissions, secretariats, congresses, conferences, plenary sessions, meetings, and assemblies at all levels—national, provincial, regional, and local. Faced with a state of emergency and a militarily organized enemy, such a mechanism is paralyzing at best, catastrophic at worst. It is the cause of the vice of excessive deliberation which Fidel has spoken of and which hampers executive, centralized, and vertical methods, combined with the large measure of tactical independence of subordinate groups which is demanded in the conduct of military operations.

This reconstitution requires the temporary suspension of "internal" party democracy and the temporary abolition of the principles of democratic centralism which guarantee it. While remaining voluntary and deliberate, more so than ever, party discipline becomes military discipline. Once the situation is analyzed, democratic centralism helps to determine a line and to elect a general staff, after which it should be suspended in order to put the line into effect. The subordinate units go their separate ways and reduce their contact with the leadership to a minimum, according to traditional rules for underground work; in pursuance of the general line they utilize to the best of their ability the greatest margin for initiative granted to them.

New ideological reflexes. Certain behavior patterns become inappropriate under conditions of an objective state of war: the basing of an entire political line on existing contradictions between enemy classes or between groups with differing interests within the same bourgeois social class; the consequent obsessive pursuit of alliances with one or another faction of the bourgeoisie, of political bargaining, and of electoral maneuvers, from which the ruling classes have so far reaped all the benefits; the safeguarding of unity at any price, regardless of revolutionary principles and interests, which has gradually turned the party and its survival in a given form into an end in itself, more sacred even than the Revolution; the siege fever, heritage of the past, and its accompanying mistrust, arrogance, rigidity and fitfulness.

Addressing himself fraternally to Party comrades during the struggle against Batista, Che Guevara made the following mordant comment: "You are capable of creating cadres who can endure torture and imprisonment in silence but not of training cadres who can capture a machine-gun nest." This remark in no way constitutes an appraisal of courage; it is a political evaluation. It is not a matter of replacing cowardice with courage, still less of one ideology with another, but of one form of courage with another, one pattern of action (and of psychic identification) with another; that is to say, of accepting the ultimate consequences of one's principles, right up to the point where they demand of the militant other forms of action and other responses from his nervous system.[2]

We can now pose the second question.

How to overcome these deficiencies? Under what conditions can these parties resume their vanguard function, including guerrilla warfare? Is it by their own political work on themselves, or is some other form of education historically necessary? If we are to answer these questions regarding the future, we must look not at the past but at the present. Briefly, the question might be posed as follows:

> II. *How is a vanguard party formed? Can the Party, under existing Latin American conditions, create the popular army, or is it up to the popular army to create the vanguard? Which is the nucleus of which?*

For reasons beyond their control, many Latin American Communist Parties made a false start, 30 or 40 years ago, thus creating a complicated situation. But parties are never anything but instruments of class struggle. Where the instrument no longer serves its purpose, should the class struggle come to a halt or should new instruments be forged?[3] A childish question: no one can make such a decision. The class struggle, especially in Latin America today, can be curbed, eroded, deflected, but it cannot be stopped. The people devise their own vanguards, making do with what is available, and the duty of revolutionaries is to hasten this development. But the development of what, precisely?

[2] Let us speak clearly. The time has passed for believing that it suffices to be "in the Party" to be a revolutionary. But the time has also come for putting an end to the acrimonious, obsessive, and sterile attitudes of those who think that in order to be a revolutionary one need only be "anti-party"; these attitudes constitute two sides of the same coin, basically identical. The Manichaeism of the Party (no revolution outside the Party) finds its reflection in anti-party Manichaeism (no revolution with the Party): both are quietist. In Latin America today a revolutionary is not defined by his formal relationship with the Party, whether he is for or against it. The value of a revolutionary, like that of a party, depends on his activity.

[3] Our description does not apply to countries where the absence of a serious struggle for power has so far permitted political organizations to escape such tensions.

We are witnessing today, here and there, strange reversals. Che Guevara wrote that the guerrilla movement is not an end in itself, nor is it a glorious adventure; it is merely a means to an end: the conquest of political power. But, lo and behold, guerrilla forces were serving many other purposes: a form of pressure on bourgeois governments; a factor in political horse-trading; a trump card to be played in case of need—such were the objectives with which certain leaderships were attempting to saddle their military instrumentalities. The revolutionary method was being utilized for reformist ends.[4] Then, after a period of marking time, the guerrillas turned away from and rejected these goals imposed from outside and assumed their own political leadership. To become reconciled with itself, the guerrilla force set itself up as a political leadership, which was the only way to resolve the contradictions and to develop militarily. Let it be noted that no part of the guerrilla movement has attempted to organize a new party; it seeks rather to wipe out doctrinal or party divisions among its own combatants. The unifying factors are the war and its immediate political objectives. The guerrilla movement begins by creating unity within itself around the most urgent military tasks, which have already become political tasks, a unity of non-party elements and of all the parties represented among the *guerrilleros*. The most decisive political choice is membership in the guerrilla forces, in the Armed Forces of Liberation. Thus gradually this small army creates rank-and-file unity among all parties, as it grows and wins its first victories. Eventually, the future People's Army will beget the party of which it is to be, theoretically, the instrument: essentially the party is the army.

Did not the Cuban Revolution experience this same paradox? It has been said with dismay that the party, the usual instrument for the seizure of power, was developed *after* the conquest of power. But no, it already existed in embryo—in the form of the Rebel Army. Fidel, its commander in chief, was already an unofficial party leader by early 1959. A foreign journalist in Cuba was astonished one day to see many Communist leaders in battle-dress; he had thought that battle-dress and pistols belonged to the folklore of the Revolution, that they were really a kind of martial affectation. Poor man! It was not an affectation, it was the history of the Revolution itself appearing before his eyes, and most certainly the future history of America. Just as the name of socialism was formally applied to the revolution after a year of socialist practice, the name of the party came into use three years after the proletarian party had begun to exist in uniform. In Cuba it was not the party that was the directive nucleus of the popular army, as it had been in Vietnam according to Giap; the Rebel Army was the leading nucleus of the party, the nucleus that created it. The first party leaders were created on July 26, 1953, at Moncada. The party is the same age as the revolution; it will be fourteen on July 26, 1967. Moncada was the nucleus of the Rebel Army, which was in turn the nucleus of the party. Around this nucleus, and only because it already had its own political-military leadership, other political forces have been able to assemble and unite, forming what is today the Communist Party of Cuba, of which both the base and the head continue to be made up of comrades from the guerrilla army.

The Latin American revolution and its vanguard, the Cuban revolution,

[4] See "Política y Guerrillas," by Fernández y Zanetti, in *El Caimán Barbudo,* No. 8, Havana.

 have thus made a decisive contribution to international revolutionary experience and to Marxism-Leninism.

> *Under certain conditions, the political and the military are not separate, but form one organic whole, consisting of the people's army, whose nucleus is the guerrilla army. The vanguard party can exist in the form of the guerrilla* foco *itself. The guerrilla force is the party in embryo.*

This is the staggering novelty introduced by the Cuban Revolution.

It is indeed a contribution. One could of course consider this an exceptional situation, the product of a unique combination of circumstances, without further significance. On the contrary, recent developments in countries that are in the vanguard of the armed struggle on the continent confirm and reinforce it. It is reinforced because, whereas the ideology of the Cuban Rebel Army was not Marxist, the ideology of the new guerrilla commands is clearly so, just as the revolution which is their goal is clearly socialist and proletarian. It is precisely because their line is so clear and their determination so unalterable that they have had to separate themselves, at a certain point, from the existing vanguard parties and propose (as in Guatemala) or impose (as in Venezuela) their own political, ideological, and organizational ideas as the foundation of any possible agreement, on a take-it-or-leave-it basis. In sum, it was necessary in both cases to discontinue all organic dependence on political parties and to replace these enfeebled political vanguards. In other words, they had to reach the point at which the Cuban Revolution started.

Thus ends a divorce of several decades' duration between Marxist theory and revolutionary practice. As tentative and tenuous as the reconciliation may appear, it is the guerrilla movement—master of its own political leadership—that embodies it, this handful of men "with no other alternative but death or victory, at moments when death was a concept a thousand times more real, and victory a myth that only a revolutionary can dream of." (Che) These men may die, but others will replace them. Risks must be taken. The union of theory and practice is not an inevitability but a battle, and no battle is won in advance. If this union is not achieved there, it will not be achieved anywhere.

The guerrilla force, if it genuinely seeks total political warfare cannot in the long run tolerate any fundamental duality of functions or powers. Che Guevara carries the idea of unity so far that he proposes that the military and political leaders who lead insurrectional struggles in America be "united, if possible, in one person." But whether it is an individual, as with Fidel, or collective, the important thing is that the leadership be homogeneous, political and military simultaneously. Career soldiers can, in the process of the people's war, become political leaders (Luis Turcios, for example, had he lived); militant political leaders can become military leaders, learning the art of war by making it (Douglas Bravo, for example).

In any case, it is necessary that they be able to make it. *A guerrilla force cannot develop on the military level if it does not become a political vanguard.* As long as it does not work out its own line, as long as it remains a pressure group or a device for creating a political diversion, it is fruitlessly marking time, however successful its partial actions may be. How can it take the initiative? On what will it build its morale? Do we perhaps believe that it will go "too far" if it is allowed to become the catalyst for popular aspirations and energies, which will *ipso facto* transform it into a directive force? Precisely because it is a mass struggle—the most radical of all—the guerrilla movement, if it is to triumph *militarily,* must *politically* assemble around it the majority of the exploited classes. Victory is impossible without their active and organized participation, since it is the general strike or generalized urban insurrection that will give the coup de grâce to the régime and will defeat its final maneuvers—a last-minute coup d'état, a new junta, elections—by extending the struggle throughout the country. But in order to reach that point, must there not be a long and patient effort by the mountain forces to coordinate all forms of struggle, eventually to coordinate action by the militia with that of the regular forces, to coordinate rearguard sabotage by the suburban guerrillas with operations carried out by the principal guerrilla group? And, beyond the armed struggle, must there not be an effort to play an ever larger role in the country's civilian life? Whence the importance of a radio transmitter at the disposition of the guerrilla forces. The radio permits headquarters to establish daily contact with the population residing outside the zone of operations. Thus the latter can receive political instructions and orientation which, as military successes increase, find an ever-increasing echo. In Cuba *Radio Rebelde,* which began transmitting in 1958, was frequently utilized by Fidel, and confirmed the role of the Rebel Army's General Staff as the directive force of the revolutionary movement. Increasingly, everyone—from Catholics to Communists—looked to the Sierra, tuned in to get reliable news, to know "what to do" and "where the action is." Clandestinity became public. As revolutionary methods and goals became more radical, so did the people. After Batista's flight, Fidel broadcast his denunciation of the maneuvers for a coup d'état in the capital, thus depriving the ruling class in a matter of minutes of its last card, and sealing the ultimate victory. Even before victory, the radio broke through government censorship on military operations, a censorship such as prevails today in all embattled countries. It is by means of radio that the guerrillas force the doors of truth and open them wide to the entire populace, especially if they follow the ethical precepts that guided *Radio Rebelde*—never broadcast inaccurate news, never conceal a defeat, never exaggerate a victory. In short, radio produces a qualitative change in the guerrilla movement. This explains the muffled or open resistance which certain party leaders offer today to the guerrilla movement's use of this propaganda medium.

Thus, in order for the small motor really to set the big motor of the masses into motion, without which its activity will remain limited, it must first be recognized by the masses as their only interpreter and guide, under penalty of dividing and weakening the people's strength. In order to bring about this recognition, the guerrillas must assume all the functions of political and military authority. Any guerrilla movement in Latin America that wishes to pursue the people's war to the end, transforming itself if necessary into a regular army and beginning a war of movement and positions, must become the unchallenged political vanguard, with the essential elements of its leadership being incorporated in the military command.

How can this "heresy" be justified? What gives the guerrilla movement the right to claim this political responsibility as its own and for itself alone?

The answer is: that class alliance which it alone can achieve, the alliance that will take and administer power, the alliance whose interests are those of socialism—the alliance between workers and peasants. The guerrilla army is a confirmation in action of this alliance; it is the personification of it. When the guerrilla army assumes the prerogatives of political leadership, it is responding to its class content and anticipating tomorrow's dangers. It alone can guarantee that the people's power will not be perverted after victory. If it does not assume the functions of political leadership during the course of emancipation itself, it will not be able to assume them when the war is over. And the bourgeoisie, with all necessary imperialist support, will surely take advantage of the situation. We have only to observe the difficulties in which Algeria finds itself today, because of yesterday's division between the internal fighters and their government outside the country. There is no better example of the risks implicit in the separation of military and political functions when there is no Marxist vanguard party. Thus it is the revolutionary civil war that strengthens the historic agencies of the new society. Lenin, in his last notes, wrote that "the civil war has *welded* together the working class and the peasantry, and this is the *guarantee of an invincible strength*."[5]

In the mountains, then, workers, peasants, and intellectuals meet for the first time. Their integration is not so easy at the beginning. Just as there are divisions into classes elsewhere, groups can arise even in the midst of an encampment. The peasants, especially if they are of Indian origin, stay to themselves and speak their own language (Quechua or Cakchiquel), among themselves. The others, those who know how to write and speak well, spontaneously create their own circle. Mistrust, timidity, custom, have to be gradually vanquished by means of untiring political work, in which the leaders set the example. These men all have something to learn from each other, beginning with their differences. Since they must all adapt themselves to the same conditions of life, and since they are all participating in the same undertaking, they adapt to each other. Slowly the shared existence, the combats, the hardships endured together, weld an alliance having the simple force of friendship. Furthermore the first law of guerrilla life is that no one survives it alone. The group's interest is the interest of each one, and vice versa. To live and conquer is to live and conquer all together. If a single combatant lags behind a marching column, it affects the speed and security of the entire column. In the rear is the enemy: impossible to leave the comrade behind or send him home. It is up to everyone, then, to share the burden, lighten his knapsack or cartridge-case, and help him all the way. Under these conditions class egoism does not long endure. Petty bourgeois psychology melts like snow under the summer sun, undermining the ideology of the same stratum. Where else could such an encounter, such an alliance, take place? By the same token, the only conceivable line for a guerrilla group to adopt is the "mass line"; it can live only with their support, in daily contact with them. Bureaucratic faintheartedness becomes irrelevant. Is this not the best education for a future socialist leader or cadre? Revolutionaries make revolutionary civil wars; but to an even greater extent it is revolutionary civil war that makes revolutionaries.

Lenin wrote: "The civil war has educated and tempered (Denikin and the others are good *teachers;* they have taught well; *all our best militants have been in the army).*"[6]

The best teacher of Marxism-Leninism is the enemy, in face-to-face confrontation during the people's war. Study and apprenticeship are necessary but

[5] Draft of a speech (not delivered) for the Tenth Congress of Russian Soviets, December 1922. Lenin's emphasis.

[6] *Ibid.* Lenin's emphasis.

not decisive. There are no academy-trained cadres. One cannot claim to train revolutionary cadres in theoretical schools detached from instructional work and common combat experiences. To think otherwise would be justifiable naïveté in Western Europe; elsewhere it is unpardonable nonsense.

The guerrilla group's exercise of, or commitment to establish, a political leadership is even more clearly revealed when it organizes its first liberated zone. It then tries out and tests tomorrow's revolutionary measures (as on the Second Front in Oriente): agrarian reform, peasant congresses, levying of taxes, revolutionary tribunals, the discipline of collective life. The liberated zone becomes the prototype and the model for the future state, its administrators the models for future leaders of state. Who but a popular armed force can carry through such socialist "rehearsals"?

The worker-peasant alliance often finds its connecting link in a group of revolutionaries of bourgeois extraction, from which a substantial part of the guerrilla command is recruited. Even if today this tendency is decreasing, because of the extreme polarization of social classes, it is far from having been eliminated.

Such is the law of "equivalent-substitutions" in countries that have been colonized even to a limited extent: one finds that a working class of restricted size or under the influence of a reformist trade union aristocracy, and an isolated and humiliated peasantry, are willing to accept this group, of bourgeois origin, as their political leadership. In the course of the struggle which awakens and mobilizes them, a kind of provisional delegation of powers is produced.[7] Inversely, in order to assume this function, this historic vicarship, and in order not to usurp a role to which they have only a provisional title, this progressive petty bourgeoisie must, to use Amilcar Cabral's phrase, "commit suicide as a class in order to be restored to life as revolutionary workers, totally identified with the deepest aspirations of their people." The most favorable time and place for this suicide is with the guerrillas, during guerrilla action: here, the small initial groups from the cities have their first daily contact with rural realities, little by little adjust themselves to its demands, and begin to understand from the inside the aspirations of their people; they cast aside political verbosity and make of these aspirations their program of action. Where better than in the guerrilla army could this shedding of skin and this resurrection take place?

Here the political word is abruptly made flesh. The revolutionary ideal emerges from the gray shadow of formula and acquires substance in the full light of day. This transubstantiation comes as a surprise, and when those who have experienced it want to describe it—in China, in Vietnam, in Cuba, in many places—they resort not to words but to exclamations.

> *The renovating spirit, the longing for collective excellence, the awareness of a higher destiny are in full flower and can develop considerably further. We had heard of these things, which had a flavor of verbal abstraction, and we accepted their beautiful meaning, but now we are living it, we are experiencing it in every sense, and it is truly unique. We have seen its incredible development in this Sierra, which is our small universe. Here the word "people," which is so often utilized in a vague and confused sense, becomes a living, wonderful and dazzling reality. Now I know who the*

[7] On this subject see "Tercer Mundo e Ideología," by Rachid, in *El Caimán Barbudo*, No. 2 (Havana).

people are: I see them in that invincible force that surrounds us everywhere, I see them in the bands of 30 or 40 men, lighting their way with lanterns, who descend the muddy slopes at two or three in the morning, with 30 kilos on their backs, in order to supply us with food. Who has organized them so wonderfully? Where did they acquire so much ability, astuteness, courage, self-sacrifice? No one knows! It is almost a mystery! They organize themselves all alone, spontaneously! When weary animals drop to the ground, unable to go further, men appear from all directions and carry the goods. Force cannot defeat them. It would be necessary to kill them all, to the last peasant, and that is impossible; this, the dictatorship cannot do; the people are aware of it and are daily more aware of their own growing strength.[8]

All these factors, operating together, gave shape to a strange band which was made to appear picturesque by certain photographs and which, because of our stupidity, impressed us only through the attire and long beards of its members. These are the militants of our time, not martyrs, not functionaries, but fighters. Neither creatures of an apparatus nor potentates: at this stage, they themselves are the apparatus. Aggressive men, especially in retreat. Resolute and responsible, each of them knowing the meaning and goal of this armed class struggle through its leaders, fighters like themselves whom they see daily carrying the same packs on their backs, suffering the same blistered feet and the same thirst during a march. The blasé will smile at this vision à la Rousseau. We need not point out here that it is not love of nature nor the pursuit of happiness which brought them to the mountain, but the awareness of a historic necessity. Power is seized and held in the capital, but the road that leads the exploited to it must pass through the countryside. Need we recall that war and military discipline are characterized by rigors unknown to the *Social Contract*? This is even truer for guerrilla armies than for regular armies. Today some of these groups have disappeared before assuming a vanguard role, having retreated or suffered liquidation. In a struggle of this kind, which involves such grave risks and is still only in the process of taking its first faltering steps, such defeats are normal. Other groups, the most important ones operating in countries whose history proves their importance for all Latin America—Venezuela, Guatemala, Colombia—have established themselves and are moving ahead. It is there, in such countries as these, that history is on the march today. Tomorrow other countries will join and supersede them in the vanguard role.

Has it been noted that nearly all of these guerrilla movements neither have nor want political commissars? The majority of the fighters come from Communist ranks. These are the first socialist guerrilla forces that have not adopted the system of political commissars, a system which does not appear to correspond to the Latin American reality.

If what we have said makes any sense at all, this absence of specialists in political affairs has the effect of sanctioning the absence of specialists in military affairs. The people's army is its own political authority. The *guerrilleros*

[8] From Fidel Castro's last letter to Frank País, written in the Sierra Maestra, July 21, 1957. The same wonderment is expressed today in the letters of Turcios, Douglas Bravo, Camilo Torres, and others. Of course this does not mean that it is easy to obtain peasant support immediately; but when it is obtained, it performs wonders. Fidel wrote the letter after eight months in the Sierra and after having escaped betrayal by several peasants.

play both roles, indivisibly. Its commanders are political instructors for the fighters, its political instructors are its commanders.

Let us sum up. Not to understand perfectly the theoretical and historical novelty of this situation is to open the way to dangerous errors at the very core of the armed struggle. To consider the existing party as different from and superior to the new type of party that grows along with the guerrilla force leads logically to two attitudes.

(1) *The guerrilla force should be subordinated to the party.* The system of political commissars is a consequence of this subordination. It implies that the guerrilla army is incapable of leading itself and that it must be guided from outside; that is, it presupposes the existence of a leader, someone who can bring revolutionary orientation from a previously existing vanguard. This hypothesis, unfortunately, does not correspond to reality.

(2) *The guerrilla force should be an imitation of the party.* In other words, the popular army should be built on the traditional party model. We have observed one effect of this system in the preference given to organizational matters over operational tasks, in the belief that the organism can create the function. Another consequence is seen in the meetings of fighters—imitations of cell meetings. This "democratist" method would seem to be to democracy among the *guerrilleros* what parliament is to socialist democracy (or pop art is to popular art): more than uprooting and transplanting a basically alien form, it is a dangerous graft. Naturally, meetings for political and ideological discussion among the combatants must be encouraged and fostered. But there are decisions that belong to the command, which presumably possesses clear and sound judgment in the military and disciplinary domain. To organize meetings at every turn leads the fighters to lose confidence in the command and, ultimately, in themselves; conscious discipline is relaxed; discord and dissension are spread among the troops; a substantial part of their military effectiveness is sacrificed. We learn from accounts of the war in Spain that Republican fighters sometimes discussed official orders at the height of a battle, refusing to attack a certain position or fall back at a given moment, holding meetings on questions of tactics while under enemy fire. We know the results only too well. In Cuba this method, occasionally adopted at the beginning of the war, led to confusion and desertions from the guerrilla group on the occasion of a public trial which almost cost the life of a highly respected captain, whose gun had gone off accidentally and killed a comrade. One could cite many other similar experiences.

A new situation calls for new methods. That is to say, we must guard against adopting forms of action, whether from error or tradition, which are inappropriate to this new content.

We can now resolve the initial dilemma. In the long run, certain regions of America, for dialectical reasons, will not need to choose between a vanguard party and a popular army. But for the moment there is a historically based *order of tasks. The people's army will be the nucleus of the party, not vice versa.* The guerrilla force is the political vanguard *in nuce* and from its development a real party can arise.

That is why the guerrilla force must be developed if the political vanguard is to be developed.

That is why, at the present juncture, *the principal stress must be laid on the development of guerrilla warfare and not on the strengthening of existing parties or the creation of new parties.*

That is why *insurrectional activity is today the number one political activity.*

REVOLUTION ON THE CAMPUS

Historically, students have been in the forefront of revolutionary movements, and today new revolutionary theories and tactics are being formulated and tested on the campuses in the Western democracies. The real thrust of the student movement in these countries is not to reform or restructure the university but rather to use the campus as a starting point for larger social revolution. The campus is for radical students a microcosm which reflects and represents larger social inequities. Racism in society is reflected by the lack of Black students and faculty on the campus; imperialism is reflected by the military research programs conducted by the university; the class nature is reflected in the elitist student-faculty-administrator structure of the university. In an even larger sense, there is a gradation of wealth and prestige among universities with the children of wealthy and prestigious families attending established, prestigious universities and the children of the working class, with few exceptions, attending the local state colleges. And the privileged few who graduate from the elite institutions become the new members of the ruling class while the graduates of the lesser institutions become members of the new working class performing the same dull and unfulfilling tasks their parents did, only using somewhat more sophisticated machinery.

In the first essay in this section, Professor George Adams points out what most college students know, that the university exists not to free the human mind and spirit but to train technicians and bureaucrats who will maintain the present economic social structure. The beginnings of student consciousness were rooted in an awareness of Professor Adams' "thirteen superstitions." But students soon realized that the university did not exist in a vacuum and was a tool and extension of the society it served. Thus the student revolt enlarged its consciousness and its goals.

Carl Davidson presents both necessary theoretical analysis and tactical considerations for student revolutionaries. Revolution is not a spontaneous event but must be based on hard, practical theory. Davidson clearly and objectively outlines the practical steps in mounting a revolutionary action on campus.

Mario Savio, perhaps the first famous American student revolutionary, is a name from the past. But the events of 1964 on the Berkeley campus of the University of California were the opening shots in what has come to be called the student revolution. Savio's brief essay "An End To History" articulates in a very general way the students' awareness of the function of the university and their decision to alter that function. Savio's essay also indicates the beginnings of student concern with the nature of the society the university serves and the university's relationship to that society. In this sense Savio's essay, though somewhat dated, is an important document in the student revolution.

The second major event in the American student revolution occurred at Columbia University in 1968. Mark Rudd, leader of the SDS chapter at Columbia, became as famous as Mario Savio, and the events at Columbia announced a new direction for the student revolution. The seizure of university buildings, the creation of new life-styles within those buildings, and the open warfare with authority announced to the world that students were no longer content with simple campus reform or "safe" constitutional issues. As Rudd points out in his essay "We Want Revolution," the students want a total restructuring of American society. The consciousness of the students at Columbia in 1968 went beyond simple issues to the larger concerns of imperialism, a warfare state, and economic exploitation.

The progress, then, from Berkeley in 1964 to Columbia in 1968 has been great. No longer concerned with simple political activity on campus, students are directing their energies to transforming society rather than simply the campus. The cry now is an end to war, racism, and imperialism around the world. It is on the campus that revolutionary theory and practice is formulated and tested. And it is from the campus as a base of operations that the students move into society.

THE FUNCTION OF A UNIVERSITY

● *george r. adams*

The function of a university is *to ensure the on-going life of the society.*

By *society* I do not mean the generally irresponsible economic system, the archaic and corrupt two-party political machine, the megalithic central government, the slow-moving legal system, the meaningless technology, the suburb syndrome, and the complex of mythology, superstition, misinformation, ignorance, custom, and the habits by which Americans lead that day-to-day life of quiet desperation which we call "the American way of life." I mean rather those activities which are meaningful in the community life of man, that is, mutual aid, uninhibited growth, guiltless sexual union, unrestricted pursuit of a life-style, perpetuation of the meaningful past, acceptance by one's peers; in short, all those actions which liberate and utilize the dynamic energies of humans, especially young humans, I see as necessary to the health, growth, and continuation of communal life, and hence as the only things that really define "society."

By *on-going life* I mean the unrepressed outflow of energies. In practice this release is seen in the sexual union of male and female for the combined and necessary aims of love-expression, gratification of sexual urges, and propagation of the species; in the natural educational process of elder teaching younger and peer helping peer; in the search by young people for something meaningful and challenging to set their hands to; in the productions of our best artists; in the beautiful milieu created by our best architects; in the scientists' demand for explanations and causes; and in the efforts by men of good will to find productive ways to live in harmony; briefly, life goes on when human activity is directed to the meaningful now and the better future, to the preservation of unity and the assurance of posterity. Any system, institution, or ideology which does not further such activity is trivial; any system, institution, or ideology which frustrates or represses such life-preserving activity, which attempts to appropriate life-energies for selfish use, is counter to life and deadly to society.

By *ensure* I would like to mean that a university has a true initiatory function, as the graduation term "commencement" implies; that is, a university should be an important stage in the on-growing growth of the young. Nowadays, unfortunately, the chief function of the university has become the *systematic dispelling of superstition.*

Because of the educational, social, familial, and economic structure of America, it is inevitable that students come to the university dragging with them, like the ghost of Jacob Marley, their chains and ledger books, the accumulated errors of seventeen years in our culture and twelve years in our schools. These errors can be classified under the heading, "13 Superstitions":

1. that "morality" means two things: you do not engage in premarital sexual intercourse, an activity which dormitory rules luckily prevent, and you accept without question all university regulations, state laws, and national aspirations;
2. that people who question, challenge, or attempt to change rules are

either insane or part of the international conspiracy to overthrow "the American way of life";

3. that if an institution exists, it obviously is supposed to exist;

4. that the administration of a school, just like Daddy at home, is always right by virtue of position and power, and if occasionally, like Daddy, the administration chooses to knock your head off for somewhat undefined reasons, that's O.K. too;

5. that a measure of "progress" at a school is a series of A's on a sheet of paper, a measure of maturity is disciplining oneself to write all the term papers required in a semester, and a measure of ethical behavior is staying out of trouble for four years;

6. that a diploma is the same thing as an education;

7. that a teacher is infallible except when he gives a D or F or questions your value-system;

8. that a fraternity is genuinely an expression of free choice in choosing a life-pattern and is an organization based on the principles of mutual aid and meaningful activity;

9. that it is the duty of a university to make sure that a student is trained for a job;

10. that it is the duty of a university to instill the values of "the American way of life";

11. that exactly 3 classes for exactly 50 minutes per class for exactly 1 semester is a sensible and efficient way to gain knowledge;

12. that a football team serves an educational function and a football stadium is a measure of academic excellence;

13. that a university should fit one for "life," a term usually not defined; in the course of preparing one for life the university can engage in research for warfare and the destruction of life, can suppress sexuality, can forestall experimentation, can deny student participation in university affairs, can avoid engaging in social reform, can encourage the construction of ugly buildings on campus, and can function as a repressive parent; in short, in fitting a student for life, the university is allowed first to kill him.

As I said earlier, the chief function of a university today is the systematic refutation of these 13 superstitions; if, in only four years, the university can in fact do this, it is pretty much a success. Hopefully, sometime in the future the university will have a more positive function, namely, to ensure the on-going life of the society by directing the young toward a life meaningful and charitable, that is, can be a genuine initiation into a vital community.

THE NEW RADICALS IN THE MULTIVERSITY: AN ANALYSIS AND STRATEGY FOR THE STUDENT MOVEMENT.

● *carl davidson*

introduction

The student movement has come under criticism from both the right and the left for its lack of a coherent ideology and strategy for social change. While there is certainly a great deal of truth in this criticism, my sensibilities tell me that this lack may be more to our advantage than to our disadvantage. To my mind, the great strength of the New Left has been its unconscious adherence to Marx's favourite motto—doubt everything. The student movement is young and inexperienced; yet, it has shown great wisdom in maintaining the principle that political truth must come from political experience. Ideology is not something sucked out of thumbs, nor found in this or that set of political catechisms. Rather, political analysis and strategy is something that grows slowly out of years of political experience and struggle. It must find its beginnings and maintain its deepest roots in people's day-to-day life-activity, for it is social reality that we are trying to understand and change.

In deepening that understanding of social reality, we must always remember that "The dispute over the reality or non-reality of thinking that is isolated from practice is a purely *scholastic* question."[1] Too often we are bogged down in theoretical disputes when the only way we can answer those questions is in *practice,* in political experimentation, in action. This is why we must remain open on many political questions. But this is not to say that we should only "do what the spirit say do." The concept of practical-critical activity (i.e. praxis) is three-sided: we must *act,* then *reflect* on the activity, and finally *criticize* the activity. The process of action, reflection, and criticism must be repeated again and again. The body of knowledge, ever changing and expanding, that grows from this process emerges as an ideology. Finally, the process is historical; it develops over a period of time.

It is for these reasons, as well as the fact that we are young and politically inexperienced, that we must emphasize an ongoing *practical-critical activity* over and above any allegiance to theoretical certitude. I hope that my following remarks on theory, strategy, and tactics will be taken in this context. All my assertions come from a limited experience; and, as such, are open to criticism, revision, and the acid-test of political practice.

the present malaise of education

"Happiness Is Student Power" was the most catching slogan emblazoned on the many banners and picket signs during the Berkeley Student Strike in December, 1966. But, as most college administrators know only too well, Berkeley and its rebellious student body is not an isolated phenomenon among the vast variety of American campuses. Far from being an exception, Berkeley

[1] Marx: *Theses on Feuerbach.*

has become the paradigm case of the educational malaise in the United States;
and, in the last few years, that malaise has been transformed into a movement. Indeed a spectre is haunting our universities—the spectre of a radical and militant nationally co-ordinated movement for *student power.*

Students began using the slogan "student power" soon after black people in the civil rights movement made the demand for "black power." Are students niggers? After studying the history of the Wobblies and labour syndicalism, students started thinking about student syndicalism. Are students workers? Power for what? Just any old kind of power? The university is a clumsy and uncoordinated machine, engulfing and serving thousands of people. Do students want to be administrators?

Obviously the cry for "power" in and of itself is a vacuous demand. Student power is not so much something we are fighting *for,* as it is something we must have in order to gain specific objectives. Then what are the objectives? What is our program? There is much variety and dispute on these questions. But there is one thing that seems clear. However the specific forms of our immediate demands and programs may vary, the long-range goal and the daily drive that motivates and directs us is our intense longing for our liberation. In short, what the student power movement is about: *freedom.*

But aren't students free? Isn't America a democracy, even if it is a little manipulative? To answer those kinds of questions and many others that are more serious, it is important to look more closely and come to an understanding of the malaise motivating the movement.

What do American students think of the educational institutions in which they live an important part of their lives? The most significant fact is that most of them don't think about them. Such young men and women made up that apathetic majority we called the "beat generation" in the 1950's. While the last few years has shown a marked and dramatic growth of a new radicalism, we should not forget that the apathetic and the cynical among the student population are still in the majority. But this need not be discouraging. In fact, we should view that apparent apathy among the majority of students with a certain qualified optimism.

What makes people apathetic? My feeling is that apathy is the *unconscious* recognition students make of the fact that they are *powerless.* Despite all the machinations and rhetoric used by hot-shot student politicos within administration-sponsored student governments, people's experience tells them that nothing changes. Furthermore, if and when change does occur, students fully recognize that they were powerless to effect those changes in one way or another. If this is in fact the case, then why shouldn't students be apathetic? The administration rules, despite the façade of student governments, of dorm councils, and of student judicials. And when *they* give us ex-officio seats on *their* academic committees, the result among most students is that deeper, more hardened kind of apathy—cynicism.

The apathetic students are correct *as far as they go.* They are powerless. The forms given us for our self-government are of the Mickey Mouse, sand-box variety. I would only be pessimistic if a majority of students really accepted the illusion that those institutions had meaning in their lives, or that they could significantly alter those institutions. But the opposite is the case. The apathy reflects the *reality* of their powerlessness. When that reality confronts the lie of the official rhetoric, the contradiction is driven home—then the apathetic become the cynical. What that contradiction—the daily living with a lie—all adds up to is a *dynamic* tension and alienation. And that, fellow organizers, is the necessary subjective condition for any revolution.

It is important to understand that students are alienated from much more than the social and extracurricular aspect of their education. In fact, their deepest alienation is directed at the education process itself. The excerpts that follow are from a letter written to the *New York Times* by a young woman student:

> *I came to this school not thinking I could even keep up with the work. I was wrong. I can keep up. I can even come out on top. My daily schedule's rough. I get up at 6:30. . . . After dinner I work until midnight or 12:30. In the beginning, the first few weeks or so, I'm fine. Then I begin to wonder just what this is all about: am I educating myself? I have that one answered . . . I'm educating myself the way they want. So I convince myself the real reason I'm doing all this is to prepare myself; meantime I'm wasting those years of preparation. I'm not learning what I want to learn . . . I don't care about the feudal system. I want to know about life. I want to think and read. When? . . . My life is a whirlpool. I'm caught up in it, but I'm not conscious of it. I'm what you call living, but somehow I can't find life . . . So maybe I got an A . . . but when I get it back I find that A means nothing. It's a letter you use to keep me going . . . I wonder what I'm doing here. I feel phony. I don't belong . . . You wonder about juvenile delinquents. If I ever become one, I'll tell you why it will be so. I feel cramped. I feel like I'm in a coffin and can't move or breathe . . . My life is worth nothing. It's enclosed in a few buildings on a campus; it goes no further. I've got to bust.*[2]

Tell the truth. Every American student knows that's the way it is. Even our administrators recognize what is going on. In 1962, a year or so *before* the first Berkeley insurrection, Clark Kerr emphasized, ". . . the undergraduate students are restless. Recent changes in the American university have done them little good . . . There is an incipient revolt . . ."[3] Kerr is not only concerned about the students. He also casts a worried glance at the faculty. "Knowledge is now in so many bits and pieces and administration so distant that faculty members are increasingly figures in a 'lonely crowd,' intellectually and institutionally."[4] The academic division of labour and depersonalization among the faculty is more than apparent to the students. Incoming freshmen scratch their heads, trying to understand *any* possible relevance of many of the courses in the catalogue, some of which they are required to take. Also, some of the best belly-laughs are had by reading the titles of master's and doctoral theses, like one granted a Ph.Ed. at Michigan State University: "An Evaluation of Thirteen Brands of Football Helmets on the Basis of Certain Impact Measures."[5] What's worse, even if a course seems as though it might be relevant to our lives, like Psychology or Political Science, we are soon told by our prof that what we'll learn only has to do with the laboratory behavior of rats, and that "political science" has nothing to do with day-to-day politics. A student from Brandeis sums it up nicely, "By the time we graduate, we have been painstakingly trained in separating facts from their meaning . . . No

[2] *New York Times,* November 29, 1964.
[3] Kerr, Clark: *Uses of the University,* p. 103.
[4] *Ibid,* p. 101.
[5] Baran and Sweezy: *Monopoly Capital.*

wonder that our classes, with few exceptions, seem irrelevant to our lives. No wonder they're so boring. Boredom is the necessary condition of any education which teaches us to manipulate the facts and suppress their meaning."[6] Irrelevancy, meaninglessness, boredom, and fragmentation are the kinds of attributes that are becoming more and more applicable to mass education in America. We are becoming a people required to know more and more about less and less. This is true not only for our students, but also for our teachers; not only in our universities, but also in our secondary and primary schools—private as well as public.

What should education be about in America? The official rhetoric seems to offer an answer: education should be the process of developing the free, autonomous, creative and responsible *individual*—the "citizen," in the best sense of that word. Furthermore, higher education ought to encourage and enable the individual to turn his personal concerns into social issues, open to rational consideration and solution. C. Wright Mills put it clearly: "The aim of the college, for the individual student, is to eliminate the need in his life for the college; the task is to help him become a self-educating man. For only that will set him free."[7]

But what is the reality of American education? Contrary to our commitment to individualism, we find that the day-to-day practice of our schools is authoritarian, conformist, and almost entirely status oriented. We find the usual relationship between teacher and student to be a disciplined form of dominance and subordination. We are told of the egalitarianism inherent in our school system, where the classroom becomes the melting-pot for the classless society of America's "people's capitalism," where everyone has the opportunity to climb to the top. Again, the opposite is the case. Our schools are more racially segregated now (1967) than ever before. There is a clear class bias contained both within and among the public schools—not even considering the clear class nature of the private schools and colleges. Within the secondary schools, students are quickly channelled—usually according to the class background of their parents—into vocational, commercial, or academic preparatory programs. Concerning the class differences among our public schools, James Conant remarks in *Slums and Suburbs,* ". . . I cannot imagine the possibility of a wealthy suburban district deliberately consolidating with other districts to achieve a truly comprehensive high school in which students of all abilities and socio-economic backgrounds will study together."[8] Even if they did consolidate the problem would only be rationalized, rather than solved. Who knows? Maybe the class struggle would break out on the playground.

Finally, what about that traditional American ideal that we were all taught to honour—the legend of the self-educated and self educating man? It seems to me that rather than enabling an individual to initiate and engage himself in a continual and coherent life-long educational process, our public programs are the sort where an individual is merely subjected to a random series of isolated training situations.

From individual freedom to national service, from egalitarianism to class and racial hierarchical ossification, from self-reliance to institutional dependence—we have come to see education as the mechanistic process of homogeneous,

[6] Golin, Steve: *New Left Notes,* October 7, 1966, p. 3.
[7] Mills, C. Wright: *Power, Politics and People,* p. 368.
[8] Conant, James: *Slums and Suburbs,* p. 77.

 uncritical absorption of "data" and development of job skills. But it is something more than that. The socialization and acculturation that goes on within American educational institutions is becoming increasingly central in the attempts to mold and shape American youth. This is mainly the result of the declining influence and, in some cases, the collapse of other traditional socializing institutions such as the church and the family. The schools, at all levels, end up with the job of maintaining, modifying, and transmitting the dominant themes of the national culture.

Quantitatively education has been rapidly increasing in the last few decades; but, as it grows in size, it decreases *qualitatively*. Rickover states in *Education and Freedom:* "We end up where we began a hundred years ago—with an elementary vocational education for the majority, and a poor college preparatory course for a minority of students." [9] Conant, who is quite concerned with the plight of the 80-85% of urban non-college bound high school students who are "social dynamite," places as a primary goal of education, giving these students ". . . the kind of zeal and dedication . . . to withstand the relentless pressures of communism." [10]

What about our school teachers? How is the nation faring on that front? Over 30% of the students in U.S. colleges and universities are going into primary and secondary education. However, despite the quantity, Mortimer Smith remarks in *The Diminished Mind,* ". . . the teacher-training institutions . . . are providing us with teachers who are our most poorly educated citizens." [11] While the job of teacher should command the highest respect in any society, many of us are well aware of the fact that in relation to other parts of the university, the college or school of education is considered to be the intellectual slum of the campus.

It seems clear that bourgeois education in the U.S. is in its historically most irrational and decadent state. Primary, secondary, and university systems are fusing together, thoroughly rationalizing and dehumanizing their internal order, and placing themselves in the service of the state, industry, and the military. Kerr is quite clear about this when he speaks of the "multiversity" making a common-law marriage with the federal government. John Hannah, president of Michigan State, was even more clear in a speech given in September, 1961, "Our colleges and universities must be regarded as bastions of our defence, as essential to the preservation of our country and our way of life as super-sonic bombers, nuclear powered submarines and intercontinental ballistics missiles." [12] The fact that none of the three weapons systems Hannah mentioned could have been designed, constructed, or operated without college-educated men proves that this is not just Fourth of July rhetoric. Hannah gives us an even better look at his idea of education in an article entitled, "The Schools' Responsibility in National Defense," where he comments: "I believe the primary and secondary schools can make education serve the individual and national interest by preparing youngsters for military service and life under conditions of stress as well as preparing them for college, or for a job or profession . . . I would not even shrink from putting the word 'indoctrination' to the kind of education I have in mind. If we do not hesitate to

[9] Rickover, Hyman: *Education and Freedom* p. 145.

[10] Conant, James: *Slums and Suburbs,* p. 34.

[11] Smith, Mortimer: *The Diminished Mind,* p. 87.

[12] Hannah, John: Speech given at Parents' Convocation at Michigan State University, September, 1961.

indoctrinate our children with a love of truth, a love of home, and a love of God, then I see no justification for balking at teaching them love of country and love of what this country means."[13]

. . .

Despite the crass attitudes of so many of our educators, or the dehumanization of the form and content of our educational institutions; it would be a mistake to think the problems are only within the educational system. While it is true that education has been stripped of any meaning it once had, and Dr. Conant is reduced to defining education as ". . . what goes on in schools and colleges,"[14] yet our system of schools and colleges are far from a point of collapse. In fact, they are thriving. The "knowledge industry," as Kerr puts it, accounts for 30% of the Gross National Product; and, it is expanding at *twice* the rate of any sector of the economy. School teachers make up the largest single occupational group of the labor force—some 3 million workers. Twenty-five years ago, the government and industry were hardly interested in education. But [in the immediate post-war period] the aggregate national outlay, public and private, amounted to 20 billions. As Kerr says, ". . . the university has become a prime instrument of national purpose. This is new. This is the essence of the transformation now engulfing our universities."[15] In short, our education institutions are becoming appendages to, and transformed by, U.S. corporate capitalism.

Education is not being done away with in favour of something called training. Rather, education is being transformed from a quasi-aristocratic classicism and petty-bourgeois romanticism into something quite new. These changes are apparent in ways other than the quantitative statistics given above. For example, we can examine the social sciences and the humanities. The social and psychological "reality" that we are given to study is "objectified" to the point of sterility. The real world, we are to understand, is "valuefree" and pragmatically bears little or no relation to the actual life-activity of men, classes, and nations. In one sense, we are separated from life. In another, we are being conditioned for life in a lifeless, stagnant, and sterile society.

For another example, there is more than a semantic connection between the academic division of labour and specialization we are so aware of, and the corresponding division of labour that has gone on in large-scale industry. But it is important to understand what this connection is. It does *not* follow that because technology becomes diversified and specialized, then academic knowledge and skills must follow suit. André Gorz makes the relevant comment, "It is completely untrue that modern technology demands specialization: quite the reverse. It demands a basic 'polyvalent' education, comprised not of fragmentary, pre-digested and specialized knowledge, but an imagination—or, put more precisely, a faculty of self-initiation—new methods of scientifico-technological research and discovery."[16] If it is not the new technological production that deems necessary this kind of isolated specialization we know so well, then what is responsible? Gorz spells it out again, "Capitalism actually needs shattered and atomized men . . ."[17] in order to maintain its system of

[13] Hannah, John: "The Schools' Responsibility in National Defense", May 5, 1955, quoted in *The Paper*, November 17, 1966, p. 1.

[14] Conant, James: Bulletin of the Council for Basic Education, January, 1960, p. 3.

[15] Kerr, Clark: *Uses of the University*, p. 87.

[16] Gorz, André: "Capitalism and the Labour Force", *International Socialist Journal*, p. 423.

[17] *Ibid*, p. 428.

 centralized, bureaucratized and militarized hierarchies, so as ". . . to perpetuate its domination over men, not only as workers, but also as consumers and citizens." [18]

From this perspective, we can begin to understand that the educational malaise we as students and faculty have felt so personally and intensely is no aberration, but firmly rooted in the American political economy. In fact, the Organized System which Paul Goodman calls "compulsory mis-education" may mis-educate us, but it certainly serves the masters of that system, the U.S. ruling class, quite well. As Edgar Z. Friedenberg wrote, "Educational evils are attributed to *defective* schools. In fact, they are as likely to be the work of *effective* schools that are being directed toward evil ends by the society that supports and controls them." [19] Furthermore, he continues later in the same article, "Schools are a definite indication that a society is divisible into a dominant and a subordinate group, and that the dominant group wants to teach the subordinate group something they could not be trusted to learn if left to themselves." [20] Clark Kerr would accept this, both for the society in general, which he divides into the "managers" and the "managed," and for the university. Kerr states: "The intellectuals (including university students) are a particularly volatile element . . . They are by nature irresponsible . . . They are, as a result, never fully trusted by anybody, including themselves." [21] But Kerr doesn't dismiss us. Even if we are by nature irresponsible (perhaps because we can perceive the contradictions?) he considers us essential. ". . . It is important who best attracts or captures the intellectuals and who uses them most effectively, for they may be a tool as well as a source of danger." [22]

I think we can conclude that the American educational system is a coherent, well-organized, and—to the extent that the rulers are still ruling—effective mechanism. However, it has turned our humanitarian values into their opposites and at the same time, given us the potential to understand and critically evaluate both ourselves and the system itself. To that extent the system is fraught with internal contradictions. Furthermore, the events comprising the student revolt in the last few years demonstrate the likelihood that those contradictions will continue to manifest themselves in an open and protracted struggle. As Kerr predicted, we *are* a source of danger and incipient revolt. And the fact that Kerr was fired and the police used in the face of that revolt only goes to prove that those contradictions are irreconcilable within the structure of corporate capitalism. As Quintin Hoare remarked in *New Left Review No. 32, " . . . a reform of the educational system involves a reform of the educators as well, and this is a political task, which immediately ricochets back to the question of transforming consciousness and ideology throughout society."* [23] The central problem of radically transforming the educational system is that of the transformation of the teaching and learning body—the faculty and students. And this transformation while it *begins* with the demands of the students' and teachers' work situation,

[18] *Ibid*, p. 428.

[19] Friedenberg, Edgar Z.: *The Nation*, September 20, 1965, p. 72.

[20] *Ibid.*

[21] Kerr, Clark: "Industrialism and Industrial Man", quoted in "The Mind of Clark Kerr", in Draper, Hal (ed.): *Berkeley: The New Student Revolt*, p. 211.

[22] *Ibid.*

[23] Hoare, Quintin: "Education: Programs and Men", *New Left Review* #32, pp. 50-51.

cannot take place unless it occurs *within* and is organically connected *to* the practice of a mass radical *political* movement. . . .

the praxis of student power strategy and tactics

Socialism on One Campus . . . an Infantile Disorder Perhaps the single most important factor for the student power movement to keep in mind is the fact that the university is intimately bound up with the society in general. Because of this, we should always remember that we cannot liberate the university without radically changing the rest of society. The lesson to be drawn is that any attempt to build a student movement based on "on-campus" issues only is inherently conservative and ultimately reactionary. Every attempt should be made to connect campus issues with off-campus questions. For example, the question of ranking and university complicity with the Selective Service System needs to be tied to a general anti-draft and "No Draft for Vietnam" movement. The question of the presence of the military on the campus in all its forms needs to be tied to the question of what that military is used for—fighting aggressive wars of oppression abroad—and not just to the question of secret research being poor academic policy. Furthermore, the student movement must actively seek to join off-campus struggles in the surrounding community. For example, strikes by local unions should be supported if possible. This kind of communication and understanding with the local working class is essential if we are ever going to have community support for student strikes.

Radicalizing the New Working Class If there is a single over-all purpose for the student power movement, it would be the development of a radical political consciousness among those students who will later hold jobs in strategic sectors of the political economy. This means that we should reach out to engineers and technical students rather than to business administration majors, education majors rather than to art students. From a national perspective, this strategy would also suggest that we should place priorities on organizing in certain *kinds* of universities—the community colleges, junior colleges, state universities, and technical schools, rather than religious colleges or the Ivy League.

One way to mount political action around this notion is to focus on the placement offices—the nexus between the university and industry. For example, when DOW Chemical comes to recruit, our main approach to junior and senior chemical engineering students who are being interviewed should not only be around the issue of the immorality of napalm. Rather, our leaflets should say that one of the main faults of DOW and all other industries as well is that their workers *have no control* over content or purposes of their work. In other words, DOW Chemical is bad, not only because of napalm, but mainly because it renders its workers *powerless*, makes them *unfree*. In short, DOW and all American industry oppresses *its own workers* as well as the people of the Third World. DOW in particular should be run off the campus and students urged not to work for them because of their complicity in war crimes. But when other industries are recruiting, our leaflets should address themselves to the interviewees' instincts of workmanship, his desires to be free and creative, to do humane work, rather than work for profit. We should encourage him, if he takes the job, to see himself in this light—as a skilled worker—and of his self-interest of organizing on his future job with his fellow workers, skilled and unskilled, for control of production and the end to which his work is directed. The need for control, for the power, on and off the job, to affect the decisions shaping one's life in all arenas; developing this kind of consciousness, on and off the campus, is what we should be fundamentally all about.

Practical, Critical Activity: Notes on Organizing There are three virtues necessary for successful radical organizing: honesty, patience, and a sense of humour. First of all if the students we are trying to reach can't trust us, who can they trust? Secondly it takes time to build a movement. Sometimes several years of groundwork must be laid before a student power movement has a constituency. It took most of us several years before we had developed a radical perspective. Why should it be any different for the people we are trying to reach? This is not to say that everyone must repeat all the mistakes we have gone through, but there are certain *forms* of involvement and action that many students will have to repeat. Finally, by a sense of humour, I mean we must be life-affirming. Lusty passionate people are the only kind of men who have the enduring strength to motivate enough people to radically transform a life-negating system.

Che Guevara remarked in *Guerrilla Warfare* that as long as people had faith in certain institutions and forms of political activity, then the organizer must work *with* the people *through* those institutions, even though we might think those forms of action are dead ends.[24] The point of Che's remark is that people must learn that those forms are stacked against them through their *own experience* in attempting change. The role of the organizer at this point is crucial. He or she should neither passively go along with the student government "reformer" types nor stand apart from the action denouncing it as "sell-out." Rather, his task is that of *constant criticism* from within the action. When the reformers fail, become bogged down, or are banging their heads against the wall, the organizer should be there as *one who has been with them throughout their struggle* to offer the relevant analysis of *why* their approach has failed and to indicate future strategies and tactics.

However, we also need to be discriminating. There are certain forms of political action, like working within the Democratic Party, that are so obviously bankrupt, that we need not waste our time. In order to discern these limits, an organizer has to develop a sensitivity to understand where people are. Many radical actions have failed on campuses because the activists have failed in laying a base for a particular action. It does no good to sit in against the CIA if a broad educational campaign, petitions, and rallies on the nature of the CIA have not been done for several days before the sit-in. It is not enough that we have a clear understanding of the oppressiveness of institutions like the CIA and HUAC before we act in a radical fashion. We must make our position clear to the students, faculty, and the surrounding community.

The Cultural Apparatus and the Problem of False Consciousness In addition to its role in the political economy, it is important to deal with the university as the backbone of what Mills called "the cultural apparatus." [25] He defined this as all those organizations and *milieux* in which artistic, scientific and intellectual work goes on, as well as the means by which that work is made avail-

[24] Guevara, Ernest "Che": *Guerrilla Warfare.*

[25] Mills, C. Wright: *Power, Politics and People,* p. 386.

able to others. Within this apparatus, the various vehicles of communication —language, the mass arts, public arts, and design arts—stand between a man's consciousness and his material existence. At present, the bulk of the apparatus is centralized and controlled by the corporate rulers of America. As a result, their use of the official communications has the effect of limiting our experience and, furthermore, expropriates much of that potential experience that we might have called our own. What we need to understand is that the cultural apparatus, properly used, has the ability both to transform power into authority and transform authority into mere overt coercion.

At present, the university's role in acculturation and socialization is the promulgation of the utter mystification of "corporate consciousness." Society is presented to us as a kind of caste system in which we are to see ourselves as a "privileged elite"—a bureaucratic man channelled into the proper bureaucratic niche. In addition to strengthening the forms of social control off the campus, the administration uses the apparatus on campus to legitimize its own power over us.

On the campus, the student press, underground newspapers, campus radio and television, literature tables, posters and leaflets, artist and lecture series, theaters, films, and the local press make up a good part of the non-academic cultural media. Most of it is both actively and passively being used against us. Any student power movement should (1) try to gain control of as much of the *established* campus cultural apparatus as possible, (2) if control is not possible, we should try to influence and/or resist it when necessary and (3) organize and develop a new counter-apparatus of our own. In short, we need our people on the staff of the school newspapers, and radio stations. We need our own local magazines. We need sympathetic contacts on local off-campus news media. Finally, we all could use some training in graphic and communicative arts.

What this all adds up to is strengthening our ability to wage an effective "de-sanctification" program against the authoritarian institutions controlling us. The purpose of de-sanctification is to strip institutions of their legitimizing authority, to have them reveal themselves to the people under them for what they are—raw coercive power. This is the purpose of singing the Mickey Mouse Club jingle at student government meetings, of ridiculing and harrassing student disciplinary hearings and tribunals, of burning the Dean of Men and/or Women in effigy. People will not move *against* institutions of power until the legitimizing authority has been stripped away. On many campuses this has already happened; but for those remaining, the task remains. And we should be forewarned: it is a tricky job and often can backfire, de-legitimizing us.

The Correct Handling of Student Governments While student governments vary in form in the United States, the objective reasons for their existence are the containment, or pacification and manipulation of the student body. Very few of our student governments are autonomously incorporated or have any powers or rights apart from those sanctioned by the regents or trustees of the university. Furthermore, most administrations hold a veto power over anything done by the student governments. Perhaps the worst aspect of this kind of manipulation and repression is that the administration uses students to control other students. Most student government politicos are lackeys of the worst sort. That is, they have internalized and embraced all the repressive mechanisms the administration has designed for use *against* them and their fellow students.

 With this in mind, it would seem that we should ignore student governments and/or abolish them. While this is certainly true in the final analysis, it is important to relate to student governments differently during the earlier stages of on-campus political struggles. The question we are left with is how do we render student governments ineffective in terms of what they are designed to do, while at the same time, using them effectively in building the movement?

Do we work inside the system? Of course we do. The question is not one of working "inside" or "outside" the system. Rather, the question is do we play by the established rules? Here, the answer is an emphatic no. The established habits of student politics—popularity contest elections, disguising oneself as a moderate, working for "better communications and dialogue" with administrators, watering down demands before they are made, going through channels—all of these gambits are stacked against us. If liberal and moderate student politicians really believe in them, then we should tell *them* to try it with all they have. But if they continue to make this ploy after they have learned from their own experience that these methods are dead-ends, then they should be soundly denounced as opportunists or gutless administration puppets.

We should face the fact that student governments are *powerless* and designed to stay that way. From this perspective, all talk about "getting into power" is so much nonsense. The only thing that student governments are useful for is their ability to be a *temporary vehicle* in building a grass-roots student power movement. This means that student elections are useful as an arena for raising real issues, combatting and exposing administration apologists, and involving new people, rather than getting elected. If our people do happen to get elected *as radicals* (this is becoming increasingly possible) then the seats won should be used as a focal point and sounding board for demonstrating the impotence of student government *from within.* A seat should be seen as a soap-box, where our representatives can stand, gaining a kind of visibility and speaking to the student body as a whole, over the heads of the other student politicians.

Can anything positive be gained through student government? Apart from publicity, one thing it can be used for is money. Many student-activities funds are open for the kinds of things we would like to see on campus: certain speakers, films, sponsoring conferences. Money, without strings, is always a help. Also, non-political services, such as non-profit used-book exchanges, are helpful to many students. But in terms of radical changes, student government can do nothing apart from a mass, radical student power movement. Even then, student government tends to be a conservative force within those struggles. In the end, meaningful changes can only come through a radical transformation of both the consciousness of large numbers of students and the forms of student self-government.

Reform or Revolution: What Kinds of Demand? Fighting for reforms and making a revolution should not be seen as mutually exclusive positions. The question should be: what kind of reforms move us toward a radical transformation of both the university and the society in general? First of all, we should avoid the kinds of reforms which leave the basic *rationale* of the system unchallenged. For instance, a bad reform to work for would be getting a better grading system, because the underlying rationale—the need for grades at all—remains unchallenged.

Secondly, we should avoid certain kinds of reform that divide students from each other. For instance, trying to win certain privileges for upper classmen but not for freshmen or sophomores. Or trying to establish non-graded courses for students above a certain grade-point average. In the course of campus political activity, the administration will try a whole range of "divide and rule" tactics such as fostering the "Greek-Independent Split," sexual double standards, intellectual vs. "jocks," responsible vs. irresponsible leaders, red-baiting and "non-student" vs. students. We need to avoid falling into these traps ahead of time, as well as fighting them when used against us.

Finally, we should avoid all of the "co-management" kinds of reforms. These usually come in the form of giving certain "responsible" student leaders a voice or influence in certain decision-making processes, rather than abolishing or winning effective control over those parts of the governing apparatus. One way to counter administration suggestions for setting up "tripartite" committees (1/3 student, 1/3 faculty, 1/3 administration, each with an equal number of votes) is to say, "OK, but once a month the committee must hold an all-university plenary session—one man, one vote." The thought of being outvoted 1000 to 1 will cause administrators to scrap that co-optive measure in a hurry.

We have learned the hard way that the reformist path is full of pitfalls. What, then, are the kinds of reformist measures that do make sense? First of all, there are the civil libertarian issues. We must always fight, dramatically and quickly, for free speech and the right to organize, advocate, and mount political action —of all sorts. However, even here, we should avoid getting bogged down in "legalitarianism." We cannot count on this society's legal apparatus to guarantee our civil liberties: and, we should not organize around civil libertarian issues *as if it could.* Rather, when our legal rights are violated, we should move as quickly as possible, without losing our base, to expand the campus libertarian moral indignation into a multi-issues *political* insurgency, exposing the repressive character of the administration and the corporate state in general.

The second kind of partial reform worth fighting for and possibly winning is the abolition of on-campus repressive mechanisms, i.e., student courts, disciplinary tribunals, deans of men and women, campus police, and the use of civil police on campus. While it is true that "abolition" is a negative reform, and while we will be criticized for not offering "constructive" criticisms, we should reply that the only constructive way to deal with an inherently destructive apparatus is to destroy it. We must curtail the ability of administrators to repress our *need to refuse* their way of life—the regimentation and bureaucratization of existence.

When our universities are already major agencies for social change in the direction of *1984,* our initial demands must, almost of necessity, be negative demands. In this sense, the first task of a student power movement will be the organization of a holding action or a resistance. Along these lines, one potentially effective tactic for resisting the university's disciplinary apparatus would be the formation of a Student Defence League. The purpose of the group would be to make its services available to any student who must appear before campus authorities for infractions of repressive (or just plain stupid) rules and regulations. The defence group would then attend the student's hearings *en masse.* However, for some cases, it might be wise to include law students or local radical lawyers in the group for the purpose of making legal counter-attacks. A student defence group would have three major goals: 1) saving as many students as possible from punishment, 2) de-sanctifying and rendering disfunctional the administration's repressive apparatus, and 3) using 1) and 2) as tactics in reaching other students for building a movement to abolish the apparatus as a whole.

When engaging in this kind of activity, it is important to be clear in our rhetoric as to what we are about. We are not trying to *liberalize* the existing order, but trying to win our *liberation* from it. We must refuse the administrations' rhetoric of "responsibility." To their one-dimensional way of thinking, the concept of responsibility has been reduced to its opposite, namely, be nice, don't rock the boat, do things according to *our* criteria of what is permissible. In actuality their whole system is geared toward the inculcation of the values of a planned irresponsibility. We should refuse *their* definitions, *their* terms, and even refuse to engage in *their* semantic hassles. We only need to define for *ourselves and other students* our notions of what it means to be free, constructive, and responsible. Too many campus movements have been co-opted for weeks or even permanently by falling into the administrators' rhetorical bags.

Besides the abolition of repressive disciplinary mechanisms within the university, there are other negative reforms that radicals should work for. Getting the military off the campus, abolishing the grade system, and abolishing universal compulsory courses (i.e., physical education) would fit into this category. However, an important question for the student movement is whether or not *positive* radical reforms can be won within the university short of making a revolution in the society as a whole. Furthermore, would the achievement of these kinds of partial reforms have the cumulative effect of weakening certain aspects of corporate capitalism, and, in their small way, make that broader revolution more likely?

At present, my feeling is that these kinds of anti-capitalist positive reforms are almost as hard to conceive intellectually as they are to win. To be sure, there has been a wealth of positive educational reforms suggested by people like Paul Goodman. But are they anti-capitalist as well? For example, we have been able to organize several good free universities. Many of the brightest and most sensitive students on American campuses, disgusted with the present state of education, left the campus and organized these counter-institutions. Some of their experiments were successful in an immediate internal sense. A few of these organizers were initially convinced that the sheer moral force of their work in these free institutions would cause the existing educational structure to tremble and finally collapse like a house of IBM cards. But what happened? What effect did the free universities have on the established educational order? At best, they had no effect. But it is more likely that they had the effect of strengthening the existing system. How? First of all, the best of our people left the campus, enabling the existing university to function more smoothly, since the "troublemakers" were gone. Secondly, they gave liberal administrators the rhetoric, the analysis, and sometimes the man-power to co-opt their programs and establish elitist forms of "experimental" colleges inside of, although quarantined from, the existing educational system. This is not to say that free universities should not be organized, both on and off the campus. They can be valuable and useful. But they should not be seen as a primary aspect of a strategy for change.

What then is open to us in the area of positive anti-capitalist reforms? For the most part, it will be difficult to determine whether or not a reform has the effect of being anti-capitalist until it has been achieved. Since it is both difficult and undesirable to attempt to predict the future, questions of this sort are often best answered in practice. Nevertheless, it would seem that the kind of reforms we are looking for are most likely to be found within a strategy of what I would call "encroaching control." There are aspects of the university's administrative, academic, financial-physical, and social apparatus that are potentially, if not actually, useful and productive. While we should try to abolish the repressive mechanisms of the university; our strategy should be to gain *control,* piece by piece, of its positive aspects.

What would that control look like? To begin, all aspects of the non-academic life of the campus should either be completely under the control of the students as individuals or embodied in the institutional forms *they* establish for their collective government. For example, an independent union of students should have the final say on the form and content of *all-university* political, social, and cultural events. Naturally, individual students and student organizations would be completely free in organizing events of their own.

Second, only the students and the teaching faculty, individually and through their organizations, should control the academic affairs of the university. One example of a worthwhile reform in this area would be enabling all history majors and history professors to meet jointly at the beginning of each semester and shape the form, content, and direction of their departmental curriculum. Another partial reform in this area would be enabling an independent union of students to hire additional professors of their choice and establish additional accredited courses of their choice independently of the faculty or administration.

Finally, we should remember that control should be sought *for some specific purpose.* One reason we want this kind of power is to enable us to meet the *self-determined* needs of students and teachers. But another objective that we should see as radicals is to put as much of the university's resources as possible into the hands of the underclass and the working class. We should use the student press to publicize and support local strikes. We should use campus facilities for meeting the educational needs of insurgent organizations of the poor, and of rank and file workers. Or we could mobilize the universities' research facilities for serving projects established and controlled by the poor and worker, rather than projects established and controlled by the government, management, and labour bureaucrats. The conservative nature of American trade unions makes activity of this sort very difficult, although not impossible. But we should always be careful to make a distinction between the American working class itself and the labour bureaucrats.

The Faculty Question: Allies or Finks? One question almost always confronts the student movement on the campus. Do we try to win faculty support before we go into action? Or do we lump them together with the administration? What we have learned in the past seems to indicate both of these responses are wrong. Earlier in this paper, I remarked on the kinds of divisions that exist among the faculty. What is important to see is that this division is not just between good and bad guys. Rather, the faculty is becoming more and more divided in terms of the objective functions of their jobs. To make the hard case on one hand, the function of the lower level of the faculty is to teach—a potentially creative and useful activity; on the other hand, the function of most administrative and research faculty is manipulation, repression, and—for the defence department hirelings—destruction. In general, we should develop our strategies so that our lot falls with the teaching faculty and theirs with ours. As for the research and administrative faculty, we should set both ourselves and the teaching faculty against them. Also, during any student confrontation with the administration, the faculty can do one of four things *as a group*. They can 1) support the administration, 2) remain neutral, 3) split among themselves, and 4) support us. In any situation, we should favor the development of one of the last three alternatives rather than the first. Furthermore, if it seems likely that the faculty will split on an issue, we should try to encourage the division indicated above. While it is important to remain open to the faculty, we should not let their support or non-support become an issue in determining whether or not we begin to mount political action. Finally, we should encourage the potentially radical sectors of the faculty to organize among themselves around their own grievances, hopefully being able to *eventually* form a radical alliance with us.

The Vital Issue of Teaching Assistants' Unions Probably the most exploited and alienated group of people on any campus *are* the graduate student teaching assistants. The forces of the multiversity hit them from two directions —both as students and as teachers. As students, they have been around long enough to have lost their awe of academia. As faculty, they are given the worst jobs for the lowest pay. For the most part, they have no illusions about their work. Their working conditions, low pay, and the fact that their futures are subject to the whimsical machinations of their department chairmen, make them a group ripe for radical organization. Furthermore, their strategic position within the university structure—makes them potentially powerful as a group if they should decide to organize and strike. If they go out, a large part of the multiversity comes grinding to a halt. The kinds of demands they are most likely to be organized around naturally connect them with a radical student power movement and with the potentially radical sector of the faculty. Furthermore, these considerations make the organization of a radical trade union of TAs a crucial part of any strategy for change. We should see this kind of labour organizing as one of our first priorities in building the campus movement.

Non-Academic Employees: On-Campus Labor Organizing Almost all colleges and especially the multiversities have a large number of blue-collar maintenance workers on campus. Within the state supported institutions in particular, these people are often forbidden to organize unions, have terrible working conditions, and are paid very low wages. Their presence on the campus offers a unique opportunity for many students to become involved in blue-collar labour organizing at the same time that they are in school. Secondly, since these workers usually live in the surrounding community, their friends and relatives will come from other sectors of the local working class. Quite naturally, they will carry their ideas, opinions, and feelings toward the radical student movement home with them. In this sense, they can be an important link connecting us with other workers, and our help in enabling them to organize a local independent and radical trade union would help tremendously. Finally, if we should ever strike as students, they could be an important ally. For instance, after SDS at the University of Missouri played a major role in organizing a militant local of non-academic employees, they learned that, were the union to strike for its own demands in sympathy with student demands, the university as a physical plant would cease to function after four days. It is obviously important to have that kind of power.

The Knowledge Machinery and Sabotage: Striking on the Job One mistake radical students have been making in relating to the worst aspects of the multiversity's academic apparatus has been their avoidance of it. We tend to avoid large classes, lousy courses, and reactionary professors like the plague. At best, we have organized counter-courses outside the class-room and off the campus. My suggestion is that we should do the opposite. Our brightest people should sign up for the large freshman and sophomore sections with the worst profs in *strategic* courses in history, political science, education, and even the ROTC counter-insurgency lectures. From this position, they should then begin to take out their frustrations with the work of the course while they are on the job, i.e., inside the classroom. Specifically, they should be constant vocal critics of the form and content of the course, the prof, class size, the educational system, and corporate capitalism in general. Their primary strategy, rather than winning debating points against the prof, should be to reach other students in the class. Hopefully, our on-the-job organizer will begin to develop a radical caucus in the class. This group could then meet outside the class, continue to collectively develop a further radical critique of the future class-work, to be presented at the succeeding sessions. If all goes well with the prof, and perhaps his department as well, they will have a full-scale academic revolt on their hands by the end of the semester. Finally, if this sort of work were being done in a variety of courses at once, the local radical student movement would have the makings of an underground educational movement that was actively engaged in mounting an effective resistance to the educational *status quo*.

Provo Tactics: Radicalization or Sublimation? There is little doubt that the hippy movement has made its impact on most American campuses. It is also becoming more clear that the culture of advanced capitalist society is becoming more sterile, dehumanized and one-dimensional. It is directed toward a passive mass, rather than an active public. Its root value is consumption. We obviously need a cultural revolution, along with a revolution in the political economy. But the question remains: where do the hippies fit in? At the present time, their role seems ambivalent.

On the one hand, they thoroughly reject the dominant culture and seem to be life-affirming. On the other hand, they seem to be for the most part, passive consumers of culture, rather than active creators of culture. For all their talk of community, the nexus of their relations with each other seems to consist only of drugs and a common jargon. With all their talk of love, one finds little deep-rooted passion. Yet, they are there; and they are a major phenomenon. Their relevance to the campus scene is evidenced by the success of the wave of "Gentle Thursdays" that swept the country. Through this approach, we have been able to reach and break loose a good number of people. Often, during the frivolity of Gentle Thursday, the life-denying aspects of corporate capitalism are brought home to many people with an impact that could never be obtained by the best of all of our anti-war demonstrations.

However, the hippy movement has served to make many of our people withdraw into a personalistic, passive cult of consumption. These aspects need to be criticized and curtailed. We should be clear about one thing: the *individual* liberation of man, the most social of animals, is a dead-end—an impossibility. And even if individual liberation were possible, would it be desirable? The sublimation of reality within the individual consciousness neither destroys nor transforms the objective reality of other men.

Nevertheless, the excitement and imagination of some aspects of hippydom can be useful in building critiques of the existing culture. Here, I am referring to the provos and the diggers. Gentle Thursday, when used as a provo (provocative) tactic on campus, can cause the administration to display some of its most repressive characteristics. Even something as blunt as burning a television set in the middle of campus can make a profound statement about the life styles of many people. However, people engaging in this kind of action should 1) not see the action as a substitute for serious revolutionary activity and 2) read up on the Provos and Situationists rather than the Haight-Ashbury scene.

From Soap-box to Student Strikes: The Forms of Protest During the development of radical politics on the campus, the student movement will pass through a multitude of organizational forms. I have already mentioned several: Student Defence League, Teaching Assistants' Unions, Non-Academic Employees' Unions, and of course, SDS chapters. Another important development on many campuses has been the formation of Black Student Unions, or Afro-American cultural groups. All of these groups are vital, although some are more important than others at different stages of the struggle. However, for the purpose of keeping a radical and multi-issue focus throughout the growth of the movement, it is important to begin work on a campus by organizing an SDS chapter.

From this starting point, how does SDS see its relation to the rest of the campus? I think we have learned that we should not look upon ourselves as an intellectual and political oasis, hugging each other in a wasteland. Rather, our chapters should see themselves as *organizing committees* for reaching out to the majority of the student population. Furthermore, we are organizing for something—the power to effect change. With this in mind, we should be well aware of the fact that the kind of power and changes we would like to have and achieve are not going to be given to us gracefully. Ultimately, we have access to only one source of power within the knowledge factory. And that power lies in our potential ability to stop the university from functioning, to render the system disfunctional for limited periods of time. Throughout all our on-campus organizing efforts we should keep this one point in mind: that sooner or later we are going to have to strike—or at least successfully threaten to strike. Because of this, our constant strategy should be the preparation of a mass base for supporting and participating in this kind of action.

What are the organizational forms, other than those mentioned above, that are necessary for the development of this kind of radical constituency? The first kind of extra-SDS organization needed is a Hyde Park or Free Speech Forum. An area of the campus, centrally located and heavily travelled, should be selected and equipped with a P.A. system. Then, on a certain afternoon one day a week, the platform would be open to anyone to give speeches on anything they choose. SDS people should attend regularly and speak regularly, although they should encourage variety and debate, and not monopolize the platform. To begin, the forum should be weekly, so that students don't become bored with it. Rather, we should try to give it the aura of a special event. Later on, when political activity intensifies, the forum could be held every day. In the early stages, publicity, the establishment of a mood and climate for radical politics, is of utmost importance. We should make our presence felt everywhere—in the campus news media, leafletting and poster displays, and regular attendance at the meetings of all student political, social, and religious organizations. We should make all aspects of our politics as visible and open as possible.

Once our presence has become known, we can begin to organize on a variety of issues. One arena that it will be important to relate to at this stage will be student government elections. The best organizational form for this activity would be the formation of a Campus Freedom Party for running radical candidates. It is important that the party be clear and open as to its radical consciousness, keeping in mind that our first task is that of building radical consciousness, rather than winning seats. It is also important that the party take positions on off-campus questions as well, such as the war in Vietnam. Otherwise, if we only relate to on-campus issues, we run the risk of laying the counter-revolutionary groundwork for an elitist, conservative and corporatist student movement. As many people as possible should be involved in the work of the party, with SDS people having the function of keeping it militant and radical in a non-manipulative and honest fashion. The party should permeate the campus with speeches, films, and leaflets, as well as a series of solidly intellectual and radical position papers on a variety of issues. Furthermore, we should remember that an election campaign should be fun. Campus Freedom Parties should organize Gentle Thursdays, jug bands, rock groups, theater groups for political skits, and homemade 8mm. campaign films. Finally, during non-election periods, the Campus Freedom Party should form a variety of CFP *ad hoc* committees for relating to student government on various issues throughout the year.

The next stage of the movement is the most crucial and delicate in the formation of a Student Strike Coordinating Committee. There are two preconditions necessary for its existence. First, there must be a quasi-radical base of some size that has been developed from past activity. Secondly, either a crisis situation provoked by the administration or a climate of active frustration with the administration and/or the ruling class it represents must exist. The frustration should be centered around a set of specific demands that have been unresolved through the established channels of liberal action. If this kind of situation exists, then a strike is both possible and desirable. A temporary steering committee should be set up, consisting of representatives of radical groups (SDS, Black Student Union, TA's Union). This group would set the initial demands and put out the call for a strike within a few weeks time. Within that time, they would try to bring in as many other groups and individuals as possible without seriously watering down the demands. This new coalition would then constitute itself as the Student Strike Coordinating Committee, with the new groups adding members to the original temporary steering committee. Also, a series of working committees and a negotiating committee should be established. Finally, the strike committee should attempt to have as many open mass plenary sessions as possible.

What should come out of a student strike? First, the development of a radical consciousness among large numbers of students. Secondly, we should try to include within our demands some issues on which we can win partial victories. Finally, the organizational form that should grow out of a strike or series of strikes is an independent, radical, and political Free Student Union that would replace the existing student government. I have already dealt with the general political life of radical movements. But some points need to be repeated. First of all, a radical student union *must* be in alliance with the radical sectors of the underclass and working class. Secondly, the student movement has the additional task of radicalizing the subsector of the labour force that some of us in SDS have come to call the new working class. Thirdly, a radical union of students should have an anti-imperialist critique of U.S. foreign policy. Finally, local student unions, if they are to grow and thrive, must become federated on regional, national, and international levels. However, we should be careful not to form a national union of students lacking in a grass-roots constituency that actively and democratically participates in all aspects of the organization's life. One NSA is enough. On the international level, we should avoid both the CIA and Soviet Union sponsored International Unions. We would be better off to establish informal relations with groups like the Zengakuren in Japan, the German SDS, the French Situationists, the Spanish Democratic Student Syndicate, and the third world revolutionary student organizations. Hopefully, in the not too distant future, we may be instrumental in forming a new International Union of Revolutionary Youth. But there is much work to be done between now and then. And even greater tasks remain to be done before we can begin to build the conditions for human liberation.

AN END TO HISTORY

● *mario savio*

Last summer I went to Mississippi to join the struggle there for civil rights. This fall I am engaged in another phase of the same struggle, this time in Berkeley. The two battlefields may seem quite different to some observers, but this is not the case. The same rights are at stake in both places—the right to participate as citizens in democratic society and the right to due process of law. Further, it is a struggle against the same enemy. In Mississippi an autocratic and powerful minority rules, through organized violence, to suppress the vast, virtually powerless, majority. In California, the privileged minority manipulates the University bureaucracy to suppress the students' political expression. That "respectable" bureaucracy masks the financial plutocrats; that impersonal bureaucracy is the efficient enemy in a "Brave New World."

In our free speech fight at the University of California, we have come up against what may emerge as the greatest problem of our nation—depersonalized, unresponsive bureaucracy. We have encountered the organized status quo in Mississippi, but it is the same in Berkeley. Here we find it impossible usually to meet with anyone but secretaries. Beyond that, we find functionaries who cannot make policy but can only hide behind the rules. We have discovered total lack of response on the part of the policy makers. To grasp a situation which is truly Kafkesque, it is necessary to understand the bureaucratic mentality. And we have learned quite a bit about it this fall, more outside the classroom than in.

As bureaucrat, an administrator believes that nothing new happens. He occupies an ahistorical point of view. In September, to get the attention of this bureaucracy which had issued arbitrary edicts suppressing student political expression and refused to discuss its action, we held a sit-in on the campus. We sat around a police car and kept it immobilized for over thirty-two hours. At last, the administrative bureaucracy agreed to negotiate. But instead, on the following Monday, we discovered that a committee had been appointed, in accordance with usual regulations, to resolve the dispute. Our attempt to convince any of the administrators that an event had occurred, that something new had happened, failed. They saw this simply as something to be handled by normal University procedures.

The same is true of all bureaucracies. They begin as tools, means to certain legitimate goals, and they end up feeding their own existence. The conception that bureaucrats have is that history has in fact come to an end. No events can occur now that the Second World War is over which can change American society substantially. We proceed by standard procedures as we are.

The most crucial problems facing the United States today are the problem of automation and the problem of racial injustice. Most people who will be put out of jobs by machines will not accept an end to events, this historical plateau, as the point beyond which no change occurs. Negroes will not accept an end to history here. All of us must refuse to accept history's final judgment that in America there is no place in society for people whose skins are dark. On campus students are not about to accept it as fact that the university has ceased evolving and is in its final state of perfection, that students and faculty are respectively raw material and employees, or that the university is to be autocratically run by unresponsive bureaucrats.

Here is the real contradiction: the bureaucrats hold history as ended. As a result significant parts of the population both on campus and off are dispossessed, and these dispossessed are not about to accept this ahistorical point of view. It is out of this that the conflict has occurred with the university bureaucracy and will continue to occur until that bureaucracy becomes responsive or until it is clear the university can not function.

The things we are asking for in our civil rights protests have a deceptively quaint ring. We are asking for the due process of law. We are asking for our actions to be judged by committees of our peers. We are asking that regulations ought to be considered as arrived at legitimately only from the consensus of the governed. These phrases are all pretty old, but they are not being taken seriously in America today, nor are they being taken seriously on the Berkeley campus.

I have just come from a meeting with the dean of students. She notified us that she was aware of certain violations of University regulations by certain organizations. University friends of SNCC, which I represent, was one of these. We tried to draw from her some statement on these great principles, consent of the governed, jury of one's peers, due process. The best she could do was to evade or to present the administration party line. It is very hard to make any contact with the human being who is behind these organizations.

The university is the place where people begin seriously to question the conditions of their existence and raise the issue of whether they can be committed to the society they have been born into. After a long period of apathy during the fifties, students have begun not only to question but, having arrived at answers, to act on those answers. This is part of a growing understanding among many people in America that history has not ended, that a better society is possible, and that it is worth dying for.

This free speech fight points up a fascinating aspect of contemporary campus life. Students are permitted to talk all they want so long as their speech has no consequences.

One conception of the university, suggested by a classical Christian formulation, is that it be in the world but not of the world. The conception of Clark Kerr, by contrast, is that the university is part and parcel of this particular stage in the history of American society; it stands to serve the need of American industry; it is a factory that turns out a certain product needed by industry or government. Because speech does often have consequences which might alter this perversion of higher education, the university must put itself in a position of censorship. It can permit two kinds of speech, speech which encourages continuation of the status quo, and speech which advocates changes in it so radical as to be irrelevant in the foreseeable future. Someone may advocate radical change in all aspects of American society, and this I am sure he can do with impunity. But if someone advocates sit-ins to bring about changes in discriminatory hiring practices, this cannot be permitted because it goes against the status quo of which the university is a part. And that is how the fight began here.

The administration of the Berkeley campus has admitted that external, extra-legal groups have pressured the University not to permit students on campus to organize picket lines, not to permit on campus speech with consequences. And the bureaucracy went along. Speech with consequences, speech in the area of civil rights, speech which some might regard as illegal, must stop.

Many students here at the University, many people in society, are wandering aimlessly about. Strangers in their own lives, there is no place for them. They are people who have not learned to compromise, who for example have come to the University to learn to question, to grow, to learn—all the standard things that sound like clichés because no one takes them seriously. And they find at one point or other that for them to become part of society, to become lawyers, ministers, businessmen, people in government, that very often they must compromise those principles which are most dear to them. They must suppress the most creative impulses that they have; this is a prior condition for being part of the system. The University is well structured, well tooled, to turn out people with all the sharp edges worn off, the well-rounded person. The University is well equipped to produce that sort of person, and this means that the best among the people who enter must for four years wander aimlessly much of the time questioning why they are on campus at all, doubting whether there is any point in what they are doing, and looking toward a very bleak existence afterward in a game in which all of the rules have been made up, which one cannot really amend.

It is a bleak scene, but it is all a lot of us have to look forward to. Society provides no challenge. American society in the standard conception it has of itself is simply no longer exciting. The most exciting things going on in America today are movements to change America. America is becoming ever more the Utopia of sterilized, automated contentment. The "futures" and "careers" for which American students now prepare are for the most part intellectual and moral wastelands. This chrome-plated consumers paradise would have us grow up to be well-behaved children. But an important minority of men and women coming to the front today have shown that they will die rather than be standardized, replaceable and irrelevant.

WE WANT REVOLUTION

mark rudd

Despite the inordinate number of reporters and commentators who have "analyzed" the New Left and events at Columbia, despite mountains of words and endless theories about conspiracies, no one outside S.D.S. (Students for a Democratic Society) and the New Left has yet to make a reasonably knowledgeable statement about the meaning of the Columbia rebellion and the rise of the New Left student movement.

There has been a qualitative shift in the purpose and identity of the student movement since the Berkeley rebellion of 1964. Young people no longer see social problems in the same light. The war in Vietnam, for example, is viewed by the New Left as an inherent part of the political-economic system that dominates our country, not as the product of one man's policies, nor the result of general "aggressive drives" in men's personalities.

The direction of S.D.S. was set in 1965 at the first March on Washington in opposition to the war. Paul Potter, at the conclusion of his speech, advised that we must take our abstract notion of "the system," ". . . analyze it, understand it," and, on the basis of what we ourselves find, change that system. Our ideas come out of our experiences with this society, not out of the dogma of any political sect. Our anger and our hopes, just as much as anyone else's, have been created by this society. Anyone who wants to understand the New Left must look at America, not Fidel Castro or Chairman Mao, to discover what we are about.

What are the realities of America's political-economic system? Why do we consider it to be our enemy and the enemy of most of the people of the world?

Everyone knows that the United States has a "capitalist" system. Theoretically, it functions through free competition for profits. Actually, the system runs by concentrations of capital, by monopolies open to very few. John Doe, next door, cannot start an automobile plant, or a railroad or even a supermarket, for want of capital, connections and political pull. But those who control the monopolies exercise tremendous power on society both economically, through the production and capital of their corporations, and politically, through their ties with the Government—they are the main contributors to Democratic and Republican Party funds, they are sponsors of intermediate institutions such as the Council on Foreign Relations, and they have personal influence as individuals.

In order for American capitalism to sustain its profits and power, it has developed two main forms of domination—racism and imperialism. The latter, working on an international scale, is the economic domination of underdeveloped countries by U.S. corporations for markets, raw materials and new areas of investment. Sometimes it is necessary for the United States Government to engage in direct political interference in order to maintain economic interests, as in Guatemala, in 1954, when the Central Intelligence Agency overthrew the Arbenz régime to protect the United Fruit Company; and the Dominican Republic, in 1965, when Johnson sent Marines to help overthrow the legal reform régime that threatened American sugar interests. In all forms of imperialism, United States domination works against the well-being of the underdeveloped countries, limiting their freedoms, sapping their wealth and restricting their development. Imperialism works against our own well-being, too. We have seen the domestic effects of the war in Vietnam—the tremendous waste of our manpower and economic resources to fight a war to maintain United States political hegemony.

Racism, far from being the product of the "American character," is, like imperialism, the result of the necessities of the capitalist system. Ghettos exist because they are profitable—they provide a source of cheap labor. For several generations white Americans have been trained to adopt racist, discriminatory attitudes, sometimes out of immediate economic self-interest. These attitudes themselves are perpetuated by policy decisions of those who control government and big business. Columbia University's expansion into Morningside Heights, to cite one such policy, is designed to create a white "respectable" neighborhood around Columbia, driving poor blacks and Puerto Ricans from one of the few integrated neighborhoods in Manhattan.

Given this analysis of our society and the workings of capitalism, New Leftists have chosen to fight imperialism and racism in order to fight capitalism —to free ourselves and others. We work where we are—in high schools, universities, unions, factories.

Many have called us a "student power" movement, implying that our goal is student control over the "educational process," taking decision-making power away from the administrators and putting it in the hands of "democratic" student groups. Presumably, the guiding principle in a university where student power is a reality would be to make possible the greatest fulfillment of human potential. Student power used to be the goal of S.D.S., but as our understanding of the society has developed, our understanding of the university's role in it has also changed.

We see the university as a factory whose goal is to produce: 1) trained personnel for corporations, government and more universities, and 2) knowledge of the uses of business and government to perpetuate the present system. Government studies at Columbia, for example, attempt to explain our society through concepts of pluralism and conflicting group interest, while the reality of the situation is quite different.

Clark Kerr, president of the University of California at Berkeley in 1964, in his book, *The Uses of the University,* explains that the purpose of universities like Berkeley and Columbia is to train the technicians who will administer our society. The University of California "educates" aeronautics engineers in the latest techniques for private aircraft companies. Columbia has received a $1.5

"gift" from I.B.M. for an expansion program. It is no accident that graduate professional schools of universities are growing most rapidly. Columbia, for example, is constructing a vast new International Affairs building to train future C.I.A. agents, State Department officers and corporate specialists, at a time when the undergraduate liberal arts college is overcrowded and fires good teachers for lack of money. Within this university factory, students are manipulated and channeled, stripped of creativity and energy, ready at the end of the assembly line to take their places in death-like offices or still more educational factories.

Student power is not the way to achieve a university structured to benefit humanity, since the problems of the university originate elsewhere. Because power and money are concentrated in corporations and government, it is impossible to create a "free" university within a society as unfree as ours; the university is the tool of society, or, in the American case, those who dominate our society. At Columbia, the all-powerful board of trustees, composed of men from banks, corporations and government, act as the representatives of this ruling class. To be sure, certain reforms are possible within the university, but these are mostly either to give the illusion of democracy, as in student or faculty senates and judicial boards, or to grant more privileges to students, such as longer dormitory visiting hours or later curfew. University administrators can well afford to make such concessions, because of their lack of social significance.

Far from being internally oriented, the rebellion at Columbia was "political" in the most important sense of the word. Our strike gave people a chance to act directly against imperialism and racism—to engage in political activity that went far out into society and linked students with other groups in the country and the world. We demanded that Columbia sever its ties with the Institute for Defense Analysis, which does weapons research for the war in Vietnam and American military ventures around the world. We demanded a stop to the construction of the university gymnasium in Morningside Heights, a demand first raised by people of the Harlem community. This was a case of white and black students at Columbia supporting the right of the people of Harlem to control their own community. We demanded an amnesty to all who participated in the demonstration. This would have forced the administration of Columbia to say we were right. If we had settled for a bipartite student-faculty committee to make decisions on discipline for the students engaged in the demonstrations, we would have been co-opted, neatly and efficiently, because Columbia president Grayson Kirk and the board of trustees could well afford to accommodate all our other demands. What they could not afford was to be among the first members of the ruling sector to be defeated on the field of political battle by a motley mob of rebelling students.

Again, this was not a question of student power; we had gone much farther. We had questioned the very foundations of our society—the capitalist system itself. And we did this in the institution where we are located—the university.

Why did so many thousands of students risk so much for issues primarily outside the university, issues that did not affect their immediate self-interest? The answer lies in the dissatisfaction we students feel with this society and our identification with the most oppressed groups—the people in the ghetto, the people of Vietnam. The young understand more clearly the oppression of others because we too are oppressed, though rarely as directly by napalm or the National Guard. At Columbia we hit out at the people responsible for the manipulation of our lives at the university, as well as the oppression of blacks and Vietnamese, by seizing the buildings. This action told the university that we would no longer allow the exploitation of our brothers or of ourselves. Ours was no group of liberals fighting for the rights of others; we felt, the entire time, that we were fighting for our own lives, for our present and future, which up to now had appeared meaningless.

Most of those who participated in demonstrations, a number reaching into the thousands, felt that the lines were very clearly drawn—whether you support oppression of human beings or you fight against it. Liberalism is bankrupt because of its inability to deal with the realities of racism and imperialism and their fundamental causes. The options are limited; to stand in the middle, to be "neutral," constitutes support for the *status quo*.

Many of the hundreds who seized the Columbia buildings said that they had never experienced such a feeling of personal liberation as during the strike; this came not only from the knowledge that they were fighting an oppressive enemy but also because we were in the process of building real communities within the buildings, which far surpassed the stiff, repressive life of Columbia.

Young people feel more strongly, too, the gap between the possibilities and the realizations of this society. The richest economy the world has ever known depends on waste production—production to satisfy created needs, not real needs—for a great part of its national income, while it leaves unbearable and degrading slums in every city. Our factories produce at a fraction of their potential capacities, yet thousands of people starve to death in the world every day. The potential for liberation from toil and want, leaving people free to create, is enormous, yet men must still work in meaningless, wasteful jobs to keep themselves and this economic system going. How meaningful, in terms of real human needs, is the work of a market research analyst developing an advertising program for a new brand of toothpaste? Or that of a worker making a part for a car he knows is designed to become obsolete in two years, working in a factory over which he has absolutely no control? We students see the huge gap between potential and realization in our lives. We see that the university prepares us for meaningless work and we see that so much remains to be done. It is true that a relatively small number—perhaps as few as 500—started the demonstrations at Columbia. Yet thousands supported the strike because the issues we were raising made sense to their own lives.

In our strike, we united with many of the people who have been affected by the university's policies—the tenants in Columbia-owned buildings, the Harlem community, the university employees. Many other people throughout the world saw us confront a symbol of those who control the decisions that are made in this country.

In France, the workers and students united to fight a common enemy. The same potential exists here in the United States. We are attempting to connect our fight with the fight of the black people for their freedom, with the fight of the Mexican-Americans for their land in New Mexico, with the fight of the Vietnamese people, and with the exploited and oppressed throughout the world. We intend to unite with all people who believe that men and women should be free to live as they choose, in a society where the government is responsive to the needs of all the people, and not the needs of the few whose enormous wealth gives them the political power. We intend to make a revolution.

6

AFTER THE REVOLUTION

Revolutionaries are often asked how they know that the society they plan to create after the revolution will be better than the one they have replaced. Often this question is posed in order to provide an escape from argument for those who instinctively distrust change, who cling to contemporary models of social organization but who cannot rationally defend the gross inequities of such organization. Although the motivation behind asking this question often seems to spring out of a desire to have revolutionaries perform like astrologers, the question itself is a pertinent and reasonable one, especially when raised in the context of other questions posed in this book. Two of the three essays included in this section—selections by Che Guevara and Michael Walzer—set about speculating upon the freedom from excessive toil and from alienation which the citizen of the future socialist state will enjoy. Walzer's article, however, outlines the difficulties in keeping such a humanely fulfilling, democratic social system running. The final selection, by workers in a Chinese factory, is included not only as a starting point for the study of transformations in social attitudes which took place in China during the last part of the sixties, but also to present for the reader's evaluation one manner of airing intra-party disputes after a revolution.

NOTES ON MAN AND SOCIALISM IN CUBA

● *che guevara*

Guevara wrote "Notes for the Study of Man and Socialism in Cuba" in the form of a letter to Carlos Quijano, editor of Marcha*, an independent radical weekly published in Montevideo, Uruguay. It bore the dateline "Havana, 1965." In addition to appearing in* Marcha*, it was printed by* Verde Olivo*, the magazine of the Cuban armed forces. It is translated in full below.*

* * *

A common argument from the mouths of capitalist spokesmen, in the ideological struggle against socialism, is that socialism, or the period of building socialism into which we have entered, is characterized by the subordination of the individual to the state. I will not try to refute this argument solely on theoretical grounds, but I will try to establish the facts as they exist in Cuba and then add comments of a general nature. Let me begin by sketching the history of our revolutionary struggle before and after the taking of power:

As is well known, the exact date on which the revolutionary struggle began—which would culminate January 1st, 1959—was the 26th of July, 1953. A group of men commanded by Fidel Castro attacked the Moncada barracks in Oriente Province on the morning of that day. The attack was a failure; the failure became a disaster; and the survivors ended up in prison, beginning the revolutionary struggle again after they were freed by an amnesty.

In this stage, in which there was only the germ of socialism, man was the basic factor. We put our trust in him—individual, specific, with a first and last name—and the triumph or failure of the mission entrusted to him depended on his capacity for action.

Then came the stage of guerrilla struggle. It developed in two distinct elements: the people, the still sleeping mass which it was necessary to mobilize; and its vanguard, the guerrillas, the motor force of the movement, the generator of revolutionary consciousness and militant enthusiasm. It was this vanguard, this catalyzing agent, which created the subjective conditions necessary for victory.

Here again, in the course of the process of proletarianizing our thinking, in this revolution which took place in our habits and our minds, the individual was the basic factor. Every one of the fighters of the Sierra Maestra who reached an upper rank in the revolutionary forces has a record of outstanding deeds to his credit. They attained their rank on this basis. It was the first heroic period and in it they contended for the heaviest responsibilities, for the greatest dangers, with no other satisfaction than fulfilling a duty.

In our work of revolutionary education we frequently return to this instructive theme. In the attitude of our fighters could be glimpsed the man of the future.

On other occasions in our history the act of total dedication to the revolutionary cause was repeated. During the October crisis and in the days of Hurricane Flora we saw exceptional deeds of valor and sacrifice performed by an entire people. Finding the formula to perpetuate this heroic attitude in daily life is, from the ideological standpoint, one of our fundamental tasks.

In January, 1959, the Revolutionary Government was established with the participation of various members of the treacherous bourgeoisie. The existence of the Rebel Army as the basic factor of force constituted the guarantee of power.

Serious contradictions developed subsequently. In the first instance, in February, 1959, these were resolved when Fidel Castro assumed leadership of the government with the post of Prime Minister. This stage culminated in July of the same year with the resignation under mass pressure of President Urrutia.

There now appeared in the history of the Cuban Revolution a force with well-defined characteristics which would systematically reappear—the mass.

This many-faceted agency is not, as is claimed, the sum of units of the self-same type, behaving like a tame flock of sheep, and reduced, moreover, to that type by the system imposed from above. It is true that it follows its leaders, basically Fidel Castro, without hesitation; but the degree to which he won this trust corresponds precisely to the degree that he interpreted the people's desires and aspirations correctly, and to the degree that he made a sincere effort to fulfill the promises he made.

The mass participated in the agrarian reform and in the difficult task of the administration of state enterprises; it went through the heroic experience of Playa Girón; it was hardened in the battles against various bands of bandits armed by the CIA; it lived through one of the most important decisions of modern times during the October crisis; and today it continues to work for the building of socialism.

Viewed superficially, it might appear that those who speak of the subordination of the individual to the state are right. The mass carries out with matchless enthusiasm and discipline the tasks set by the government, whether economic in character, cultural, defensive, athletic, or whatever.

The initiative generally comes from Fidel or from the Revolutionary High Command, and is explained to the people who adopt it as theirs. In some cases the party and government utilize a local experience which may be of general value to the people, and follow the same procedure.

Nevertheless, the state sometimes makes mistakes. When one of these mistakes occurs, a decline in collective enthusiasm is reflected by a resulting quantitative decrease of the contribution of each individual, each of the elements forming the whole of the masses. Work is so paralyzed that insignificant quantities are produced. It is time to make a correction. That is what happened in March, 1962, as a result of the sectarian policy imposed on the party by Aníbal Escalante.

Clearly this mechanism is not adequate for insuring a succession of judicious measures. A more structured connection with the masses is needed and we must improve it in the course of the next years. But as far as initiatives originating in the upper strata of the government are concerned, we are presently utilizing the almost intuitive method of sounding out general reactions to the great problems we confront.

In this Fidel is a master, whose own special way of fusing himself with the people can be appreciated only by seeing him in action. At the great public mass meetings one can observe something like a counterpoint between two musical melodies whose vibrations provoke still newer notes. Fidel and the mass begin to vibrate together in a dialogue of growing intensity until they reach the climax in an abrupt conclusion culminating in our cry of struggle and victory.

The difficult thing for someone not living the experience of the revolution to understand is this close dialectical unity between the individual and the mass, in which the mass, as an aggregate of individuals, is interconnected with its leaders.

Some phenomena of this kind can be seen under capitalism, when politicians capable of mobilizing popular opinion appear, but these phenomena are not really genuine social movements. (If they were, it would not be entirely correct to call them capitalist.) These movements only live as long as the persons who inspire them, or until the harshness of capitalist society puts an end to the popular illusions which made them possible.

Under capitalism man is controlled by a pitiless code of laws which is usually beyond his comprehension. The alienated human individual is tied to society in its aggregate by an invisible umbilical cord—the law of value. It is operative in all aspects of his life, shaping its course and destiny.

The laws of capitalism, blind and invisible to the majority, act upon the individual without his thinking about it. He sees only the vastness of a seemingly infinite horizon before him. That is how it is painted by capitalist propagandists who purport to draw a lesson from the example of Rockefeller —whether or not it is true—about the possibilities of success.

The amount of poverty and suffering required for the emergence of a Rockefeller, and the amount of depravity that the accumulation of a fortune of such magnitude entails, are left out of the picture, and it is not always possible to make the people in general see this.

(A discussion of how the workers in the imperialist countries are losing the spirit of working-class internationalism due to a certain degree of complicity in the exploitation of the dependent countries, and how this weakens the combativity of the masses in the imperialist countries, would be appropriate here; but that is a theme which goes beyond the aim of these notes.)

In any case the road to success is pictured as one beset with perils but which, it would seem, an individual with the proper qualities can overcome to attain the goal. The reward is seen in the distance; the way is lonely. Further on it is a route for wolves; one can succeed only at the cost of the failure of others.

I would now like to try to define the individual, the actor in this strange and moving drama of the building of socialism, in his dual existence as a unique being and as a member of society.

I think it makes the most sense to recognize his quality of incompleteness, of being an unfinished product. The sermons of the past have been transposed to the present in the individual consciousness, and a continual labor is necessary to eradicate them. The process is two-sided: On the one side, society acts through direct and indirect education; on the other, the individual subjects himself to a process of conscious self-education.

The new society being formed has to compete fiercely with the past. The latter makes itself felt in the consciousness in which the residue of an education systematically oriented towards isolating the individual still weighs heavily, and also through the very character of the transitional period in which the market relationships of the past still persist. The commodity is the economic cell of capitalist society; so long as it exists its effects will make themselves felt in the organization of production and, consequently, in consciousness.

Marx outlined the period of transition as a period which results from the explosive transformation of the capitalist system of a country destroyed by its own contradictions. However in historical reality we have seen that some countries, which were weak limbs of the tree of imperialism, were torn off first—a phenomenon foreseen by Lenin.

In these countries capitalism had developed to a degree sufficient to make its effects felt by the people in one way or another; but, having exhausted all its possibilities, it was not its internal contradictions which caused these systems to explode. The struggle for liberation from a foreign oppressor, the misery caused by external events like war whose consequences make the privileged classes bear down more heavily on the oppressed, liberation movements aimed at the overthrow of neo-colonial régimes—these are the usual factors in this kind of explosion. Conscious action does the rest.

In these countries a complete education for social labor has not yet taken place, and wealth is far from being within the reach of the masses simply through the process of appropriation. Underdevelopment on the one hand, and the inevitable flight of capital on the other, make a rapid transition impossible without sacrifices. There remains a long way to go in constructing the economic base, and the temptation to follow the beaten track of material interest as the moving lever of accelerated development is very great.

There is the danger that the forest won't be seen for the trees. Following the will-o'-the-wisp method of achieving socialism with the help of the dull instruments which link us to capitalism (the commodity as the economic cell, profitability, individual material interest as a lever, etc.) can lead into a blind alley.

Further, you get there after having traveled a long distance in which there were many crossroads and it is hard to figure out just where it was that you took the wrong turn. The economic foundation which has been formed has already done its work of undermining the development of consciousness. To build communism, you must build new men as well as the new economic base.

Hence it is very important to choose correctly the instrument for mobilizing the masses. Basically, this instrument must be moral in character, without neglecting, however, a correct utilization of the material stimulus—especially of a social character.

As I have already said, in moments of great peril it is easy to muster a powerful response to moral stimuli; but for them to retain their effect requires the development of a consciousness in which there is a new priority of values. Society as a whole must be converted into a gigantic school.

In rough outline this phenomenon is similar to the process by which capitalist consciousness was formed in its initial epoch. Capitalism uses force but it also educates the people to its system. Direct propaganda is carried out by those entrusted with explaining the inevitability of class society, either through some theory of divine origin or through a mechanical theory of natural selection.

This lulls the masses since they see themselves as being oppressed by an evil against which it is impossible to struggle. Immediately following comes hope of improvement—and in this, capitalism differed from the preceding caste systems which offered no possibilities for advancement.

For some people, the ideology of the caste system will remain in effect: The reward for the obedient after death is to be transported to some fabulous other-world where, in accordance with the old belief, good people are rewarded. For other people there is this innovation: The division of society is predestined, but through work, initiative, etc., individuals can rise out of the class to which they belong.

These two ideologies and the myth of the self-made man have to be profoundly hypocritical: They consist in self-interested demonstrations that the lie of the permanence of class divisions is a truth.

In our case direct education acquires a much greater importance. The explanation is convincing because it is true; no subterfuge is needed. It is carried on by the state's educational apparatus as a function of general, technical and ideological culture through such agencies as the Ministry of Education and the party's informational apparatus.

Educational takes hold of the masses and the new attitude tends to become a habit; the masses continue to absorb it and to influence those who have not yet educated themselves. This is the indirect form of educating the masses, as powerful as the other.

But the process is a conscious one; the individual continually feels the impact of the new social power and perceives that he does not entirely measure up to its standards. Under the pressure of indirect education, he tries to adjust himself to a norm which he feels is just and which his own lack of development had prevented him from reaching theretofore. He educates himself.

In this period of the building of socialism we can see the new man being born. His image is not yet completely finished—it never could be—since the process goes forward hand in hand with the development of new economic forms.

Leaving out of consideration those whose lack of education makes them take the solitary road toward satisfying their own personal ambitions, there are those, even within this new panorama of a unified march forward, who have a tendency to remain isolated from the masses accompanying them. But what is important is that everyday men are continuing to acquire more consciousness of the need for their incorporation into society and, at the same time, of their importance as the movers of society.

They no longer travel completely alone over trackless routes toward distant desires. They follow their vanguard, consisting of the party, the advanced workers, the advanced men who walk in unity with the masses and in close communion with them. The vanguard has its eyes fixed on the future and its rewards, but this is not seen as something personal. The reward is the new society in which men will have attained new features: the society of communist man.

The road is long and full of difficulties. At times we wander from the path and must turn back; at other times we go too fast and separate ourselves from the masses; on occasions we go too slow and feel the hot breath of those treading on our heels. In our zeal as revolutionists we try to move ahead as fast as possible, clearing the way, but knowing we must draw our sustenance from the mass and that it can advance more rapidly only if we inspire it by our example.

The fact that there remains a division into two main groups (excluding, of course, that minority not participating for one reason or another in the building of socialism), despite the importance given to moral stimuli, indicates the relative lack of development of social consciousness.

The vanguard group is ideologically more advanced than the mass; the latter understands the new values, but not sufficiently. While among the former there has been a qualitative change which enables them to make sacrifices to carry out their function as an advance guard, the latter go only half way and must be subjected to stimuli and pressures of a certain intensity. That is the dictatorship of the proletariat operating not only on the defeated class but also on individuals of the victorious class.

All of this means that for total success a series of mechanisms, of revolutionary institutions, is needed. Fitted into the pattern of the multitudes marching towards the future is the concept of a harmonious aggregate of channels, steps, restraints, and smoothly working mechanisms which would facilitate that advance by ensuring the efficient selection of those destined to march in the vanguard which, itself, bestows rewards on those who fulfill their duties, and punishments on those who attempt to obstruct the development of the new society.

This institutionalization of the revolution has not yet been achieved. We are looking for something which will permit a perfect identification between the government and the community in its entirety, something appropriate to the special conditions of the building of socialism, while avoiding to the maximum degree a mere transplanting of the commonplaces of bourgeois democracy—like legislative chambers—into the society in formation.

Some experiments aimed at the gradual development of institutionalized forms of the revolution have been made, but without undue haste. The greatest obstacle has been our fear lest any appearance of formality might separate us from the masses and from the individual, might make us lose sight of the ultimate and most important revolutionary aspiration, which is to see man liberated from his alienation.

Despite the lack of institutions, which must be corrected gradually, the masses are now making history as a conscious aggregate of individuals fighting for the same cause. Man under socialism, despite his apparent standardization, is more complete; despite the lack of perfect machinery for it, his opportunities for expressing himself and making himself felt in the social organism are infinitely greater.

It is still necessary to strengthen his conscious participation, individual and collective, in all the mechanisms of management and production, and to link it to the idea of the need for technical and ideological education, so that he sees how closely interdependent these processes are and how their advancement is parallel. In this way he will reach total consciousness of his social function, which is equivalent to his full realization as a human being, once the chains of alienation are broken.

 This will be translated concretely into the regaining of his true nature through liberated labor, and the expression of his proper human condition through culture and art.

In order for him to develop in the first of the above categories, labor must acquire a new status. Man dominated by commodity relationships will cease to exist, and a system will be created which establishes a quota for the fulfillment of his social duty. The means of production belong to society, and the machine will merely be the trench where duty is fulfilled.

Man will begin to see himself mirrored in his work and to realize his full stature as a human being through the object created, through the work accomplished. Work will no longer entail surrendering a part of his being in the form of labor-power sold, which no longer belongs to him, but will represent an emanation of himself reflecting his contribution to the common life, the fulfillment of his social duty.

We are doing everything possible to give labor this new status of social duty and to link it on the one side with the development of a technology which will create the conditions for greater freedom, and on the other side with voluntary work based on a Marxist appreciation of the fact that man truly reaches a full human condition when he produces without being driven by the physical need to sell his labor as a commodity.

Of course there are other factors involved even when labor is voluntary: Man has not transformed all the coercive factors around him into conditioned reflexes of a social character, and he still produces under the pressures of his society. (Fidel calls this moral compulsion.)

Man still needs to undergo a complete spiritual rebirth in his attitude towards his work, freed from the direct pressure of his social environment, though linked to it by his new habits. That will be communism.

The change in consciousness will not take place automatically, just as it doesn't take place automatically in the economy. The alterations are slow and are not harmonious; there are periods of acceleration, pauses and even retrogressions.

Furthermore we must take into account, as I pointed out before, that we are not dealing with a period of pure transition, as Mark envisaged it in his *Critique of the Gotha Program,* but rather with a new phase unforeseen by him: an initial period of the transition to communism, or the construction of socialism. It is taking place in the midst of violent class struggles and with elements of capitalism within it which obscure a complete understanding of its essence.

If we add to this the scholasticism which has hindered the development of Marxist philosophy and impeded the systematic development of the theory of the transition period, we must agree that we are still in diapers and that it is necessary to devote ourselves to investigating all the principal characteristics of this period before elaborating an economic and political theory of greater scope.

The resulting theory will, no doubt, put great stress on the two pillars of the construction of socialism: the education of the new man and the development of technology. There is much for us to do in regard to both, but delay is least excusable in regard to the concepts of technology, since here it is not a question of going forward blindly but of following over a long stretch of road already opened up by the world's more advanced countries. This is why

Fidel pounds away with such insistence on the need for the technological training of our people and especially of its vanguard.

In the field of ideas not involving productive activities it is easier to distinguish the division between material and spiritual necessity. For a long time man has been trying to free himself from alienation through culture and art. While he dies every day during the eight or more hours that he sells his labor, he comes to life afterwards in his spiritual activities.

But this remedy bears the germs of the same sickness; it is as a solitary individual that he seeks communion with his environment. He defends his oppressed individuality through the artistic medium and reacts to esthetic ideas as a unique being whose aspiration is to remain untarnished.

All that he is doing, however, is attempting to escape. The law of value is not simply a naked reflection of productive relations: The monopoly capitalists—even while employing purely empirical methods—weave around art a complicated web which converts it into a willing tool. The superstructure of society ordains the type of art in which the artist has to be educated. Rebels are subdued by its machinery and only rare talents may create their own work. The rest become shameless hacks or are crushed.

A school of artistic "freedom" is created, but its values also have limits even if they are imperceptible until we come into conflict with them—that is to say, until the real problem of man and his alienation arises. Meaningless anguish and vulgar amusement thus become convenient safety valves for human anxiety. The idea of using art as a weapon of protest is combated.

If one plays by the rules, he gets all the honors—such honors as a monkey might get for performing pirouettes. The condition that has been imposed is that one cannot try to escape from the invisible cage.

When the revolution took power there was an exodus of those who had been completely housebroken; the rest—whether they were revolutionaries or not—saw a new road open to them. Artistic inquiry experienced a new impulse. The paths, however, had already been more or less laid out and the escapist concept hid itself behind the word "freedom." This attitude was often found even among the revolutionaries themselves, reflecting the bourgeois idealism still in their consciousness.

In those countries which had gone through a similar process they tried to combat such tendencies by an exaggerated dogmatism. General culture was virtually tabooed, and it was declared that the acme of cultural aspiration was the formally exact representation of nature. This was later transformed into a mechanical representation of the social reality they wanted to show: the ideal society almost without conflicts or contradictions which they sought to create.

Socialism is young and has made errors. Many times revolutionaries lack the knowledge and intellectual courage needed to meet the task of developing the new man with methods different from the conventional ones—and the conventional methods suffer from the influences of the society which created them.

(Again we raise the theme of the relationship between form and content.)

Disorientation is widespread, and the problems of material construction preoccupy us. There are no artists of great authority who at the same time have great revolutionary authority. The men of the party must take this task to hand and seek attainment of the main goal, the education of the people.

But then they sought simplification. They sought an art that would be understood by everyone—the kind of "art" *functionaries* understand. True artistic values were disregarded, and the problem of general culture was reduced to taking some things from the socialist present and some from the dead past (since dead, not dangerous). Thus Socialist Realism arose upon the foundations of the art of the last century.

But the realistic art of the nineteenth century is also a class art, more purely capitalist perhaps than this decadent art of the twentieth century which reveals the anguish of alienated man. In the field of culture capitalism has given all that it had to give, and nothing of it remains but the offensive stench of a decaying corpse, today's decadence in art.

Why then should we try to find the only valid prescription for art in the frozen forms of Socialist Realism? We cannot counterpose the concept of Socialist Realism to that of freedom because the latter does not yet exist and will not exist until the complete development of the new society. Let us not attempt, from the pontifical throne of realism-at-any-cost, to condemn all the art forms which have evolved since the first half of the nineteenth century for we would then fall into the Proudhonian mistake of returning to the past, of putting a straitjacket on the artistic expression of the man who is being born and is in the process of making himself.

What is needed is the development of an ideological-cultural mechanism which permits both free inquiry and the uprooting of the weeds which multiply so easily in the fertile soil of state subsidies.

In our country we don't find the error of mechanical realism, but rather its opposite, and that is so because the need for the creation of a new man has not been understood, a new man who would represent neither the ideas of the nineteenth century nor those of our own decadent and morbid century.

What we must create is the man of the twenty-first century, although this is still a subjective and not a realized aspiration. It is precisely this man of the next century who is one of the fundamental objectives of our work; and to the extent that we achieve concrete successes on a theoretical plane—or, vice versa, to the extent we draw theoretical conclusions of a broad character on the basis of our concrete research—we shall have made an important contribution to Marxism-Leninism, to the cause of humanity.

Reaction against the man of the nineteenth century has brought us a relapse into the decadence of the twentieth century; it is not a fatal error, but we must overcome it lest we open a breach for revisionism.

The great multitudes continue to develop; the new ideas continue to attain their proper force within society; the material possibilities for the full development of all members of society make the task much more fruitful. The present is a time for struggle; the future is ours.

To sum up, the fault of our artists and intellectuals lies in their original sin: They are not truly revolutionary. We can try to graft the elm tree so that it will bear pears, but at the same time we must plant pear trees. New generations will come who will be free of the original sin. The probabilities that great artists will appear will be greater to the degree that the field of culture and the possibilities for expression are broadened.

Our task is to prevent the present generation, torn asunder by its conflicts, from becoming perverted and from perverting new generations. We must not bring into being either docile servants of official thought, or scholarship students who live at the expense of the state—practicing "freedom." Already there are revolutionaries coming who will sing the song of the new man in the true voice of the people. This is a process which takes time.

In our society the youth and the party play an important role.

The former is especially important because it is the malleable clay from which the new man can be shaped without any of the old faults. The youth is treated in accordance with our aspirations. Its education steadily grows more full, and we are not forgetting about its integration into the labor force from the beginning. Our scholarship students do physical work during their vacations or along with their studying. Work is a reward in some cases, a means of education in others, but it is never a punishment. A new generation is being born.

The party is a vanguard organization. The best workers are proposed by their fellow workers for admission into it. It is a minority, but it has great authority because of the quality of its cadres. Our aspiration is that the party the vanguard, that is, when they are educated for communism.
will become a mass party, but only when the masses have reached the level of

Our work constantly aims at this education. The party is the living example; its cadres should be teachers of hard work and sacrifice. They should lead the masses by their deeds to the completion of the revolutionary task which involves years of hard struggle against the difficulties of construction, class enemies, the sicknesses of the past, imperialism. . .

Now, I would like to explain the role played by personality, by man as the individual leader of the massses which make history. This has been our experience; it is not a prescription.

Fidel gave the revolution its impulse in the first years, and also its leadership. He always strengthened it; but there is a good group who are developing in the same way as the outstanding leader, and there is a great mass which follows its leaders because it has faith in them, and it has faith in them because they have been able to interpret its desires.

This is not a matter of how many pounds of meat one might be able to eat, nor of how many times a year someone can go to the beach, nor how many ornaments from abroad you might be able to buy with present salaries. What is really involved is that the individual feels more complete, with much more internal richness and much more responsibility.

The individual in our country knows that the illustrious epoch in which it was determined that he live is one of sacrifice; he is familiar with sacrifice. The first came to know it in the Sierra Maestra and wherever else they fought; afterwards all of Cuba came to know it. Cuba is the vanguard of the Americas and must make sacrifices because it occupies the post of advance guard, because it shows the road to full freedom to the masses of Latin America.

Within the country the leadership has to carry out its vanguard role, and it must be said all sincerity that in a real revolution, to which one gives himself entirely and from which he expects no material remuneration, the task of the revolutionary vanguard is at one and the same time glorious and agonizing.

At the risk of seeming ridiculous, let me say that the true revolutionary is guided by a great feeling of love. It is impossible to think of a genuine revolutionary lacking this quality. Perhaps it is one of the great dramas of the leader that he must combine a passionate spirit with a cold intelligence and make painful decisions without contracting a muscle. Our vanguard revolutionaries must idealize this love of the people, the most sacred cause, and make it one and indivisible. They cannot descend, with small doses of daily affection, to the level where ordinary men put their love into practice.

The leaders of the revolution have children just beginning to talk, who are not learning to call their fathers by name; wives, from whom they have to be separated as part of the general sacrifice of their lives to bring the revolution to its fulfillment; the circle of their friends is limited strictly to the number of fellow revolutionists. There is no life outside of the revolution.

In these circumstances one must have a great deal of humanity and a strong sense of justice and truth in order not to fall into extreme dogmatism and cold scholasticism, into an isolation from the masses. We must strive every day so that this love of living humanity will be transformed into actual deeds, into acts that serve as examples, as a moving force.

The revolutionary, the ideological motor force of the revolution, is consumed by this uninterrupted activity which can come to an end only with death until the building of socialism on a world scale has been accomplished. If his revolutionary zeal is blunted when the most urgent tasks are being accomplished on a local scale and he forgets his proletarian internationalism, the revolution which he leads will cease to be an inspiring force, and he will sink into a comfortable lethargy which imperialism, our irreconcilable enemy, will utilize well. Proletarian internationalism is a duty, but it is also a revolutionary necessity. So we educate our people.

Of course there are dangers in the present situation, and not only that of dogmatism, not only that of weakening the ties with the masses midway in the great task. There is also the danger of weaknesses. If a man thinks that dedicating his entire life to the revolution means that in return he should not have such worries as that his son lacks certain things, or that his children's shoes are worn out, or that his family lacks some necessity, then he is entering into rationalizations which open his mind to infection by the seeds of future corruption.

In our case we have maintained that our children should have or should go without those things that the children of the average man have or go without, and that our families should understand this and strive to uphold this standard. The revolution is made through man, but man must forge his revolutionary spirit day by day.

Thus we march on. At the head of the immense column—we are neither afraid nor ashamed to say it—is Fidel. After him come the best cadres of the party, and immediately behind them, so close that we feel its tremendous force, comes the people in its entirely, a solid mass of individualities moving toward a common goal, individuals who have attained consciousness of what must be done, men who fight to escape from the realm of necessity and to enter that of freedom.

This great throng becomes organized; its clarity of program corresponds to its consciousness of the necessity of organization. It is no longer a dispersed force, divisible into thousands of fragments thrown into space like splinters from a hand grenade, trying by any means to achieve some protection against an uncertain future, in desperate struggle with their fellows.

We know that sacrifices lie before us and that we must pay a price for the heroic act of being a vanguard nation. We leaders know that we must pay a price for the right to say that we are at the head of a people which is at the head of the Americas. Each and every one of us must pay his exact quota of sacrifice, conscious that he will get his reward in the satisfaction of fulfilling a duty, conscious that he will advance with all toward the image of the new man dimly visible on the horizon.

Let me attempt some conclusions:

We socialists are freer because we are more complete; we are more complete because we are freer.

The skeleton of our complete freedom is already formed. The flesh and the clothing are lacking. We will create them.

Our freedom and its daily maintenance are paid for in blood and sacrifice.

Our sacrifice is conscious: an installment payment on the freedom that we are building.

The road is long and in part unknown. We understand our limitations. We will create the man of the twenty-first century—we, ourselves.

We will forge ourselves in daily action, creating a new man with a new technology.

Individual personality plays a role in mobilizing and leading the masses insofar as it embodies the highest virtues and aspirations of the people and does not wander from the path.

It is the vanguard group which clears the way, the best among the good, the party.

The basic clay of our work is the youth. We place our hope in them and prepare them to take the banner from our hands.

* * *

If this inarticulate letter clarifies anything it has accomplished the objective which motivated it. I close with our greeting—which is as much of a ritual as a handshake or an "Ave Maria Purissima"—Our Country or Death!

A DAY IN THE LIFE OF A SOCIALIST CITIZEN

● *michael walzer*

Imagine a day in the life of a socialist citizen. He hunts in the morning, fishes in the afternoon, rears cattle in the evening, and plays the critic after dinner. Yet he is neither hunter, fisherman, herdsman nor critic; tomorrow he may select another set of activities just as he pleases. This is the delightful portrait that Marx sketches in *The German Ideology* as part of a polemic against the division of labor. Socialists since have worried that it is not economically feasible; perhaps it isn't. But there is another difficulty that I want to consider: that is, the curiously apolitical character of the citizen Marx describes. Certain crucial features of socialist life have been omitted altogether.

In light of the recent discussions about participatory democracy, Marx's sketch needs to be elaborated. Before hunting in the morning, this unalienated man of the future is likely to attend a meeting of the Council on Animal Life, where he will be required to vote on important matters relating to the stocking of the forests. The meeting will probably not end much before noon, for among the many-sided citizens there will always be a lively interest even in highly technical problems. Immediately after lunch, a special session of the Fishermen's Council will be called to protest the maximum catch recently voted by the Regional Planning Commission. And the Marxist man will participate eagerly in these debates, even postponing a scheduled discussion of some contradictory theses on cattle-rearing. Indeed, he will probably love argument far better than hunting, fishing, *or* rearing cattle. The debates will go on so long that the citizens will have to rush through dinner in order to assume their roles as critics. Then off they will go to meetings of study groups, clubs, editorial boards, and political parties where criticism will be carried on long into the night.

Socialism, Oscar Wilde once wrote, would take too many evenings. This is, it seems to me, one of the most significant criticisms of socialist theory that has ever been made. The fanciful sketch above is only intended to suggest its possible truth. Socialism's great appeal is the prospect it holds out for the development of human capacities. An enormous growth of creative talent, a new and unprecedented variety of expression, a wild proliferation of sects, associations, schools, parties: This will be the flowering of the future society. But underlying this new individualism and exciting group life must be a broad, self-governing community of equal men. A powerful figure looms behind Marx's hunter, fisherman, herdsman, and critic: the busy citizen attending his endless meetings. "Society regulates the general production," Marx writes, "and thus makes it possible for me to do one thing today and another tomorrow . . . ." If society is not to become an alien and dangerous force, however, the citizens cannot accept its regulation and gratefully do what they please. They must participate in social regulation; they must be social men, organizing and planning their own fulfillment in spontaneous activity. The purpose of Wilde's objection is to suggest that just this self-regulation is incompatible with spontaneity, that the requirements of citizenship are incompatible with the freedom of hunter, fisherman, and so on.

Politics itself, of course, can be a spontaneous activity, freely chosen by those men and women who enjoy it and to whose talents a meeting is so much exercise. But this is very unlikely to be true of all men and women all the time—even if one were to admit what seems plausible enough: that political life is more intrinsic to human nature than is hunting and cattle-rearing or even (to drop Marx's rural imagery) art or music. "Too many evenings" is a shorthand phrase that describes something more than the sometimes tedious, sometimes exciting business of resolutions and debates. It suggests also that socialism and participatory democracy will depend upon, and hence require, an extraordinary willingness to attend meetings, and a public spirit and sense of responsibility that will make attendance dependable and activity consistent and sustained. None of this can rest for any long period of time or among any substantial group of men upon spontaneous interest. Nor does it seem possible that spontaneity will flourish above and beyond the routines of social regulation.

Self-government is a very demanding and time-consuming business, and when it is extended from political to economic and cultural life, and when the organs of government are decentralized so as to maximize participation, it will inevitably become more demanding still. Ultimately, it may well require almost continuous activity, and life will become a succession of meetings. When will there be time for the cultivation of personal creativity or the free association of like-minded friends? In the world of the meeting, when will there be time for the tête-à-tête.

I suppose there will always be time for the tête-à-tête. Men and women will secretly plan love affairs even while public business is being transacted. But Wilde's objection isn't silly. The idea of citizenship on the Left has always been overwhelming, suggesting a positive frenzy of activity, and often involving the repression of all feelings except political ones. Its character can best be examined in the work of Jean Jacques Rousseau, from whom socialists and, more recently, New Leftists directly or indirectly inherited it. In order to guarantee public-spiritedness and political participation, and as a part of his critique of bourgeois egotism, Rousseau systematically denigrated the value of private life:

> *The better the constitution of a state is, the more do public affairs encroach on private in the minds of the citizens. Private affairs are even of much less importance, because the aggregate of the common happiness furnishes a greater proportion of that of each individual, so that there is less for him to seek in particular cares.*

Rousseau might well have written these lines out of a deep awareness that private life will not, in fact, bear the great weight that bourgeois society places upon it. We need, beyond our families and jobs, a public world where purposes are shared and cooperative activity is possible. More likely, however, he wrote them because he believed that cooperative activity could not be sustained unless private life were radically repressed, if not altogether eradicated. His citizen does not participate in social regulation as one part of a round of activities. Social regulation is his entire life. Rousseau develops his own critique of the division of labor by absorbing all human activities into the idea of citizenship: "Citizens," he wrote, "are neither lawyers, nor soldiers, nor priests by profession; they perform all these functions as a matter of duty." *As a matter of duty:* Here is the key to the character of that patriotic, responsible, energetic man who has figured also in socialist thought, but always in the guise of a new man, freely exercising his human powers.

It is probably more realistic to see the citizen as the product of collective repression and self-discipline. He is, above all, *dutiful,* and this is only possible if he has triumphed over egotism and impulse in his own personality. He embodies what political theorists have called "republican virtue"—that means, he puts the common good, the success of the movement, the safety of the community, above his own delight or well-being, *always.* To symbolize his virtue, perhaps, he adopts an ascetic style and gives up every sort of self-decoration: He adopts a sansculotte style or wears unpressed khakis. More important, he foregoes a conventional career for the profession of politics; he commits himself entirely. It is an act of the most extreme devotion. Now, how is such a man produced? What kind of conversion is necessary? Or what kind of rigorous training?

Rousseau set out to create virtuous citizens, and the means he chose are very old in the history of republicanism: an authoritarian family, a rigid sexual code, censorship of the arts, sumptuary laws, mutual surveillance, the systematic indoctrination of children. All these have been associated historically (at least until recent times) not with tyrannical but with republican régimes: Greece and Rome, the Swiss Protestant city-states, the first French republic. Tyrannies and oligarchies, Rousseau argued, might tolerate or even encourage license, for the effect of sexual indulgence, artistic freedom, extravagant self-decoration, and privacy itself was to corrupt men and turn them away from public life, leaving government to the few. Self-government requires self-control: It is one of the oldest arguments in the history of political thought.

But if that argument is true, it may mean that self-government also leaves government to the few. For, if we reject the discipline of Rousseau's republicanism (as we have, and for good reasons), then only those men and women will be activists who volunteer for action. How many will that be? How many of the people you and I know? How many ought they to be? Certainly no radical movement or socialist society is possible without those ever-ready participants, who "fly," as Rousseau said, "to the public assemblies."

Radicalism and socialism make political activity for the first time an option for all those who relish it and a duty—sometimes—even for those who don't. But what a suffocating sense of responsibility, what a plethora of virtue would be necessary to sustain the participation of everybody all the time! How exhausting it would be! Surely there is something to be said for the irresponsible nonparticipant and something also for the part-time activist, the half-virtuous man (and the most scorned among the militants), who appears and disappears, thinking of Marx and then of his dinner? The very least that can be said is that these people, unlike the poor, will always be with us.

We can assume that a great many citizens, in the best of societies, will do all they can to avoid what Mel Tumin has nicely called "the merciless masochism of community-minded and self-regulating men and women." While the necessary meetings go on and on, they will take long walks, play with their children, paint pictures, make love, and watch television. They will attend sometimes, when their interests are directly at stake or when they feel like it. But they won't make the full-scale commitment necessary for socialism or participatory democracy. How are these people to be represented at the meetings? What are their rights? These are not only problems of the future, when popular participation has finally been established as the core of political and economic life. They come up in every radical movement; they are the stuff of contemporary controversy.

Many people feel that they ought to join this or that political movement; they do join; they contribute time and energy—but unequally. Some make a full-time commitment; they work every minute; the movement becomes their whole life and they often come to disbelieve in the moral validity of life outside. Others are established outside, solidly or precariously; they snatch hours and sometimes days; they harry their families and skimp on their jobs, but yet cannot make it to every meeting. Still others attend no meetings at all; they work hard but occasionally; they show up, perhaps, at critical moments, then they are gone. These last two groups make up the majority of the people available to the movement (any movement), just as they will make up the majority of the citizens of any socialist society. Radical politics radically increases the amount and intensity of political participation, but it doesn't (and probably oughtn't to) break through the limits imposed on republican virtue by the inevitable pluralism of commitments, the terrible shortage of time, and the day-to-day hedonism of ordinary men and women.

Under these circumstances, words like citizenship and participation actually describe the enfranchisement of only a part, and not necessarily a large part, of the movement or the community. Participatory democracy means the sharing of power among the activists. Socialism means the rule of the men with the most evenings to spare. Both imply also an injunction to the others: Join us, come to the meetings, participate!

Sometimes young radicals sound very much like old Christians, demanding the severance of every tie for the sake of politics. "How many Christian women are there," John Calvin once wrote, "who are held captive by their children!" How many "community people" miss meetings because of their families! But there is nothing to be done. Ardent democrats have sometimes urged that citizens be legally required to vote: That is possible, though the device is not attractive. Requiring people to attend meetings, to join in discussions, to govern themselves: That is not possible, at least not in a free society. And if they do not govern themselves, they will, willy-nilly, be governed by their activist fellows. The apathetic, the occasional enthusiasts, the part-time workers: All of them will be ruled by full-timers, militants, and professionals.

But if only some citizens participate in political life, it is essential that they always remember and be regularly reminded that they are . . . only some. This isn't easy to arrange. The militant in the movement, for example, doesn't represent anybody; it is his great virtue that he is self-chosen, a volunteer. But since he sacrifices so much for his fellowmen, he readily persuades himself that he is acting in their name. He takes their failure to put in an appearance only as a token of their oppression. He is certain he is their agent, or rather, the agent of their liberation.

He isn't in any simple sense wrong. The small numbers of participating citizens in the United States today, the widespread fearfulness, the sense of impotence and irrelevance: All these are signs of social sickness. Self-government is an important human function, an exercise of significant talents and energies, and the sense of power and responsibility it brings is enormously healthy. A certain amount of commitment and discipline, of not-quite-merciless masochism, is socially desirable, and efforts to evoke it are socially justifiable.

But many of the people who stay away from meetings do so for reasons that the militants don't understand or won't acknowledge. They stay away not because they are beaten, afraid, uneducated, lacking confidence and skills (though these are often important reasons), but because they have made other commitments; they have found ways to cope short of politics; they have created viable subcultures even in an oppressive world. They may lend passive support to the movement and help out occasionally, but they won't work, nor are their needs and aspirations in any sense embodied by the militants who will.

The militants represent themselves. If the movement is to be democratic, the others must *be represented*. The same thing will be true in any future socialist society: Participatory democracy has to be paralleled by representative democracy. I'm not sure precisely how to adjust the two; I am sure that they have to be adjusted. Somehow power must be distributed, as it isn't today, to small groups of active and interested citizens, but these citizens must themselves be made responsible to a larger electorate. Nothing is more important than that responsibility; without it we will only get one or another sort of activist or *apparatchik* tyranny. And that we have already.

Nonparticipants have rights; it is one of the dangers of participatory democracy that it would fail to provide any effective protection for these rights. But nonparticipants also have functions; it is another danger that these would not be sufficiently valued. For many people in America today, politics is something to watch, an exciting spectacle, and there exists between the activists and the others something of the relation of actor and audience. Now for any democrat this is an unsatisfactory relation. We rightly resent the way actors play upon and manipulate the feelings of their audiences. We dislike the aura of magic and mystification contrived at on stage. We would prefer politics to be like the new drama with its alienation effects and audience participation. Fair enough.

But even the new drama requires its audience, and we ought not to forget that audiences can be critical as well as admiring, enlightened as well as mystified. More important, political actors, like actors in the theater, need the control and tension imposed by audiences, the knowledge that tomorrow the reviews will appear, tomorrow people will come or not come to watch their performance. Too often, of course, the reviews are favorable and the audiences come. That is because of the various sorts of collusion which presently develop between small and co-opted cliques of actors and critics. But in an entirely free society, there would be many more political actors and critics than ever before, and they would, presumably be self-chosen. Not only the participants, but also the nonparticipants would come into their own. Alongside the democratic politics of shared work and perpetual activism, there would arise the open and leisurely culture of criticism, second-guessing, and burlesque.

It would be a mistake to underestimate the importance of all these, even if they aren't marked, as they generally won't be, by responsibility and virtue. They are far more important in the political arena than in the theater. For activists and professionals in the movement or the polity don't simply contrive effects; their work has more palpable results. Their policies touch us all in material ways, whether we go or don't go to the meetings. And those who don't go may well turn out to be more effective critics than those who do: No one who was one of its first guessers can usefully second-guess a decision. That is why the best critics in a liberal society are men-out-of-office. In a radically democratic society they would be men who stay away from meetings, perhaps for months at a time, and only then discover that something outrageous has been perpetrated that must be mocked or protested. The proper response to such protests is not to tell the laggard citizens that they should have been active these past many months, not to nag them to do work that they don't enjoy and in any case won't do well, but to listen to what they have to say. After all, what would democratic politics be like without its kibbitzers?

MORTAL FOE OF THE WORKING CLASS, RUNNING DOG OF THE CAPITALISTS

● *by the workers' revolutionary mass criticism and repudiation team of the tientsin soda plant*

On May 7, 1949, just at the historic moment of impending nationwide victory in the Chinese people's democratic revolution, labour traitor Liu Shao-chi made his way into our Tientsin Soda Plant and handed over the power of factory management to the capitalists, criminally selling out the working class.

It was less than two months after the Second Plenary Session of the Seventh Central Committee of the Communist Party of China at which our great leader Chairman Mao called on the Party, the army and the people to "Carry the revolution through to the end" and "build China into a great socialist state". To fulfil this historic task, he said, "We must wholeheartedly rely on the working class." He stressed that "after the victory of the people's democratic revolution, the state power of the people's republic under the leadership of the working class must not be weakened but must be strengthened." This was Chairman Mao's proletarian revolutionary line. But the renegade, traitor and scab, Liu Shao-chi, opposed this. As part of his manoeuvres, he stealthily rushed to Tientsin and began issuing sinister reports and directives in a big way.

liu shao-chi and the capitalists, the same dream

Birds of a feather flock together. When Liu Shao-chi arrived at the Tientsin Soda Plant, he showed no concern for the workers but threw himself into the arms of the capitalists. They shook hands, hugged each other, had pictures taken together and held a capitalists' forum. At this forum, Liu Shao-chi pushed his absurd "exploitation has its merits" theory, shamelessly praising the reactionary capitalist, now dead, who had ruthlessly oppressed and exploited us workers. "He has made contributions," said Liu Shao-chi. "I have great respect and admiration for him." The capitalist vampires at the forum were astonished by the "big shot" himself showing them such concern and favour. They hastened to show Liu Shao-chi plans which they had drawn up before liberation for getting richer by monopolizing China's chemical industry. Since these coincided with his own desire to develop capitalism, Liu Shao-chi at once expressed his firm support and praise: "You private factories can still hire men in the future. Run more factories. The government gives you firm support. Make every effort to develop them!" The vampires, delirious with joy, smiled and hurried to send this report to their company headquarters in Shanghai: "On May 7, Liu Shao-chi and others honoured our plant with their presence, expressed concern and protection for the plant's work and the wish to exert all possible effort to help us expand the plant."

What nonsense it is for Liu Shao-chi to cry, "Make every effort to develop them!" In the old society under the oppression of these very capitalists, we workers were beasts of burden. We had this song at the soda plant:

As soon as we come into the plant yard,
We cover our bodies with pieces of gunny sacks,

In our hands we carry beggars' pots,
Every hair on our body is baked dry,
Our backs and arms become crooked with fatigue.

In the brine shop, for example, the workers, naked the year round, had to rake salt on ground heated to very high temperatures. The ruthless capitalists also forced the workers to stand on planks placed over the boiling cauldrons to stir the brine to prevent the salt from clogging. Many fell into the cauldrons and were scalded to death.

Capitalists built their paradise on heaps of workers' bones. When the reactionary capitalist started this soda factory, he had a capital of only 400,000 yuan. Thirty-one years later, by the time of liberation, his capital had "developed" to 30 million yuan and he had opened other chemical plants in Nanking, Szechuan and Hunan. Each yuan of the capitalists' "accumulation" was soaked in the workers' blood. Yet the dog Liu Shao-chi applauded them for developing capitalism—exactly his scheme to pull the newly liberated working class back into the dark old society and plunge us once more into misery! Liu Shao-chi's cry to the Tientsin capitalists to "make every effort" to develop capitalism is only another in a long list of facts which prove his ambitious design to reverse and sabotage Chairman Mao's proletarian revolutionary line.

Chairman Mao had already pointed out clearly at the Second Plenary Session of the Seventh Central Committee of the Party: "In this period, all capitalist elements in the cities and countryside which are not harmful but beneficial to the national economy should be allowed to exist and expand. . . . But the existence and expansion of capitalism in China will not be unrestricted and uncurbed as in the capitalist countries. It will be restricted from several directions—in the scope of its operation and by tax policy, market prices and labour conditions. We shall adopt well-measured and flexible policies for restricting capitalism from several directions according to the specific conditions in each place, each industry and each period." Liu Shao-chi, however, said nothing whatsoever about restriction and did his best to pull the country back to capitalism.

Chairman Mao said: "When the people overthrew the rule of imperialism, feudalism and bureaucrat-capitalism, many were not clear as to which way China should head—towards capitalism or towards socialism. Facts have now provided the answer: only socialism can save China." But Liu Shao-chi stubbornly adhered to the bourgeois stand and served as the general representative of the bourgeoisie The report by the capitalists of the soda plant to their Shanghai headquarters is iron-clad proof of Liu Shao-chi's scab betrayal of working-class interests and his attempt to develop capitalist monopoly enterprises.

liu shao-chi handed power to the capitalists

The great victory of the Chinese revolution brought immense joy and encouragement to the working class and the broad labouring masses. But the capitalists ground their teeth with hatred and waged a last-ditch struggle against it. Those of our plant smuggled, speculated and slyly withdrew capital. Then, with the cry that "resources are dried up" and "there's no money to pay wages", they tried to discharge workers. We fought them resolutely. We surrounded their offices and homes and all of them became scared as stray dogs. Fearing the workers' struggle against him, the capitalist director scurried into hiding and did not dare enter the plant. With our revolutionary action, we workers dealt a severe blow to the capitalists and they no longer dared to mention firing workers.

The scab Liu Shao-chi, afraid that the capitalists would suffer losses, hurried to call a forum of industrial and commercial capitalists in Tientsin to encourage and incite them. "You must struggle with the workers," he told them. "If you don't struggle against them, don't blame the Communist Party if the workers struggle until your factories collapse." Afraid that the capitalists would not be bold enough for lack of support, the traitor came to the Tientsin Soda Plant himself and handed power over to the capitalists. He described this: "You have three powers—the power of financial disposal, the power of administration and management, and the power of using the personnel."

To his agents in Tientsin he spelled it out in detail: "The capitalist side has the freedom to engage or discharge the workers." He had this written as an article of law into the "Temporary Measures in Dealing with Labour-Capital Relations". This gave the green light to the capitalists for exercising bourgeois dictatorship over the working class.

Chairman Mao says: "The aim of every revolutionary struggle in the world is the seizure and consolidation of political power." When we have political power, we have everything; when we lose political power, we lose everything. In 1949, Chairman Mao liberated us, the working class, from the oppression of the three big mountains of imperialism, feudalism and bureaucrat-capitalism, and we became masters of the country. But precisely at this historic point, the dog Liu Shao-chi tried to hand over our political power, seized through decades of bloody battle by the revolutionary people under Chairman Mao's leadership, to the capitalists.

liu shao-chi phrases the laws of capitalism

To maintain capitalist exploitation, Liu Shao-chi, with a slavish filial piety towards his capitalist masters, issued sinister directives to his agents in Tientsin in April 1949. "In case of labour-capital dispute, equal rights must be given to both sides after agreement is reached between the labour unions and the trade and commercial associations . . . ." On his visit to the Tientsin Soda Plant, he fawned on the capitalists and suggested that "A labour-capital consultative conference must be organized in order henceforth to deal suitably with matters concerning labour-capital relations." Thus the evil wind of "labour-capital consultative conferences" blew from our plant all over Tientsin.

"Labour-capital consultative conferences", "equal rights to both sides"—it all sounded good, just and fair and not partial to either side! But "Sham is sham, and the mask must be stripped off." Rip off their mask, and what do we find? The regulations ran: "Both labour and capital send their representatives to take part. Naturally the capitalist director of the plant is the chairman and has the power of final decision. The workers have the right to protest . . ." —capitalist exploitation and oppression of the workers made legal! "Right to protest"? Protest or not, the capitalist director had the final decision! Under the mask was true bourgeois dictatorship over the working class!

Our great leader Chairman says: "For decades the old-line Social Democrats, and for over ten years the modern revisionists, have never allowed the proletariat equality with the bourgeoisie. They completely deny that the several thousand years of human history are a history of class struggle. They completely deny the class struggle of the proletariat against the bourgeoisie, the proletarian revolution against the bourgeoisie and the dictatorship of the proletariat over the bourgeoisie. On the contrary, they are faithful lackeys of the bourgeoisie and the imperialists. Together with the bourgeoisie and the imperialists, they cling to the bourgeois ideology of oppression and exploitation of the proletariat and to the capitalist system, and they oppose Marxist-Leninist ideology and the socialist system." This great teaching of Chairman Mao perfectly describes the reactionary nature of China's arch traitor to the working class, Liu Shao-chi.

The Enlarged 12th Plenary Session of the Eighth Central Committee of the Communist Party of China unanimously adopted a resolution "to expel Liu Shao-chi from the Party once and for all, to dismiss him from all posts both inside and outside the Party". This is a great victory for Chairman Mao's proletarian revolutionary line. Under Chairman Mao's leadership we have seized back that part of the power which Liu Shao-chi had handed on a platter to the capitalists. We will follow Chairman Mao closely and answer the call of the Plenary Session to "carry on deep-going revolutionary mass criticism and repudiation and eradicate the counter-revolutionary revisionist ideas of Liu Shao-chi". We will carry the great proletarian cultural revolution through to the end!